BRUTAL

The Myth and Reality of
BANASTRE TARLETON

Anthony J. Scotti, Jr.

HERITAGE BOOKS, INC.

Copyright 1995, 2002
Anthony J. Scotti, Jr.

Cover illustration:
Slaughter of Col. Buford's Regiment at Charleston, Waxhaws, May 29, 1780;
line engraving, circa 1860-1870
(Anne S. K. Brown Military Collection,
Brown University Library, Providence, R.I.)

Published 2002 by
HERITAGE BOOKS, INC.
1540E Pointer Ridge Place, Bowie, Maryland 20716
1-800-398-7709
www.heritagebooks.com

ISBN 0-7884-2099-2

A Complete Catalog Listing Hundreds of Titles
On History, Genealogy, and Americana
Available Free Upon Request

for
Laura

Contents

List of Illustrations..vi

Acknowledgments... vii

Chapter I: Introduction 1

Chapter II: Banastre Tarleton...13

Chapter III: The British Legion..31

Chapter IV: The Legion on Campaign 71

Chapter V: Perceptions..91

Chapter VI: Virtue 125

Chapter VII: Discipline..155

Chapter VIII: Terror...201

Chapter IX: Epilogue and Conclusions 231

Bibliography 251

Index..283

About the Author 303

List of Illustrations

Slaughter of Col. Buford's Regiment at Charleston, Waxhaws, May 29, 1780; line engraving, circa 1860-1870 (Anne S. K. Brown Military Collection, Brown University Library, Providence, R.I.). .... Cover and page 174

Colonel Banastre Tarleton (1782), oil painting by Sir Joshua Reynolds (© National Gallery, London)..12

The author in the uniform of an infantry sergeant, British Legion, Captain Patrick Stewart's Company, circa 1780 (Historic Camden Revolutionary War Site, Camden, S.C., November 2001; photograph courtesy of the author)................. facing page 34

Military reenactor John T. Truelove in the uniform of an infantry lieutenant, British Legion, Captain Patrick Stewart's Company, circa 1780 (Historic Camden Revolutionary War Site, Camden, S.C., November 2001; photograph courtesy of the author)... facing page 35

Map of the Southern Theater
Source: Mark Mayo Boatner III, *Encyclopedia of the American Revolution* (Mechanicsburg, Penn.: Stackpole Books, 1994), endpaper...70

Map of the Western Carolinas
Source: Mark Mayo Boatner III, *Encyclopedia of the American Revolution* (Mechanicsburg, Penn.: Stackpole Books, 1994), endpaper...76

Acknowledgments

The writing of any book is truly a collaborative effort, and I cannot express enough my gratitude to all those who provided assistance in this endeavor. Professors Robert Weir, Owen Connelly, Simon Paul Mackenzie, and Charles Kovacik, all of the University of South Carolina, reviewed the manuscript as a doctoral dissertation in 1995. Dr. Dennis Showalter of Colorado College also looked at an early draft and made some helpful suggestions.

Appreciation should be accorded to the following libraries and archives: Alderman Library, University of Virginia, Charlottesville; Colonial Williamsburg, Inc., Williamsburg, Virginia; Library of Congress, Washington, D.C.; Liverpool Record Office, Liverpool, England; National Archives, Washington, D.C.; New-York Historical Society, New York; Princeton University Library, Princeton, New Jersey; Public Archives of Canada, Ottawa, Ontario; Public Record Office, Kew, England; South Carolina Department of Archives and History, Columbia; South Caroliniana Library and Thomas Cooper Library, University of South Carolina, Columbia; Sterling Memorial Library, Yale University, New Haven, Connecticut; and William L. Clements Library, University of Michigan, Ann Arbor.

Stackpole Books of Mechanicsburg, Pennsylvania, the Anne S.K. Brown Military Collection at Brown University Library, and the National Gallery in London all graciously allowed the reproduction of pictures for this volume.

Joanna Craig and her staff at Historic Camden Revolutionary War Site, Camden, South Carolina, always encouraged my work, identifying a real need for a revisionist study of Tarleton and the Legion.

I would like to thank Matthew J. Bruccoli and Richard Layman for teaching me the finer skills of editing. Janet E. Hill, Marie Parker, and Zoe R. Cook helped with the scanning of photos.

A debt of gratitude is due the publisher Heritage Books for agreeing to take on this project. Roxanne Carlson has shown much enthusiasm for the volume and her editing made the manuscript into a better book. Indeed, every author should be fortunate enough to have such a fine editor.

Participating in living history events has provided me with useful insight into the trials and tribulations of the Loyalist foot soldier during the Revolutionary War. John T. Truelove of Raleigh, North Carolina, has been my mentor and boon companion for more than twelve years of reenacting in Captain Patrick Stewart's company of infantry, British Legion. John's knowledge of Revolutionary War era uniforms, weaponry, tactics, and camp life is immense. He has been a true comrade and friend on the "battlefield" and in "bivouac." He and the other members of the unit have been the real driving force behind this historical work appearing in print.

Finally, I wish to thank my wife Laura and step-son Anderson for allowing me the many hours in the study to complete this book. Ultimately, it would mean little without them.

Tony Scotti
Irmo, South Carolina
April 8, 2002

CHAPTER I

Introduction

This work addresses one of the most commonly held notions to come out of the Revolutionary War. Over two hundred years have passed since the end of that fratricidal struggle and many Americans still view Lieutenant Colonel Banastre Tarleton, commandant of the British Legion, as a vile and despicable character. Why? The following account provides striking illustration.

In 1835, Moses Hall, an enfeebled seventy-five-year-old man, applied to the federal government for a pension based on military service in the Revolutionary War. His memory of his service in North Carolina between 1780 and 1781 was still vivid. One incident made a lasting impression on him, and perhaps turned a sensitive youth of twenty-one into a hardened soldier.

One evening after a fierce engagement with the Tories, Hall and some comrades approached six Loyalist prisoners standing together. Said Hall, "some discussion taking place, I heard some of our men cry out, 'Remember Buford,' and the prisoners were immediately hewed to pieces with broadswords." Shocked, Hall spent a sleepless night, his mind on "the cruelties of war until overcome and unmanned by a distressing gloom."

The next morning before daybreak, his detachment of North Carolina militia cautiously moved to a recently abandoned campsite of the British Legion. Fires built from a nearby rail fence still burned brightly, casting eerie shadows upon the surroundings. In the cold predawn darkness, Hall stumbled over something which proved to be a sixteen-year-old boy. He was still able to speak, although bleeding from a mortal wound. The youth had come out to view the British out of curiosity, hoping to catch a glimpse of the infamous Banastre Tarleton. The soldiers, however, thought he might be a Rebel spy. A Legionnaire ran him through with a bayonet and left him for dead. In the words of Moses Hall:

> The sight of this unoffending boy, butchered rather than be encumbered...on the march, I assume, relieved me of my distressful feelings for the slaughter of the Tories, and I desired nothing so much as the opportunity of participating in their destruction.[1]

The above narrative shows the basis for Banastre Tarleton's reputation. Popular imagination has characterized Lieutenant Colonel Banastre Tarleton and the British Legion as evil, pure and simple. In practically all histories of the Revolutionary War in the South, Tarleton and his green-coated Legionnaires thunder down dusty country lanes, leaving burnt farmsteads and destitute families in their wake. They left such an indelible impression upon the historical landscape that, supposedly, long after the war, house servants would use their names in order to frighten troublesome children.

There are no truly objective studies of Banastre Tarleton and the British Legion. He and his men are basically relegated to a few pages in the standard histories of the war, and these are hardly flattering. Their "eager" implementation of a terror policy is usually affirmed, while their more "colorful" depredations are mentioned. When Tarleton and the Legion are discussed in detail, it is frequently in relation to the defeat at the Cowpens in 1781.[2]

It is necessary "to move beyond the prevailing posture of contempt" for Banastre Tarleton. Indeed, the man is a controversial subject even to this day, but understanding him is undoubtedly more useful to historical inquiry than merely condemning him. Part of the problem is the average American's strong attraction to the "usable past." He remembers those events which show his nation at its best, while simultaneously ignoring those incidents which illustrate it at its worst. All nations actually exhibit this type of selective memory; it is after all a matter of patriotism and pride, but Americans tend to carry it a step further. They are infected with what one historian calls "a lethal delusion:" a belief that they are God's Chosen People and can do no wrong. By the same token, Americans are infatuated with their enemies' mistakes, poor judgment, and occasional wrongdoing.

Much of this delusion comes from the colonial experience. Early Americans were confronted with a harsh environment, both in a physical and mental sense. Life in this frontier environment made them very hardy and resourceful. What faith they had was directed to their king, and more importantly, to a God of their understanding. Especially in New England, colonial Americans lived in a "Christian Sparta," where sermon after sermon assured them that God was at their side in all things, even battle. William Bradford attributed the Pilgrims' success against the Pequots in 1637 to the Almighty, "who had wrought so wonderfuly (*sic*) for them...so speedy a victory over so proud & insulting an enimie (*sic*)." As Brigadier General Daniel Morgan proclaimed after his victory over Tarleton at the Cowpens on January 17, 1781, "our success must be attributed to the justice of our cause."[3]

At the victorious conclusion of the Revolutionary War, God's benevolence and grace upon the American people were confirmed. Like a lithograph, the images and reminiscences of that glorious struggle became etched upon the national conscience, to be cherished and never forgotten. Yet, these recollections transformed themselves over time and became even more refined and acceptable. Indeed, John Adams' lament is very appropriate:

"What are we to think of history? When in less than 40 years, such [diversity] appears in the memories of living men who were witnesses."[4]

In the case of Banastre Tarleton and the British Legion, too much myth began to surround them. As a result, we are today left with vivid stories about these "abominable fiends." They seem to be almost inhuman, other worldly. For instance, in May 1780 near Camden, South Carolina, a Legion lieutenant reportedly and for no apparent reason cut down a Quaker boy in his own front yard. Later on in the same summer near St. John's Parish, a terrified woman dropped her baby and fled into the woods upon the mere approach of Legion dragoons.

Robert D. Bass is partially to blame for American opinion. This eloquent English professor wrote the only biography of Tarleton, *The Green Dragon: The Lives of Banastre Tarleton and Mary Robinson* (New York: Henry Holt, 1957). It is a flowing narrative of the British officer and his times. It is also a popularized account, written much in the same vein as Bass's works on Francis Marion and Thomas Sumter. Bass utilized any story about Tarleton which would grab the public's attention and enhance his subject's reputation for butchery. However, most of what he reported is unsubstantiated as well as poorly cited. As a result, we have Tarleton engaging in sundry but questionable activities. For example, he manages to tame a wild steed even though a "witness" states that "the mad brute will certainly be the death of him." At another time, the young Briton supposedly had his dragoons dig up the recently interred body of General Richard Richardson, although no one actually saw them do it.[5]

A myth is

> Any real or fictional story, recurring theme, or character type that appeals to the consciousness of a people by embodying its cultural ideals or by giving expression to deep, commonly felt emotions.[6]

Myth, therefore, by its very nature, deals with expectations rather than reality. Americans cling to traditional myths of valor, honor, and decency because they *expect* their ancestors to have been virtuous and noble human beings. Moreover, their motivation for studying someone like Tarleton has been to review what he and his men did to their forefathers, not to look at the more controversial issue of American involvement. Yet to affix blame on either side is not a true historical issue. One must see Tarleton's ride through the Southern provinces in context, which is a civil war. This is a struggle in which the civilian population turns on itself and "war becomes an ambiguous, dangerous occupation." Both sides in a civil war are responsible for their actions and *re*actions. All are innocent and all are guilty.[7]

A student of the Revolution wrote this judgment of the myth-making process:

> It is curious that American myth-making is so unlike the ancient myth-making which as time went on made its gods and goddesses more and more human with mortal loves and passions. Our process is just the reverse. Out of a man who actually lived among us and of whose life we have many truthful details we make an impossible abstraction of idealized virtues.[8]

By logical reasoning, we can also make an impossible abstraction of imperfect virtues. This man would lack honor and decency; he would be a man like Banastre Tarleton.

In 2000, Hollywood reached the extremes of myth-making with *The Patriot*, a movie based loosely on the lives of Francis Marion and Banastre Tarleton. The historical inaccuracies of this film are numerous and perpetuate common misconceptions of basic U. S. history. Indeed, the scene in which Colonel William Tavington (Tarleton) locks civilians in a church and then orders the structure to be burned is more reminiscent of Nazi tactics in World War II than British policy in the Revolutionary War.[9]

The purpose of this study is to analyze the myth and reality surrounding Banastre Tarleton and the British Legion. However, before proceeding, we must become better acquainted with our subjects. The next two chapters provide objective background information on this officer and his regiment.

[1] John C. Dann, ed., *The Revolution Remembered: Eyewitness Accounts of the War for Independence* (Chicago: University of Chicago Press, 1980), 201-203. This volume is an excellent collection of Revolutionary War pension applications held in the National Archives. There are eighty thousand applications all told, with Dann choosing seventy-nine of the more significant reminiscences. The executed Loyalists were members of Colonel John Pyle's command, which was routed near the Haw River, February 23, 1781. "Remember Buford" is in reference to Colonel Abraham Buford, the Continental officer whose troops were reportedly massacred by Tarleton and the British Legion at the Waxhaws, May 29, 1780. Moses Hall eventually did receive his pension.

Loyalist and *Tory* are names which designate an American who remained loyal to Britain during the Revolution; *Patriot* and *Whig* are used to identify a colonial who rebelled against Crown law.

[2] According to Francis Jennings, "objectivity requires honesty in the citation and reportage of evidence, recognition of differing interpretations, and fairness of presentation." *Empire of Fortune: Crowns, Colonies and Tribes in the Seven Years War in America* (New York: WW Norton, 1990), xxii-xxiii; James Ferguson, *Two Scottish Soldiers, a Soldier of 1688 and Blenheim, a Soldier of the American Revolution and a Jacobite Laird and His Forbears* (Aberdeen: D. Wyllie & Son, 1888), 78; Tarleton is comparable to Walter Butler in popular Revolutionary history, "a dark mysterious portent of evil." The son of a prominent Loyalist, Walter Butler served as a captain in his father's Rangers and has been accused of various atrocities in the upstate New York area. See Howard Swiggett, *War Out of Niagara*, Empire State Historical Publication 20 (Port Washington, NY: Ira J. Friedman, 1963), vii-x, 96, 247; Christopher Ward's interpretation of Tarleton is worth repeating: He

> Was shrewd, sudden, and swift to strike. As a leader of cavalry, he was unmatched on either side for alertness and rapidity of movement, dash, daring, and vigor of attack. As a man, he was cold-hearted, vindictive, and utterly ruthless. He wrote his name in letters of blood all across the history of the war in the South.

See Ward's *The War of the Revolution*, 2 vols. (New York: Macmillan Company, 1952), 2:701; for the standard treatment of Tarleton and the British Legion, consult Henry Lumpkin, *From Savannah to Yorktown: The American Revolution in the South* (Columbia: University of South Carolina Press, 1981); John S. Pancake, *This Destructive War: The British Campaign in the Carolinas, 1780-1782* (Tuscaloosa: University of Alabama Press, 1985); William J. Wood, *Battles of the Revolutionary War, 1775-1781* (Chapel Hill: Algonquin Books, 1990); Dan Morrill, *Southern Campaigns of the American Revolution* (Baltimore, MD: Nautical and Aviation Publishing, 1993).

[3] In *Paul Revere's Ride* (New York and Oxford: Oxford University Press, 1994), xviii, David Hackett Fischer addresses the "prevailing posture of contempt" for a less infamous British soldier, Major General Thomas Gage, commander-in-chief of Crown forces in North America, 1763-1775; Ian K. Steele begins *Betrayals: Fort William Henry and the "Massacre"* (New York and Oxford: Oxford University Press, 1990), vii-viii, with the following sentence: "This reopening of a sensitive subject is offered with the hope that readers will agree that understanding is preferable to forgetting." For the "usable past," see page 149; "a lethal delusion" is discussed in Jennings, *Empire of Fortune*, 482. He is also adamant that "truth is the first casualty of war," 109; Michael Kammen, *Mystic Chords of Memory: The Transformation of Tradition in American Culture* (New York: Alfred A. Knopf, 1991). "Memory is always selective," 13; Jacques Barzun believes that great figures appear more frequently in European history than American history because the US has no cultural tradition of feudalism, monarchy, or aristocracy. As a result, Americans are more shocked and even intrigued by the behavior of "villains." *The Modern Researcher*, 4th ed. (San Diego: Harcourt Brace Jovanovich, 1985), 225, 232; for a "Christian Sparta," see John Ferling, *A Wilderness of Miseries: War and Warriors in Early America* (Westport, Conn: Greenwood Press, 1980), 154, 199-200; John Morgan Dederer, *War in America to 1775 Before Yankee Doodle* (New York: New York University Press, 1990), 180; William Bradford, *Of Plimoth Plantation* (1856; repr., Boston: Wright & Potter, 1898), 426; General Daniel Morgan to General Nathanael Greene, January 19, 1781, *The Papers of General Nathanael Greene*, ed. Richard K. Showman, 7 vols. (Chapel Hill: University of North Carolina Press, 1994), 7:155; "The revolutionaries based their Revolution on their claim to superior moral strength." In Charles Royster, *Light-Horse Harry Lee and the Legacy of the American*

Revolution (New York: Alfred A. Knopf, 1981), 46; also see Royster's *A Revolutionary People at War: The Continental Army and American Character, 1775-1783* (New York: WW Norton, 1981), 368. Mason Locke Weems, *The Life of George Washington; With Curious Anecdotes, Equally Honourable to Himself and Exemplary to His Young Countrymen*, 9th ed. (Philadelphia: Mathew Carey, 1809).

[4] James West Davidson and Mark Hamilton Lytle, *After the Fact: The Art of Historical Detection*, 3rd ed. (New York: McGraw-Hill, 1992), 51. Ralph Barton Perry wrote:

> Tradition is as inalienable as blood inheritance. In short, we shall resemble our past as a son his father, but we shall be so different that our past would scarcely recognize us and would probably disown us.

Meanwhile, Ralph Ellison states:

> That which we remember is, more often than not, that which we would like to have been; or that which we hope to be. Thus our memory and our identity are ever at odds; our history ever a tall tale told by inattentive idealists.

Both quotes are found in Kammen, *Mystic Chords*, 2; Lester H. Cohen, *The Revolutionary Histories: Contemporary Narratives of the American Revolution* (Ithaca: Cornell University Press, 1980), 15, 18-19, 228-229.

[5] These are but a few of the myths surrounding Tarleton and the Legion. More interesting and indeed gory ones will be discussed later on. For the Quaker boy, see George F. Scheer and Hugh F. Rankin, *Rebels and Redcoats* (Cleveland: World Publishing, 1957), 402; the abandoned baby was picked up by a dragoon who "tied it in a pocket handkerchief, and carried it into camp, at Monk's Corner." The child was later returned to the relieved mother. See Joseph Johnson, *Traditions and Reminiscences Chiefly of the American Revolution in the South: Including Biographical Sketches, Incidents and Anecdotes, Few of Which Have Been Published, Particularly of Residents in the Upper Country* (Charleston: Walker and James, 1851), 310-311; the story of the crazed horse and its "dauntless rider" is long and quite fanciful. The unnamed "witness" was an individual employed by Cornwallis to carry dispatches to Tarleton. He told his tale to the Petersburg *Intelligencer* after the war.

His comment about the rider's safety provoked the following statement from a nearby servant: "Never fear for him, never fear for him. His time has not come yet." At the conclusion of the ride, "the horse was completely subdued," and followed its new master around "like a dog." For the story in its entirety, consult James Parton, *Life of Andrew Jackson*, 3 vols. (Boston: Houghton, Mifflin & Company, 1859-1860), 1:82-84. It is also reprinted in Bass, *The Green Dragoon*, 2-4. For the Richardson incident, see Bass, 110-111. Tarleton's reported pretense for digging up the six-week-old corpse was that he might "look upon the face of such a brave man." This exceedingly ghoulish act seems unlikely, although not impossible. Kenneth A. Lockridge, *The Diary, and Life, of William Byrd II of Virginia, 1674-1744* (Chapel Hill and London: University of North Carolina Press, 1987), 43-44; also consult Anthony J. Scotti, Jr., "'This Disagreeable Exertion of Authority': Banastre Tarleton and the British Legion in the Southern Campaigns, 1780-1781" (MA thesis, Wake Forest University, 1991), 71-72; Henry P. Johnston takes the liberty of changing Tarleton's first name to "Banastré" in *The Yorktown Campaign and the Surrender of Cornwallis, 1781* (New York, 1881); one really cannot blame Bass too much, for the lives of Tarleton, Marion and Sumter are quite romantic and make for good stories. Bass, *Swamp Fox: The Life and Campaigns of General Francis Marion* (New York: Henry Holt, 1959) and *Gamecock: The Life and Campaigns of General Thomas Sumter* (New York: Henry Holt, 1961).

[6] Davidson and Lytle, *After the Fact*, 361; Kammen in *Mystic Chords*, 25, defines myth as:

> A traditional or legendary story, usually concerning some superhuman being or some alleged person or event, with or without a determinable basis of fact or a natural explanation.

[7] "The best history recognizes those deep-seated emotions that myths address." It also allows us "a method by which we may come to appreciate the authentic truths that the best myths reveal." In Davidson and Lytle, *After the Fact*, 372, 378-379, 381, 383; Benjamin Franklin observed: "Historians relate, not so much what is done, as what they would have believed." See Norman Gelb, *Less than Glory* (New York: G. P. Putnam's Sons, 1984), 9, 11, 17, 172.

[8] Kammen, *Mystic Chords*, 27-28. The student of the Revolution is Syndney George Fisher, author of *The True Benjamin Franklin* (Philadelphia, 1899). The quote is on p. 6.

[9] There is simply no documentation of such an incident ever occurring during the American rebellion. Roland Emmerich, director, *The Patriot* (Culver City, CA: Sony Pictures Entertainment, 2000). Anthony J. Scotti, Jr., "The Myths of Bloody Tarleton," paper presented at the Banastre Tarleton Symposium, Kershaw County Historical Society and Historic Camden Revolutionary War Site, Camden, S.C., April 26, 2002.

Colonel Banastre Tarleton (1782), oil painting by Sir Joshua Reynolds (© National Gallery, London)

CHAPTER II

Banastre Tarleton

There is a portrait of Lieutenant Colonel Banastre Tarleton that has left an indelible mark upon the American psyche. When the renowned Sir Joshua Reynolds put brush to canvas in 1782, he not only created a superb likeness of Tarleton, he also captured the personality, the very essence of his subject. This painting shows a young, dashing cavalryman standing before two wild-eyed mounts. He is clad in a gold-laced green uniform with a large saber. A dragoon helmet sits firmly on the head, black swan feathers adding a touch of elegance and grandiosity. The man himself is short and muscular, "a perfect model of manly strength and vigor," as one admirer observed. His countenance is rather boyish, almost to the point of feminine beauty. However, it is the eyes which prevent the face from being totally such, for they are cold and determined, seemingly gazing toward some faraway goal, plotting victory. His stance is relaxed yet tense, ready to spring into action. All in all, a rather impudent looking man, sure of himself and his abilities, someone not to be taken lightly.[1]

Banastre Tarleton was born on August 21, 1754, the second oldest son of John Tarleton, Sr. (1718-1773), one of the most prosperous Liverpool merchants in the second half of the eighteenth century. The father made his money in the West Indian sugar trade. During this time, the elder Tarleton also managed several slaving vessels, including the *John*, the *Swan*, and the *Tarleton*. In 1764, the "Great T," as his friends and admirers called him, became mayor of his home city. At his death nine years later, John Tarleton possessed an estate named "Fairfield" in Derby, a house and store on both the islands of Curacao and Grenada, plus a home on Water Street in Liverpool. His estate's net worth was approximately eighty thousand pounds sterling, or close to eight million dollars by today's standards.[2]

It is interesting to note that during his numerous dealings with the West Indies and mainland North American colonies, John Tarleton struck up an amiable as well as profitable business relationship with Henry Laurens of South Carolina. Starting in 1760, the Charles Town company of Austin, Laurens, and Appleby regularly loaded Tarleton's brigantine *Fanny* with sundry merchandise bound for Montserrat, Jamaica and other West Indian islands. The usual cargo consisted of rice, pork, peas, corn, pitch, tar, turpentine, hogshead staves, cypress shingles, and pine boards. Henry Laurens obviously felt John Tarleton to be a valuable customer, writing to the Englishman that he was "always glad to receive your commands." In April 1772, Laurens, who was in Westminster, wrote Tarleton that he was looking forward to meeting him in Bristol, and thanked him for his politeness and many favors.[3]

What makes this Tarleton-Laurens business relationship so interesting is that both men fathered sons who participated prominently in the Revolutionary War. Banastre Tarleton and John Laurens represented opposite extremes of that conflict. The former led Loyalist troops through bloody fighting in the South and is generally remembered as a "devil incarnate." Meanwhile, the latter acted as an aide-de-camp on Washington's staff and died at the end of the war, the very epitome of Patriot virtue and courage. Undoubtedly, both these young men knew about each other, and it is possible that they had some type of direct contact after the siege of York Town in October 1781.⁴

Little is known of Banastre Tarleton's childhood except that he was a dutiful son and followed his father's wishes to enter Oxford, which he did by enrolling in University College in 1771. He never showed any interest in mercantile activities, and when his father died he let his older brother Thomas handle the family business. In fact, young Banastre attempted to study law at one of the inns of court, and made a rather poor show of it; he drank and gambled away most of his inheritance of five thousand pounds. He then withdrew from Middle Temple, a brooding, restless youth.

A young man who does not know what to do with himself is often a good candidate for military service, and Banastre Tarleton was no exception. On April 20, 1775, ironically one day after Lexington and Concord, a commission as cornet in the First or King's Dragoon Guards was purchased for him. His mother Lady Jane seems to have advanced the money, more than likely after lengthy discussion with Thomas.⁵

He did not have much time to enjoy the novelty of military life as a junior officer for news of war soon reached England. Seeing an opportunity to prove himself and also to gain valuable experience (not to mention simple excitement), Cornet Tarleton eagerly volunteered for service in North America. On December 26, 1775, he embarked with other troops under the command of Earl Cornwallis. His Lordship and the other senior officers must have been decidedly impressed with this inexperienced volunteer.

The energy, confidence, and ambition, which normally accompany youth, can only take one so far. As a cornet in a dragoon regiment not assigned for service in North America, Banastre Tarleton was basically an unattached officer. As a result, when the troops under Cornwallis arrived in New York after the abortive attempt to take Charles Town, the cornet immediately applied for service with the Sixteenth or Queen's Own Light Dragoons, Lieutenant Colonel William Harcourt commanding. This unit along with the Seventeenth Light Dragoons were the only regular British cavalry regiments to serve in the American war.

The Northern theater of operations granted this junior officer many opportunities for recognition. In the New York campaign of 1776, he was present at White Plains on October 28 and the capture of Fort Washington and Fort Lee, on November 16 and 20, respectively. The sight of these two posts falling to His Britannic Majesty's forces thrilled young Tarleton. He observed that "Genl. Washingtons Army is retreating farther back into the Country every Day." Meanwhile, the Sixteenth Light Dragoons penetrated twelve miles into New Jersey, alarming the Rebels and cutting up their pickets. The confident subaltern bragged that "Great Courage animates all the British Troops."[6]

A month later Tarleton participated in an event that undoubtedly brought him to his superiors' attention. On December 13, 1776 at an obscure inn called White's Tavern in Basking Ridge, New Jersey, General Charles Lee of the Rebel Army finished his breakfast and began to write some dispatches. A sudden loud commotion caused him to stop and peer outside. Lieutenant Colonel Harcourt and twenty-nine dragoons surprised his headquarters, with Cornet Tarleton and five other horsemen leading the way. The cornet exhibited the reckless bravery that would make him more famous later. Apparently he charged the tavern at full speed, making enough noise to fool Lee's staff into believing that a larger enemy force was outside. After Lee had been placed in custody, Tarleton jubilantly remarked: "This is a most miraculous Event, it appears like a Dream." Whether or not he exaggerated his role in this affair is not really important, for a youth enamored with glorious and quick victory probably would brag. What is more important is his mere participation in this event and the credit it lent to his reputation, especially among his superiors.[7]

In January 1777, Tarleton participated in operations near Princeton and Trenton. That summer he accompanied the Howe expedition to the Delaware and Chesapeake, disembarking on the Elk River in late August. He then participated in the battles of

Brandywine on September 11 and Germantown on October 4. At Monmouth Courthouse on June 28, 1778, he distinguished himself with the rear guard.[8]

As can be seen, in a matter of only a few months this young man saw heavy service. In wartime, many officers get promotions, but Tarleton is special for he rose through the ranks very fast. These promotions should not be dismissed as simple good fortune. A detailed examination of Tarleton's ascension in rank can yield some very significant findings concerning this man.

In the military institutions of eighteenth-century Europe, it was common practice for officers to buy their rank. Two-thirds of all officers in the British Army obtained their commissions through purchase. Therefore, an officer without substantial wealth rarely rose above the junior ranks, the lowest priced of all commissions. What is significant in Tarleton's case is that during his service in North America, he never once had to buy another commission. Aside from the cornetcy, it was solely by merit that Tarleton gained his rank for he did not have the financial means to buy commissions. Granted, he did come from a wealthy family, but it does not seem that brother Thomas or Lady Jane were too forthcoming with major monetary aid. In fact, Tarleton's family apparently disapproved of his extravagance. On May 25, 1777, Tarleton wrote his mother that he felt ashamed of his past conduct. When the family stopped honoring his drafts upon them, Banastre complained to Thomas in a letter dated October 21, 1778: "Nothing can equal the Compunction I feel for my Bills being dishonor'd but the shame I feel for having done a wrong thing." Two months later, he wrote his mother again, asking her assistance in paying bills amounting to 2,500 pounds.[9]

As may be seen, valor alone brought this individual to a substantial rank in His Majesty's forces. The long-standing accusation that he "acquired power without any extraordinary degree of merit" has absolutely no basis. However, the charge that he was a favorite of his superiors certainly does have some foundation.[10]

Lieutenant Colonel William Harcourt, commander of the Sixteenth Light Dragoons and Tarleton's immediate superior, became the first officer to take notice of the cornet. It appears that as early as December 1776, Tarleton acted in the capacity of a lieutenant. With the capture of General Lee later that month, Harcourt was even more impressed with his young charge. After conferring with Sir William Erskine, overall commander of British cavalry forces, Harcourt promoted Tarleton to captain as well as brigade major in the Sixteenth Light Dragoons.[11]

Tarleton must have been extremely grateful for these advancements, but even he realized that they were merely temporary. The ranks bestowed upon him were strictly local appointments or, in the parlance of eighteenth century military terminology, "provincial commissions." They meant nothing outside the North American theater of operations and would cease to function once the war ended. Regardless of Harcourt's and Erskine's good intentions, what Tarleton needed was a regular commission in the British Army. Such a commission would be permanent and entitle him to better pay, prestige, and avenues for advancement.

Fortunately for Tarleton such a position soon materialized. On January 8, 1778, the city of Liverpool elected him to a post in the newly created Seventy-Ninth Foot or Royal Liverpool Volunteers, a regular British regiment. The first company muster rolls listed one "Banestre Tarleton" as the new captain. If that was not enough, he received a second captaincy on June 13 in the King's Dragoon Guards. Undoubtedly some people in high places back home heard good things about this active and zealous young man. One possible example of the stories circulating about Tarleton concerns what he did near Kingsbridge, New York, on August 31, 1778. In a skirmish with some Stockbridge Indians, the brigade major had a narrow escape. He charged the enemy and while attempting to saber a fleeing Indian, he fell from his horse. Fortunately for Tarleton, the Indian had already discharged his musket and had no bayonet.[12]

Sir Henry Clinton, British commander-in-chief in North America from 1778-1782, was another one of Tarleton's benefactors. Indeed, he probably did the most to further Tarleton's budding career in the military. On August 1, 1778, he was so taken with the cavalry officer that he conferred upon Major Tarleton the rank by which he is most well-known, lieutenant colonel of the British Legion, a newly formed Loyalist corps. Again, this was only a local appointment, but Clinton worked behind the scenes to get the new Loyalist commander a regular commission as major. On July 4, 1779, Sir Henry wrote Lord George Germain, Secretary of State for the American Colonies, and recommended Tarleton for promotion. Germain evidently referred the matter to the King's military adviser, Lord Jeffrey Amherst. On October 30, Baron Amherst penned his reply, denying Clinton's request and insisting that officers in America needed to choose between their regular or provincial commissions. What probably influenced Amherst's decision is that Tarleton had already been promoted to brevet major on August 11.[13]

While Clinton awaited an answer from the ministry, he granted Tarleton in late October-early November 1779 the additional title of commandant of the British Legion. If this was a face-saving measure for the younger officer, it probably helped. Nevertheless, Clinton persisted in his petition for Tarleton, again writing Germain on May 15, 1780. It finally paid off, for Germain wrote the commander-in-chief on July 5, approving Tarleton's regular promotion to major and brevet lieutenant colonel. However, he quickly pointed out that this was an exception to the rule, and that no more officers would be allowed to hold both regular and provincial commissions.[14]

Meanwhile, by this time Lieutenant Colonel Banastre Tarleton and the British Legion had been sent to the southern provinces with Earl Cornwallis. There, the Legion commander continued to impress his superiors, and Lord Cornwallis soon joined the chorus singing Tarleton's praise. The earl observed that "he is indefatigably laborious and active, cool and intrepid in action, discerns as by intuition, seizes rapidly, and improves with skill the short, but favorable and decisive moments of victory." On August 21, 1780, Cornwallis wrote directly to Lord Amherst, recommending Tarleton for a regular lieutenant colonelcy and describing him as "one of the most promising officers" he had ever known. However, on November 6, Amherst wrote Germain that the King was sensible of Tarleton's services but did not think he should be promoted to a regular lieutenant colonelcy. Three days later, Germain notified Cornwallis of the King's decision.

Tarleton did not receive another promotion until June 15, 1781, when he became a lieutenant colonel in the Seventy-Ninth Regiment. He still, though, remained a provincial lieutenant colonel in the British Legion for another eighteen months. On December 25, 1782, His Majesty commended his service, advancing him to become a full lieutenant colonel of "Light Dragoons, America."[15]

This analysis of Tarleton's quick ascension through the ranks reveals several things. First, it shows a capable young man eager to please his superiors. He obviously knew that he was a favorite and that much was expected from him. Therefore, he was not willing to disappoint Clinton, Cornwallis and the others. Second, this meteoric rise illustrates that ambition definitely motivated Tarleton. Third, it reveals how this twenty-four-year-old obtained a mark of special favor, i.e., command of the British Legion. Fourth, it also discloses to a lesser extent how a promising young officer commissioned in regiments not serving in North America was ideal for a newly created Loyalist regiment.

Tarleton received commendations from his commanding officers for obvious reasons. Although the Basking Ridge and Kingsbridge incidents showed him to be somewhat reckless, he still demonstrated a profound ability to "get the job done." However, Tarleton and his commanding officers were not the only ones to realize this—his peers did as well. How Tarleton interacted with and was viewed by his fellow officers is also extremely important to our understanding of the man.

Such a young officer, visibly a favorite of his superiors, must have made some other officers extremely jealous and Tarleton thus a target of resentment. As may be gathered from the earlier discussion, promotions were delicate subjects in eighteenth century armies. The dating of those commissions, in order to grant seniority, was also a very sensitive subject. The French cavalry officer the Duc de Lauzun, for instance, became so angry by an associate's promotion that he protested directly to King Louis XVI. Ensign George Hanger resigned his commission in the British First Regiment of Foot Guards because he felt he was unjustly treated concerning another's advancement.[16]

In the case of Tarleton, his promotion to major was initially denied because Amherst believed his advancement would cause many senior captains to be "most severely mortified." Lieutenant Colonel John Graves Simcoe, commander of the Loyalist unit the Queen's Rangers, in many respects the British Legion's sister regiment, also hotly contested Tarleton's advancement on at least one occasion. On December 12, 1780, Simcoe wrote Clinton, complaining that his brevet as major was later in date than Tarleton's. Clinton's appeasement may be seen in a letter to Lord Germain dated November 8, 1781. In it he requested that Simcoe's commission as brevet lieutenant colonel should be antedated to that of Tarleton's, as the the latter officer was technically junior in rank and length of service.[17]

What makes Simcoe's complaint even more interesting is that he considered Tarleton to be a good friend. If such a good friend would complain about the favoritism shown Tarleton, then it does not take too much speculation to determine what other less congenial officers were saying around the mess tables. However, this is only half the story, for Tarleton did have friends among his peers.

Tarleton was just one young officer in the close circle of dandies surrounding the first commander-in-chief, Sir William Howe (1775-1778). The group included John André (1751-1780), Oliver De Lancey, Jr. (1749-1822), William Schaw Cathcart (1755-1843),

Patrick Ferguson (1744-1780), and John Simcoe (1752-1806). Tarleton apparently struck up a friendship with each one of these men. When Clinton replaced Howe, these officers organized an extravaganza to commemorate Howe's departure. At the "Mischianza" in Philadelphia on May 18, 1778, they appeared as knights accompanied by beautiful maidens. Tarleton had for his device a light dragoon, and, as he was never one for subtlety, had for his motto "Swift, Vigilant, and Bold."[18]

Lieutenant Colonel Banastre Tarleton: young, energetic, confident, courageous, ambitious. He was undoubtedly seen by his fellow officers in many lights. At the least, some probably viewed him as nothing more than a sycophant. At the most, others presumably recognized him as a gallant comrade. However, what is more likely is the middle ground of a general consensus: a young, arrogant officer who demonstrated ability and skill and was rewarded for his promise. If his commanding officers took a personal liking to him and saw something more in him than a dutiful subordinate, it was his good fortune to be bestowed with their favors, especially the British Legion. The formation and early operations of this Loyalist corps will be discussed in the next chapter.

---

[1] Tarleton sat for the artist in London on various occasions between January 28 and April 15, 1782. The Reynolds portrait currently hangs in the British National Gallery (93 inches by 57.5 inches). J.R. Smith of London engraved a hand-colored mezzotint (25 inches by 16 inches) of Reynolds' painting soon after its completion. It appears frequently in modern publications, but it is not a very good likeness of Tarleton. In fact, the mezzotint distorts his facial features. It emphasizes the boyish aspects of the countenance at the expense of its intensity. For the mezzotint, see Craig L. Symonds, *A Battlefield Atlas of the American Revolution* (Baltimore: The Nautical and Aviation Publishing Company, 1986), 80. Two other paintings of Tarleton can be found in Robert D. Bass, *The Green Dragoon: The Lives of Banastre Tarleton and Mary Robinson* (New York: Henry Holt, 1957)—as a cornet (facing page 362) and as an older man (facing page 363). Some scholars debate whether

or not the cornet painting is really that of Banastre or a relative. A good modern rendition was done by Robert Wilson in 1976. See Henry Lumpkin, *From Savannah to Yorktown: The American Revolution in the South* (Columbia: University of South Carolina Press, 1981), 117. The admirer who commended Tarleton's manliness also stated that his bearing displayed "all the elasticity which usually accompanies elegance of proportion." See James Parton, *Life of Andrew Jackson*, 3 vols. (Boston: Houghton, Mifflin and Company, 1859-1860), 1:83. Another observer who saw Tarleton ride into Philadelphia in 1777 gave this impression of him: "Rather below middle size, stout, strong, and heavily made, large muscular legs, and an uncommonly active person. His complexion dark, and his eye small, dark and piercing." In James B. Atlay, "Tarleton of the Legion," *Cornhill Magazine* (August 1905): 235n1. Anthony J. Scotti, Jr., "'This Disagreeable Exertion of Authority': Banastre Tarleton and the British Legion in the Southern Campaigns, 1780-1781" (MA thesis, Wake Forest University, 1991), 3-4. W.Y. Carman, "Banastre Tarleton and the British Legion," *Journal of the Society for Army Historical Research* 62 (1984): 127-128.

[2] *The Papers of Henry Laurens*, 13 vols., eds. David R. Chesnutt and C. James Taylor (Columbia: University of South Carolina Press, 1968-1992): 3:26-27n9 (hereafter cited as *PHL*). Bass, *Green Dragoon*, 12; Robert H. Vetch, "Sir Banastre Tarleton, 1754-1833," *The Dictionary of National Biography*, 22 vols., eds. Sir Leslie Stephen and Sir Sidney Lee (London: Oxford University Press, 1921-1922), 19:364-365. John Tarleton came to eminence during "the silver age of sugar." He also owned Belfield Estate on Dominica. *British Records Relating to America in Microform*, ed. W.E. Minchinton, *American Material from the Tarleton Papers in the Liverpool Record Office*, introduction by P.D. Richardson (University of Hull, 1974), 10-15. John Tarleton had six other children: Thomas, John, Jr., William, Clayton, Bridget, and Jane.

[3] "Invoice, Charles Town, February 29, 1760," 3:26; "Invoice, Charles Town, January 20, 1761," 3:57; "Invoice, Charles Town, March 18, 1762," 3:90; "Henry Laurens to John Tarleton, Charles Town, March 29, 1763," 3:389; "Henry Laurens to John Tarleton, Charles Town, November 9, 1763," 4:38-39; "Henry Laurens to John Tarleton, Charles Town, December 27, 1768," 6:241; "Henry Laurens to John Tarleton, Westminster, April 16, 1772," 8:273; "Henry Laurens to Thomas Tarleton, Charles Town, February 20, 1775," 10:80-81, all in

PHL; John Tarleton had at least two other ships involved in this trade, the *Clayton* and the *Elizabeth*. For the Tarleton accounts with Austin, Laurens, and Appleby, see Tarleton Papers, Liverpool Record Office, 920 TAR 2/8-10.

[4] For the "devil incarnate," consult Parton, *Life of Andrew Jackson*, 3:85; Gregory D. Massey, "A Hero's Life: John Laurens and the American Revolution" (PhD diss., University of South Carolina, 1992). When Laurens and Tarleton met in private after the siege of York Town, the young American reportedly admonished his British counterpart for discharging his duty with too much cruelty. This story, which very well may be apocryphal, will be discussed in much greater detail later. It is found in George Washington Parke Custis, *Recollections and Private Memoirs of Washington* (New York: Derby and Jackson, 1860), 251-252.

[5] *Dictionary of National Biography*, 19:364-365; the *London Chronicle* of October 14, 1780, gave the following description of his plight:

> Being of a lively disposition and rather involved in his circumstances, he had recourse to the Army, as a profession in which, from his natural activity and courage, he would be sure of making his fortune or dying in the pursuit of it.

Lady Jane purchased the cornetcy from one John Trotter. "New War Letters of Banastre Tarleton," ed. Richard M. Ketchum, *New York Historical Society Quarterly* 51 (January 1967): 63. *American Material from the Tarleton Papers in the Liverpool Record Office*, intro. Richardson, 15-19; Thomas inherited most of his father's property and, along with John, Jr. and Clayton, continued the family's partnership with the Backhouses, another Liverpool mercantile family. The business relationship with Daniel Backhouse proved to be quite stormy in subsequent years. See Tarleton Papers, Liverpool Record Office, 920 TAR 4/5, 4/10, 4/26, 4/41; Captain Walter Harold Wilkin, *Some British Soldiers in America* (London: Hugh Rees, 1914), 118; "Sir Banastre Tarleton," *Blackwoods Magazine* 116 (October 1874): 433-437; Benson J. Lossing, *The Pictorial Field-Book of the Revolution*, 2 vols. (New York, 1855), 2:401n1; a cornetcy in 1776 cost one thousand pounds. See "Prices of Commissions, 1776: Dragoon Guards and Dragoons," in Edward E. Curtis, *Organization of the British Army in the American Revolution* (New Haven, Connecticut, 1926), 160; dragoons were so named because of the firearm they initially used was called a *dragon*. This weapon produced a very fiery blast. Technically mounted infantrymen, dragoons could fight on horseback or foot. In the Revolutionary War, they acted chiefly as cavalry. See Scotti, "'Disagreeable Exertion,'" 4, 13, 15, 29n3.

[6] For the quotes, see the letter dated "Camp at New Bridge Jerseys Novr. 23 1776," in "New War Letters," ed. Ketchum, 63, 65. Lieutenant Colonel Robert Sloper, commander of the First Dragoon Guards, approved the cornet's request on December 24, 1775. The muster rolls for that date note that he was "absent by the King's leave." Carman, "Banastre Tarleton and the British Legion," 127; the first British attempt to take Charles Town occurred in June 1776. The Sixteenth Light Dragoons arrived in America in late October. Wilkin, *British Soldiers*, 118-119; Scotti, "'Disagreeable Exertion,'" 4-5.

[7] See the letter dated "Princes Town Decr. 17 1776," in "New War Letters," ed. Ketchum, 68-72; a former British Army officer, Charles Lee commanded the Sixteenth Light Dragoons in Portugal in 1762. His army of two thousand Americans was only three miles away at Vealtown. Why General Lee did not encamp with his troops remains a matter of some speculation. Washington caustically noted that Lee was indulging in "folly and imprudence...for the sake of a little better lodging." Christopher Ward, *The War of the Revolution*, 2 vols. (New York: Macmillan Company, 1952), 1:288-289. A.J. Langguth suggests a possible amorous encounter influenced Lee's decision. See Langguth's *Patriots: The Men Who Started the American Revolution* (New York: Simon and Schuster, 1988), 404.

[8] It is interesting to note that Tarleton accompanied the troops who attacked Anthony Wayne's men at Paoli, Pennsylvania on September 21, 1777. The Americans made much of the fact that the British used only the bayonet in this surprise night assault. For the so-called "Paoli Massacre," see Ward, *War of the Revolution*, 1:358-359, 469n21. "New War Letters," ed. Ketchum, 78-79; Wilkin, *British Soldiers*, 118-119; *Dictionary of National Biography*, 19:365.

[9] "Banastre Tarleton to Jane Tarleton, Brunswick, May 25, 1777," 32-33; "Banastre Tarleton to Thomas Tarleton, New York Oct.21, 1778," 51; "Banastre Tarleton to Jane Tarleton, Long Island New York

Province Dec.25, 1778," 52-53, all in Bass, *Green Dragoon*; Scotti, "'Disagreeable Exertion,'" 10n10; *Dictionary of National Biography*, 19:368. Tarleton simply loved the high life, as his post-war activities exhibit. In fact, he went to France on at least one occasion to escape his creditors. See George Hanger, *The Life, Adventures, and Opinions of Col. George Hanger*, 2 vols. (London: J. Debrett, 1801), 2:442. Also consult "Sir Banastre Tarleton," *Blackwoods Magazine*, 116:443-449; at the end of the war, the British officer wrote: "My affairs are greatly deranged by a stay of upwards of five years in this country." Atlay, "Tarleton of the Legion," 244-245; many British officers lived beyond their means during this period. Captain John Knox, *An Historical Journal of the Campaigns in North-America, for the Years 1757, 1758, 1759, and 1760*, 3 vols. (London: W. Johnston and J. Dodsley, 1769), 1:139.

[10] For one of Tarleton's greatest detractors, consult Charles Stedman, *The History of the Origin, Progress, and Termination of the American War*, 2 vols. (1794; repr., New York: Arno Press, 1969), 2:325. A more positive view of Tarleton is found in Lieut. Col. J.G. Simcoe, *A History of the Operations of a Partisan Corps Called the Queen's Rangers* (New York, 1844; repr., New York: Arno Press, 1968), 80. "In Lt. Col. Tarleton, he (Simcoe) had a colleague, full of enterprise and spirit, and anxious for every opportunity of distinguishing himself."

[11] As brigade major, Tarleton supervised the daily paper work and guard details of all the British cavalry regiments. Such a post went to exemplary captains, but it was only temporary. Robert K. Wright, Jr., *The Continental Army*, Army Lineage Series (Washington, DC: Center of Military History, 1989), 30, 32; Carman, "Banastre Tarleton and the British Legion," 127-128; *Dictionary of National Biography*, 19:365; "New War Letters," ed. Ketchum, 79; Wilkin, *British Soldiers*, 118.

[12] The *Army List* of 1780 has "Banister Tarleton." *Journals of the House of Commons*, 1547-1803, 57 vols. (London, 1803), 36:622; Bass, *Green Dragoon*, 44; the Royal Liverpool Volunteers or the "Blues" served in Jamaica, Honduras, and Nicaragua during the war and did not return to England until 1784. It is just as well that Tarleton did not accompany this regiment to the West Indies as it suffered horrendous casualties due to illness. Only eighty-four men disembarked in Liverpool out of an original complement of 1,100. Philip R.N. Katcher, *Encyclopedia of British, Provincial, and German Army Units, 1775-1783* (Harrisburg,

Pennsylvania: Stackpole Books, 1973), 71. The holding of multiple commissions was not uncommon in the eighteenth century. For a good discussion of the "officer class," see Christopher Duffy, *The Military Experience in the Age of Reason* (New York: Atheneum, 1988), 35-88. Tarleton did not serve with the First Dragoon Guards either during the American rebellion, and he certainly never commanded that regiment as claimed by Symonds, *Battlefield Atlas*, 80. In fact, this unit never left Great Britain between 1775 and 1783. "Estimate of the charge of Guards, Garrisons, and other land forces in Great Britain, including those on Jersey and Guernsey," *Journals of the House of Commons*, 35:35, 36:22, 37:17, 38:33, 39:242-243. Tarleton's close call with the Indian is in Simcoe, *History of the Operations*, 85. Sir Henry Clinton erroneously states that Tarleton was a captain in the Manchester (Seventy-Second) Regiment. "Sir Henry Clinton to Lord Germain, Philipsborough, July 4, 1779," *Documents of the American Revolution: 1770-1783*, ed. K.G. Davies, Colonial Office Series, 21 vols. (Dublin: Irish University Press, 1972-1981), 16:131 (hereafter cited as *DAR*). The Manchester Volunteers, commanded by Colonel Charles Mawhood, served at Gibraltar. Mark M. Boatner III, *Encyclopedia of the American Revolution* (New York: David McKay, 1966), 686.

[13] Brevet status gives a military officer higher nominal rank than that for which he receives pay. Wilkin, *British Soldiers*, 119; *Dictionary of National Biography*, 19:365; it seems that Germain and Amherst were of the same opinion. "Clinton to Germain, Philipsborough, July 4, 1779," 16:131; "Amherst to Germain, Whitehall, October 30, 1779," 16:203; "Germain to Clinton, Whitehall, November 4, 1779," 17:251-252, all in *DAR*.

[14] Bass, *Green Dragoon*, 57-58; Clinton also urged that Tarleton not be required to report for service with the Liverpool Blues. Apparently a junior captain summoned him to do so. "Clinton to Germain, Charleston, May 15, 1780," 18:91-92; Simcoe was also promoted to the same rank. "Germain to Clinton, Whitehall, July 5, 1780," 16:359, both in *DAR*. Carman, "Banastre Tarleton and the British Legion," 128n2. See "Adjt. Timothy Russell to Capt. Bannister Tarleton, Kingston Jamaica 23rd Jany. 1780," in Sir Henry Clinton Papers, Volume 83, item 23, William L. Clements Library, University of Michigan.

[15] Cornwallis's evaluation is in "New War Letters," ed. Ketchum, 81; "Cornwallis to Amherst, Camden, August 21, 1780," Cornwallis Papers, Public Record Office, Kew 30/11/79, ff. 29-30 (hereafter cited as PRO). The earl heard rumors of Tarleton's possible promotion in November and berated the younger officer for not mentioning it to him. "You say nothing to me about your rank of Lieut. Colo., which if it is true that you have it, I take very ill, as you must be convinced that it is an event in which I feel myself much interested." "Cornwallis to Tarleton, Winnsboro, November 8, 1780," Cornwallis Papers, PRO, 30/11/82, ff. 12-13. Carman, "Banastre Tarleton and the British Legion," 128; *Dictionary of National Biography*, 19:367-368; "Amherst to Germain, Whitehall, November 6, 1780," 16:431; "Germain to Cornwallis, Whitehall, November 9, 1780," 16:433; "Germain to Clinton, Whitehall, July 7, 1781," 20: 174-176, all in *DAR*; War Office Records, PRO, Kew 26/31/328 has the list of officers in the British Legion, December 25, 1782. Another source lists Tarleton's rank of lieutenant colonel in the regular army as being dated 15 July 1781. *Army List, 1781.*

[16] Scotti, "'Disagreeable Exertion,'" 6-7; Duffy, *Military Experience*, 63-64; *Memoirs of the Duc de Lauzun*, trans., C.K. Scott Moncrieff (London: George Routledge and Sons, 1928), 188; Hanger, *Life*, 2:57.

[17] The Queen's Rangers will be discussed in much greater detail later. "Germain to Clinton, Whitehall, November 4, 1779," 17:251-252; "Simcoe to Clinton, New York, December 12, 1780," 16:455; "Clinton to Germain, New York, November 8, 1781," 19:210, all in *DAR*; Simcoe also felt "much affected" by Lord Cathcart's promotion to colonel of provincials on July 18, 1778. Simcoe, *History of the Operations*, 79-80.

[18] Tarleton also became good friends with Lord Francis Rawdon (1754-1826), an acquaintance from his Oxford days. All these officers except for André and De Lancey commanded Loyalist units: British Legion (Cathcart, until May 1780), American Volunteers or Rangers (Ferguson), Queen's Rangers (Simcoe), Volunteers of Ireland (Rawdon). Oliver De Lancey, Jr. of the Seventeenth Light Dragoons succeeded John André as Clinton's adjutant general in 1780. The Mischianza lasted from 4 p.m. to 4 a.m. A London company reportedly sold twelve thousand pounds of silk, laces, and other fineries to the organizers of this event. Boatner, *Encyclopedia of the American*

Revolution, 21-22, 189-190, 326-327, 364-365, 710, 918-921, 1009-1010. *The American Rebellion: Sir Henry Clinton's Narrative of His Campaigns, 1775-1782, With an Appendix of Original Documents*, ed. William B. Willcox (New Haven: Yale University Press, 1954), 111, 215; David H. Murdoch, ed., *Rebellion in America: A Contemporary British Viewpoint, 1765-1783* (Santa Barbara, California: Clio Books, 1979), 621-625.

CHAPTER III

The British Legion

A few months after the preliminary peace had been signed in Paris, Major George Hanger, second in command of the British Legion, set out for Philadelphia to visit some old friends. The Duc de Lauzun, a French cavalry officer, guaranteed him safe passage, but the major was nonetheless "rather doubtful and diffident." He met some of his acquaintances in Princeton where he found them "in great humour." They introduced him to a well-known doctor and then proceeded to describe the embarrassed Hanger in such a manner as to turn the physician pale. Hanger later reflected that the doctor surely would have hidden his silverware ten feet underground if given the chance. Nevertheless, his friends among the French officers and leading American families treated him with great civility. Hanger felt somewhat taken aback, as he was after all, an officer in the British Legion, "*a corps not much esteemed by the Americans.*"[1]

The bad reputation of the British Legion for wanton killing and destruction is well known in popular Revolutionary War literature. To a large extent it is unjustified. In order to understand how this reputation developed, it is necessary to examine the unit's origins, formation, and early operations.

The birth of the British Legion occurred during a time in which the British ministry revamped its policy toward the war in general and the Loyalists in particular. The British needed to consolidate their holdings and counter the new threat from France after the debacle of Saratoga. Furthermore, the ministry needed a viable argument to combat rising criticism of the war. "The potential of loyalist support in the Southern back country was the only evidence that could begin to prove that the war was still worth prosecuting."[2] As a result, greater reliance would be placed upon Loyalist forces and the Provincial Line reconstructed.

Starting in 1778 each new Provincial recruit received a royal grant of fifty acres and the same pay as a regular. The term of service would now be for two years or "during the present war in North America." These reforms, proposed by a board of general officers, became effective in December. They also included a bounty of three guineas for each new Provincial recruit, a one guinea reward for the capture of each Provincial deserter, and an annual allowance of forty pounds to each Provincial regiment for hospital expenses, nurses and orderly rooms. The May 1779 reforms concentrated on the Loyalist officer. He would now have permanent rank in America and half-pay upon reduction, providing his unit had a full complement and was also "properly officered and fit for service." A wounded officer received a gratuity of one year's pay in advance just like his regular comrade. An additional bounty was intended to encourage deserters from the Continental Army while fugitives from justice were assured that every effort would be made to secure their pardon.[3]

New Loyalist regiments were to be created while existing units would be brought up to the current wartime establishment of fifty-six men per company. Furthermore, they would no longer be clothed in green but in red uniforms. Presumably, this last change was implemented to save money, improve morale, and to give the

Provincials a greater semblance, both visually and psychologically, to regulars.[4]

The formation of what became known as the British Legion coincides with these developments. Toward the middle of 1778 in Philadelphia, Sir Henry Clinton authorized the creation of two new Provincial regiments. According to Clinton's *An Historical Detail of Seven Year's Campaigns In North America From 1775 to 1782*, he initially formed a unit of Irishmen known as the Volunteers of Ireland, under the command of Lord Francis Rawdon. "The foundation of a legionary corps was also at the same time laid, for the reception of such other Europeans as might choose to join it, the command of which I gave to a Scotish (*sic*) nobleman, Lord Cathcart."[5] Reportedly, both these regiments filled fast with recruits.

The British Legion was based upon a military organization which had become popular during the War of Austrian Succession. A legion was a small, semi-independent command consisting of both dragoons and light infantry. As stated earlier, dragoons were mounted infantry who could fight on foot or horseback. During the war in America, they acted primarily as cavalry. Light infantry were generally small, quick marksmen wearing short coats and leather jockey caps. When combined in a legion, dragoons and light infantry represented an extremely mobile force. Both sides employed them during the war, with the British Legion being the most famous in the Royal camp while Lee's and Pulaski's legions were in the Rebel camp.[6]

The topography of North America rendered the Revolutionary War different from conflicts on the European continent and therefore required a greater use of light, mobile troops. Lord William Howe deemed every movement in North America "an enterprise." Major General Charles Grey called it the strongest country he was ever in and the best suited for the defensive. "The country was wholly unsuited to the art of war as conceived and practised in Europe."[7] Today, the area which comprised the Thirteen Colonies is essentially the same: heavily wooded rough terrain with swift-flowing rivers. The only flat open country is to be found in the South.[8]

The British Army came to North America wholly unprepared to counter this problem. It brought only two dragoon regiments with it, the Sixteenth and Seventeenth Light Dragoons. Only one of these, the Seventeenth, stayed for the duration of the conflict. In 1778, troopers of the under-strength Sixteenth Light Dragoons were drafted into the Seventeenth while the officers returned home to recruit.[9] Thus, the need for a legion became evident from the beginning of the conflict, and the British Legion came about as a result. There are several factors, however, which made its origins and formation unique.

The physical appearance of the British Legion was the most obvious. It was not dressed like other Provincial units. While other Loyalist battalions changed to redcoats in late 1778-early 1779, the British Legion kept its green uniforms. The only other Loyalist regiment to do so was Simcoe's Queen's Rangers. Simcoe claimed with just cause that green was the best color for light troops with dark accoutrements, as the uniform would fade after several months' wear and tear and would be "scarcely discernable (*sic*) at a distance." A Hessian officer described the Legion cavalry uniforms as "Short Round Green Tight Jacketts (*sic*), Black Collar and Cuffs," and that of the infantry as a "Short Coat-Green with same lappel (*sic*), variety button hole & Black Cuff & Collar."[10] It is probable that all ranks, cavalry as well as infantry, wore leather dragoon helmets. As a specialized unit, the Legion would have been given such a mark of distinction. In time, the British Legion became popularly known as the "Green Horse."[11]

The intended purpose of the British Legion is a second factor which made it unique. As with other Provincial battalions, it was meant to shore up Loyalist confidence and to enhance the war effort. Moreover, as a "legion," it acted in a very mobile manner. This mobility tied into the third factor, capability.

It is pertinent at this time to discuss the Queen's Rangers, the best known and most active Loyalist corps next to the British

The author in the uniform of an infantry sergeant, British Legion, Captain Patrick Stewart's Company, circa 1780 (Historic Camden Revolutionary War Site, Camden, S.C., November 2001; photograph courtesy of the author)

Military reenactor John T. Truelove in the uniform of an infantry lieutenant, British Legion, Captain Patrick Stewart's Company, circa 1780 (Historic Camden Revolutionary War Site, Camden, S.C., November 2001; photograph courtesy of the author)

Legion. In many respects this unit was the Legion's sister regiment. They frequently operated together and shared cantonments on Long Island, New York during the winter months. Created in 1776, the Rangers undoubtedly had more experience and helped train the Legion. Moreover, Lieutenant Colonel John Graves Simcoe provides probably the best analysis of cavalry and light infantry tactics as practiced in the Revolutionary War.[12]

In his book, *A Journal of the Operations of the Queen's Rangers, from the End of the Year 1777, to the Conclusion of the Late American War*, Simcoe argues that the key to victory in battle rests upon individual courage, initiative, and close fighting with the bayonet. He took much pride in his regiment and trained it thoroughly. His Rangers became accustomed to ninety miles of marching per week, with the flank companies and hussars going even farther. While encamped at Oyster Bay, Long Island during the winter of 1778-1779, the corps exercised constantly in firing and charging. The Ranger had instructions to "keep his head well up, and erect," in order to look intimidating as well as graceful. Simcoe maintained that a soldier who looks his enemy in the eye and simultaneously thrusts his bayonet "is certain of conquest." The light infantry also were trained to run alongside the cavalry through the woods by clinging to the horses' manes. The dragoons, meanwhile, practiced galloping through infantry files while the foot soldiers lay flat upon the ground.[13]

Very few military units in the Revolutionary War were capable of such agility and mobility. Undoubtedly, the British Legion received some of the same thorough training. With an individual like Banastre Tarleton in command, the Green Horse utilized its agility to deliver swift, stunning attacks. Subsequently, this type of offensive capability designated an element of dread and fear to a group of men already despised for their political beliefs.

The organization of the British Legion also made it different. It was one of only three legions in the British Army during the rebellion in America. The Queen's Rangers, although not a legion in name, certainly had the characteristics of one. It consisted of eleven infantry companies and four cavalry troops. The American Legion, formed by Benedict Arnold after his defection to the royal cause in 1780, came too late in the war to be truly effective.[14] The other Loyalist cavalry units which existed also saw limited service. Lieutenant Colonel Andreas Emmerick's Chasseurs occasionally served mounted in New York until drafted into other regiments in 1779. Meanwhile, the King's American Dragoons under Lieutenant Colonel Benjamin Thompson did not arise until 1781.[15]

An analysis of British Legion numerical strength can reveal some interesting findings concerning that organization. In studying any regiments of the Provincial Line difficulties arise. First, attrition rates are not readily discernible, especially with the appearance and disappearance of various units on the rolls. Second, there exist few accurate and complete tabulations of killed, died of disease, discharged for wounds, etc. As a result, the rates of desertion and bounty-jumping are also very hard to ascertain. Last, the number of officers for many units is vague because of transfers, promotions, illnesses and wounds, and capture. Altogether, these account for glaring contradictions in the British Legion muster rolls.[16]

It is helpful to remember that any muster roll or official return stating only the "rank and file" is an indication of approximately 85% of the total regimental complement. The terms "rank and file" and "effectives" were used interchangeably and represented the corporals and privates but not the sergeants or drummers. The term "men" apparently referred to all ranks below the commissioned level, and included all noncommissioned officers (sergeants, corporals), musicians (drummers, trumpeters, fifers, pipers, hautboisiers), and private soldiers.[17]

One of the greatest myths surrounding the British Legion is that it contained strictly Loyalists and deserters from the Rebel Army. There is no real way of verifying this statement because Legion muster rolls are silent on the matter. Nevertheless, the Green Horse probably had its share of both these elements. Loyalist battalions also frequently had a number of soldiers who were not

Loyalists in the true sense of the word. Many officers and noncommissioned officers (NCO's) in these units were actually British regulars, not Provincials. Regular volunteers in the British Legion included captains James Edwards, Thomas Miller, Donald McPherson, lieutenants Donald McCrimmin, James McDonald, Jeremiah Denovan, Sorrel McDonald, ensigns John Miller, William Jordan, George Browne, and Adjutant Thomas Stanley.[18]

Part of the misconception concerning deserters stems from a January 2, 1779 *Cambridge Chronicle and Journal* report. It states that four hundred deserters came in to specifically join the Legion after "a noble Earl's" proclamation and pardon in September. There is no evidence, however, to substantiate this claim. Four hundred deserters seems like an unusually high number to come in at one time. Furthermore, if four hundred such individuals appeared there is no reason to assume that they all joined the British Legion.[19]

Some of the confusion also comes from what is known about the organization of other Loyalist units. Lord Rawdon's Volunteers of Ireland reportedly consisted of nothing but deserters and Simcoe's Queen's Rangers frequently recruited prisoners. Tarleton himself mentions that his regiment had some "bad materials," and this could pertain to deserters. As it stands, in light of these two well-known Loyalist units, it is easy to see why many would assume the same for the Legion. At present, it is not known what percentage of the Legionnaires were Loyalists, deserters, British regulars or even German auxiliaries.[20]

Indeed, little is known about the officers and men who comprised the ranks of the British Legion. As a result, their lack of identity makes it all the more easy to demonize them in popular history. They appear merely as names on the muster lists with brief notations attached: Private John Dun – orderly with Lieut Colonel Tarleton; Trumpeter Francis Miles – enlisted November 23, 1777; Sergeant Peter McDonald – transferred to the Royal Garrison Battalion; Lieutenant William Robins – prisoner with the Rebels; Captain Patrick Stewart – died October 24, 1782.[21]

Research on the officers yields only limited results. For instance, Legion infantry Captain Donald McPherson at one time commanded the Black Pioneers, a small Loyalist battalion of only six officers and sixty-eight men. Why McPherson left this regiment and what kind of service record it had are uncertain. Dragoon Captain Christian Huck, a former Philadelphia lawyer, gained a notorious reputation in South Carolina for his profane language. Huck, along with Isaac Bullock, Abraham and Amos Chapman, Richard Hovenden, Jacob James, Nathaniel Vernon, and Walter Willet were all convicted of treason by their respective colonies and had their estates confiscated.[22]

In the case of two enlisted personnel, research has produced more fruitful results. Private Isaac Green was captured and tried in Pennsylvania for treason. On July 5, 1781, the court granted him a pardon on condition that he serve on board the rebel frigate *Trumbull* for the war's duration. Green attempted to reverse the decision, but met with failure. He then escaped and, if it is the same individual, he reenlisted in the Legion later that year on August 25.[23]

The second enlisted man is Michael Docherty. He started his military career in the Rebel army as a sergeant. At Brandywine Creek, Pennsylvania in September 1777 he found himself captured. To avoid an English jail, he enlisted in the Seventeenth Regiment of Foot. Assigned to the royal garrison at Stony Point, New York, he was soon recaptured by his former comrades in the Delaware Regiment on the night of July 16, 1779. He then rejoined his old regiment and suffered the ignominy of capture once again at Camden, South Carolina in August 1780. Given the choice a second time of imprisonment or enlistment in the royal army, he opted for the latter and became a private in the British Legion infantry. At the Cowpens on January 17, 1781, he was recaptured a final time and rejoined the Delaware Regiment.[24]

The above-mentioned individuals represent only a small fraction of those who served in the British Legion throughout the war. The Legion's estimated cumulative total is an impressive 773 officers and men. Yet, it appears that its maximum strength at any one time never exceeded 550, as reported on January 1, 1781. The southern campaigns did not treat the regiment kindly. Its attrition rate, assigned by Loyalist historian Paul H. Smith, is a broad "moderate to heavy." Indeed, only 208 rank and file (including twenty-four sick and wounded) surrendered at York Town in October 1781, and this seems to warrant a "heavy" and not a "moderate" rating.[25]

The wartime establishment of the British Legion was 754 officers and men, but it was always at least 204 short. The figure of 754 is much higher than the wartime establishment for a regular British regiment, which was 560 rank and file. Most Loyalist units seem to have had higher establishments, the rationale being that recruits would be easy to obtain. The Queen's Rangers had 744 while the Volunteers of Ireland had 612. Nevertheless, few Provincial corps, or regular British regiments for that matter, ever got very near to their intended establishment figures.[26]

A comparison of the following Provincial units reveals that the British Legion was a fairly large sized organization:

Regiment	Known Maximum Strength
King's American Regiment	588
New York Volunteers	364
Queen's Rangers	616
Volunteers of Ireland	632

These units in no way compare to DeLancey's Brigade (three battalions of 1,218 rank and file), the King's Royal Regiment of New York (two battalions of 1,070 rank and file), or the New Jersey Volunteers (six battalions of 1,972 rank and file), which were anomalies. The British Legion and the four other regiments listed above represent the norm for Loyalist units.[27]

There is some confusion over the exact birth of the British Legion. As already discussed, Clinton maintains that it was formed from scratch. Robert H. Vetch's *Dictionary of National Biography* sketch of Tarleton, however, asserts that Lord Cathcart formed the

Legion out of the "Caledonian Volunteers." Meanwhile, Robert Bass claims that Cathcart created the Legion from three existing dragoon troops. Whatever the exact sequence of events, it appears that it was an original idea and that small Loyalist units already in existence were combined to make the British Legion.[28]

The British Legion had six cavalry troops during the war. These six were commanded by captains Francis Gildart, Richard Hovenden, Jacob James, David Ogilvy, Thomas Sandford, and Nathaniel Vernon. The initial troops were those of Hovenden, James, and Sandford, all raised in Philadelphia during the British occupation of that city (September 1777-June 1778). In fact, these troops were actually independent organizations. The Bucks County Light Dragoons or Volunteers under Sandford had its first formation on December 25, 1777 and had thirty-eight effectives. The First Troop of Philadelphia Light Dragoons under Hovenden mustered on January 8, 1778, while the Second Troop of Philadelphia (or Chester County) Light Dragoons under James mustered on February 5. These two troops each had thirty-seven privates.[29]

Initially, these three units were attached to the Queen's Rangers. Only later when the idea for a legionary corps came up did British officials decide to attach these provincial cavalry units to newly raised Loyalist infantry companies. On August 15 and September 7, 1778, Hovenden's and James's troops, respectively, were assigned to the new Legion infantry companies encamped at Kingsbridge, New York. The Bucks County Volunteers did not officially transfer to the Legion until October 25, 1780, when the latter was already in South Carolina.[30]

Meanwhile, during the summer of 1778 infantry companies for the new Legion were also being raised in Philadelphia as well as New York. The regiment ended the war with six companies of infantry technically on the muster rolls. The six companies were commanded by captains Charles McDonald, Thomas Miller, John Rousselet, Patrick Stewart, James Edwards, and Donald McPherson.[31]

The initial foot companies seem to have been like the first cavalry troops, i.e. independent organizations. One of these, a group of Scottish volunteers collectively known as the Caledonian Volunteers, had for its commander Captain William Sutherland, Sir Henry Clinton's aide-de-camp. Lord William Cathcart acted as the colonel. Although Bass states that they consisted of only one company, they appear to have had two or three companies and numbered 151 effectives. Of the six infantry companies mentioned above, it is not certain which ones were in the Caledonian Volunteers.[32]

The first time that these cavalry troops and infantry companies appear as a single unit is on August 15, 1778. A muster roll for that date in New York gives "Tarleton's Legion" only ninety-eight rank and file. The growth rate must have been steady because five months later on January 1, 1779, an official return of Provincial troops in North America reveals that Lord Cathcart's newly raised corps numbered 323 effectives. This figure appears to represent both cavalry and infantry.[33] On July 10, 1779, two Legion deserters came into the Rebel lines in New Jersey and reported their former regiment to be composed of four companies of infantry and four troops of light horse—all told, 450 officers and men.[34]

By January of the next year, the British Legion would be in the South where combat, disease, and the climate took their toll upon the corps. Tarleton gave a return of 308 officers and men on the night of August 15, 1780, while the British Army awaited battle outside of Camden, South Carolina.[35]

Two months later on October 25, 1780, the British Legion's five dragoon troops had three hundred men while its four infantry companies had 221 effectives. The discrepancy with the previous return can be attributed to the numerous detachments of Legionnaires scattered throughout South Carolina. On January 1, 1781, Tarleton reported that he had 550 officers and men.[36]

After the debacle at Cowpens on January 17, 1781, there is a noticeable drop in Legion ranks. On April 25, 1781, there were 247 dragoons and only ninety-one infantrymen, for a total of 338 effectives. The same total is recorded for two months later. Even then, these figures are misleading because they include those who were sick, in the provost, on detached duty at different locales and with other regiments, as well as those who had deserted. Furthermore, these numbers include the captured, the bulk of whom were infantrymen lost on January 17. The true figures include only those fit and present for duty; these range from 168 to 174 rank and file on various dates between February 1 and October 1, 1781.[37]

By the war's end, the six cavalry troops and four infantry companies of the British Legion were in poor shape, as exhibited in an embarkation return dated September 15, 1783 for those regiments traveling to Nova Scotia and exile. The cavalry had twenty-three officers, twelve sergeants, six trumpeters, and 128 troopers. The infantry had eight officers, five sergeants, and twenty-six privates. These men were all that remained of the British Legion.[38]

One of the best regular cavalry regiments in the British Army had a troop assigned to the British Legion during the southern campaigns. The detachment from the Seventeenth Light Dragoons enhanced the professionalism of the British Legion, most likely training new recruits and teaching them proper care techniques for their mounts. Nevertheless, the men of this troop were a fiercely proud lot and refused to trade their redcoats for Legion green, thus undoubtedly causing some hard feelings with the Legionnaires.[39]

His Majesty George III near the end of the war recognized the meritorious service of some of his provincial regiments by placing them upon the "Regular Establishment." Battalions belonging to the Regular or British Establishment "were administered in accordance with laws and regulations that governed pay, promotion, retirement, etc."[40] As may be expected, Loyalist regiments did not serve under the same stipulations and belonged to the Provincial or American Establishment, created in May 1779. It was a mark of special favor to be placed upon the Regular Establishment, and only five Provincial regiments received this distinction. The

British Legion, along with the Queen's Rangers, Volunteers of Ireland, the New York Volunteers, and the King's American Regiment, all saw hard campaigning. On March 7, 1781, three months before Tarleton's promotion to regular lieutenant colonel, his organization was officially placed on the Provincial Establishment as the Fifth American Regiment. It made the leap to Regular Establishment on December 25, 1782, after much petitioning by Tarleton.[41]

The last but far from least factor which made the British Legion a truly unique Provincial regiment was its leader. Banastre Tarleton did not originally command the unit. On July 18, 1778, Sir Henry Clinton's adjutant general, Lord William Schaw Cathcart, became colonel of the regiment while on August 1 Major Banastre Tarleton became its lieutenant colonel. During this time, Cathcart also acted as temporary quartermaster general. Thus, the time he actually spent with his Legionnaires was rather limited and left young Tarleton in *de facto* command. The green-clad members of the regiment became popularly known as "Tarleton's Green Horse," although officially it was still referred to as Cathcart's Legion until after the fall of Charles Town in May 1780.[42] During the siege of that southern city, Cathcart became sick and returned to New York. There, he recovered from his illness and then decided to return to a post with the Thirty-Eighth Regiment of Foot instead of the Legion.[43]

In a letter to Lord George Germain on May 15, 1780, Sir Henry Clinton made a very insightful observation concerning the commanders of the British Legion and the Queen's Rangers.

> These corps I must observe, my lord, exist in their chiefs, and I am persuaded that losing them they might shortly be reduced to the state of some other provincial battalions, very weak in numbers and not trained with the same exemplary degree of care or discipline, though they are now such as I can place the highest confidence in.[44]

Although he does not directly state it, Clinton is referring to something that Tarleton and Simcoe both possessed, a key facet to their personalities: charisma. These men undoubtedly had to possess this quality in order to lead their troops and to inspire them to the point that both the British Legion and the Queen's Rangers became very reliable Loyalist units. Unfortunately, no direct observation along the same lines from Legion officers and enlisted personnel exists, if one excludes George Hanger's fawning comments in his memoirs and *An Address to the Army* (London: James Ridgway, 1789). Simcoe, one of Tarleton's friends and admirers, reflected: "In Lt. Col. Tarleton, [Simcoe] had a colleague, full of enterprise and spirit, and anxious for every opportunity of distinguishing himself."[45]

Banastre Tarleton also obviously possessed bravery, a characteristic which always inspires military subordinates. He constantly exhibited this quality. Aside from examples already cited, Tarleton demonstrated it at Blackstocks Hill, South Carolina on November 20, 1780, when he rescued a wounded officer under heavy fire. At Guilford Courthouse, North Carolina on March 15, 1781, the young Legion commander rode into battle already wounded. His right arm in a sling and his left hand upon the reins, he was totally defenseless.[46]

This British officer had the stamina of a leader and the appearance of invincibility. During August or September 1780, Tarleton came down with either malaria or yellow fever, an almost certain death sentence in the eighteenth century. He made a full recovery. His second in command, Major George Hanger, almost died from his bout of yellow fever. The Legion major and five other sick officers were placed in wagons. Within a week, the others had died. The disease reduced Hanger to a "skeleton," for his ribs and hips "came fairly through the skin." For three weeks, the major subsisted on nothing but opium and port wine. When he could travel, he temporarily left the service in order to complete his recovery in Bermuda.[47]

The loyalty the Legionnaires felt for their lieutenant colonel was indeed extreme. This may help to explain their actions at the Waxhaws, South Carolina in May 1780. This battle will be discussed later; it will suffice for now to state that Tarleton's men reacted with hideous rage when they thought he had been killed.

Without his leadership, they behaved differently. At Charlotte, North Carolina in September 1780, while Tarleton was still ill, Major Hanger ordered the Legion cavalry to charge a fence held by American militia. They did so twice, sustaining heavy casualties each time. Upon Hanger's third request, they refused until Earl Cornwallis himself pleaded with them. Afterwards, the British general wrote: "Indeed the whole of them are very different when Tarleton is present or absent."[48]

Unfortunately, there exists no detailed observations or testimony about Tarleton from his subordinates, whether commissioned or enlisted. However, it may be surmised with some degree of certainty that the Legionnaires saw something in Tarleton besides charisma and courage that inspired them. He apparently gave his men, especially the Loyalist members of the Legion, a sense of self-worth. His Legionnaires, in turn, looked up to him as some sort of protector, a champion of their well-being. John Simcoe mentions that his Rangers viewed him as such. Tarleton does appear to have taken some interest in the personal plight of his men, if not their cause. A strong indication of this can be seen in his actions after the Cowpens. On January 19, 1781, Tarleton, under a flag of truce, sent a letter to Daniel Morgan, alerting the American brigadier general that he was sending a doctor and surgeon's mate of the Seventh Regiment to look after the British wounded. Also, he "sent some money for the use of the Prisoners."[49] The Loyalist members of the British Legion more than likely took notice of this action on the part of their commander and felt deeply grateful.

Loyalists were a desperate lot. Their fellow Americans despised them. Essentially exiles in their own country, they acted upon what they believed to be "firm principle" with their political attachment to the Crown. They had much to lose for many colonies passed confiscation acts directed at the King's friends.[50] Moreover, loyal Americans had to contend with their British comrades-in-arms, who treated all colonial soldiers with a certain amount of contempt, frequently ill concealed. This superiority complex had been present in all the previous colonial wars and had naturally carried over into the Revolutionary War. Major General James Wolfe, victor of the Battle of Quebec in 1759, stated that the colonials were totally unfit for military service and described them as "dilatory, ignorant, and irresolute." Furthermore,

> The Americans are in general the dirtiest, the most contemptible, cowardly dogs you can conceive. There is no depending on 'em in action. They fall down dead in their own dirt and desert by battalions, officers and all.[51]

James Wolfe was never one to mince words, but his assessment was shared by many British officers. Major General Edward Braddock maintained "that scarce any military service can be expected of them." It would "cost indefinite pains and labor to bring them to any sort of regularity and discipline."[52]

In the case of Banastre Tarleton, there is no indication that he felt this way about provincial soldiers. If he did, then he did not show it, for his Legionnaires certainly would have noticed. The consequences on their morale would have been dire, but there is no overt evidence.

Like John Simcoe and Patrick Ferguson, Banastre Tarleton took pride in his regiment. On several occasions, the British Legion received arms and accoutrements actually destined for other regiments. At another time, Tarleton obtained Cornwallis's permission to take the best mounts in the Crown's southern army for Legion use.[53]

A strong *esprit de corps* pervaded the British Legion, instilled no doubt by Tarleton's demands on training and discipline and also fostered by the unit's many successes in battle. Even more significant, their leader encouraged a keen sense amongst Legionnaires of being in an elite organization. As a specialized unit the British Legion probably had what one student has termed a "fighter pilot mentality." The Legionnaires felt capable of handling all contingencies and reveled in the charge and ultimately close combat, like today's fighter pilots. Tarleton would concur with Simcoe that the bayonet was the key to victory. This ageless phenomenon of "chivalric encounters" gave this battalion a sense of being apart from and even better than the average Loyalist regiment.[54]

There was also an "extra-specific" factor at work in the Legion. One modern historian has suggested that men on horseback feel superior to and different from men on foot, and thus have less qualms about killing them out of hand. This superiority complex comes from the traditional and well-known animosity between cavalrymen and infantrymen. In the eighteenth century, armies frequently utilized mounted troops to assist the provost marshal and to suppress infantry mutinies.[55]

Tarleton's energy was well known to his Legionnaires. He once told a fellow officer: "The more difficulty, the more glory." His hatred of all things "Rebel" also became apparent to his soldiers, and Tarleton vocalized his feelings on numerous occasions. In a letter to Lord Cornwallis on August 5, 1780, at the height of the southern campaigns, Tarleton said that he felt the need to "discriminate with severity." At another time, he described his activities in the South Carolina low country as "this disagreeable exertion of authority."[56]

Early operations of the British Legion occurred in the Northern theater and were limited in scope. However, it did gain a reputation as a reliable battalion. In the summer and early fall of 1778, the Green Horse patrolled Westchester County, New York in the area above Kingsbridge and bivouacked with the Queen's Rangers on frequent occasions. It engaged in a couple of minor skirmishes in July. For the winter of 1778-1779, the British Legion and the Queen's Rangers entered cantonments on Long Island, ideal horse country with its rolling plains and plentiful forage. While the Rangers quartered at Oyster Bay, the Legionnaires stayed at Setalket.[57]

In mid May 1779, both regiments moved back to the Kingsbridge area. During this summer, the Legion engaged in a raid on Poundridge and Bedford, New York. This appears to be the only time that it was ever used to its full potential before the southern campaigns. Tarleton's goal was to surprise Colonel Elisha Sheldon's Second Continental Dragoons as well as capture Major Ebenezer Lockwood, both at Poundridge. Under the cover of night and a thunderstorm, Tarleton and two hundred mounted troops set out from Mile Square along the Bronx River on July 1. At Poundridge, Tarleton missed his quarry and became annoyed with Rebel sniping from behind stone walls, trees, and fences. In a harbinger of things to come, he ordered Major Lockwood's home to be set on fire. At Bedford, he encountered the same obstinacy and reacted accordingly.

> I proposed to the militia terms, that if they would not fire from the buildings, I would not burn [them]. They interpreted my mild proposal wrong, imputing it to fear. They persisted in firing until the torch stopped their progress, after which not a shot was fired.[58]

During the retreat, Tarleton had eight or ten known Rebels placed into custody. His Legionnaires continued their burning of buildings and running off of cattle. By 10:30 p.m. they arrived back at Mile Square, having ridden sixty-four miles in twenty-three hours. Although essentially a failure, since Sheldon's command and Lockwood both got away, this raid did contribute to the new unit's reputation.[59]

In October 1779, the Legion was back on Long Island at Jericho. Apparently, it stayed there until its embarkation for South Carolina in December. However, at least one company of infantry found itself detached for service in Georgia prior to this date.

During the Franco-American siege of Savannah in the fall of 1779, Captain Charles Stewart's company manned the most northerly battery.[60]

The British Legion was formed during a time of change and high hopes for English military officials. It had a strong *esprit de corps*, instilled by its training and an aggressive leader. It performed well on outpost duty, but desultory skirmishing gave the Green Horse only limited experience. Not until the southern campaigns would the regiment reach its full potential.

---

[1] Emphasis added. US and British commissioners agreed upon a preliminary treaty on November 5, 1782 in Paris. It is peculiar to eighteenth-century warfare and aristocratic manners that Lauzun and Hanger, just so recently enemies, could now become friends. What makes this story even more astonishing is that the American families involved had sided with the Rebels during the war. George Hanger, *The Life, Adventures, and Opinions of Col. George Hanger*, 2 vols. (London: J. Debrett, 1801), 2:422-424. George Hanger (1751?-1824) had a rambunctious lifestyle, just like his close friend Tarleton. A companion of the profligate Prince of Wales, (the future George IV), Hanger became in December 1814 the fourth Baron Coleraine, but refused to be called by that title.

Armand-Louis de Gontaut-Biron, Duc de Lauzun (1747-1793) commanded the Second Legion of the *Volontaires étrangers de la Marine*, a regiment very similar in composition to Tarleton's Legion. The duke was a romantic character and even had a brief relationship with Mary Robinson, Tarleton's love interest for many years. However, this did not stop the former adversaries from becoming friends after the war. Lauzun died under the guillotine during the French Revolution. See his *Memoirs*, trans. C. K. Scott Moncrieff (London: George Routledge & Sons, 1928).

[2] A British army under Major General John Burgoyne surrendered to the Rebels at Saratoga, New York on October 17, 1777. France signed a military and commercial treaty with the US in 1778; Robert McCluer Calhoon, *The Loyalists in Revolutionary America: 1760-1781* (New York: Harcourt Brace Jovanovich, 1965), 479-483; William B. Willcox, ed., *The American Rebellion: Sir Henry Clinton's Narrative of His Campaigns, 1775-*

1782, With an Appendix of Original Documents (New Haven: Yale University Press, 1954), xlvi, 149-156; in late 1778, Clinton's army lost thirteen regular regiments. These had been sent back to England and to other places, such as Halifax, Pensacola, Savannah, and the West Indies. The need for Loyalist troops now became even greater. Greg Novak, *A Guide to the American War of Independence in the North*, Campaign Book #7A (Champaign, Illinois: Ulster Imports, 1990), 65; Lord George Germain to Sir Henry Clinton (Most Secret), Whitehall, March 8, 1778, 15:57-62; Germain stated the King's intention was to attack Georgia and South Carolina and rouse the loyal inhabitants. See Secret Instructions for General Sir Henry Clinton, St. James's, March 21, 1778, 15:74-76. This letter ordered Clinton to send five thoussand troops to St. Lucia and three thousand to Florida, plus to evacuate Philadelphia as well as New York if the latter could not be held; Germain to Clinton, Whitehall, May 4, 1778, 15:114-115. "A French war appears to be inevitable"; Lt. Col. Archibald Campbell to Sir Henry Clinton, Savannah, March 4, 1779, 17:73-76; Governor Sir James Wright to Lord Germain, Savannah, August 9, 1779, 17:185-186. Wright claimed that the conquest of South Carolina would not be difficult. All in *Documents of the American Revolution: 1770-1783*, Colonial Office Series, ed. K.G. Davies, 21 vols. (Dublin: Irish University Press, 1972-1981) (hereafter cited as *DAR*).

[3] Reduction meant that a regiment had been disbanded. John Mollo, *Uniforms of the American Revolution* (Blandford Press, 1975; repr., New York: Sterling Publishing, 1991), 36. The royal grant of fifty acres was in lieu of levy money. Until May 1779, provincial officers ranked junior to regular officers with the same commissions. This mindset represented a leftover from previous colonial wars and caused much animosity.

Loyalists represented 16% (513,000 out of 3,210,000) of the total population, or 19.8% of white Americans. Between 1775 and 1781, fifty Provincial regiments were established, comprising 312 companies. Approximately 21,000 saw service in these battalions. Provincials were a type of regular soldier and had the same type of uniform and accoutrements. They should not be confused with volunteer "associators" or militiamen.

The overall British policy toward the loyal Americans failed. Ministry officials consistently overestimated their numbers and never formulated realistic goals concerning their use. This can be seen in the returns for December 1778 and December 1779 when the number of Provincial soldiers rose from 7,400 to only nine thousand. See Paul H. Smith, *Loyalists and Redcoats: A Study in British Revolutionary Policy* (Chapel Hill: University of North Carolina Press, 1964), 60-78; Paul H. Smith, "The American Loyalists: Notes on Their Organization and Numerical Strength," *William and Mary Quarterly* 25 (1968): 263, 266-267, 269.

[4] It became a point of honor among young officers to be given the command of such units. C.T. Atkinson, "British Forces in North America, 1774-1781: Their Distribution and Strength," *Journal of the Society for Army Historical Research* 16 (1937): 4 (hereafter cited as *JSAHR*). Thirty-eight privates represented the peacetime establishment for a regular British company. Edward E. Curtis, *The Organization of the British Army in the American Revolution* (New Haven, 1926), 4. For the change to red uniforms, see Lieut. Col. J.G. Simcoe, *A History of the Operations of a Partisan Corps Called the Queen's Rangers* (New York: Bartlett and Welford, 1844; repr., New York: Arno Press, 1968), 38.

[5] Clinton's book is reproduced as Willcox, ed., *The American Rebellion*, 111. Francis Rawdon (1754-1826), an Irish nobleman, attended Oxford with Tarleton. Known as Lord Moira, he became in February 1817 the First Marquess of Hastings. For his biography as well as the one of William Schaw Cathcart, tenth Baron Cathcart (1755-1843), consult L. Edward Purcell, *Who was Who in the American Revolution* (New York: Facts on File, 1993), 87, 401-402.

[6] During this time in Europe, cavalry consisted of three types: cuirassier (heavy), dragoon (medium), and hussar (light). The name "cuirassier" came from the iron breastplate or *cuirass*, an extremely uncomfortable protective device. Hussars went by various other names, such as light dragoons, chevaux légers, chasseurs à cheval, and lancers.

Light infantry represented the elite of any regiment. At the time of Lexington and Concord, a peacetime English regiment on the Regular Establishment consisted of 474 men of all ranks, subdivided into ten companies: eight battalion companies known as "hatmen" for their tricorn headgear and one flank company each of grenadiers and light infantry. Grenadiers were usually the tallest and strongest men in the regiment and wore high bearskin caps. By 1774 they no longer threw grenades. With their special skills and appearance, flank companies frequently were battalioned separately while on campaign. Four battalions of each saw service in America.

In 1775, light infantrymen were a fairly new commodity on the European military scene. Frederick the Great utilized them often in the first line of attack and never truly grasped their potential as skirmishers. There was even a hesitant approach in the British Army to use light infantry because many considered them "a most ruinous drain" on the line regiments, depriving the latter of some of their best men. Anthony J. Scotti, Jr., "'This Disagreeable Exertion of Authority': Banastre Tarleton and the British Legion in the Southern Campaigns, 1780-1781," (MA thesis, Wake Forest University, 1991), 13-15, 17-18. Legions remained popular in the armies of Europe through the Napoleonic era. A good discussion of European light troops is found in Christopher Duffy, *The Military Experience in the Age of Reason* (New York: Atheneum, 1988), 268-279; for George Washington's view on mounted troops, see Leszek Szymanski, *Casimir Pulaski: A Hero of the American Revolution* (1979; New York: Hippocrene Books, 1994), 157-177, 202-203, 210-211, 242-243, 284; Robert K. Wright, Jr., *The Continental Army*, Army Lineage Series (Washington, DC: Center of Military History, 1989), 48-49, 105-106, 126, 133-134, 160-161, 184.

[7] Scotti, "'This Disagreeable Exertion of Authority,'" 14.

[8] *Ibid*.

[9] "Drafted" means that the troops were simply transferred. The British did have previous military experience in North America. Why they did not bring more light troops might have to do with peacetime reductions and a poor opinion of colonial resistance. The cavalry of the British Army at this time consisted of seventeen dragoon regiments, four light dragoon regiments, two troops each of Horse Guards and Horse Grenadier Guards, and the Royal Regiment of Horse Guards (Blue). The Irish Establishment had four additional horse regiments. A regiment of cavalry had 230 effectives, divided into six troops. Anthony D. Darling, *Red Coat and Brown Bess*, Historical Arms Series No. 12 (Bloomfield, Ontario: Museum Restoration Service, 1970), 7. Robin May and G.A. Embleton, *The British Army in North America*

1775-1783, Men-at-Arms Series 39 (London: Osprey Publishing, 1974), 38-39. The Brunswick Dragoon Regiment Prinz Ludwig Ernst, a German auxiliary unit, arrived in the American colonies without mounts in 1776. It never obtained horses and most of the regiment was either killed or captured at Bennington, Vermont the next year.

[10] Most English and German regiments had only one battalion, and for that reason the terms "regiment" and "battalion" were used interchangeably. Other European powers during this time period had two or more battalions per regiment. See Wright, *The Continental Army*, 4. Simcoe, *History of the Operations*, 38, 209-210. During the summer months in the South the Legion wore white sleeved waistcoats; M. S. Almanack for the year 1783, comp. Bernhard de Wiederhold, New York Historical Society; the *Boston New England or Independent Chronicle*, August 10 and September 7, 1780, described four Legion officers who escaped from Rebel custody as wearing "short green Coats trimmed with narrow Gold Lace." At least one had a fur cap while another wore striped trousers. The *Ipswich (Connecticut) Journal* of October 21, 1780 gave a similar description of the coat.

[11] The eighteenth century was an age of gaudy military uniforms and exotic headgear. The Legion head-dress, worn by English light dragoons until 1814, was called a "Tarleton helmet." Mollo, *Uniforms of the American Revolution*, 211. Also, Anthony J. Scotti, Jr., "'The Lost Sons': British Legion Light Infantry in the Revolutionary War," *Loyalist Gazette* 33 (Spring 1995): 24-26. The Queen's Rangers and Lee's Legion had uniforms very similar in appearance to that of the British Legion. For the Rangers, see Lt. Charles M. Lefferts, *Uniforms of the American, British, French, and German Armies in the War of the American Revolution, 1775-1783* (New York, 1926; repr., Old Greenwich, Connecticut: W. E. Inc., 1971), 229. For Lee's Legion, see Christopher Ward, *War of the Revolution*, 2 vols. (New York: Macmillan, 1952), 2: 778-779. Scotti, "'Disagreeable Exertion of Authority,'" 12. One source has the Legion infantry wearing light infantry style caps. What these looked like is uncertain, especially since there was no standard light infantry cap in the British Army at the time. "400 Helmets are preparing for the Cavalry and 400 Leather Caps for the Infantry." See "Return of Arms, Accoutrements & Clothing wanting for the Cavalry of the British Legion Commanded by Lt. Colo. Banastre Tarleton Charlestown 14th June 1780," in PRO, Chancery,

Class 106, Volume 90. Don Troiani, *Military Buttons of the American Revolution* (Gettysburg, Penn.: Thomas Publications, 2001), Troiani, *Soldiers In America 1754-1865* (Mechanicsburg, Penn.: Stackpole Books, 1998), 39-40.

[12] Tarleton's *A History of the Campaigns of 1780 and 1781, in the Southern Provinces of North America* (London: T. Cadell, 1787), is an excellent and thorough history, but offers nothing in the way of tactical discussions.

[13] Reprinted as Simcoe, *History of the Operations*, 18-20, 28, 32, 37, 98-99. He also wanted his hussars to be armed with daggers, "to lead the minds of the soldiers to expect that decisive mode of combat." Duke of Cumberland, "Standing orders for the dragoons, circa 1755," *JSAHR* 23 (1945): 98-106; Henry Earl of Pembroke, *Military Equitation: Or, a Method of Breaking Horses, and Teaching Soldiers to Ride*, 3rd ed. (London: E. Easton, 1778); William Richardson Davie, *Instructions to be Observed for the Formations and Movements of the Cavalry* (Halifax, North Carolina: Abraham Hodge, 1799).

[14] The eleven Ranger infantry companies consisted of eight riflemen and one each of grenadiers, light infantry, and Highlanders; the cavalry troops included one of hussars and three of light dragoons. Simcoe, *History of the Operations*, 20, 150; Lefferts, *Uniforms*, 222 (plate); Mollo, *Uniforms of the American Revolution*, 211-213; Smith, "The American Loyalists," 271; the intended strength of the American Legion was to be 684 men, but it never exceeded 201. Willard Sterne Randall, *Benedict Arnold: Patriot and Traitor* (New York: William Morrow, 1990), 577-578. Arnold attempted to fill his ranks with Continental deserters. Washington viewed this as an "unparalleled piece of assurance...I am at a loss which to admire most, the confidence of Arnold in publishing, or the folly of the enemy in supposing that a production signed by so infamous a character will have any weight with the people of these states." George Washington to the President of Congress, Head Quarters near Passaic Falls, October 29, 1780, *Writings of George Washington: 1745-1799*, ed. John Fitzpatrick, 39 vols. (Washington, DC: US Government Printing Office, 1931-1944), 20:263-264. The American Legion finally mustered out with only three companies and forty-four rank and file. See the embarkation return in Colonial Office

Records, Public Record Office, Kew, 5/111, f. 149 (hereafter cited as PRO).

[15] A recruiting advertisement for chasseurs and dragoons, commanded by Lt. Col. Emmerick, can be found in the *New York Royal Gazette*, July 8, 1778. The Saturday, June 29, 1782 issue of the *New York Royal Gazette* offers a ten-guinea bounty for volunteers in the King's American Dragoons. In the French and English armies, "chasseur" was another name for light infantry. The Germans called such troops jägers (also spelled yagers), which is somewhat confusing because they also called riflemen by the same name. See Mark M. Boatner III, *Encyclopedia of the American Revolution* (New York: David McKay, 1966), 218. Smith, "The American Loyalists," 272-273, 275; the known maximum total for Emmerick's command is 215, while for Thompson's unit it is 290. The King's American Dragoons combined members of the Queen's Rangers, British Legion, Volunteers of New England, and Stewart's Provincial Dragoons. Philip Katcher and Michael Youens, *The American Provincial Corps 1775-1784*, Men-at-Arms Series (Reading, England: Osprey, 1973), 29. The English also gave mounts to eighty-six German jägers in Philadelphia in March 1778. Captain Frederick de Diemar's Hussars and Captain Gilles' North Carolina Dragoons were very small organizations, having only seventy-three and fifty-four men, respectively. Two other small mounted Provincial units were the Georgia Light Dragoons (Rangers) and the South Carolina Loyalists. Atkinson, "British Forces in North America," *JSAHR* 16 (1937): 13, 17, 19, 21. During the last six months of the war in South Carolina, the British formed an Independent Troop of Black Dragoons. A shortage of manpower as well as the psychological effects upon the enemy induced royal officials to turn to slaves and freedmen. Although only thirty in number, the Black Dragoons frightened inhabitants north of Charles Town with their nightly raids. The cavalrymen kept British markets in the town well supplied with livestock. See Pay Abstract Nr 163, Independent Troop of Black Dragoons, for 92-days pay, July 1 to September 30, 1782, PRO, T50, Vol. 2. Also, Sylvia R. Frey, *Water from the Rock: Black Resistance in a Revolutionary Age* (Princeton: Princeton University Press, 1991), 139, 190-191.

[16] Lack of differentiation in Legion rolls between officers and enlisted personnel and between cavalry troops and infantry companies also presents some confusion. Smith, "The American Loyalists," 265;

"warrant men" must also be taken into account when reviewing muster rolls. A regular English regiment had six of these fictitious individuals. Their pay was for the widows of regimental officers, recruiting purposes, replacing clothes lost by deserters, etc. "Contingent men" were actually non-effectives maintained in each company to repair arms and to cover other expenses. Darling, *Red Coat and Brown Bess*, 12n9. The British Legion infantry had three contingent men per company. See British Legion, Minutes of Muster for December 25, 1780, April 25, 1781, and June 25 to August 24, 1781, Loyalist Regiment Muster Rolls, 1777-1783 (vols. 1851-1908), Public Archives of Canada, Ottawa, RG8I "C" Series, Vols. 1883 and 1884 (hereafter cited as PAC).

[17] Smith, *Loyalists and Redcoats*, 60n2; J.A. Houlding, *Fit for Service: The Training of the British Army, 1715-1795* (Oxford: Clarendon Press, 1981), 116n31; Boatner presents some different percentages. He claims that if the effective rank and file number of an English unit is known, then 17.5% should be added to get the total combatant strength. For Rebel battalions, 28% should be added to get the corresponding figure. Boatner, *Encyclopedia of the American Revolution*, 916.

[18] Confusion can develop over a definition of "Loyalist." How long did one have to reside in the colonies to become a Loyalist? Six months? Three years? It is known that Loyalist recruiters actively sought deserters. Mollo, *Uniforms of the American Revolution*, 36; for regulars in the ranks of Provincial battalions, see Smith, "The American Loyalists," 263; some of the regiments that these regular volunteers came from were the Sixteenth Light Dragoons (John Miller), Seventeenth Light Dragoons (Stanley), Fifty-Fourth Foot (Jordan), and Thirty-Seventh Foot (Browne). Murtie June Clark, *Loyalists in the American Southern Campaign of the Revolutionary War*, 3 vols. (Baltimore: Genealogical Publishing Company, 1981), 3:343, 354-355, 379. By the same token, there were many Loyalists in regular British regiments. See Atkinson, "British Forces in North America," *JSAHR* 16 (1937): 4-5.

[19] The "noble Earl" was Lord Cathcart. *Cambridge Chronicle and Journal* (England), January 2, 1779.

[20] For the Volunteers of Ireland, see Willcox, ed., *American Rebellion*, 110-111; Sir John Fortescue, *A History of the British Army*, 13 vols. (London, 1899-1930; repr., New York: AMS Press, 1976), 3:270. The Queen's Rangers had a high turnover of American Loyalists, "old countrymen" or Europeans, and deserters. Simcoe, *History of the Operations*, 18-19, 91-92. Around August 1778, some deserters came in and enlisted in the British Legion. For Tarleton's quote, see Lt. Gen. Ban. Tarleton to the Duke of York, Richmond, Sept. 28th, 1801, in Robert D. Bass, *The Green Dragoon: The Lives of Banastre Tarleton and Mary Robinson* (New York: Henry Holt, 1957), 406-408. It will be interesting to see if more research can reveal the percentage of militia and Continental deserters in Provincial battalions. For a preliminary study, see Lawrence E. Babits, "Continentals in the British Legion, August 1780-October 1781," paper presented at Guilford Courthouse National Military Park, Greensboro, N.C., March 16, 2001.

As the war progressed, desertion became pandemic and both sides had a serious problem with it. Nathanael Greene reflected: "At the close of the war, we fought the enemy with British soldiers, and they fought us with those of America." In John S. Pancake, *This Destructive War: The British Campaign in the Carolinas, 1780-1782* (Tuscaloosa: University of Alabama Press, 1985), 217; Alexander Garden, *Anecdotes of the Revolutionary War in America, With Sketches of Character of Persons the Most Distinguished, in the Southern States, For Civil and Military Services* (Charleston: A.E. Miller, 1822), 396-398, 409.

[21] Muster Roll of Captain Richard Hovenden's Troop of the British Legion, December 25, 1780 to February 24, 1781; Muster Roll of the First Troop of Philadelphia Light Dragoons Commanded by Captain Richard Hovenden, February 23, 1778; Muster Roll of Captain Charles McDonald's Company, British Legion Infantry, from February 24, 1782 to April 24, 1782; Muster Roll of Captain David Ogelvey's Troop, British Legion Cavalry, from December 25 to February 23, 1782, all in Loyalist Regiment Muster Rolls, 1777-1783, PAC, RG8I "C" Series, Vols. 1884 and 1894; British Legion, Abstract of 61 days pay for the commissioned officers of the infantry, October 25, 1782 to December 25, 1782, PRO, 30/55, Doc. 6493; Clark, *Loyalists in the American Southern Campaign*, 3:343, 354, 379; twenty-four Legion officers received half-pay upon the conclusion of the war. See the letter of Thomas Townshend to the Secretary at War, Whitehall, January 14, 1783, and Commissions for the following Gentlemen to be Officers in a

Regiment of Light Dragoons, Home Office Records, PRO, 51/146, f. 52, 57.

[22] Pioneer troops acted as engineers and constructed fortifications, cleared roadways, maintained bridges, etc. Smith, "The American Loyalists," 271. The Black Pioneers had a known cumulative total of eighty. Twelve men are listed as dead, discharged, and deserted. Benjamin Quarles, *The Negro in the American Revolution* (Chapel Hill, 1961), 146-149; Lorenzo Sabine, *Biographical Sketches of Loyalists of the American Revolution, With an Historical Essay*, 2 vols. (Boston: Little, Brown, and Company, 1864), 1:79-86, 309, 546, 552-553, 569; 2:387, 489, 494, 596. James was a renowned horse thief. Samuel Chapman, a lieutenant in Hovenden's troop of Legion cavalry, was tried and acquitted for treason by the state of Pennsylvania. Vernon's four sons eventually received their father's property.

[23] Sabine, *Biographical Sketches of Loyalists*, 2:522, asserts that Green held the rank of corporal. Muster Roll of the Second Troop of Philadelphia Light Dragoons, Commanded by Captain Jacob James, July 27, 1778 and Muster Roll of Captain Jacob James' Troop of the British Legion, Hussars, from October 25 to December 24, 1781, in Loyalist Regiment Muster Rolls, 1777-1783, PAC, RG8I "C" Series, Vols. 1884 and 1894.

[24] Garden, *Anecdotes of the Revolutionary War in America*, 396-398. Docherty's name is also spelled Dogharty, Doharty, and Dockerty in the muster rolls. The dates of his enlistment in the British Legion (September 3, 1780) and his subsequent capture at the Cowpens (officially reported on February 23, 1781) are verified in Muster Rolls of Captain Donald McPherson's Company, British Legion, Infantry, from October 25, 1780 to December 24, 1780, and from October 25, 1781 to December 24, 1781, Loyalist Regiment Muster Rolls, 1777-1783, PAC, RG8I "C" Series, Vol. 1884. Also see PRO, 30/55, Doc. 10253.

[25] Smith, "The American Loyalists," 271; Tarleton, *History of the Campaigns*, 210; State of the Troops, Number XXI, in Earl Cornwallis, *An Answer to That Part of the Narrative of Lieutenant-General Sir Henry Clinton, K.B., Which Relates to the Conduct of Lieutenant-General Earl*

Cornwallis, During the Campaign in North-America, in the Year 1781 (London, 1783; repr., Philadelphia, 1865), facing p. 236.

[26] Atkinson, "British Forces in North America," *JSAHR* 16 (1937): 4-5; 20 (1941): 192. This last citation reports 570 rank and file for a wartime establishment. All units in the British Army were chronically undermanned due to combat, disease, desertion, and drafting. British officials always had high hopes for the British Legion. The issue of clothing for the Legion in March 1782 included coats for 640 privates. W.Y. Carman, "Banastre Tarleton and the British Legion," *JSAHR* 62 (1984): 130.

Apparent exaggerations of Legion strength exist in at least two sources. In December 1779, a jäger captain named Johann von Hinrichs reported Lord Cathcart's Legion to be seven hundred strong. Certainly Tarleton himself would have bragged of such an impressive muster in his book. Bernhard A. Uhlendorf, trans., *The Siege of Charleston, With an Account of the Province of South Carolina: Diaries and Letters of Hessian Officers From the von Jungkenn Papers in the William L. Clements Library* (Ann Arbor: University of Michigan Press, 1938), 105. Lord Germain claimed that as of December 31, 1780, there were over six hundred Legion rank and file in South Carolina. Germain to Clinton, Whitehall, March 7, 1781, *DAR*, 20:77-78.

[27] Smith, "The American Loyalists," 271-277. Forty-one units are surveyed in this article.

[28] Willcox, ed. *American Rebellion*, 111; Robert H. Vetch, "Sir Banastre Tarleton, 1754-1833," *The Dictionary of National Biography*, eds. Sir Leslie Stephen and Sir Sidney Lee, 22 vols. (Oxford: Oxford University Press, 1921-1922), 19:365; Bass, *Green Dragoon*, 46-47; Pancake is mistaken when he states that "the Legion consisted of 300 Loyalist infantry recruited in New York and 150 dragoons of the 17th Regiment." Pancake, *This Destructive War*, 49, 59.

[29] Muster Roll of Captain Francis Gildart's Troop of Light Dragoons belonging to the British Legion, October 24, 1781 to December 24, 1781; Muster Roll of Captain Richard Hovenden's Troop of the British Legion, October 25 to December 24, 1780; Muster Roll of Captain Jacob James' Troop of the British Legion, October 25, 1780 to December 24, 1780; Muster Roll of Captain David Ogilvy's Company,

British Legion Cavalry, October 25 to December 24, 1780; Muster Roll of Captain Thomas Sandford's Troop of Light Dragoons, October 25 to December 24, 1780; Muster Roll of Captain Nathaniel Vernon's Troop, British Legion, December 25, 1781 to February 23, 1782. Ogilvy's name is also spelled Ogilvie and Ogelvey. Sandford is sometimes spelled Sanford, and Hovenden is sometimes spelled Hovedon. David Kinlock commanded the seventh troop. Muster Roll of Captain David Kinlock's Troop under the Command of Lieut Colonel Tarleton, October 25 to December 24, 1780. All found in Loyalist Regiment Muster Rolls, 1777-1783, PAC, RG8I "C" Series, Vols. 1883 and 1884. For the unit's final muster, see the embarkation return, September 15, 1783, Colonial Office Records, PRO, 5/111, f. 149; Capt. Robert Mackenzie to Capt. Hovedon, Philadelphia, November 7, 1777, vol. 5, No. 130, 1p; June 25 to August 24, 1782, Sixty-one days' pay abstract for the British Legion, vol. 43, No. 212, 2p; February 24 to April 24, 1783, Sixty days' pay abstract for the British Legion, vol. 31, Nos. 63 and 64, 3p, all in *Report on American Manuscripts in the Royal Institution of Great Britain*, prepared by The Historical Manuscripts Commission Great Britian, 4 vols., Introduction by George A. Billias (Boston: Gregg Press, 1972), Vol. 3, calendar, July 1782 to March 1783, Carleton Papers (microfilm) (hereafter cited as Carleton Papers); Carman, "Banastre Tarleton and the British Legion", 128-129; Dr. Carlos E. Godfrey, "Muster Rolls of Three Troops of Loyalist Light Dragoons Raised in Pennsylvania 1777-1778," *The Pennsylvania Magazine of History and Biography* 34 (1910): 1-8. One report states that the Philadelphia troop had "112 horse" in March 1778. See Bernhard A. Uhlendorf, trans., *Revolution in America: Confidential Letters and Journals 1776-1784 of Adjutant General Major Baurmeister of the Hessian Forces* (New Brunswick: Rutgers University Press, 1957), 158.

[30] Simcoe, *History of the Operations*, 74, 79, 107. Godfrey, "Muster Rolls of Three Troops of Loyalist Light Dragoons Raised in Pennsylvania 1777-1778," 2-3.

[31] Muster Roll of Captain James Edwards' Company of British Legion, October 25 to December 24, 1781; Muster Roll of Captain Charles McDonald's Company, British Legion Infantry, October 25 to December 24, 1780; Muster Roll of Captain Donald McPherson's Company, British Legion, October 25 to December 24, 1781; Muster Roll of Captain Thomas Miller's Company, British Legion, October 25,

1780; Muster Roll of Captain John Rousselet's Company, Infantry of the British Legion, October 25 to December 24, 1780; Muster Roll of Captain Patrick Stewart's Company of Infantry British Legion, October 25 to December 24, 1780. See Loyalist Regiment Muster Rolls, 1777-1783, PAC, RG8I "C" Series, Vols. 1883 and 1884. The four companies to survive the war were those of Stewart, Rousselet, Miller, and McDonald. April 25 to June 24, 1782, British Legion Infantry, Abstract of sixty-one days' pay, vol. 41, No. 220, 2pp; Board of General Officers, January 10, 1783, New York, abstract of pay for Edwards' and McPherson's companies, vol. 45, No. 128, 2pp; Warrant, September 6, 1783, New York, to pay Lieutenant Moore Hovenden, paymaster, British Legion, vol. 37, No. 9, 1p, all in Carleton Papers; Embarkation return, September 15, 1783, Colonial Office Records, PRO, 5/111, f. 149. Scotti, "'Lost Sons,'" 24-26.

[32] A recruiting advertisement for the Caledonian Volunteers is in the *New York Royal Gazette*, July 11, 1778. Philip R.N. Katcher, *Encyclopedia of British, Provincial, and German Army Units, 1775-1783* (Harrisburg, Pennsylvania: Stackpole Books, 1973), 83-84. Katcher asserts that the Caledonians were a mounted/foot company. According to Bass, the Legion had one company each of Scots and Americans and two of Englishmen. Bass, *Green Dragoon*, 47-48. The Orderly Book of Captain Thomas Scott's (American) Company of the British Legion, Andre de Coppet Collection, Princeton University Library, Manuscript Division, Department of Rare Books and Special Collections, Princeton, New Jersey.

[33] Atkinson, "British Forces in North America," *JSAHR* 16 (1937): 13-14. Provincial troops in North America. Return of numbers of effectives, New York, January 1, 1779, *DAR*, 16:244. In October 1778, the New York garrison had six unattached cavalry troops, amounting to 193 rank and file. Katcher, *Encyclopedia of British, Provincial, and German Army Units*, 135. The Legion under Lord Cathcart had thirty officers and 246 other ranks fit for duty in August 1778. Carman, "Banastre Tarleton and the British Legion," 128.

[34] Lewis Nicola to John Jay, July 10, 1779, *The Papers of the Continental Congress*, comp. John P. Butler (Washington, DC: US Government Printing Office, 1978), 2p., M247, reel 180, i163, page 72. Uhlendorf,

trans., *Revolution in America*, 264. Lord Cathcart had 350 horse in April 1779.

[35] The Legion cavalry on this date had eleven officers, twelve sergeants, two trumpeters, and 157 rank and file; the Legion infantry had eight officers, nine sergeants, three drummers, and 106 rank and file. Tarleton, *History of the Campaigns*, 136. Uhlendorf, trans., *Revolution in America*, 352.

[36] Troops listed as "on command" were on detached duty, either in the immediate vicinity of camp or at a great distance. See, Wright, *The Continental Army*, 40n43. In April 1781, the Legion had four rank and file "on command within the district," and one sergeant and thirty rank and file "without the district." See State of the Army with Earl Cornwallis at Wilmington, North Carolina, April 15, 1781, Cornwallis Papers, PRO, 30/11/103, ff. 27-28. British Legion, Minutes of Muster for October 25, 1780, Loyalist Regiment Muster Rolls, 1777-1783, PAC, RG8I "C" Series, Vol. 1883; Tarleton, *History of the Campaigns*, 210; Etat des différens corps sous le commandement du comte Cornwallis..., *Correspondance du Lord G. Germain, Avec Les Généraux Clinton, Cornwallis & les Amiraux dans la station de l'Amérique, avec plusieurs lettres interceptées du Général Washington, du Marquis de la Fayette & de M. de Barras, chef d'Escadre* (Berne: Chez la Nouvelle Société Typographique, 1782), after page 304. State of His Majesty's provincial forces in the southern district of North America, Charleston, December 31, 1780, *DAR*, 16:470. During this time the Legion had 230 cavalry fit for duty out of 285.

[37] British Legion, Minutes of Muster for April 25, 1781; British Legion, Minutes of Muster For June 25 to August 24, 1781. Both are located in Loyalist Regiment Muster Rolls, 1777-1783, PAC, RG8I "C" Series, Vol. 1884. No Date (1782 or 1783), Account of cash paid to prisoners in Philadelphia jail belonging to the British Legion Infantry, Carleton Papers, vol. 27, No. 228, 1p; contrary to common belief, the Legion infantry were not all lost at the Cowpens. Some apparently survived and were sent back to Charles Town, while others became dragoons or were drafted into other regiments. See Scotti, "'Lost Sons,'" 24-26. Uhlendorf, trans., *Revolution in America*, 436. In May 1781, prison camps at Fredericktown, Maryland interned 411 Cowpens soldiers. The British officers taken at the engagement received paroles and

went to Charles Town. See Lt. Gen. Alexander Leslie to Sir Henry Clinton, Charleston, December 27, 1781, *DAR*, 20:286-288. "I beg to know what is to be done with the officers of the Legion, many are here and no men, and all of them of their infantry." A muster roll is available for the Legion on the first of each month between February and October 1781. See State of the Troops, Number VI, VII, XX, XXI, in Cornwallis, *Answer*, 53, 77, facing page 236. The figures are as follows: February to April, 174 effectives; May to July, 173; August, 183; September to October, 168. At the York Town capitulation on October 18, 1781, Cornwallis listed 208 effectives plus twenty-four sick and wounded. State of the troops left in South Carolina under the command of ... Lord Rawdon, January 15, 1781, 30/11/103, ff. 15-16; State of the army with Earl Cornwallis at Wilmington, North Carolina, April 15, 1781, 30/11/103, ff. 27-28, both in Cornwallis Papers, PRO. Tarleton's *History of the Campaigns* (p. 450) lists a total of 241 officers and men for the British Legion: 1 lieutenant colonel, 6 captains, 8 lieutenants, 3 cornets, 6 quartermasters, 1 surgeon, 17 sergeants, 7 trumpeters, and 192 rank and file.

[38] Embarkation return, September 15, 1783, Colonial Office Records, PRO, 5/111, f. 149; Carleton to Brig. Gen. H.E. Fox, New York, September 12, 1783, vol. 49, No. 141, 4p; Abstract, 61 days' pay for the British Legion, June 25 to August 24, 1783, vol. 37, Nos. 91 and 92, 2p; Warrant, September 6, 1783, New York, to pay Lt. Moore Hovenden, paymaster, vol. 37, No. 9, 1p, all in Carleton Papers.

[39] Simcoe said that the Seventeenth had "superior discipline." These dragoons, in fact, trained his hussars. Simcoe, *History of the Operations*, 97, 290; Scotti, "'Disagreeable Exertion,'" 27-28; The troop is not enumerated on Legion muster rolls. It does appear on Earl Cornwallis's returns for June 1, 1781. On that date, a separate heading is provided for the twenty-five rank and file fit for duty. By October 1, this figure was down to twenty-one. State of the Troops, Number XX, Cornwallis, *Answer*, facing page 236. The men of the Seventeenth wore brass helmets with long red horsehair crests. The regimental motto, a death's head with the words "OR GLORY" underneath it, were painted on the helmet's front. This badge is still in use today and commemorates the death of James Wolfe at Quebec as well as his victory (1759). May and Embleton, *The British Army in North America*, 38.

⁴⁰ Boatner, *Encyclopedia of the American Revolution*, 115, 927-928.

⁴¹ The five American Regiments in numerical order were the Queen's Rangers (First), Volunteers of Ireland (Second), New York Volunteers (Third), King's American Regiment (Fourth), and the British Legion (Fifth). When the Volunteers of Ireland became the 105th Regiment of Foot and vacated its position as the Second American Regiment, the three subordinate Provincial units moved up one slot. That is why some sources note the Legion as being the Fourth American Regiment. Mollo, *Uniforms of The American Revolution,* 36; the positions of the British Legion and the King's American Regiment are reversed in Smith, "The American Loyalists," 271, 273, 275-277; Simcoe, *History of the Operations,* 100; Lt. Col. Turnbull to Sir Guy Carleton, August 18, 1783, vol. 52, No. 123, 1p; only the Legion cavalry were so honored, causing Captain Donald McPherson of the infantry to feel "most sensibly" about the discrimination. See McPherson to Carleton, August 1783, vol. 38, No. 145, 2p, both in Carleton Papers; Thomas Townshend to the Secretary at War, Whitehall, January 14, 1783, and Commissions for the following Gentlemen to be Officers in a Regiment of Light Dragoons, Home Office Records, PRO, 51/146/ p. 52, 57; formation and list of officers, "Dec. 25, 1782, Lt. Dragoons," War Office Records, PRO, 26/31/ p. 328; eulogy of the corps of Tarleton's Light Dragoons prior to placing on Establishment, Colonial Office Records, PRO, 5/237/ p. 359; Carman, "Banastre Tarleton and the British Legion," 130; Katcher, *Encyclopedia of British, Provincial, and German Army Units,* 83.

⁴² An adjutant general supervised the daily administrative paperwork of an army. The quartermaster general had the responsibility of housing, feeding, equipping, and moving troops. Wright, *The Continental Army,* 435, 439. Scotti, "'Disagreeable Exertion,'" 22.

⁴³ Cathcart, a major in the Thirty-Eighth Foot and a former captain in the Seventeenth Dragoons, was "invalided" back to New York in April. Boatner, *Encyclopedia of the American Revolution,* 115, 189-190. It is interesting to note that colonels rarely ever accompanied their regiments abroad, thus leaving the lieutenant colonels to act as the field commanders. As stated earlier, Tarleton became commandant of

the Legion just before the Charles Town expedition. Duffy, *The Military Experience*, 70-73.

[44] Clinton to Germain, May 15, 1780, Charleston, *DAR*, 18:91-92.

[45] Simcoe, *History of the Operations*, 80.

[46] The officer, Lieutenant John Money, an aide-de-camp to the Earl Cornwallis, later died of his wounds. Henry Lumpkin, *From Savannah to Yorktown: The American Revolution in the South* (Columbia: University of South Carolina Press, 1981), 113, 169; Franklin and Mary Wickwire, *Cornwallis: The American Adventure* (Boston: Houghton Mifflin Company, 1970), 226; Tarleton, *History of the Campaigns*, 311-312; "I am hit at last in the right Hand and Arm." Tarleton to Dr. Collyer, N Carolina April 10th, 1781, in Richard M. Ketchum, ed., "New War Letters of Banastre Tarleton," *New York Historical Society Quarterly* 51 (January 1967): 81; Tarleton received a gunshot wound during the running cavalry skirmish before the main battle occurred around the courthouse. Elijah Coffin, a young Quaker boy at the time, remembered that: "A soldier came in great haste to my mother at the dwelling, having two fingers shot off and bleeding, which she kindly dressed for him as well as she could and he hastened back to the conflict." Whether or not this was Banastre Tarleton has never been ascertained. Consult Algie I. Newlin, *The Battle of New Garden* (Greensboro, North Carolina: The North Carolina Friends Historical Society and the North Carolina Yearly Meeting of Friends, 1977), 1, 23, 34-35.

[47] Tarleton, *History of the Campaigns*, 100, 159, 165. The Englishman implies that a "fever" started to plague him in July. Bass claims that he had both diseases. On page 90 of the Tarleton biography, Bass states that Tarleton had malaria in August 1780. Sixteen pages later, he asserts that the Legion commander had yellow fever in September 1780. Malaria and yellow fever are two separate diseases. It is possible that Tarleton had both, but it is not very likely that he would have lived considering his already weakened condition just after one of them. See Bass, *The Green Dragoon*, 90, 106; in the 1700s, yellow fever was more lethal than malaria with an 85% mortality rate among those infected. It was a viral infection from the West African forest and was carried by the domesticated mosquito (*Aedes aegypti*). These

mosquitoes were found usually in water containers. The malaria mosquito (*Anopheles*) frequented swamps and puddles. Tarleton probably had malaria. See John McNeill, "The Ecological Basis of Warfare in the Caribbean, 1700-1804," in Maarten Ultee, ed., *Adapting to Conditions: War and Society in the Eighteenth Century* (University of Alabama Press, 1986), 27-29; Wickwire, *Cornwallis*, 199; Tarleton "is exceedingly ill at White's on Fishing Creek: He cannot be removed; & I am obliged to have his Corps there, for his protection." Lord Cornwallis to Major Richard England, September 20, 1780, Waxhaws, 30/11/80, p. 31-32; "I have been very uneasy about him." Cornwallis to Lt. Col. Nisbet Balfour, September 21, 1780, Waxhaw (*sic*), 30/11/80, p. 35-36; "We are fortunate to save him." Cornwallis to Balfour, September 23, 1780, Waxhaw (*sic*), 30/11/80, p. 39-40, all in Cornwallis Papers, PRO; two years after his return to England, Hanger was a guest at Earl Moira's home where some other officers of the American war were amazed to see him still alive. Hanger, *Life, Adventures, and Opinions*, 2:408-414.

[48] Quoted in Bass, *Green Dragoon*, 107. His Legionnaires also rescued Tarleton from French lancers outside of Gloucester, Virginia in October 1781. "There was no officer with them capable of commanding them." Cornwallis to Balfour, September 23, 1780, Waxhaw (*sic*), Cornwallis Papers, PRO, 30/11/80, p. 39-40; Tarleton, *History of the Campaigns*, 30-31, 377; Hanger, *An Address to the Army; in Reply to Strictures, by Roderick M'Kenzie (Late Lieutenant in the 71st Regiment) on Tarleton's History of the Capaigns of 1780 and 1781*, (London: James Ridgway, 1789), 54-58; Wickwire, *Cornwallis*, 198-199.

[49] Simcoe, *History of the Operations*, 153; Tarleton to Morgan, January 19, 1781, in Theodorus Bailey Myers, *Cowpens Papers, Being Correspondence of General Morgan and the Prominent Actors* (Charleston, 1881), 29. This British dragoon was "a gentleman in adversity."

[50] Simcoe claims that the Queen's Rangers became "close knit" and that he was "obliged to preserve this spirit." The Rebels, on the other hand, did not engage in an honorable cause. Simcoe, *History of the Operations*, 18-19; Sabine, *Biographical Sketches of Loyalists*, 1:79-86, 546, 552-553, 569; 2:387, 489, 596; John Richard Alden, *The South in the Revolution: 1763-1789* (Louisiana State University Press, 1957) 162-163, 323-328; Don Higginbotham, *The War of American Independence: Military*

Attitudes, Policies, and Practice, 1763-1789 (New York: Macmillan, 1971), 133-139.

[51] Wolfe did not have a good opinion of the common English soldier either. Quoted from Francis Jennings, *Empire of Fortune: Crowns, Colonies and Tribes in the Seven Years War in America* (New York: WW Norton, 1990), 220. Smith, *Loyalists and Redcoats*, 78.

[52] Lee McCardell, *Ill-Starred General: Braddock of the Coldstream Guards* (University of Pittsburgh Press, 1958), 212; in March 1758, rumors reached English troops in Nova Scotia that New England troops would be used to reduce Canada in the upcoming campaign. This caused one officer to remark: "Then the French will be finely humbled in America." Captain John Knox, *An Historical Journal of the Campaigns in North America For the Years 1757, 1758, 1759, and 1760*, 3 vols. (London: W. Johnston and J. Dodsley, 1769; repr., Toronto: The Champlain Society, 1914), 1:145.

[53] For a new biography of Ferguson, see M. M. Gilchrist, *Patrick Ferguson: "A Strange Adventurer, Tho' A Man of Some Genius,"* Scots' Lives Series (Edinburgh: National museums of Scotland Publications, 2002). Major Patrick Ferguson (1744-1780) led a group of rangers during the war and acted as Inspector of Militia in the Southern Provinces. He raised about four thousand Loyalist militia in the Ninety-Six District of South Carolina before meeting his demise at Kings Mountain. See Purcell, *Who was Who in the American Revolution*, 161-162; one of the regiments which lost its equipment to Tarleton's Legion was none other than the Queen's Rangers. See Simcoe, *History of the Operations*, 303; Tarleton, *History of the Campaigns*, 103; Wickwire, *Cornwallis*, 139; Memorandum to Cornwallis, No Date, (May 1780?), Carleton Papers, vol. 19, No.22, 3p.; The Inspector General of Provincial Forces (Alexander Innes) Report to His Excellency the Commander in Chief, New York, May 30, 1781, 30/11/6, ff. 162-163; Cornwallis to Lt. Col. Nisbet Balfour, Winnsboro, November 4, 1780, 30/11/82, ff. 6-7, both in Cornwallis Papers, PRO. At least one officer claims that some owners never received any compensation for their mounts. See Roderick Mackenzie, *Strictures on Lt. Col. Tarleton's History of the Campaigns of 1780 and 1781, in the Southern Provinces of North America; Wherein Characters and Corps are Vindicated from Injurious Aspersions, and Several Important Transactions Placed in Their Proper Point*

of View (London: R. Faulder, 1787), 39-40; Hanger vehemently denies this accusation. Hanger, *An Address to the Army*, 48-50.

[54] Major Dik A. Daso, "Chariots, Chivalry, and Cockpits: Evolution of the Fighter Pilot, 500 BC - AD 1918, 1993," (photocopy). Author, Columbia, South Carolina, 3-4, 16-18, 24-25. John Keegan, *A History of Warfare* (New York: Alfred A. Knopf, 1993), 139. Charioteers and horsemen "were the first great aggressors in human history;" Simcoe, *History of the Operations*, 98-99.

[55] The provost marshal supervised the military police. John Keegan, *The Face of Battle: A Study of Agincourt, Waterloo and the Somme* (London: Penguin Books, 1978), 203. War enhances the feeling of power associated with being mounted. Note that Tarleton's first commission was in the King's Dragoon Guards. For more on the psychology of the mounted man, see Winston Churchill to Lord Randolph Churchill, 53 Seymour Street, September 10, 1893, 1:209-210; Winston to Lady Randolph, Sandhurst, May 1, 1894, 1:226, both in Randolph S. Churchill and Martin Gilbert, *Winston S. Churchill*, 8 vols. (London: Heinemann, 1966-1988).

[56] Tarleton to Lieutenant Haldane, December 24, 1780, 30/11/4, ff. 383-384; Tarleton to Cornwallis, August 5, 1780, 30/11/63, ff. 19-20; Tarleton to Lt. Col. George Turnbull, near Singletons, November 5, 1780, 30/11/4, ff. 63-64, all in Cornwallis Papers, PRO; Tarleton, *History of the Campaigns*, 100; Tarleton to Captain John André, February 19, 1779, Sir Henry Clinton Papers, William L. Clements Library, University of Michigan, Ann Arbor, Michigan.

[57] Westchester County became known as the "Neutral Ground," thirty miles of no man's land between the British positions around New York City and the Rebel lines in the Highlands. Lawless bands of "Cowboys" (Loyalists) and "Skinners" (Rebels) terrorized the region and stole cattle. Robert Kyff, "Tarleton's Raid on Bedford and Poundridge," *The Westchester Historian* 44 (Summer 1968), 50; *Lieutenant-General Royal Engineers Archibald Robertson: His Diaries and Sketches in America 1762-1780*, ed. Harry Miller (Lydenberg, New York: New York Public Library, 1930), 186-187 (hereafter cited as Robertson, *Diaries*). The British Legion infantry was at Huntington on December

21, 1778 and Setalket on December 22; Simcoe, *History of the Operations*, 79-92; Uhlendorf, *Revolution in America*, 189, 212, 229.

[58] Quoted in Kyff, "Tarleton's Raid," 53. Tarleton's command had members of his own Legion as well as the Queen's Rangers, the Seventeenth Light Dragoons, and some German jägers. Poundridge is twenty miles northeast of White Plains. Tarleton to Sir Henry Clinton, Camp on the Brunx, July 2, 1779, Eleven P.M., in Bass, *The Green Dragoon*, 55-56; Simcoe, *History of the Operations*, 101-107; Robertson, *Diaries*, 193-194, 198-199; Uhlendorf, trans., *Revolution in America*, 273-274, 280, 291; *New York Royal Gazette*, July 7, 1779.

[59] Kyff, "Tarleton's Raid," 54-58. Each side suffered minimal casualties.

[60] Simcoe, *History of the Operations*, 108, 209-210. After the fall of Charles Town, the Legion and the Rangers did not serve together again until the 1781 British operations in Virginia; Ward, *War of the Revolution*, 2:689. The siege of Savannah lasted from September 23 until October 20, 1779. Some dismounted dragoons under a Captain Tawes manned the Spring Hill Redoubt. Whether these were Legion dragoons is not certain. Major General Augustine Prevost sent dispatches to Sir Henry Clinton via Captain Charles Stewart, "who having been here through the siege has behaved as an officer of merit." Charles Stewart should not be confused with Patrick Stewart, also a captain in the Legion. Prevost to Clinton, November 22, 1779, Savannah, Carleton Papers, vol. 15, Nos. 228 and 229, 2pp. and 3pp.; Robertson, *Diaries*, 206, 218; Eliza Wilkinson complained in June 1779(?) of red-coated and green-coated horsemen plundering the communities on Yonge's Island, thirty miles south of Charles Town. See *Letters of Eliza Wilkinson*, ed. Caroline Gilman (New York Times and Arno Press, 1969), 39-43.

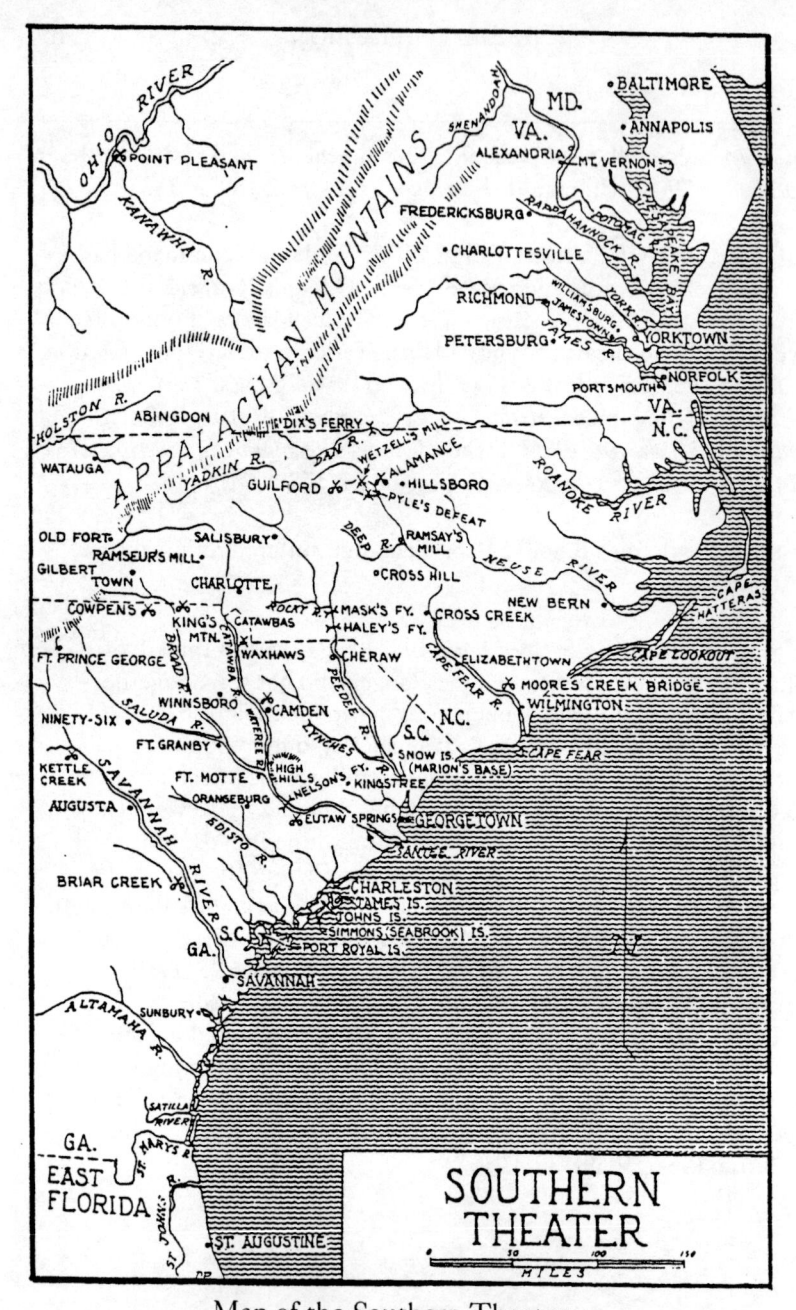

Map of the Southern Theater
Source: Mark Mayo Boatner III, *Encyclopedia of the American Revolution* (Mechanicsburg, Penn.: Stackpole Books, 1994), endpaper

CHAPTER IV

The Legion On Campaign

Along the misty James River, the door to a slumbering brick mansion crashes open, revealing a horse and rider. Both are perspiring profusely in the early morning heat. The horse is evidently uneasy about his surroundings, eyes wide with excitement, his nostrils flaring. The rider, possessing a youthful, handsome countenance, is clad in a green uniform and exudes confidence and determination. He abruptly spurs his reluctant mount across the foyer while simultaneously unsheathing his dragoon saber. Clumsily, the horse takes the black walnut stairs while the rider yells about an approaching enemy patrol. He wildly swings his sword, repeatedly sinking the blade into the banister. The upstairs inhabitants awake from their sleep and frantically assemble their gear. Racing down the stairs, they pass the horseman, who bids them haste. Within minutes, Lieutenant Colonel Banastre Tarleton and his Legionnaires ride forth to meet the enemy.[1]

The above is just one of the many stories concerning Banastre Tarleton which survive to this day, especially in the Old South. Along with the tales of Moses Hall and George Hanger related earlier, it is from such stories that we form our perceptions of Banastre Tarleton and the British Legion. Yet, before analyzing these perceptions it will first be necessary to summarize Legion operations in the southern colonies.

The British Legion had a brief but illustrious career in the South. The regiment disembarked at Savannah, Georgia in January 1780 and surrendered at York Town, Virginia in October 1781. In the course of that time, it participated in most of the major engagements fought in the region, including the siege of Charles Town and the battles of Camden and Guilford Courthouse. Its most complete victory occurred at the Waxhaws while its most stunning defeat happened at the Cowpens. The innumerable smaller battles and skirmishes in which it had an active part include MacPherson's Plantation, Monck's Corner or Biggins Bridge, Lenud's Ferry, Williamson's Plantation, Hanging Rock, Fishing Creek, Wahab's Plantation, Charlotte, Blackstocks Hill, Tarrant's Tavern, and Gloucester Point.[2]

The southern provinces differed in two ways from their northern counterparts. As can be seen today, the topography is quite different. An even plain with open woods dominates eighty to one hundred miles inland from the coast. From that point westward, gentle hills rise to vast mountain ridges. The major rivers of the area, the Savannah, Santee, Pee Dee, Cape Fear, Roanoke, and the James run a general northwest to southeast course. Numerous creeks and morasses dot the landscape. The winters are mild without the extremes of a Yankee wind and eight months of the year are tolerable. The summers are decidedly hot.[3]

Overall, the area was and still is ideal horse country. Not until the southern campaigns did a true cavalry spirit develop on either side. Anticipating the bountiful opportunities for mobile warfare, Sir Henry Clinton included in the British expedition to Charles Town three cavalry organizations: the British Legion, the Queen's Rangers and a detachment of the Seventeenth Light Dragoons. However, only the Legion and one troop from the Seventeenth remained in the South after the reduction of the city.

Unfortunately for the royal cause, these would prove to be not enough.[4]

In fact, this lack of cavalry regiments indicated a larger problem. Peacetime reductions and a general lack of respect for colonial military prowess caused the British Army to come to North America unprepared for mobile warfare. Until the middle of the conflict, British military commanders concentrated their operations in the Northern colonies. There, the need for mounted troops could be met by provincial cavalry organizations, especially since it was cheaper and less time consuming to arm, mount, and accoutre Loyalists. However, France entered the war in 1778, which stretched British manpower reserves. Consequently, Clinton's army suffered "a severe dismemberment." The commander-in-chief had to dispatch thirteen regiments to England, Halifax, Pensacola, and the West Indies. The flank companies also had been withdrawn from the First and Second Battalions of Grenadiers and Light Infantry. Moreover, the Sixteenth Light Dragoons had returned home.[5]

Politically, the South also differed from the North. In fact, this is the reason why the British targeted the region for major offensive operations after 1778. They believed that a majority of the populace remained loyal to King George III and would flock to His Majesty's standard upon sight. However, this proved to be a serious overestimation. Furthermore, the civil war waged between Whig and Tory rendered loyalties frail. The old estimate indicating one-third of the American population as each Rebel, Loyalist, and Neutral is indeed too high for the last two categories. Loyalists actually comprised 16% (513,000 out of 3,210,000) of the total population, or 19.8% of white Americans.[6]

When the English invaded South Carolina in early 1780, they were unprepared for the vicious civil war plaguing the land. Loyalist versus Rebel was a conflict found in all the Thirteen Colonies, but it seems to have had a most intense and ferocious quality in the South. Whigs were viewed as traitors despicable in their perfidy. Meanwhile, Tories were deemed cowards who lacked the courage to defend their nation's rights and collaborators willing to sell themselves and fellow countrymen into slavery. One rarely granted mercy to the other. The countryside "exhibited scenes of distress which were shocking to humanity." The Ninety-Six District of South Carolina alone supposedly contained 1,400 widows and orphans by the war's end.[7]

The British presence only inflamed this bitterness even more. "King's Men," driven from their homes into hideouts in neighboring swamps, came out in full force after the royal victories at Charles Town and Camden, perpetuating "rapine, outrage and murder." Many joined the provincial units attached to the British Army—Turnbull's New York Volunteers, Ferguson's American Volunteers, and Tarleton's British Legion. Meanwhile, partisan bands led by three revolutionaries in particular harassed the English—Francis Marion ("Swamp Fox"), Thomas Sumter ("Carolina Gamecock"), and Andrew Pickens. The Rebels also committed the most heinous crimes; indeed, their "purity and nobility" are much exaggerated.[8]

Before Sir Henry Clinton left the Southern theater in the hands of his able subordinate, Charles, Earl Cornwallis, he issued three decrees which had a profound effect upon the populace. On May 22, 1780, ten days after the surrender of Charles Town, Clinton declared that anyone taking up arms or persuading "faithful and peaceable subjects" to rebel would suffer punishment and confiscation of property. On June 1, he granted a full pardon to those who returned to their allegiance. However, two days later the third decree proclaimed that all paroled civilians had to resume all the duties of citizenship (in other words, prove one's loyalty by possibly serving in Provincial military formations). If not, they would be considered rebels.

Much debate has occurred among scholars over the implications of these proclamations. According to one historian, the last decree initiated a "counter-revolution." Paroled Rebels viewed it as treachery for they could not now live as neutrals. While some fled to the backcountry to take up resistance, others took the oath without any intention of obeying it. The latter gained the King's protection and disgusted many authentic Loyalists in the process. The mood in the South changed overnight from one of resignation under British occupation to suspicion with this "arbitrary fiat of the commander-in-chief."[9]

Charles, Earl Cornwallis, commanded a virtual hornet's nest after Clinton sailed back to New York on June 8, 1780. He was ill-prepared for a light, mobile war with partisans raiding the countryside. Communications and supply lines between the various South Carolina outposts—Charles Town, Camden, Ninety-Six, Hanging Rock, Rocky Mount, Cheraw, George Town, plus the little river forts of Granby, Motte, and Watson—had to be kept open. And, as already stated, the only cavalry he had belonged to the British Legion.[10]

Consequently, Cornwallis came to rely heavily upon Tarleton's command. He once wrote to his subordinate: "I wish you would get three Legions, and divide yourself in three parts: We can do no good without you."[11] The Legion soon attained "seasoned" status, but at a high price. It became scattered while the cavalry rode about the countryside on various missions and the infantry garrisoned numerous posts. Moreover, the constant use of the regiment fatigued it greatly. A glaring example of this, which had dire consequences, concerns the fate of Major Patrick Ferguson. On October 6, 1780, Cornwallis wrote Ferguson, who had been marching through western South Carolina and became greatly alarmed about approaching enemy backwoodsmen. His request for reinforcements met with the following reply from Cornwallis: "Tarleton shall pass at some of the upper fords, and clear the country; for the present both he and his corps want a few days rest."[12] The next day at Kings Mountain, Rebel riflemen killed Ferguson and all but annihilated his command.[13]

The British Legion represented a highly visible element of the southern Crown forces in 1780-1781, partially because of its mobility and especially since it frequently operated far from the main army. Its distinctive uniform also made the Green Horse noticeable.

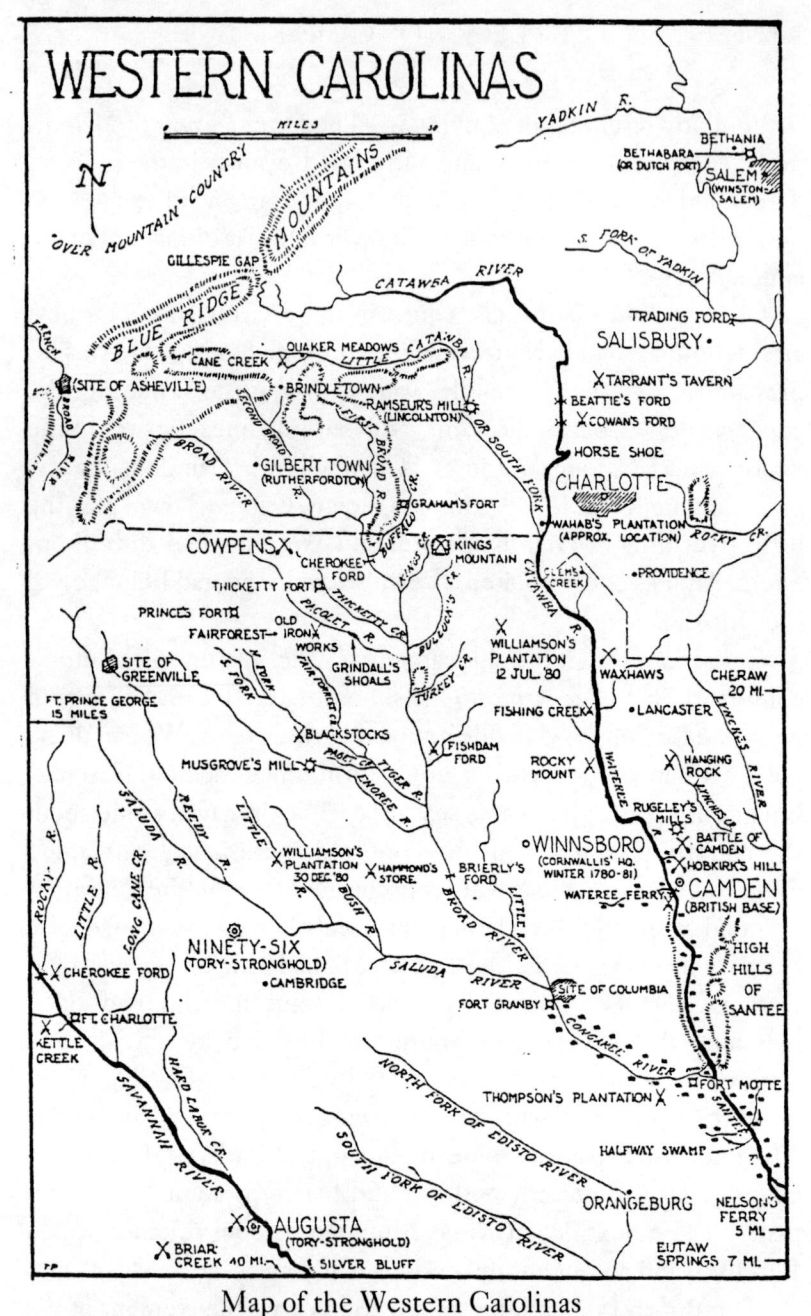

Map of the Western Carolinas
Source: Mark Mayo Boatner III, *Encyclopedia of the American Revolution* (Mechanicsburg, Penn.: Stackpole Books, 1994), endpaper

Given the circumstances, both the Legion cavalry and infantry performed remarkably well. To discuss in detail the battles of the Legion or its numerous hit-and-run raids is unnecessary here since they are well chronicled in Tarleton's *History of the Campaigns of 1780 and 1781, in the Southern Provinces of North America* (London: T. Cadell, 1787) and other more contemporary accounts. Several themes, though, can be discerned[14]

Tarleton relied upon shock and relentless pursuit to ensure victory over his opponents. Even though he was sometimes outnumbered, this policy worked more often than not. Lenud's Ferry (May 6, 1780), Fishing Creek (August 18, 1780), and Tarrant's Tavern (February 1, 1781) were all surprise attacks resulting in significant enemy losses in men and material while British casualties were minimal. The Legion commander also utilized the cover of night to have the maximum effect, as occurred at MacPherson's Plantation (March 14, 1780) and Monck's Corner (April 14, 1780).[15]

The swiftness of these attacks was certainly not lost upon those on the receiving end. Nevertheless, Tarleton's impetuosity did get him into trouble in at least two engagements. At Blackstocks Hill, South Carolina (November 20, 1780), the Legion lieutenant colonel rushed forward with only 170 Legion cavalry and eighty mounted infantry of the Sixty-Third Regiment in order to engage Thomas Sumter and one thousand Rebel militia before they crossed the Tyger River. The fighting was fierce, with the young lieutenant colonel and his dragoons charging uphill to rescue the eighty infantrymen. Approaching darkness concluded the battle, and the Americans managed to escape across the river. Although Tarleton admitted his losses to be only fifty-one killed and wounded, American sources put British losses much higher, including one report that states ninety-two killed and one hundred wounded. Whatever the correct figures may be, Tarleton's figures are indeed high in proportion to the number of English troops engaged.[16]

The other example of Tarleton's impetuosity getting the best of him is the famous battle at the Cowpens, South Carolina (January

17, 1781). So much has been written on this engagement that it is somewhat daunting to add to the commentary. Let it be sufficient to state that fate along with simple fatigue had a hand in Tarleton's defeat that day. Although some may attribute the dragoons' refusal to charge the advancing Americans to poor discipline, it must be remembered that the British had been chasing Morgan's command without respite for two weeks. Furthermore, on the day of the battle, Tarleton had his men awake at 2 a.m. and marching within the hour. No time was even allowed for breakfast.[17]

This mention of fatigue alerts us to the fact that even the Green Horse had its breaking point. By September 1780, the British Legion had already seen nine months of hard service in the South, including one full summer. The strain of constant duty had taken its toll. The example of the Charlotte, North Carolina skirmish (September 26, 1780), in which the dragoons refused Hanger's third request to charge, has already been cited. Another example occurred five days earlier in an incident at Wahab's Plantation. At this site ten miles southwest of Charlotte, eighty American cavalry led by Colonel William Davie surprised the Legion dragoons. Caught in the process of saddling their mounts, they tried to form but quickly panicked and fled. Sixty Legionnaires were killed and wounded while 120 stand of arms and ninety-six fully equipped horses were captured.[18]

Nonetheless, the British Legion could distinguish itself as capable of sustaining and giving assaults like a conventional eighteenth-century line regiment. The prime example of this occurred at Hanging Rock, South Carolina. On August 6, 1780, in the heat of a fierce battle, 160 Legion infantry charged an enemy force three times as strong. This event caused Roderick MacKenzie, one of Tarleton's greatest detractors, to state: "The infantry of the legion had seen much service, and had always behaved well: this our author will surely not deny."[19]

The forced marches of the Green Horse also are impressive. As already stated, in July 1779 it rode sixty-four miles in twenty-three hours during the Poundridge-Bedford, New York raid. In the most well-known example, Tarleton gave chase to Colonel Abraham Buford's command before it could flee into North Carolina, and cornered it at the Waxhaws on May 29, 1780. The Legionnaires, some mounted two to a horse, rode 105 miles in fifty-four hours, quite a feat for late May in South Carolina. Several horses died from fatigue and by the time they reached the Waxhaws, "many of the British cavalry and mounted infantry were totally worn out."[20]

At the Battle of Camden, South Carolina (August 16, 1780), the Legion chased the fleeing Americans twenty-two miles, taking in the process "many prisoners of all ranks, twenty ammunition wagons, one hundred and fifty carriages, containing the baggage, stores, and camp equipage of the American army."[21] In a raid on Charlottesville, Virginia in June 1781, Tarleton and the Legion dragoons rode seventy miles in twenty-four hours. Later that same summer, they raided Bedford and Prince Edward counties and returned to the main British army at Suffolk after covering four hundred miles in fifteen days.[22]

In order to enhance his mobility, Tarleton would sometimes send captured enemy personnel to Cornwallis or parole them, as he did with those captured in Charlottesville. As he was constantly on the move, he received specific orders from Cornwallis concerning enemy stores. Those he could not remove, he had the authority to burn.[23]

Lieutenant Colonel Banastre Tarleton also exploited the psychological impact of his mobility. He usually kept his numbers concealed by advancing on roads and then abruptly retiring. More drastic measures were taken at times, as with the incident first related in this work involving the sixteen-year-old boy. The Legionnaires occasionally removed their jackets to hide their identity, and they would also "leave tokens of fear, by leaving camps abruptly & provisions cooked, in order to [frighten] the enemy."[24] The cooking fires at the abandoned Legion bivouac along the Haw River in February 1781 undoubtedly kept Moses Hall and his comrades from making a hasty approach.[25]

This brief summary of Legion operations in the South is helpful in determining how the regiment and its leader were perceived by their contemporaries. Knowledge of such perceptions and how they became magnified is essential to any understanding of the myths surrounding Banastre Tarleton. The next chapter will examine the manner in which revolutionaries as well as fellow Britons viewed Tarleton and his command.

---

[1] The author is indebted to Robert Gerling, Manager of Interpretive Programs at Carter's Grove, for verification of this story. The Grove is the restored mansion of Carter Burwell, located eight miles east of Williamsburg, Virginia. There is extant evidence which suggests that Tarleton and his Legionnaires occupied the house. Archaeologists in the early 1970's excavated from the grounds a brass insignia bearing Tarleton's personal crest. The horse ride up the stairs is probably an embellishment. Even though the stairwell is large enough to accommodate a horse and rider, it does not seem likely that any cavalryman would risk a good mount on such an act of bravado. However, there remains the question of the slash marks on the banister, which the author saw for himself in a visit to the Grove in the autumn of 1988. A piece of metal is still embedded in the black walnut railing and could possibly be from a saber. For further information see Alan Simpson, "The Legends of Carter's Grove—Fact or Fiction?," *Colonial Williamsburg* 11 (1989): 32-38.

[2] Lenud's is also spelled Lenneau's and Lenew's in various contemporary accounts. Most of this chapter comes from Chapter 3 of the author's MA thesis. See Anthony J. Scotti, Jr., "'This Disagreeable Exertion of Authority': Banastre Tarleton and the British Legion in the Southern Campaigns, 1780-1781" (MA thesis, Wake Forest University, 1991), especially pp.34-37, 40-49.

[3] David Ramsay, *The History of the Revolution of South-Carolina, from a British Province to an Independent State*, 2 vols. (Trenton, New Jersey, 1785), 1:2-3; Lieutenant Colonel Banastre Tarleton, *A History of the Campaigns of 1780 and 1781, in the Southern Provinces of North America* (London: T. Cadell, 1787), 4; Christopher Ward, *The War of the Revolution*, 2 vols. (New York: Macmillan Company, 1952), 2:656.

[4] The basically flat countryside of the European continent provides ideal cavalry ground, whether for eighteenth century horsemen or modern day tanks. European history rings with the din of classic cavalry battles, such as occurred at Mollwitz (1741), Hohenfriedeberg (1745), Soor (1745), and Torgau (1760). The famous maxim of Frederick the Great sets the tone for cavalry warfare in the Age of Reason: "Above all attack with impetuosity." Scotti, "'This Disagreeable Exertion of Authority,'" 13; Frederic G. Bauer, "Notes on the Use of Cavalry in the American Revolution," *US Cavalry Association Journal* 47 (1938): 136-143; the British Legion was shipped South in two detachments. The first section went to Georgia and marched north to South Carolina with Brigadier General James Paterson's command in March 1780. The second detachment of the Legion arrived in the siege lines outside of Charles Town sometime before its fall. The Queen's Rangers went back to New York with Clinton and did not serve with the Legion again until the Virginia operations of mid-1781. See C.T. Atkinson, "British Forces in North America, 1774-1781: Their Distribution and Strength," *Journal of the Society for Army Historical Research* 16 (1937): 18-22 (hereafter cited as *JSAHR*); *Archibald Robertson, Lieutenant-General Royal Engineers: His Diaries and Sketches in America 1762-1780*, ed. Harry Miller Lydenberg (New York: New York Public Library, 1930), 206, 218.

[5] Greg Novak, *A Guide to the American War of Independence in the North*, Campaign Book #7A (Champaign, Illinois: Ulster Imports, 1990), 64-65. "I have rejected all plans for raising cavalry except the augmentation of the Legion to seventy men a troop." Earl Cornwallis to Sir Henry Clinton, July 14, 1780, Charles Town, in *Documents of the American Revolution: 1770-1783*, Colonial Office Series, ed. K.G. Davies, 21 vols. (Dublin: Irish University Press, 1972-1981), 18:118-120 (hereafter cited as *DAR*); "The necessity for cavalry in this province is daily increasing." Lieutenant Colonel Nisbet Balfour to Sir Henry Clinton, February 13, 1781, Charles Town, 30/11/5, pp.55-56; Cornwallis to Balfour, November 4, 1780, Winnsboro, 30/11/82, pp.6-7, Cornwallis Papers, Public Record Office, Kew, (hereafter cited as PRO); Balfour to Major General Alexander Leslie, January 25, 1781, Charlestown, in Alexander Leslie Letterbook, 1781-1782, Nisbet Balfour, Letters, January to December 1781, South Carolina Department of Archives and History, Columbia, South Carolina

(microfilm); low provincial turnout contributed to the lack of cavalry. Paul H. Smith, *Loyalists and Redcoats: A Study in British Revolutionary Policy* (Chapel Hill: University of North Carolina Press, 1964), 75-77. The amount of time needed for training may have had something to do with the limited number of cavalry recruits. It took approximately five years to properly train a trooper to full proficiency. Christopher Duffy, *The Military Experience in the Age of Reason* (New York: Atheneum, 1988), 117.

[6] "The number of Americans alive during the period 1775-83 was about 3,210,000, or the 1783 population of 2,950,000 plus the 260,000 persons buried during that interval (discounting the infant mortality rate)." The black population in 1780 was probably around 575,000. Paul H. Smith, "The American Loyalists: Notes on Their Organization and Numerical Strength," *William and Mary Quarterly* 25 (1968): 269-270; John Richard Alden, *The South in the Revolution, 1763-1789* (Louisiana State University Press, 1957), 5-8; Lord George Germain to Sir Henry Clinton (Most Secret), March 8, 1778, Whitehall, *DAR*, 15:57-62; in the South specifically, Loyalists represented anywhere from 25 to 33% of whites. Don Higginbotham, *The War of American Independence: Military Attitudes, Policies, and Practice, 1763-1789* (New York: Macmillan Company, 1971), 134; Robert Calhoon, *The Loyalists in Revolutionary America: 1760-1781* (New York: Harcourt Brace Jovanovich, 1965), 482-483; for other studies on Loyalists and the South in general see Carole Watterson Troxler, *The Loyalist Experience in North Carolina* (Raleigh: North Carolina Department of Cultural Resources, Division of Archives and History, 1976); Ronald Hoffman, Thad W. Tate, and Peter J. Albert, eds., *An Uncivil War: The Southern Backcountry during the American Revolution* (Charlottesville: The University Press of Virginia, 1985); Jeffrey J. Crow and Larry E. Tise, eds., *The Southern Experience in the American Revolution* (Chapel Hill: University of North Carolina Press, 1978).

[7] Ramsay, *History of the Revolution of South-Carolina*, 2:215, 275; a good but popularized history of the Ninety-Six District in the Revolutionary War is Robert D. Bass, *Ninety Six: The Struggle for the South Carolina Back Country* (Lexington, South Carolina: The Sandlapper Store, 1978).

[8] Ramsay, *History of the Revolution of South-Carolina*, 2:271; Charles Stedman, *The History of the Origin, Progress, and Termination of the*

American War, 2 vols. (London, 1794), 2:197, 348; Robert Stansbury Lambert, *South Carolina Loyalists in the American Revolution* (Columbia: University of South Carolina Press, 1987), 33-77, 198-215; M. F. Treacy, *Prelude to Yorktown: The Southern Campaign of Nathanael Greene, 1780-1781* (Chapel Hill: University of North Carolina Press, 1963), 43; "partisan" is the eighteenth century term for guerrilla. Marion operated in the low country of South Carolina while Pickens and Sumter generally stayed in the upstate region. Ward, *War of the Revolution*, 2:661-662; also see the two biographies by Bass, *Swamp Fox: The Life and Campaigns of General Francis Marion* (New York: Henry Holt, 1959) and *Gamecock: The Life and Campaigns of General Thomas Sumter* (New York: Henry Holt, 1961); another active but less well-known partisan was William Richardson Davie. See Blackwell P. Robinson, ed., *The Revolutionary War Sketches of William R. Davie* (Raleigh: North Carolina Department of Cultural Resources, Division of Archives and History, 1976); John S. Pancake, *This Destructive War: The British Campaign in the Carolinas, 1780-1782* (University of Alabama Press, 1985), xiv; passions for revenge ran high in this civil war. One form of torture for captured soldiers was "spicketing," or driving a sharp pin through the foot. Consult John C. Dann, ed., *The Revolution Remembered: Eyewitness Accounts of the War for Independence* (Chicago: University of Chicago Press, 1980), 188-189; "In the most complete gesture of triumph, of revenge, of contempt," the American backwoodsmen who killed Patrick Ferguson at Kings Mountain on October 7, 1780 reportedly urinated on his naked corpse. See Hank Messick, *King's Mountain: The Epic of the Blue Ridge "Mountain Men" in the American Revolution* (Boston: Little, Brown and Company, 1976), 152.

[9] All three decrees can be found verbatim in Tarleton, *History of the Campaigns*, 71-76; "derived from the French *parole d'honneur* (word of honor), a parole is a pledge or oath under which a prisoner of war is released with the understanding that he will not again bear arms until exchanged." Mark Mayo Boatner III, *Encyclopedia of the American Revolution* (David McKay, 1966; repr., Mechanicsburg, PA: Stackpole Books, 1994), 832; Lambert, *South Carolina Loyalists*, 97-98; Calhoon, *Loyalists in Revolutionary America*, 485-486; Stedman, *History of the American War*, 2:198-199; John Shy, "British Stategy for Pacifying the Southern Colonies, 1778-1781," in Crow and Tise, eds., *Southern Experience in the American Revolution*, 155-173. Also see Shy's "The

American Revolution: The Military Conflict Considered as a Revolutionary War," in Stephen G. Kurtz and James H. Hutson, eds., *Essays on the American Revolution* (Chapel Hill: University of North Carolina Press, 1973), 121-156; Pancake, *This Destructive War*, 67-72; Ira D. Gruber, "Britain's Southern Policy," in Robert W. Higgins, ed., *The Revolutionary War in the South: Power, Conflict, and Leadership. Essays in Honor of John Richard Alden* (Durham: Duke University Press, 1979), 205-238. Robert M. Weir, *Colonial South Carolina: A History* (New York: KTO Press, 1983).

[10] "The many work details required of it weakened the Legion as a fighting force." Franklin and Mary Wickwire, *Cornwallis: The American Adventure* (Boston: Houghton Mifflin Company, 1970), 135, 137-138; Atkinson, "British Forces in North America," *JSAHR* 16 (1937): 18-20. Fort Granby was located along the Congaree River, near modern Columbia. The site of Fort Motte was at the strategic confluence of the Congaree and Wateree where they become the Santee River. Fort Watson could be found along the Santee. Sol Stember, *The Bicentennial Guide to the American Revolution*, 3 vols. (New York: Saturday Review Press, 1974), 3:79-81. In the late summer-early fall of 1780, Cornwallis had to rely upon mounted infantry of the Sixty-Third Regiment under Major James Wemyss to suppress Rebel activity along the Santee River. Pancake, *This Destructive War*, 126, 200-203; Tarleton usually gave mounts to the Legion infantry during the southern campaigns. Ward, *War of the Revolution*, 2:702; Bauer, "Notes on the Use of Cavalry," 136-143; Whig and Tory militia in the South generally rode horses to battle, but fought on foot. Lieutenant Colonel Louis D.F. Frasché, "Problems of Command: Cornwallis, Partisans and Militia, 1780," *Military Review* 57 (April 1977): 60-74 ; the need for mounted infantry in Cornwallis's army became even greater after the loss of Legion infantry at the Cowpens in January 1781. Tarleton at times had to employ mounted infantry of the Sixty-Third, Twenty-Third, Seventy-Sixth, Eighty-Second, and Hamilton's North Carolina Volunteers. Tarleton, *History of the Campaigns*, 222, 252, 286, 295-296, 299, 309, 341-342, 345, 387.

[11] Cornwallis to Tarleton, November 11, 1780, Winnsborough, in Tarleton, *History of the Campaigns*, 201-202.

[12] Cornwallis to Ferguson, October 6, 1780, 30/11/81, f. 23; for scattered detachments of the Legion, see State of the army with Earl Cornwallis at Wilmington, North Carolina, April 15, 1781, 30/11/103, ff. 27-28, both in Cornwallis Papers, PRO; in *History of the Campaigns*, pp. 165-168, Tarleton blames Cornwallis for not sending the British Legion to rescue Ferguson. When this book was published in 1787, the Earl became rather angry by this and other comments. Cornwallis maintained that he ordered Ferguson *not* to engage the enemy and entreated Tarleton to march to his aid. However, the dragoon officer "pleaded weakness from the remains of a fever, and refused to make the attempt." (This would have been the time that Tarleton was recovering from malaria.) Cornwallis to the Bishop of Lichfield and Coventry, December 12, 1788, in *Correspondence of Charles, First Marquis Cornwallis*, ed. Charles Ross, 3 vols., 2nd ed. (London: John Murray, 1859), 1:315-316. By mid-August 1780, Tarleton complained that the Legion cavalry was "nearly destroyed by the constant duties of detachment and patrol." Tarleton, *History of the Campaigns*, 86-88, 101.

[13] For Kings Mountain, see Ward, *War of the Revolution*, 2:737-747; Messick, *King's Mountain*; Pancake, *This Destructive War*, 108-121.

[14] Aside from the sources already cited, one should consult the following for the southern operations of the Revolutionary War: Henry Lumpkin, *From Savannah to Yorktown: The American Revolution in the South* (Columbia: University of South Carolina Press, 1981); Dan L. Morrill, *Southern Campaigns of the American Revolution* (Baltimore, MD: The Nautical and Aviation Publishing Company, 1993); W.J. Wood, *Battles of the Revolutionary War 1775-1781* (Chapel Hill, NC: Algonquin Books, 1990).

[15] All these battle sites are in South Carolina except for Tarrant's Tavern, which is in North Carolina. The Legion commander was outnumbered at Lenud's Ferry, Waxhaws, Fishing Creek, Blackstocks Hill, and Tarrant's Tavern. Tarleton, *History of the Campaigns*, 15-17, 19-20, 27-31, 113-115, 175-181, 225-226. His assault at Lenud's Ferry occurred so suddenly that Lieutenant Colonel William Washington and some of the other American officers had to swim the Santee in order to escape. Thomas Sumter was sleeping under a wagon when the Green Horse made its appearance at Fishing Creek. Ward, *War of the Revolution*, 2:733-734. For the confused scuffle at MacPherson's

Plantation in which Ferguson accidentally received a bayonet wound from a Legion infantryman, consult James Ferguson, *Two Scottish Soldiers, a Soldier of 1688 and Blenheim, a Soldier of the American Revolution and a Jacobite Laird and His Forbears* (Aberdeen: D. Wyllie and Son, 1888), 76-79. Ferguson commended the Legionnaire and even gave him some money for being such a good soldier. "We should have known our friends sooner from their mode of attack"; Lawrence Linfield Stirling, "Banastre Tarleton: A Reevaluation of His Career in the American Revolution" (MA thesis, Louisiana State University and Agricultural and Mechanical College, 1964), 25-49.

[16] The British Legion lieutenant colonel stated that one hundred Americans had been killed and wounded and fifty captured. Tarleton, *History of the Campaigns*, 175-180; Sumter's men collected most of the dead and wounded from both sides. Ward, *War of the Revolution*, 2:746-747; this same American report claims that the English commander had three hundred Legion cavalry and 130 men of the Sixty-Third present. It also asserts that Sumter lost only three killed and four wounded. See Hugh Middleton, Report re battle at Blackstocks, undated, *The Papers of the Continental Congress: 1774-1789*, comp. John P. Butler (Washington, DC: US Government Printing Office, 1978), 2p., M247, reel 175, i155, vol. 1, pp. 493-494 (microfilm).

[17] In defense of the British Legion lieutenant colonel, it must be stated that many of his officers and NCOs had been killed during the initial charge on the American lines. Consequently, the infantry ranks quickly lost not only direction but cohesion as well. When the retiring Americans abruptly turned about to fire at a staggering ten yards, the British infantry, leaderless and extremely fatigued, broke physically as well as psychologically. In addition, Tarleton asserts with some justification:

> The extreme extension of the files always exposed the British regiments and corps....If infantry who are formed very open, and only two deep, meet with opposition, they can have no stability: But when they experience an unexpected shock, confusion will ensue, and flight, without immediate support, must be the inevitable consequence.

Of course, the bravery and good conduct of the Americans must be taken into account. Morgan certainly handled his command better than Tarleton managed his on that cold January morning. The role of "some unforeseen event" is usually scoffed at by many historians, but upon further reflection it is not so easily dismissed. For instance, the First Maryland, a veteran Continental regiment, broke and ran at the Battle of Hobkirk's Hill, South Carolina on April 25, 1781. All attempts to rally it during the battle proved fruitless.

Tarleton, *History of the Campaigns*, 210-222; he is hotly vilified in Roderick MacKenzie's *Strictures on Lt. Col. Tarleton's History of the Campaigns of 1780 and 1781, in the Southern Provinces of North America; Wherein Characters and Corps are Vindicated from Injurious Aspersions, and Several Important Transactions Placed in Their Proper Point of View* (London: R. Faulder, 1787), 81-118; the Legion commander is defended by George Hanger, *An Address to the Army; in Reply to Strictures, by Roderick M'Kenzie (Late Lieutenant in the 71ST Regiment) on Tarleton's History of the Campaigns of 1780 and 1781* (London: James Ridgway, 1789), 89-118. Piers Mackesy is skeptical about the infantry files. See Mackesy, "What the British Army Learned," in Ronald Hoffman and Peter J. Albert, eds., *Arms and Independence: The Military Character of the American Revolution* (Charlottesville: University Press of Virginia, 1984), 202-203. Scotti, "'This Disagreeable Exertion of Authority,'" 46-50; Ward, *War of the Revolution*, 2:748-762, 802-808; the British advance met "with a very warm reception." William Seymour, "A Journal of the Southern Expedition, 1780-1783," *Pennsylvania Magazine of History and Biography* 7 (1883): 286-298; Don Higginbotham, *Daniel Morgan: Revolutionary Rifleman* (Chapel Hill: University of North Carolina Press, 1961), 129-144; also consult Treacy's *Prelude to Yorktown*; Lumpkin, *From Savannah to Yorktown*; Burke Davis, *The Cowpens-Guilford Courthouse Campaign* (Philadelphia: J.B. Lippincott Company, 1962); Hugh F. Rankin, "Cowpens: Prelude to Yorktown," *North Carolina Historical Review* 31 (1954): 336-369; Wood, *Battles of the Revolutionary War*, 208-226; William Seymour, *The Price of Folly: British Blunders in the War of American Independence* (London: Brassey's, 1995), passim. A good recent account of the battle from the American perspective is Lawrence E. Babits, *A Devil of a Whipping: The Battle of Cowpens* (Chapel Hill: University of North Carolina Press, 1998).

[18] This occurred during Tarleton's bout with malaria. The Legionnaires' sad performance under Major Hanger is worth noting. Whether it is a poor reflection upon Hanger's leadership ability, lack of discipline, a desire for Tarleton's inspiring presence, or a combination of all three factors is difficult to determine. This situation will be analyzed further in Chapter VII.

Hanger, who was wounded in the fight, deemed Charlotte "a trifling insignificant skirmish," but admitted he should have sent the infantry in first to clear the town. Hanger, *An Address to the Army*, 55-58; when Cornwallis arrived at the scene, he reportedly said: "Legion, remember you have everything to lose, but nothing to gain." Wickwire, Cornwallis, 196-199; Stedman, *History of the American War*, 2:239; for Wahab's Plantation, see Robinson, ed., *War Sketches of William R. Davie*, 21-26; the loss of ninety-six cavalry horses was a serious matter. Tarleton, *History of the Campaigns*, 159.

[19] MacKenzie, *Strictures*, 26, 113; Tarleton, *History of the Campaigns*, 94-95; the American forces under Thomas Sumter numbered approximately eight hundred men. Aside from the Legion infantry detachment, the royal forces included elements of the Prince of Wales Loyal American Volunteers, North Carolina Provincials, and South Carolina Rangers—in all, about five hundred men. Note that this was a battle fought entirely between Americans. Ward, *War of the Revolution*, 2:709-711.

[20] Tarleton, *History of the Campaigns*, 27-28, 83; Lieutenant-Colonel Banastre Tarleton to Sir Henry Clinton, Camp on the Brunx, July 2, 1779, Eleven P.M., in Robert D. Bass, *The Green Dragoon: The Lives of Banastre Tarleton and Mary Robinson* (New York: Henry Holt, 1957), 55-56. Assyrian horse troops could make thirty miles a day along roads. After researching armies from antiquity to the First World War, John Keegan maintains that twenty miles a day is the best speed to be achieved by men on foot. John Keegan, *A History of Warfare* (New York: Alfred A. Knopf, 1993), 170, 302. The British troops which raided Lexington and Concord, Massachusetts on April 18-19, 1775 traveled 34.5 miles in 11.45 hours. News of the raid reached Providence, RI by the evening of April 19, Williamsburg, VA by April 28, and Charles Town, SC on May 9. See Appendix M: The British March: Time, Distance, Velocity, and Appendix S: Spread of the News of the First Shots at Lexington, both in David Hackett Fischer, *Paul*

Revere's Ride (New York and Oxford: Oxford University Press, 1994), 317, 324-325.

[21] Tarleton, *History of the Campaigns*, 104-108.

[22] *Ibid.*, 295-296, 358-359.

[23] Tarleton, *History of the Campaigns*, 296, 358; Tarleton to Cornwallis, December 14, 1780, Woodwards, 30/11/4, ff. 325-326; see the paroles of Dudley Digges, Robert Nelson, Wm. Nelson, Peter Lyons and Col. John Syms, all signed by Tarleton on June 4, 1781, 30/11/93, ff. 12-15, 17; Cornwallis to Tarleton, November 8, 1780, Winnsboro, 30/11/82, ff. 10-11, in Cornwallis Papers, PRO.

[24] Tarleton to Cornwallis, November 11, 1780, Singleton's Mills, Cornwallis Papers, PRO, 30/11/4, ff. 96-97; Tarleton, *History of the Campaigns*, 101, 353; Bass, *The Green Dragoon*, 93, 117-118; the Briton even fooled an American into believing that he was William Washington, the American cavalry leader. In August 1780, James Bradley, a paroled SC assemblyman, guided the Legion commander to the upper Black River fords (Bradley's and Nelson's). Along the way, Bradley "was severe in his denunciations against the British officers and soldiers, and warm in commendation of the heroic spirit of his supposed friends and guests." Stirling, "Banastre Tarleton: A Reevaluation," 47-49; the British Legion and Lee's Legion had similar coats. One would occasionally be mistaken for the other, as Loyalist Colonel John Pyle and his unfortunate command discovered along the Haw River, North Carolina on February 25, 1781. Pyle's men marched right up to Lee's Legion before realizing their mistake. Ward, *War of the Revolution*, 2:778-779; in the summer of 1781, Tarleton used a popular trick and sent a black slave and a dragoon into Marquis de Lafayette's camp at Green Spring Farm, Virginia. Both claimed to be British deserters but were actually spies sent to communicate false intelligence. Charlemagne Tower, Jr., *The Marquis De La Fayette in the American Revolution. With Some Account of the Attitude of France toward the War of Independence*, 2 vols. (Philadelphia: J. B. Lippincott Company, 1895), 2:357-358.

[25] As already discussed in the Introduction, Moses Hall was the NC militiaman who found the mortally wounded youth at the Legion campsite. Dann, ed. *The Revolution Remembered*, 202.

CHAPTER V

Perceptions

Several months after the surrender of Charles Town, the Earl Cornwallis dispatched Banastre Tarleton on an errand to suppress Rebel activity in the low country of South Carolina. While he gathered his men at Lenud's Ferry on the sultry Santee, the leader of the Green Horse had a brief time to reflect upon the war and the proper way to conduct it. These reflections manifested themselves in a letter to the English commander-in-chief:

> I have promised the young men who chose to assist me in this expedition the plunder of the leaders of the faction. If warfare allows me, I shall give these disturbers of the peace no quarter. If humanity obliges me to spare their lives, I shall convey them close prisoners to Camden. For a confiscation must take place in their effects. I must discriminate with severity.[1]

This attitude toward the rebellion soon became clearly apparent to the enemies of the Crown. As he rode along the Black River shortly after writing this letter, the Legionnaire dispersed the Rebel militia, an activity he termed as "this disagreeable exertion of authority."[2] Later, he added that it was not the intention of Britons to be cruel, but "nothing will serve these people but fire & sword, ... [and] small pox."[3]

Banastre Tarleton and the British Legion appeared practically everywhere in the South. As already stated, the Legion acted in a mobile manner and became a highly visible element of the southern Crown forces. Few areas, especially in South Carolina, did not receive a visit from it, and as a result the British Legion became quickly known throughout the southern provinces. For instance, during the above mentioned operation, Tarleton rode from Charles Town to the Black River communities of Kingstree and Salem, and then proceeded onto Camden, all within a matter of ten days. Three months later in November 1780, the Green Horse returned to the same area. Within eighteen days, it traveled from Winnsboro to Singleton's Mills in the High Hills of the Santee. After fruitlessly chasing Francis Marion, Tarleton rode back to Winnsboro and then on to the upper Tyger River and the battle at Blackstocks Hill.[4]

This mobility, combined with Tarleton's attitude, had a direct relationship upon how Americans perceived the Englishman and his command. It is impossible to place a number on how many Americans had firsthand experience with his tactics and activities. However, given the scope of Legion operations, it is apparent that many combatants engaged the regiment in battle and numerous civilians encountered his troops on the march or in bivouac. These individuals who lived through the internecine strife of the Revolutionary War in the South undoubtedly had many memories of that conflict. In the case of Tarleton, most of them were bad.

The overall American view of Tarleton was one of simple condemnation and hatred. John Williams, a North Carolina justice of the peace, felt that the name of young Tarleton was synonymous with inhumanity and cruelty.[5] Major General Nathanael Greene, commander of American forces in the South after Horatio Gates's defeat at Camden, complained to his adversary, Lord Cornwallis: "The feelings of mankind will forever decide when the rights of humanity are invaded. I leave them to judge...Lt. Colonel Tarleton's conduct in laying waste the country and distressing the inhabitants...."[6]

Francis Marion, the object of the Legion's chase in the low country during early November, came out of his lair on Snow Island after Tarleton left. The South Carolina partisan observed:

> Colonel Tarleton has behaved to the poor Women, he has destroyed, with great Barbarity—he beat Mrs. Richardson, the Relick (*sic*) of General Richardson to make her tell where I was—and has not left her a Shift of Clothes;...It is beyond Measure distressing to see the Women and Children in the open air round a Fire without a Blanket or any Clothing but what they had—and Women of family and of ample Fortunes; for he spares neither Whig or Tory.[7]

Lord Cornwallis noticed early on in the southern campaigns that Legion prisoners of war "by all accounts have been most cruelly treated." Reportedly, Lieutenant Colonel Tarleton had apprehensions for his safety after the York Town and Gloucester Point garrisons surrendered in October 1781. According to another contemporary, "it was generally observed of Tarleton and his corps, that they not only exercised more acts of cruelty than any one in the British Army, but also carried further the spirit of depredation."[8]

The rebellious colonials clearly felt a certain amount of fear and respect toward Lieutenant Colonel Banastre Tarleton. In the process, they conformed to two basic premises of military science. It is natural to be a little intimidated by one's enemy. Moreover, it is never advisable to underestimate him. Both these maxims ring true for our subject.

Rebel commanders saw Tarleton as a constant threat to their operations and security. Once Nathanael Greene took command of the southern American army on December 3, 1780, he realized that in addition to all his other myriad problems, he had a formidable enemy cavalry force to contend with.[9]

The British Legion by this time had been in the southern colonies for close to a year, gaining experience as well as a name for quick, stunning victories. The American cavalry had suffered grievous losses at Monck's Corner, Lenud's Ferry, and Camden. Lieutenant Colonel William Washington had only ninety horsemen and these constituted a destitute lot. On January 13, 1781, Greene wrote to Brigadier General Daniel Morgan, who was detached from the main army. He warned that Tarleton was on his way "to pay you a visit."[10]

Fortunately for the American cause, Morgan soon defeated Tarleton at the Cowpens. However, he quickly left the field of battle in order to rejoin Greene's force. The fear that Tarleton would return with his dragoons and the rest of Cornwallis's army motivated Morgan to do so.[11]

Months later in Virginia, the Marquis de Lafayette had his own anxious moments with Tarleton. To Major General Anthony Wayne he wrote a letter from Richmond on July 15, 1781. He ordered Wayne to make in conjunction with Morgan "a stroke against Tarleton" if at all practicable. However, he cautioned him not to stray too far southward from his main force, as the possible results would be disastrous.[12]

The next month the young marquis lamented to Major General Frederick von Steuben that the cavalry of Tarleton was now stronger than ever. "I dread the consequences of such a superiority of horse."[13] Four days later, he wrote again, and claimed that without at least two hundred dragoons, "the consequences will be fatal—not only to this state and army—but to the whole system of our campaign."[14]

North Carolina partisan leader William R. Davie encountered the British Legion on various occasions, especially at Wahab's Plantation and Charlotte in September 1780. He called the Legion officer "an enterprising enemy," a mark of evident respect coming from the likes of Davie, who held Tarleton in utter contempt.[15]

Armand-Louis de Gontaut-Biron, Duc de Lauzun, who commanded a legion in the French army, desired to be sent immediately southward when he arrived at Newport, Rhode Island in mid-1780. He wished to meet Tarleton's corps, "which had proved irresistible."[16]

This healthy respect for the Green Horse became mingled with fear. Especially among the militia of the Rebel Army, the mere mention of Tarleton's name caused deep concern.[17] Francis Marion noted in November 1780 that the militia of the lower Santee was slow to turn out, being "in great Dread of Tarleton's Horse."[18] At Tarrant's Tavern, North Carolina on February 1, 1781, the American militia and civilians along the road panicked when word circulated of Tarleton's imminent arrival. As a result, many were caught out in the open and suffered accordingly.[19]

Lieutenant Colonel Henry "Light Horse Harry" Lee observed that American militia "entertained dreadful apprehensions" of cavalry, especially when associated with the name of Tarleton. The Englishman's reputation had a "destructive effect" on many occasions.[20] Another American officer confirmed Lee's observation in a letter dated February 2, 1781. Although Tarleton had only 250 dragoons, Major Ichabod Burnet stated that the militiamen would "not assemble or annoy the enemy" until "a superiority in cavalry" appeared in the American ranks.[21] Further proof of the intimidation that the Green Horse caused can be seen with Moses Hall's actions on that morning he discovered the mortally wounded boy. Hall and his comrades slowly approached the Legion encampment and assuredly had a tense few moments before they realized it had just been abandoned.[22]

A more graphic example of how much fear surrounded Tarleton concerns one John Postell. An American soldier who had surrendered at Charles Town, he received a parole and returned home. Two weeks later, a couple of Legion dragoons arrived at the residence and confiscated his prize horse. In mid-October, three more dragoons appeared and took another horse and told Mrs. Postell that they were going to kill her husband. Fortunately, John

Postell was not home at the time, but when he learned of the unwelcome visit he decided to quickly seek refuge with the partisans.[23]

French views of Banastre Tarleton could be equally scathing. Although they arrived relatively late on the scene and had limited experience with the British Legion, they picked up on the prevailing opinion of their American allies.[24] Brigadier General Claude Gabriel de Choisy took enough notice of him to write his superior in October 1781: "Le bruit court que Tarleton a été blessé."[25] Lieutenant General Jean Baptiste Donatien de Vimeur, Comte de Rochambeau, commander of the French expeditionary force to America in 1780, had a low opinion of the British Army and this officer in particular. He maintained that the English and German troops were renowned for "violent doings" in the South. Of the Legion commander, Rochambeau stated: "Colonel Tarleton has no merit as an officer—only that bravery that every Grenadier has—but is a butcher and a barbarian."[26]

Other French officers were just as ready to accept Rochambeau's assessment. Jean-Baptiste-Antoine de Verger, a sous-lieutenant in the Royal Deux-Ponts Régiment, and Joachim du Perron, Comte de Revel, a sous-lieutenant in the Régiment d'Infanterie de Monsieur, both accused Tarleton's men of committing abominable atrocities. In fact, Verger blames the Legionnaires for killing a pregnant woman and mutilating her corpse and unborn infant. Du Perron also mentions the story, but reserves condemning anyone in particular, just the English in general. He does note that Tarleton's name made the American people tremble.[27]

However, not all encounters with Legionnaires resulted in trauma. In one instance, a Major Coughran of the Legion prevented the destruction of American homes.[28] Eliza Wilkinson, a young widow from Yonge's Island, South Carolina, mentions in her memoirs that she conversed with a Captain Sanford at her home after the surrender of Charles Town. This officer, very likely Captain Thomas Sandford of the British Legion cavalry, acted like a gentleman and even stopped his men from butchering her hogs.[29] Captain Miller, a participant in the attack on Buford, had a reputation among the survivors of the engagement as a man of "humanity."[30] An unnamed Legion officer reportedly helped the widow Richardson and her three children gather a few possessions before Tarleton had her house torched in November 1780.[31]

Thomas Jefferson, someone who had probably the most to fear from the British Legion because of his leading role in the revolutionary movement, had a remarkably "uneventful" visit from one of its cavalry detachments. It occurred during Tarleton's raid on Charlottesville, Virginia in June 1781. Tarleton himself ordered Captain Kenneth McLeod to disturb nothing at Monticello. After a stay of eighteen hours at the residence, McLeod and his troopers departed without Jefferson and any plunder as well.[32]

Perceptions of Tarleton in the royal camp were naturally different. Aside from the Cowpens, the young Englishman was the usual winner of impressive victories. Consequently, he became a hero to his troops and the public back home. *The Annual Register* called him "a striking specimen of that active gallantry, and of those peculiar military talents, which have since so highly distinguished his character."[33] *The London Chronicle* and *London Gazette Extraordinary* frequently published his dispatches to his superiors.[34] The British public saw him as a "brave and active officer," who "could not avoid being particularly distinguished."[35]

Some of his fellow British soldiers shared this admiration for an active and gallant officer. As already stated, he was a favorite of Sir Henry Clinton. After the reduction of Charles Town, the young lieutenant colonel approached Clinton and asked a favor. He desired that his friend, Captain George Hanger of the Hessian jäger corps, be made a major of Legion cavalry and therefore his second in command. The British commander-in-chief ordered this promotion before he returned to New York.[36]

What is even more significant is his close relationship with Earl Cornwallis. As stated earlier, he commanded the English southern operations between 1780 and 1781. Not only was he a favorite of his lordship, but both Robert Bass and Franklin and Mary Wickwire maintain with much justification that these men shared a father-son relationship, at least until the Cowpens. It is evident to see in their correspondence, especially in those missives concerning Tarleton's bout with malaria.[37]

Tarleton gained the earl's admiration as well as his confidence. The British Legion represented the earl's eyes in a hostile land because it was the only cavalry available to his lordship. And young Tarleton, very ambitious and eager to please, desired to put his regiment through its paces. As a result, nothing was too good for Cornwallis's Legion commander. As already exhibited, he put much effort into gaining for Tarleton advanced rank. More proof of favoritism concerns the procurement of horses.[38]

Horses naturally represented a precious commodity to the young commander. His *History of the Campaigns of 1780 and 1781, in the Southern Provinces of North America* (London: T. Cadell, 1787) abounds with the exact numbers lost during various engagements -- thirty-one at the Waxhaws, twenty at Fishing Creek, thirty at Blackstocks Hill. In fact, Tarleton's greatest critic, Lieutenant Roderick MacKenzie, found this preoccupation with mere animals to be insulting to the honor of dead officers who served in America.[39]

Nevertheless, the Legion needed proper mounts to be effective as a mobile force. When the Legion landed on Port Royal Island in early 1780, practically all their horses had died during the stormy voyage from New York. In March and April, the British Legion occupied Beaufort, South Carolina, and used local horses of very inferior quality (by cavalry standards). On April 14, after the Green Horse routed three regiments of Continental cavalry at Monck's Corner, this problem was rectified. The Legion captured four hundred fully accoutred dragoon horses. At Lenud's Ferry three weeks later, the remnants of the cavalry from Monck's Corner were dispersed and their mounts also captured. Not surprising, Article VI of the Charles Town surrender terms prohibited all horses from leaving the city.[40]

Yet, there were never enough. "The rapidity of the march, and the heat of climate" killed the poor animals quickly, as seen in the pursuit of Colonel Buford. Therefore, Cornwallis, who "was not unmindful of his cavalry" and upon application of his subordinate, assembled at Camden in August 1780 all the horses of the army. The Legionnaires then proceeded to choose the best ones for themselves. The disgruntled owners received either direct payment or receipts.[41]

Tarleton found the need to purchase horses from the civilian population as well. In December 1780, he sent Lieutenant Walter Willet with one hundred guineas to buy mounts along the Congaree River. However, at times, he believed that "Coolness Apathy & Civil Law will never supply Hussars with Horses," and basically confiscated what he needed, as John Postell's account confirms.[42]

The best accoutrements also became earmarked for Legion use. Sometime in late October or early November 1780, equipment for three hundred cavalry horses arrived at Savannah, Georgia. Unfortunately, most was damaged. Cornwallis nevertheless ordered its immediate disbursement to the Legion, stating that Tarleton would have the best and give up the worst of his own.[43]

As may be expected, Lord Cornwallis became very protective of the British Legion and was reluctant to squander it. During the summer of 1780, Lord Francis Rawdon, commanding at Camden, frequently detached small units of the provincial regiment on various missions. Tarleton, although on good terms with Rawdon, saw this service combined with the intense heat of the season as destroying his regiment. He evidently brought the matter to Cornwallis's attention, for on July 15, 1780, Cornwallis wrote Rawdon: "Let me conjure you to take care of the cavalry, and to give the most positive orders against small detachments; they are always distressing."[44]

Banastre Tarleton probably knew that he was special in the earl's eyes, and so did everyone else in the English army. All this obvious favoritism bestowed upon a young subordinate naturally would cause jealousy and a certain amount of resentment in any army. Rawdon, although a friend of Tarleton from their Oxford days, assuredly felt the sting of Cornwallis's reproach. As mentioned in a previous chapter, John Graves Simcoe became angry because the Legion received equipment earmarked for the Queen's Rangers. Even Cornwallis himself could lose his patience with the younger man.

Tarleton's demands evidently exceeded their bounds on at least one occasion with the general. In January 1781, an exasperated Cornwallis wrote a bitter complaint to Tarleton concerning the Legion quartermaster. Apparently, the latter had pressed into service some army wagons destined for other use. The commissaries argued with him, but "he swore he did not care, that he had Colonel Tarleton's orders to press wagons, and he would have them and appealed to the *ratio ultima* of the broad sword." The usual patient earl demanded the man be "severely" punished.[45]

The defeat at the Cowpens represents the low point in Tarleton's career. The stigma of such a severe loss to the royal cause could not be easily removed and many fellow officers made negative remarks concerning the Legion commander. It even temporarily cooled some of the popular acclaim over Tarleton. *The Annual Register* reported that although the defeat could be attributed to "one of those unexpected events," Tarleton in subsequent actions became more circumspect and prudent.[46]

Sir Henry Clinton and Earl Cornwallis certainly felt the magnitude of the loss. Both asserted that the defeat contributed to the ultimate demise of British control in North America, but neither assigned blame to Tarleton *per se*.[47] In fact Cornwallis, who reportedly broke his sword upon learning of the American victory, wrote the Legion commander in an attempt to soothe his wounded pride after much unsolicited commentary by his fellow officers.[48] In his letter of January 30, 1781, he wrote:

> You have forfeited no part of my esteem as an officer by the unfortunate event of the action of the

17th: The means you used to bring the enemy to action were able and masterly, and must ever do you honour. Your disposition was unexceptionable; the total misbehaviour of the troops could alone have deprived you of the Glory which was so justly your due.[49]

Others were not so forgiving. Charles Stedman, a commissary for Cornwallis, reflected: "During the whole period of the war no other action reflected so much dishonour upon the British arms...."[50] Furthermore, "Colonel Tarleton acquired power without any extraordinary degree of merit, and upon most occasions exercised it without discretion."[51]

Members of the Seventy-First Highlanders, a regiment which lost its first battalion at the battle, became Tarleton's most vocal critics. Lieutenant Roderick MacKenzie, a participant in the battle, wrote an eloquent attack upon him soon after the war. His *Strictures on Lt. Col. Tarleton's History of the Campaigns of 1780 and 1781, in the Southern Provinces of North America; Wherein Characters and Corps are Vindicated from Injurious Aspersions, and Several Important Transactions Placed in Their Proper Point of View* (London: R. Faulder, 1787) is at times utterly blistering.[52] Major Archibald McArthur suffered the ignominy of surrendering the first battalion and commented "that he was an officer before Tarleton was born; that the best troops in the service were put under 'that boy' to be sacrificed."[53] Officers of the second battalion of the Seventy-First felt so strongly that they later signed a petition and refused to serve with the Legion commander.[54]

One American, who happened to be in Charles Town when news arrived of the Cowpens, noticed that the defeat "chagrined and disappointed" the British officers and Loyalists "exceedingly." Many appeared on the street corners with sullen countenances, whispering hurriedly in small groups. When paroled British officers reached the city, they added fuel to the fire and commented more on that "boy."[55]

The whispering behind Tarleton's back must have made him feel uncomfortable and embarrassed. For some who wished to smirk at his misfortune, it appeared that too much responsibility had been heaped upon a young, inexperienced officer. An utter lack of respect for his ability to command anything above a troop of dragoons underlines many of their criticisms. However, this is not an entirely fair assessment, for it appears that part of their motivation was fueled by resentment and jealousy.[56]

What all these individuals witnessed, whether American, French, or British, be they soldier or civilian, left an indelible mark upon their memories. Even before the conclusion of the war, their stories began to circulate and grow. In St. Johns Parish, South Carolina, a woman and her nurse became so frightened at the approach of Legion dragoons that they fled into the woods to hide and dropped the lady's baby. Joseph Johnson, an early historian of the Revolution, reportedly heard this story firsthand from one of those involved, and remarked that "the incident serves to show the pervading terror in the inhabitants."[57] The name of Tarleton became so terrifying that another historian, James Ferguson, assures his readers that long after the war it was common practice for house servants to use his name in order to frighten troublesome children.[58]

Aside from Ferguson's assessment of Tarleton as some proverbial "boogyman," it is interesting and highly significant to note that none of the above mentioned contemporary accounts, including the British ones, identify him as "Bloody Tarleton."[59] It is very likely, in fact even probable, that contemporaries referred to him as "Bloody Tarleton," but it is at the same time extremely odd that none wrote it down in their memoirs, diaries, correspondence, or histories. They at times make reference to his brutal nature and the depredations of his Legionnaires, and even "Tarleton's Quarter," but that is it.[60] In all their loathing for the man, none of these individuals follows through and calls him by this sobriquet so commonly used by the general public today. Other contemporaries, such as John Rutledge, James Thacher, John Bell Tilden, John Davis, William Seymour, John Taylor, Guilford Dudley, Carl

Leopold Baurmeister, Robert Gray, and Archibald Robertson follow suit and make no mention of Tarleton by this appellation.[61] Even Moses Hall, who had very good reason to call him "Bloody Tarleton," did not do so in his petition.[62]

The first generation of Revolutionary War historians are also silent about "Bloody Tarleton." Early histories by Alexander Garden, William Gordon, Abiel Holmes, John Lendrum, John Marshall, Jedidiah Morse, William Moultrie, David Ramsay, and Mercy Otis Warren[63] do not mention Tarleton by that name. While Garden, Gordon, Ramsay, and Warren condemn Tarleton for his excesses,[64] Holmes, Lendrum, Marshall, Morse and Moultrie[65] are very matter-of-fact when speaking of the Legion officer. Surprisingly, Timothy Pitkin's 1831 history of the United States contains no apparent mention of Tarleton.[66]

An overview of later nineteenth century histories of the war proves to be equally fruitless. Joseph Johnson has Tarleton engaging in the ghoulish practice of grave robbing, while James Parton calls him "a devil incarnate."[67] Meanwhile, George Washington Parke Custis relates that American officers after York Town refused to dine with such a cruel individual.[68] Even the outspoken William Gilmore Simms has no reference of "Bloody Tarleton." In his historical novel *The Partisan*, Tarleton is merely a "fierce legionary."[69] George Bancroft, Richard Hildreth, and George Tucker, the first great professional historians of the United States, also reserve any commentary on "Bloody Tarleton."[70]

It appears that "Bloody Tarleton" is a relatively recent development in the historiography of the Revolution. Stories about the Legion lieutenant colonel circulated and have done much to perpetuate his memory. Consequently, his "evil" stature grew in the popular imagination and continues to do so.[71] Only one person was needed to express the popular opinion, and that individual was Tarleton's one and only biographer.

It can be stated with some degree of certainty that Robert D. Bass in his *The Green Dragoon: The Lives of Banastre Tarleton and Mary Robinson* (New York: Henry Holt, 1957) is one of the first historians to call him "Bloody Tarleton" and to make this sobriquet a household phrase.[72] John Pancake follows suit but uses a twist on Bass's sinister nickname. In his *This Destructive War: The British Campaign in the Carolinas, 1780-1782* (Tuscaloosa: University of Alabama Press, 1985), Pancake alludes to Tarleton as "Bloody Ban."[73] Yet, that these modern historians call him "Bloody Tarleton" is really not that important. What is more significant is that they feel justified in doing so.[74]

This idea of "Bloody Tarleton" represents a natural progression in the historiography of the Revolutionary War as well as patriotism and some poetic license. It is a vital element of the myth making process surrounding Tarleton and the Legion. Its origins are found in preconceived notions about warfare and virtue.

---

[1] Tarleton to Cornwallis, August 5, 1780, Leneu's Ferry, Cornwallis Papers, Public Record Office, Kew, 30/11/63, ff. 19-21 (hereafter cited as PRO). Lt. Col. Banastre Tarleton, *A History of the Campaigns of 1780 and 1781, in the Southern Provinces of North America* (London: T. Cadell, 1787), 100-101. Many of the inhabitants broke their parole, hence the reason for Tarleton's visit. The area between the lower Santee and lower Pee Dee proved to be a trouble spot for royal forces throughout the war.

[2] Tarleton, *History of the Campaigns*, 100; Benjamin Franklin Stevens, comp. and ed., *The Campaign in Virginia 1781. An exact Reprint of Six rare Pamphlets on the Clinton-Cornwallis Controversy with very numerous important Unpublished Manuscript Notes By Sir Henry Clinton K.B. And the Omitted and hitherto Unpublished portions of the Letters in their Appendixes added from the Original Manuscripts*, 2 vols. (London: 4 Trafalgar Square, Charing Cross, 1888), 1:47.

[3] Tarleton to Lieutenant Colonel George Turnbull, November 5, 1780, near Singletons, 30/11/4, ff. 63-64; also see Tarleton's proclamation, November 11, 1780, announcing a pardon for "all people concerned in the late revolt," between Nelson's Ferry, Thompston Bridge and Santee Hills, 30/11/4, f. 95, Cornwallis Papers, PRO.

[4] From early 1780 to late 1781, Cornwallis's army marched through South Carolina, North Carolina, and Virginia, with the British Legion usually in the vanguard. Tarleton, *History of the Campaigns*, 100-101, 171-180. During the August 1780 excursion, the Legion traveled a minimum of 120 miles. The November ride covered at least 150 miles. Although these distances do not seem great by today's standards, it must be remembered that they are very modest estimates and that these horsemen traveled without the benefit of paved roadways.

[5] Thomas Dark, a captain in David Fanning's Loyalist militia, "from his approved inhumanity and cruelties in cutting, hacking and wounding his prisoners had acquired among those of his own Party the name of young Tarleton." Judge John Williams to Governor Alexander Martin, Hillsborough, January 27, 1782, in *The State Records of North Carolina*, ed. Walter Clark, 26 vols. (Goldsboro, North Carolina: Nash Brothers, 1886-1907), 22:610. This quote also hints at some recognition among the British of Tarleton's reputation; Lawrence Linfield Stirling, "Banastre Tarleton: A Reevaluation of His Career in the American Revolution" (MA thesis, Louisiana State University and Agricultural and Mechanical College, August 1964), 96. Stirling acknowledges the American condemnation of the Englishman, but downplays the numbers actively engaged in combat against him.

[6] Greene to Cornwallis, December 17, 1780, *The Papers of the Continental Congress: 1774-1789*, comp. John Butler (Washington, DC: US Government Printing Office, 1978), 4p. Copy, M247, reel 175, i155, vol.1, pp.521-523 (microfilm). Greene was referring to Tarleton's November operations along the Santee.

[7] Marion to General Horatio Gates, Benbow's Ferry, Black River, November 9, 1780, *Papers of the Continental Congress*, 1p., Copy, M247, reel 174, i154, vol.2, p.334 (microfilm). Snow Island is located at the confluence of the Pee Dee and Lynches Rivers. Robert D. Bass, *Swamp Fox: The Life and Campaigns of General Francis Marion* (New York: Henry Holt, 1959), 104.

[8] Cornwallis to Lord Francis Rawdon, July 26, 1780, Charlestown, Cornwallis papers, PRO, 30/11/78, ff. 48-49; for Tarleton at York Town, see Henry Lee, *Memoirs of the War in the Southern Department of the United States*, 2 vols. (Philadelphia: Bradford & Inskeep, 1812),

2:362-363; William Dobein James, A.M., *A Sketch of the Life of Brig. Gen. Francis Marion and a History of His Brigade From Its Rise in June 1780 until Disbanded in December, 1782 With Descriptions of Characters and Scenes Not Heretofore Published* (Charleston, 1821), 64. James was a former member of Marion's brigade.

[9] Christopher Ward, *The War of the Revolution*, 2 vols. (New York: Macmillan Company, 1952), 2:748-750. The Legion cavalry mustered 273 troopers on December 25, 1780, while the foot soldiers numbered 154. The dragoons essentially survived the Battle of Cowpens intact. On February 24, 1781, they numbered 218 privates. See Loyalist Regiment Muster Rolls, 1777-1783, British Legion, Minutes of Muster for December 25, 1780 and February 24, 1781, Public Archives of Canada, Ottawa, RG8I "C" Series, Vols. 1883 and 1884 (hereafter cited as PAC).

[10] Greene to Gen. Daniel Morgan, Camp on the Pedee, SC, January 13, 1781, *The Papers of General Nathanael Greene*, ed. Richard K. Showman, 7 vols. to date (Chapel Hill: University of North Carolina Press, 1976-), 7:106; Tarleton, *History of the Campaigns*, 15-20, 105-108. Ward, *War of the Revolution*, 2:698-702, 749. The remnants of three Continental cavalry regiments at Monck's Corner were the First (Bland's), Third (Baylor's), and Fourth (Moylan's). Also present were some dragoons from Pulaski's Legion, Horry's Horse, and about one hundred men under William Washington. Altogether, they numbered five hundred troopers. Brigadier General Isaac Huger commanded at this post. Robert K. Wright, Jr., *The Continental Army*, Army Lineage Series (Washington, DC: Center of Military History, United States Army, 1983), 345-347, 349.

[11] Morgan began his retreat within eight hours of the battle. John S. Pancake, *This Destructive War: The British Campaign in the Carolinas, 1780-1782* (Tuscaloosa: University of Alabama Press, 1985), 157. Tarleton's dragoons concerned Greene too during his subsequent retreat to the Dan River. See Col. Otho H. Williams to Greene, Mitchell's Mill 16 miles from Hillsborough, NC, 25 February 1781, 6 PM, *The Papers of Nathanael Greene*, 7:350.

[12] Lafayette to Wayne, dated Richmond, July 15, 1781, 4:248-249; Lafayette to Daniel Morgan, Richmond, July 16, 1781, 4:251, both in

Lafayette in the Age of the American Revolution: Selected Letters and Papers, 1776-1790, ed. Stanley J. Idzerda, 5 vols. to date (Ithaca: Cornell University Press, 1977-). Wayne operated in the Chesterfield Courthouse area along the Appomattox River, north of Petersburg. After Cowpens, Daniel Morgan claimed ill health, resigned his command, and returned home to Virginia. According to different accounts, he suffered from arthritis, rheumatism, and sciatica. Consult Don Higginbotham, *Daniel Morgan: Revolutionary Rifleman* (Chapel Hill: University of North Carolina Press, 1961).

[13] Lafayette to Baron Steuben, August 9, 1781, in Charlemagne Tower, Jr., *The Marquis De La Fayette in the American Revolution. With Some Account of the Attitude of France Toward the War of Independence*, 2 vols. (Philadelphia: J. B. Lippincott Company, 1895), 2:414-415.

[14] Lafayette to the Baron von Steuben, Montock Hill, August 13, 1781, 4:320-321; the threat of enemy cavalry had been plaguing the young Frenchman's mind for some time. See the earlier letter to the Baron von Steuben, Wilton, May 17, 1781, 4:106-108, *Lafayette in the Age of the American Revolution*. By this time Tarleton's British Legion and Simcoe's Queen's Rangers had been reunited. The Rangers had come to Virginia with Brigadier General Benedict Arnold's expedition in December 1780. William B. Willcox, ed., *The American Rebellion: Sir Henry Clinton's Narrative of His Campaigns, 1775-1782, With An Appendix of Original Documents* (New Haven: Yale University Press, 1954), 235-237, 249-258. C. T. Atkinson, "British Forces in North America, 1774-1781: Their Distribution and Strength," *Journal of the Society for Army Historical Research* 16 (1937): 20-21 (hereafter cited as *JSAHR*). Cornwallis now had about four hundred cavalry, "in excellent order." Tarleton, *History of the Campaigns*, 368-369.

[15] Davie could be just as utterly ruthless as his English counterpart. At Wahab's Plantation, he ordered his men to take no prisoners because the Legionnaires had burned the buildings. He claimed that Tarleton suffered from "boyish Temerity" and "had the merit of audacity and good fortune." *The Revolutionary War Sketches of William R. Davie*, ed. Blackwell P. Robinson (Raleigh: North Carolina Department of Cultural Resources, Division of Archives and History, 1976), 19-26.

[16] *Memoirs of the Duc de Lauzun*, trans. C. K. Scott Moncrieff (London: George Routledge and Sons, 1928), 185-186, 189-191, 193, 207-208, 248n221. Lauzun's Legion had eight hundred infantry and four hundred cavalry. However, a shortage of transports caused one-half of the regiment to remain in France. It skirmished with the British Legion at Gloucester Point, Virginia on October 3, 1781. During this encounter, the duke and his uhlans (lancers) nearly captured Tarleton.

[17] The better trained Continental troops probably did not fear Tarleton as much as the militia feared him. As regular troops, Continentals were trained to repel a cavalry assault by maintaining their line and presenting bayonets. Nevertheless, this proved to be at times a disconcerting affair for them as the Waxhaws clearly demonstrates. The infantry square did not become popular until the Napoleonic period. See Christopher Duffy, *The Military Experience in the Age of Reason* (New York: Atheneum, 1988), 214-216. The British Legion was a military organization not seen before in North America. Its ability to move far and fast undoubtedly frightened militiamen. By the end of the war, the Continental Army had four legionary and two partisan corps. (Both types of units were actually legions, the only difference being the ratio between mounted and dismounted troops). Wright, *The Continental Army*, 160-161, 184.

[18] "Colonel Tarleton has burnt all the Houses, and destroyed all the Corn from Camden down to Nelson's Ferry." Marion to Gen. Gates, Benbow's Ferry, November 26, 1780, *Papers of the Continental Congress*, 1p. Copy, M247, reel 174, i154, vol. 2, p. 334 (microfilm).

[19] This tavern is called Torrence's by Burke Davis. See Burke Davis, *The Cowpens-Guilford Courthouse Campaign* (Philadelphia and New York: J.B. Lippincott Company, 1962), 89-91, 94. Tarleton told his men to "*remember the Cowpens*" at this engagement. Tarleton, *History of the Campaigns*, 225-226.

[20] Lee, *Memoirs*, 1:315.

[21] Burnet to Colonel Henry Lee, Jr. Camp at Mask's Ferry, NC (On Pee Dee), February 2, 1781, *The Papers of General Nathanael Greene*, 7:234-235. Burnet's intelligence overestimated Legion strength by seventy-six men. See "State of the Troops that marched with the

Army under the Command of Lieutenant-General Earl Cornwallis," Number VI, in Earl Cornwallis, *An Answer to That Part of the Narrative of Lieutenant-General Sir Henry Clinton, K.B. Which Relates to the Conduct of Lieutenant-General Earl Cornwallis, During the Campaign in North-America, in the Year 1781* (London: J. Debrett, 1783), 53. These 174 dragoons represent the rank and file fit and present for duty.

[22] John C. Dann, ed., *The Revolution Remembered: Eyewitness Accounts of the War for Independence* (Chicago: The University of Chicago Press, 1980), 201-203.

[23] John Postell. Charleston Jail. Statement re his actions while a prisoner. June 24, 1781, in *Papers of the Continental Congress*, 4p. Copy. M247, reel 175, i155, vol. 2, p. 294 (microfilm). Postell's story makes a very strong statement about the failure of terror to subdue a population. Terror will be examined in Chapter VIII.

[24] Direct French military assistance did not occur until the summer of 1778 with the assault upon Newport, Rhode Island. The next Franco-American effort occurred in the siege of Savannah, September to October 1779, where one company of British Legion infantry served. Ward, *War of the Revolution*, 2:587-595, 688-694.

[25] "It is rumored that Tarleton has been wounded." In Robert D. Bass, *The Green Dragoon: The Lives of Banastre Tarleton and Mary Robinson* (New York: Henry Holt, 1957), 2. De Choisy is making reference to a sharp cavalry skirmish outside of Gloucester, Virginia.

[26] For "violent doings," see *Memoirs of the Marshal Count De Rochambeau* (Paris, 1838; repr., New York Times and Arno Press, 1971), 106; Rochambeau's opinion of the English officer can be found in Bass, *The Green Dragoon*, 4.

[27] A sous-lieutenant was equivalent to an ensign in the British Army. This is an unsubstantiated story which circulated among French officers. It will be analyzed in more detail later. Verger's "Journal of the Most Important Events that occurred to the French Troops under the Command of M. le Comte de Rochambeau," is reproduced in *The American Campaigns of Rochambeau's Army 1780, 1781, 1782, 1783*, trans. and eds. Howard C. Rice, Jr. and Anne S. K. Brown, 2 vols. (Princeton

University Press, 1972). Volume I, page 137 has the story of the murdered woman; le colonel Talton, "qui les avait fait trembler pendant longtemps...Son nom seul faisait frémir un Américain." (Colonel Tarleton, who made them tremble for a long time...only his name caused an American to shudder). Joachim du Perron, Comte de Revel, *Journal particulieur d'une campagne aux Indes Occidentales (1781-1782)* (Paris: H. Charles-Lavauzelle, 1898?), 124-125, 169.

[28] Coughran is also spelled Cochrane. Captain Charles Cochrane (1749-1781) commanded the light company of the 4th Regiment until 1778 when the unit went to the West Indies. He then purchased a lieutenancy in the 1st Guards and accepted a brevet major's commission in the newly formed British Legion. In early June 1780 he received permission from Earl Cornwallis to go home on leave. He returned to New York in October 1781 and Sir Henry Clinton sent him on to York Town with dispatches. Cochrane arrived there on the 10th; Cornwallis assigned him to his staff as an aide-de-camp. While inspecting the outer defenses with his Lordship, Cochrane was decapitated by an enemy cannon ball. See Mellon Chamberlain, "Memorial of Captain Charles Cochrane, A British Officer in the Revolutionary War," *Proceedings of the Massachusetts Historical Society*, May 1891. He stopped the burning of American houses probably during the Poundridge-Bedford, New York raid of July 1779. See Thomas Portlock, Phila. Deposition re alleged British atrocities. July 24, 1779. Sworn before John Ord, in *Papers of the Continental Congress*, 1p., M247, reel 180, i163, p. 94 (microfilm). James Ferguson, *Two Scottish Soldiers, a Soldier of 1688 and Blenheim, a Soldier of the American Revolution and a Jacobite Laird and His Forbears* (Aberdeen: D. Wyllie and Son, 1888), 76.

[29] *Letters of Eliza Wilkinson*, ed. Caroline Gilman (New York, 1839; repr., New York Times and Arno Press, 1969), v-vi, 103-108. Yonge's Island is thirty miles south of Charles Town. Captain Thomas Sandford's troop of British Legion light dragoons was in the Charles Town area during this time. See this troop's muster rolls for October 25 to December 24, 1780, October 25 to December 24, 1781, and December 25, (1781) to February 23, 1782, in Loyalist Regiment Muster Rolls, 1777-1783, British Legion, PAC, RG8I "C" Series, Vol. 1884.

[30] Lee, *Memoirs of the War*, 1:284; This Captain Miller's first name is not known. In Sabine's *Biographical Sketches*, there are three Millers of distinction: Thomas Millar, John Miller, and Thomas Miller. All three were officers of cavalry in the Legion, but Thomas Millar is the only captain. See Lorenzo Sabine, *Biographical Sketches of Loyalists of the American Revolution, With an Historical Essay*, 2 vols. (Boston: Little, Brown and Company, 1864), 2:80, 557.

[31] Edward McCrady, *The History of South Carolina in the Revolution 1775-1783*, 2 vols. (New York and London: The Macmillan Company, 1901-1902), 1:817.

[32] *The Writings of Thomas Jefferson: Being His Autobiography, Correspondence, Reports, Messages, Addresses, And Other Writings, Official And Private*, ed. H.A. Washington, 9 vols. (Washington, DC: Taylor and Maury, 1853-1854), 2:424-427. The Legion commander "behaved very genteelly (*sic*) with me." McLeod "preserved everything with sacred care." Jefferson's house at Elk Hill along the James River received far worse treatment at the hands Lord Cornwallis. The Earl's troops left the plantation "an absolute waste," having burned all the buildings and excess crops plus consumed every cow, sheep, and hog. Furthermore, they confiscated thirty slaves "and carried off all the horses capable of service; of those too young for service he cut the throats." Tarleton, *History of the Campaigns*, 295-298. His near capture by Legion dragoons terrified Jefferson. Several members of the Virginia legislature became prisoners. See "New Documentary Light on Tarleton's Raid: Letters of Newman Brockenbrough and Peter Lyons," ed. John Cook Wyllie, *The Virginia Magazine of History and Biography* 74 (October 1966): 452-461.

[33] *The Annual Register* was a journal published by the government. This quote is in reference to Tarleton's victory at Biggin's Bridge. See *The Annual Register, or a View of the History, Politics, and Literature, For the Year 1780*, vol. XXIII (London: J. Dodsley, 1788), 220; Bernard Berelson and Gary A. Steiner, *Human Behavior: An Inventory of Scientific Findings* (New York: Harcourt, Brace & World, 1964), 363-381, 443-449; John Keegan, *The Mask of Command* (New York: Viking, 1987), 10-11; "I should wish to have as many of the Militia as possible sent to Colonel Tarleton. If anybody can put spirit into them he will."

Cornwallis to Lt. Col. John Harris Cruger, Wynnesborough, November 25, 1780, in Bass, *The Green Dragoon*, 123.

[34] *The London Chronicle*, July 18, 1780 has an account of the battle at the Waxhaws. "Col. Tarleton knew, that having taken a command of the King's troops, the duty he owed to his country directed him to fight and conquer." *London Gazette Extraordinary*, July 5, 1780 also reprints letters concerning the Waxhaws. The October 9, 1780 issue recounts Tarleton's exploits at Camden and Fishing Creek; *Ruddiman's Weekly Mercury* of January 2, 1782 reported: "It must give pleasure to every lover of this country, to be assured, that by a letter from the gallant Col. Tarleton to his brother, now in Ipswich, that distinguished character was in perfect health in the middle of last month, and is daily expected in England."

[35] *The Annual Register, or a View of the History, Politics, and Literature, For the Year 1780*, vol. XXIII, 233-234.

[36] George Hanger, *The Life, Adventures, and Opinions of Col. George Hanger*, 2 vols. (London, 1801), 2:58, 62, 406-407.

[37] Of Cowpens, Cornwallis wrote: "The late affair almost broke my heart." Quoted from Bass, *The Green Dragoon*, 160; Franklin and Mary Wickwire, *Cornwallis: The American Adventure* (Boston: Houghton Mifflin Company, 1970), 175-176. "We can do no good without you." Cornwallis to Tarleton, November 11, 1780, *History of the Campaigns*, 201-202. For Tarleton's near fatal fever, see Cornwallis to Major Richard England, Waxhaws, September 20, 1780, 30/11/80, ff. 31-32; Cornwallis to Lt. Col. Nisbet Balfour, Waxhaw, September 21, 1780, 30/11/80, ff. 35-36; "We are fortunate to save him." Cornwallis to Balfour, Waxhaw, September 23, 1780, 30/11/80, ff. 39-40, all in Cornwallis Papers, PRO.

[38] The dragoon leader's string of successes spoke loudly to the earl. Wickwire, *Cornwallis*, 135-138, 175-177; when Cornwallis dispatched Tarleton after Marion, he wrote his subordinate: "You will of course not be long absent, and let me hear from you constantly." Without the Legion cavalry, his Lordship could not "hear of any considerable body of the enemy." See Cornwallis to Tarleton, Winnsboro, November 2, 1780, 30/11/82, f. 5; "Tarleton alone can settle matters." Cornwallis to

Lieutenant Richard Money, Winnsborough, November 13, 1780, 30/11/4, ff. 112-113, Cornwallis Papers, PRO.

[39] Tarleton, *History of the Campaigns*, 6-7, 16, 27, 30, 62, 103, 115, 180; Roderick MacKenzie, *Strictures on Lt. Col. Tarleton's History of the Campaigns of 1780 and 1781, in the Southern Provinces of North America: Wherein Characters and Corps are Vindicated from Injurious Aspersions, and Several Important Transactions Placed in Their Proper Point of View* (London: R. Faulder, 1787), 30-31; when horses were transported from England to America, few if any survived the six to eight week ocean crossing. Therefore, purchasing them from the colonial civilian population became an absolute necessity. In just one month in 1782, General Clinton's commissary general bought a staggering nine hundred horses. It is interesting to note that Captain Jacob James of the Legion was an accomplished horse thief. See Anthony J. Scotti, Jr., "'This Disagreeable Exertion of Authority': Banastre Tarleton and the British Legion in the Southern Campaigns, 1780-1781" (MA thesis, Wake Forest University, May 1991), 16-17.

[40] Tarleton, *History of the Campaigns*, 4, 6-8, 15-17, 19-20, 62; Henry Lee asserts that American cavalry had an inherent superiority over British cavalry because they had better mounts obtained from Virginia. Also, Americans were just simply better horsemen. Lee ignores the fact that the British Legion was a Loyalist unit and that the mounts seized at Monck's Corner came primarily from three Continental cavalry regiments formed in the Virginia region. Lee, *Memoirs*, 1:315-316, 324, 330-331; Wright, *The Continental Army*, 345-347. Also see the advertisement in the *New York Royal Gazette* for Saturday, April 12, 1783. "To be Sold by Auction, Upwards of Two Hundred excellent Dragoon Horses."

[41] Tarleton, *History of the Campaigns*, 87-88, 101, 103; George Hanger, An *Address to the Army; in Reply to Strictures, by Roderick M'Kenzie (Late Lieutenant in the 71st Regiment) on Tarleton's History of the Campaigns of 1780 and 1781* (London: James Ridgway, 1789), 48-50.

[42] For the quote, see Tarleton to Captain John André, February 19, 1779, Clinton Papers, William L. Clements Library, Ann Arbor, Michigan; Tarleton to Cornwallis, Woodwards, December 14, 1780, Cornwallis Papers, PRO, 30/11/4, ff. 325-326; John Postell, Statement

re his actions while a prisoner, June 24, 1781, in *Papers of the Continental Congress*, 4p. Copy. M247, reel 175, i155, vol. 2, p. 294 (microfilm).

[43] Captain Dunlap, who was raising two or three cavalry troops for the Ninety-Six District, SC, received the rejected accoutrements. These troops represent further evidence of the extreme need for royal cavalry in the South. British officials intended to give horses to approximately 190 men from among the loyal militia and Rebel prisoners of war. Cornwallis to Balfour, Winnsboro, November 4, 1780, 30/11/82, ff. 6-7; Cornwallis to Lt. Col. John Cruger, Winnsboro, November 4, 1780, 30/11/82, f. 8; Cornwallis to Major Dunlap, Winnsboro, November 11, 1780, 30/11/82, ff. 24-25; Cornwallis to Cruger, Winnsboro, November 11, 1780, 30/11/82, ff. 26-27; Alex. Innes, Inspector General of Provincial Forces, "The Inspector General of Provincial Forces Report to His Excellency the Commander in Chief," New York, May 30, 1781, 30/11/6, ff. 162-163; Major General Alexander Leslie to Cornwallis, Portsmouth, July 15, 1781, 30/11/6, ff. 299-300, all in Cornwallis Papers, PRO. As testimony to its hard service, by the spring of 1781 the British Legion needed new kits again. "The Legion being in the utmost distress for want of arms, cloathing (*sic*), boots, and indeed appointments of all kinds, I must beg that your Excellency will be pleased to direct the Inspector General to forward a supply of every article with the greatest dispatch." Cornwallis to Clinton, Petersburg, VA, May 20, 1781, in Cornwallis, *An Answer*, 64-66. Evidently, this was the equipment meant for Simcoe's Rangers and appropriated by the Legion. See Lieut. Col. J.G. Simcoe, *A History of the Operations of a Partisan Corps Called the Queen's Rangers* (New York: Bartlett and Welford, 1844; repr., New York: Arno Press, 1968), 303-304.

[44] Cornwallis to Rawdon, Charleston, July 15, 1780, Cornwallis Papers, PRO, 30/11/78, ff. 18-19; Tarleton, *History of the Campaigns*, 87-95. Captain Christian Huck led one of the small parties sent out. At Williamson's Plantation, South Carolina, on July 12, 1780, 260 Rebel militia attacked Huck's 115 men (Legion dragoons, New York Volunteers, and Loyalist militia). Only twenty-four Crown troops escaped. Huck, known as the "Swearing Captain," died in the fighting. See Sabine, *Biographical Sketches of Loyalists*, 1:552-553.

[45] Cornwallis to Tarleton, Wynnsborough, January 7, 1781, Cornwallis Papers, PRO, 30/11/84, ff. 29-30. Simcoe, *History of the Operations*, 303-

304. A commissary performed various logistical duties. Although considered an officer, he held no military rank per se. Wright, *The Continental Army*, 436. During the march through North Carolina in February 1781, no officer from the Legion appeared at a court of enquiry concerning the exact number of horses in the regiment. See General Orders, Head Quarters, Armstrong's [NC], February 19, 1781, in A.R. Newsome, "A British Orderly Book, 1780-1781," *North Carolina Historical Review* 9 (1932): 370. The officers of the Legion cavalry were entitled to at least thirty-six horses. All servants needed to have signed passes for the horses they rode.

[46] *The Annual Register, or a View of the History, Politics, and Literature, For the Year 1781*, vol. XXIV, 55-57, 64-66. After the war when Tarleton became a Member of Parliament, he openly criticized Sir Arthur Wellesley for his Portugal campaign. The latter responded that "he would much rather follow his example in the field than his advice in the senate." *The Annual Register...For the Year 1809*, vol. LI, 60. *The London Chronicle* of March 29, 1781 voiced a more magnanimous opinion of the Cowpens. "By all accounts Col. Tarleton was never more distinguished for spirit and gallantry than on this occasion."

[47] "I am most exceedingly concerned, my Lord, at the very unfortunate affair of the 17th of January, (Cowper's). I confess I dread the consequences." Clinton to Cornwallis, March 5, 1781, in Sir Henry Clinton, K.B., *Narrative of the Campaign in 1781 in North America* (London, 1783), 5-6, 113-115; "The disaster of the 17th of January cannot be imputed to any defect in my conduct, as the detachment was certainly superior to the force against which it was sent, and put under the command of an officer of experience and tried abilities. This misfortune, however, did not appear irretrievable." In Cornwallis, *An Answer*, iv. After the war, Clinton and Cornwallis conducted a "pamphlet battle" over who was to blame for the failure of the 1781 campaign. See Stevens, comp. and ed., *The Campaign in Virginia 1781. An exact Reprint of Six rare Pamphlets on the Clinton-Cornwallis Controversy....*

[48] Wickwire, *Cornwallis*, 269-270. The Legion officer requested that he be allowed to retire and a court-martial be convened in order to determine the responsibility for the defeat. Tarleton, *History of the Campaigns*, 222.

⁴⁹ Tarleton, *History of the Campaigns*, 252; Cornwallis knew that his Legion commmander worried about the past. Moreover, his Lordship realized that Tarleton needed to hear from him directly that all was forgiven. Cornwallis wrote: "You must be sensible that, in the present instance, I put the greatest confidence in you... [Ignore] the sanguine opinions of friends and your own prejudices...Distinguish between *is* and *has been*" (original emphasis). Cornwallis to Tarleton, Nahunta Creek, May 5, 1781, in Tarleton, *History of the Campaigns*, 330; On June 9, 1781, Cornwallis wrote to Tarleton that he placed "the greatest confidence in your zeal and abilities." Tarleton, *History of the Campaigns*, 344-345.

⁵⁰ "Every disaster that befel (*sic*) lord Cornwallis, after Tarleton's most shameful defeat at the Cowpens, may most justly be attributed to the imprudence and unsoldierly conduct of that officer in the action...Is it possible for the mind to form any other conclusion, than that there was a radical defect, and a want of military knowledge on the part of colonel Tarleton?" Stedman had much respect for Cornwallis and despised Tarleton for his postwar criticisms of the general. Charles Stedman, *The History of the Origin, Progress, and Termination of the American War*, 2 vols. (London, 1794), 2:324.

⁵¹ While his personal bravery was superior and undeniable, his talents were that of "a partizan (*sic*) captain of light dragoons, daring in skirmishes." *Ibid*., 2:324-325.

⁵² "He led a number of brave men to destruction, and then used every effort in his power to damn the same [to] posterity." MacKenzie, *Strictures*, 105-118.

⁵³ "A rash, foolish boy." George F. Scheer and Hugh F. Rankin, *Rebels and Redcoats* (Cleveland and New York: The World Publishing Company, 1957), 432; Henry Lee, Jr., *The Campaign of 1781 in the Carolinas* (Philadelphia, 1824), 98n.

⁵⁴ The officers drew up the remonstrance against Tarleton "from a recollection of his conduct at the Cowpens." This occurred in Virginia during the summer of 1781. Stedman, *The History of the American War*, 2:387n.

[55] William Moultrie, *Memoirs of the American Revolution, So Far As It Related to the States of North and South-Carolina, and Georgia*, 2 vols. (New York: David Longworth, 1802), 2:256-259. Moultrie saw service in the war and became a national hero for his defense of the fort on Sullivan's Island, South Carolina in 1776; Richard Wheeler, comp., *Voices of 1776* (New York: Thomas Y. Crowell, 1972), 361-364. Tarleton frequently exhibited "boyish Temerity." Robinson, ed., *The Revolutionary War Sketches of William R. Davie*, 19.

[56] The Rebel view of the Cowpens will be dealt with later in the discussion of American virtue. For now, it will suffice to repeat David Ramsay's assessment that Tarleton had a "distinguished reputation, but he was greatly indebted for his military fame to good fortune and accident. In all his previous engagements [before Cowpens] he either had the advantage of surprising an incautious enemy—of attacking them when panick-struck (*sic*) after recent defeats—or of being opposed to undisciplined militia. He had gathered no laurels by hard fighting against an equal force." David Ramsay, *The History of the Revolution of South-Carolina, From a British Province to an Independent State*, 2 vols. (Trenton: Isaac Collins, 1785), 2:200. Ramsay was an eminent South Carolina physician who also served in the state legislature during the war. In August 1780, royal authorities exiled him to St. Augustine, Florida, where he remained for a year. Upon his return, he resumed his political career and became a delegate to the Continental Congress. He apparently plagiarized the British *Annual Register* to write to his *History of the Revolution of South-Carolina*. See Arthur H. Shaffer, *To Be An American: David Ramsay and the Making of the American Consciousness* (Columbia: University of South Carolina Press, 1991), 58, 62, 87-90, 97-98, 100, 104-105, 113, 175, 187, 234.

[57] Joseph Johnson, *Traditions and Reminiscences Chiefly of the American Revolution in the South: Including Biographical Sketches, Incidents and Anecdotes, Few of Which Have Been Published, Particularly of Residents in the Upper Country* (Charleston: Walker and James, 1851), 310-311.

[58] Ferguson, *Two Scottish Soldiers*, 78.

[59] "Bloody" used in this manner meant exceedingly, abominably, or desperately. It also expressed anger, resentment, and detestation.

The lowest classes constantly used the word, which was in general colloquial use from around the mid-seventeenth to the mid-eighteenth century. The upper elements of English society considered it a "horrid word," on a par with obscene or profane language. Newspaper accounts and police reports during this era usually printed it as "b----y." *The Oxford English Dictionary*, prepared by J. A. Simpson and E. S. C. Weiner, 20 vols., 2nd ed. (Oxford: Clarendon Press, 1989), 2:308.

[60] Ramsay describes the consequences of the Waxhaws as follows: "This barbarous massacre gave a more sanguinary turn to the war. Tarleton's quarters became proverbial, and in the subsequent battles a spirit of revenge gave a keener edge to military resentments." Ramsay, *History of the Revolution of South-Carolina*, 2:110. As a noun, the word "quarter" means clemency granted to a defeated enemy. In response to the Waxhaws, the expression "Tarleton's Quarter" arose and meant "no quarter." J. Tracy Power, "'The Virtue of Humanity Was Totally Forgot': Buford's Massacre, May 29, 1780," *South Carolina Historical Magazine* 93 (January 1992): 5-14. The American riflemen at Kings Mountain reportedly cried out "Buford! Buford! Tarleton's quarter!" Ward, *War of the Revolution*, 2:742. Another account has the Americans saying "Give them Buford's play!" Lyman C. Draper, *King's Mountain and Its Heroes: History of the Battle of King's Mountain, October 7th, 1780, and the Events Which Led To It* (Cincinnati: Peter G. Thomson, 1881), 282; at least one contemporary thought of Tarleton as a "criminal." Shaffer, *To Be An American*, 102.

[61] See Joseph Barnwell, "Letters of John Rutledge," *South Carolina Historical and Genealogical Magazine* 18 (January 1917): 42-49; Tarleton was "a bold and impetuous leader." In September 1781, his dragoons had the "baseness" to shoot Colonel Alexander Scammell as he reconnoitered the York Town fortifications and after he had surrendered. James Thacher, *Military Journal of the American Revolution, From the Commencement to the Disbanding of the American Army; Comprising a Detailed Account of the Principal Events and Battles of the Revolution, With Their Exact Dates, And a Biographical Sketch of the most Prominent Generals* (Hartford, Connecticut: Hurlbut, Williams and Company, American Subscription Publishing House, 1862), 280-281, 292; John Bell Tilden Phelps, "Extracts from the Journal of Lieutenant John Bell Tilden, Second Pennsylvania Line, 1781-1782," *Pennsylvania Magazine of History and Biography* 19 (1895): 51-63, 208-233 (hereafter cited as

PMHB). "The Yorktown Campaign. Journal of Captain John Davis, of the Pennsylvania Line," *PMHB* 5 (1881): 290-311; William Seymour, Sergeant-Major of the Delaware Regiment, "A Journal of the Southern Expedition, 1780-1783," *PMHB* 7 (1883): 286-298; the accounts of John Taylor and Guilford Dudley are in Dann, ed., *The Revolution Remembered*, 204-228; *Revolution in America: Confidential Letters and Journals 1776-1784 of Adjutant General Major Baurmeister of the Hessian Forces*, trans. Bernhard A. Uhlendorf (New Brunswick, New Jersey: Rutgers University Press, 1957), 363, 378-382, 393, 443; "Colonel Robert Gray's Observations on the War in Carolina," *The South Carolina Historical and Genealogical Magazine* 11 (July 1910): 139-159; *Archibald Robertson, Lieutenant-General Royal Engineers: His Diaries and Sketches in America 1762-1780*, ed. Harry Miller Lydenberg (New York: New York Public Library, 1930), 186-187, 193-194, 198-199, 206, 218, 230; British cavalry plundered the home of Mrs. Eliza Wilkinson after Charles Town fell. As they left, they told her "that they had favored us a great deal—that we might thank our stars it was no worse." *Letters of Eliza Wilkinson*, ed. Gilman, 28-31, 39-43, 88-89, 103-108.

[62] Dann, *The Revolution Remembered*, 196-204.

[63] Michael Docherty, an American deserter who served with the Legion infantry stated: "I never before had kept such bad company." Alexander Garden, *Anecdotes of the Revolutionary War in America, with Sketches of Character of Persons the Most Distinguished, in the Southern States, For Civil and Military Services* (Charleston: A.E. Miller, 1822), 259, 267, 269, 284-288, 396-398; Alexander Garden, *Anecdotes of the American Revolution, Illustrative of the Talents and Virtues of the Heroes and Patriots, Who Acted the Most Conspicuous Parts Therein*, 2nd Series (Charleston: A.E. Miller, 1828), 126-127, 129-130, 135-140; William Gordon, *The History of the Rise, Progress, and Establishment, of the Independence of the United States of America: Including an Account of the Late War; and of the Thirteen Colonies, From Their Origin to that Period*, 4 vols. (London: Charles Dilly and James Buckland, 1788), 3:360, 447, 471, 4:35, 402; Abiel Holmes, *The Annals of America, From the Discovery by Columbus in the Year 1492, to the Year 1826*, 2 vols. (Cambridge: Hilliard and Brown, 1829), 2:309, 321-322; John Lendrum, *A Concise and Impartial History of the America Revolution. To Which is Prefixed, a General History of North and South America. Together with an Account of the Discovery and Settlement of North America, and a View of the Progress, Character, and Political State*

of the Colonies previous to the Revolution, 2 vols. (Boston: I. Thomas and E.T. Andrews, 1795), 2:278, 289-290, 299-300, 347-350, 366; John Marshall, *The Life of George Washington, Commander in Chief of the American Forces, During the War Which Established the Independence of His Country, and First President of the United States*, 5 vols. (Philadelphia: C.P. Wayne, 1804-1807; repr., Fredericksburg, Virginia: Citizens' Guild of Washington's Boyhood Home, 1926), 3:167, 172, 174, 179, 194, 199, 297, 303, 305, 317, 319, 323, 329, 367, 398; Jedidiah Morse, *Annals of the American Revolution; Or a Record of the Causes and Events Which Produced, and Terminated in the Establishment and Independence of the American Republic. Interspersed with Numerous Appropriate Documents and Anecdotes* (Hartford, 1824), 331-335, 347-348; William Moultrie, *Memoirs of the American Revolution*, 2:203-208, 253-259; David Ramsay, *History of the Revolution of South-Carolina*, 2:63-67, 109-110, 196-200; Mercy Otis Warren, *History of the Rise, Progress and Termination of the American Revolution. Interspersed with Biographical, Political and Moral Observations*, 3 vols. (Boston: Manning and Loring, 1805), 2:196-197, 202-203, 244, 309-312, 315-316, 3:27, 33-34.

[64] Garden, *Anecdotes of the American Revolution*, 2nd Series, 129-130, 139-140; Gordon, *The History of the United States of America*, 4:33-36; Ramsay, *History of the Revolution of South-Carolina*, 2:109-110, 199-200; Warren was simply appalled that he had the effrontery "to boast in the presence of a lady of respectability, that he had killed more men, and ravished more women, than any man in America." Warren, *History of the American Revolution*, 2:197.

[65] Holmes, *The Annals of America*, 2:309, 321-322; Lendrum, *A Concise and Impartial History*, 2:289-290; Marshall, *The Life of George Washington*, 3:179-181; Morse, *Annals of the American Revolution*, 331; Moultrie, *Memoirs of the American Revolution*, 2:203-208.

[66] Timothy Pitkin, *A Political and Civil History of the United States of America, From the Year 1763 to the Close of the Administration of President Washington, in March, 1797: Including A Summary View of the Political and Civil State of the North American Colonies, Prior to that Period*, 2 vols. (New Haven: Hezekiah Howe and Durrie and Peck, 1831). Postwar newspaper accounts also have no reference to "Bloody Tarleton." "Anecdote of Colonel Tarleton," in *Philadelphia American Museum or Universal Magazine* 4 (1788): 94; "Lt. Col. Tarleton: His Character,"

and "Notice of Lt. Col. Tarleton's *History of the Campaigns*," both in *The Cambridge (Massachusetts) General Repository and Review* 3 (January 1813): 106, 124, 126.

[67] Johnson, *Traditions and Reminiscences of the Revolution*, 162, 165-166. James Parton, *Life of Andrew Jackson*, 3 vols. (Boston and New York: Houghton, Mifflin and Company, 1859-1860), 1:82-85.

[68] *Recollections and Private Memoirs of Washington, by his adopted son, George Washington Parke Custis, with a memoir of the author, by his daughter; and illustrative and explanatory notes by Benson J. Lossing* (New York: Derby and Jackson, 1860), 251-252.

[69] William Gilmore Simms, *The Partisan: A Romance of the Revolution* (Chicago: Belford, Clarke and Company, 1887), 15-16, 95, 372-373, 429, 461-465, 474. Also see Simms, *The Revolutionary War in South Carolina: An Anthology*, comp. Stephen Meats (Columbia: Southern Studies Program, University of South Carolina, 1975).

[70] George Bancroft, *History of the United States, From the Discovery of the American Continent*, 10 vols. (1834-1874; repr., Boston: Little, Brown, and Company, 1861-1875), 10:306-307, 319, 325, 327, 342-343, 461, 463-464, 504-505, 508, 518; Richard Hildreth, *The History of the United States of America*, 6 vols. (1849-1852; repr., New York: Harper and Brothers, 1877-1880), 3:306, 315, 325, 327, 341, 343, 345, 355, 357; George Tucker, *The History of the United States, From Their Colonization to the End of the Twenty-Sixth Congress, In 1841*, 4 vols. (Philadelphia: J. B. Lippincott and Company, 1856-1857), 1:252, 254, 270, 280; Tarleton "had a sanguinary and resentful temper, which made him unmerciful to his enemies." Benson J. Lossing, *The Pictorial Field-Book of the Revolution*, 2 vols. (New York, 1855), 2:401.

[71] John Fiske, *The American Revolution*, 2 vols. (Boston: Houghton, Mifflin and Company, 1891), 2:177-178, 192, 195, 249, 254, 271; Sir George Otto Trevelyan, *The American Revolution*, 4 vols. (New York: Longmans, Green, and Company, 1898-1907), 3:281, 285; J. W. Fortescue, *A History of the British Army*, 13 vols. (London: Macmillan and Company, 1899-1930), 3:315-318; McCrady, *The History of South Carolina in the Revolution 1775-1783*, 1:816-819; George M. Wrong, *Washington and His Comrades in Arms: A Chronicle of the War of*

Independence (New Haven: Yale University Press, 1921), 216-217, 219-221, 248, 252-253, 263-264; Willard Wallace claims that Tarleton was a "huge dashing cavalryman," which is an exaggeration, given that all contemporary accounts state that Banastre Tarleton was rather short. Willard M. Wallace, *Appeal to Arms: A Military History of the American Revolution* (New York: Harper and Brothers, 1951), 209-210, 214-215, 229, 232-234, 236-238, 250, 256; Tarleton is the "Red Raider" in Hugh F. Rankin, "Cowpens: Prelude to Yorktown," *North Carolina Historical Review* 31 (1954): 336-369; John Richard Alden, *The South in the Revolution 1763-1789* (Louisiana State University Press, 1957), 240-241, 245-246, 250, 252-254, 257-259, 294, 298; in George F. Scheer and Hugh F. Rankin, *Rebels and Redcoats* (Cleveland: World Publishing Company, 1957), 457, Tarleton's countenance ran "a little to grossness about the eyes and mouth." Again, this is an exaggeration for all one has to do is look at the Reynolds portrait to see otherwise. Scheer and Rankin are trying to make the "monster" in Tarleton appear more real; for "the terrible Tarleton...one of the real villains of the Revolution," see Elswyth Thane, *The Family Quarrel: A Journey Through the Years of the Revolution* (New York: Duell, Sloan and Pearce, 1959), 25, 100, 105, 108-109, 155, 160-161, 166, 179, 181-183, 189, 194, 196-200, 210-211, 213, 254, 288; Tarleton was "that indefatigable brewer of hatred for the British." M. F. Treacy, *Prelude to Yorktown: The Southern Campaign of Nathanael Greene 1780-1781* (Chapel Hill: University of North Carolina Press, 1963), 16-17, 20, 42-45, 48, 67, 88-93, 97-116, 127-128; Piers Mackesy, *The War for America 1775-1783* (Cambridge: Harvard University Press, 1964), 341-343, 405-406; Robert McCluer Calhoon, *The Loyalists in Revolutionary America: 1760-1781* (New York: Harcourt Brace Jovanovich, 1965), 491-492, 494-495; Henry Lumpkin, *From Savannah to Yorktown: The American Revolution in the South* (Columbia: University of South Carolina Press, 1981), 45-50, 61, 80, 102, 109-133, 164-169, 218-219, 250; M. Foster Farley, "The 'Old Wagoner' and the 'Green Dragon,'" *History Today* 25 (March 1975): 190-195.

[72] Bass, *The Green Dragon*, 72, 83. There exists ample evidence, if not actual proof, that Bass utilized some poetic license after reading Christopher Ward's *War of the Revolution*, which came out in 1952, five years before his biography. In vol. 2, p.701, Ward states that Tarleton *"wrote his name in letters of blood all across the history of the war in the South"* (emphasis added). Bass also evidently consulted Hugh Rankin, "Cowpens: Prelude to Yorktown," 346, who appears to be among the

first to have called him "Bloody Tarleton." It is also interesting to note that Bass refers to the Loyalist partisan William Cuningham as "Bloody Bill." Cuningham, whose name is generally spelled Cunningham, operated throughout Georgia and the Carolinas. See Robert Bass, *Ninety Six: The Struggle for the South Carolina Back Country* (Lexington, SC: Sandlapper Store, 1978), 451. Don Higginbotham, *The War of American Independence: Military Attitudes, Policies, and Practice, 1763-1789* (New York: The Macmillan Company, 1971), 361. One of the earliest references to "Bloody Tarleton" is in Thomas J. Kirkland and Robert M. Kennedy, *Historic Camden*, 2 vols. (Columbia, S.C.: State Company, 1905 and 1926), 1:194.

[73] Pancake, *This Destructive War*, 71; "Bloody Ban" is also found in Craig L. Symonds, *A Battlefield Atlas of the American Revolution* (Baltimore: Nautical and Aviation Publishing, 1986), 80; Christopher Hibbert refers to him as "the Butcher" in *Redcoats and Rebels: The American Revolution Through British Eyes* (New York: Avon Books, 1991), 266.

[74] Other sources which have "Bloody Tarleton" include the following: Bart McDowell, *The Revolutionary War* (Washington, DC: National Geographic Society, 1967), 165; Power, "'The Virtue of Humanity Was Totally Forgot,'" 5; Thomas Fleming, *"Downright Fighting": The Story of Cowpens*, Official National Park Handbook 135 (Washington, DC: US Department of the Interior, 1988), 23, 25; James L. Stokesbury, *A Short History of the American Revolution* (New York: William Morrow, 1991), 231-232, 233, 237.

CHAPTER VI

Virtue

In a work entitled *Recollections and Private Memoirs of Washington*, published in 1860, George Washington Parke Custis relates many an interesting tale concerning the illustrious General Washington and the War for American Independence. Included in these is an intriguing story about Banastre Tarleton. Although it is probably apocryphal, it is worth reciting.[1]

According to Custis, following the siege of York Town in 1781 Banastre Tarleton and Lieutenant Colonel John Laurens, an aide-de-camp to General Washington, had a brief but tense encounter concerning a matter of military etiquette. It was considered most polite and proper in the armies of the eighteenth century to show courtesy to a defeated foe. For instance, Washington and the French commander Comte de Rochambeau sent their compliments to Earl Cornwallis and even exchanged visits on several occasions. Other American officers followed suit and invited their British counterparts to dine at their tables.[2]

However, not a single American officer invited Banastre Tarleton to his table. Concerned by what he construed as an insult, Tarleton approached the Marquis de Lafayette who in turn kindly directed him to Lieutenant Colonel Laurens. The commandant of the British Legion asked Laurens if the neglect was perhaps accidental. Laurens replied: "No, Colonel Tarleton, no accident at all; intentional, I can assure you, and meant as a reproof for certain cruelties practiced by the troops under your command in the campaigns in the Carolinas."

Taken somewhat aback, the Englishman demanded: "What, sir, and is it for severities inseparable from war, which you are pleased to term cruelties, that I am to be disgraced before junior officers? Is it, sir, for a faithful discharge of my duty to my king and my country, that I am thus humiliated in the eyes of three armies?"

Such a question did not faze the American officer. He coolly retorted: "Pardon me. There are modes, sir, of discharging a soldier's duty, and where mercy has a share in the mode, it renders the duty more acceptable to both friends and foes."[3]

Regardless of this story's authenticity, the statements made by the two participants are quite in character for them. In the course of the conversation, each officer reveals his notions of what war entails and how it should be conducted. What is even more significant is that this conversation illustrates how John Laurens and Banastre Tarleton, both the epitome of their respective causes, defined "virtue."

This chapter will analyze the American and British views of virtue and how past experiences shaped these perceptions in the Revolutionary War. How each side defined the word correlated to the manner in which they conducted themselves during the conflict and, more important, the way in which they viewed their opponent's actions. This is significant for our purposes because the legacy of American virtue explains in part how we are today left with the perception of "Bloody Tarleton."

"Virtue" in the eighteenth century is somewhat difficult to define. It was a vogue word, a cliché, so widely used that it had no precise meaning. However, its main qualities could be stated to have been restraint and sacrifice. A virtuous person did not engage in excess during times of plenty and certainly did not betray his cause in times of adversity. Virtue was, in essence, the desire to put the public good ahead of personal interest. A person had to daily make steady self-conscious choices in order to maintain his virtue and to check any of the more base human desires. Moreover, the virtuous individual acted with courage, no matter what the circumstances.[4]

The American and British combatants in the Revolutionary War developed their own styles of virtue. However, neither style was right nor wrong; they simply represented that respective side's perception of what needed to be done and how to go about it.

An American brand of virtue grew out of the colonial military experience. Many of the initial English settlements coincided with a period of military transition in Europe. In the Thirty Years' War (1618-1648), a frenzy of bloodletting caused the population of Germany alone to fall from twenty-one to thirteen million. Europe responded to this brutal period by attempting to rationalize war and to limit it. "Limited war" placed restraints upon duration, location, objectives, intensity or mode of fighting, and impact upon civilian populations. The colonists naturally brought this paradoxical European heritage with them and it profoundly influenced their dealings with the native peoples inhabiting North America.[5]

What the colonists encountered in the New World was a tough, indigenous adversary, someone who taught them many a valuable and painful lesson about warfare. In what some historians justifiably term an armed invasion, colonists and Native Americans became locked in a total war, a contest which pitted the very survival and existence of one culture against another. No semblance to limited war could be found. War generally raged throughout the year, with noncombatants regarded as fair game. Little quarter was granted in battle. The European colonist participated wholeheartedly in such activity and as time passed became even more aggressive and expansionistic. Armed conflict became seen as an inevitable occurrence with the Amerindian, and in the process, it became justifiable too. The colonist legitimized his fighting with the Native American by maintaining that he had a right to defend his property, acquire land, and to redress wrongs.[6]

An ethos developed among the provincials. The good, courageous, citizen soldier exemplified the prime virtues of discipline, valor, zeal for right, and Christianity. Clerical as well as secular leaders embraced this ethos and gave it reinforcement, especially in New England. As Old Testament Christians, the New England colonials believed that Yahweh would lead them to victory and that "an eye for an eye" had divine approval. From early childhood onward, sermon after sermon drilled it into their heads that God was at their side in all things, including battle. It is hardly surprising that such a people, governed by self-preservation while they established settlements on a distant and at times inhospitable shore, could turn feral war into just war. They were God's Select, His Chosen People. The Native Americans were simply "other," non-Christians, and inferior. Such people normally deserved brutal treatment.[7]

This ideal for self-preservation and just war is no better demonstrated than in William Bradford's *Of Plimoth Plantation*. This work rings with resounding righteousness, especially when discussing European encounters with the Native Americans. Bradford, the long term governor of Plymouth Colony (1621-1656), described the destruction of a Pequot village along the Mystic River in 1637 as follows:

> It was conceived they [colonists] thus destroyed about 400. at this time. It was a fearfull sight to see them thus frying in ye fyer, and ye streams of blood quenching ye same, and horrible was ye stinck & sente ther of; but ye victory seemed a sweete sacrifice, and they gave the prays therof to God, who had wrought so wonderfuly for them, thus to inclose their enimise in their hands, and give them so speedy a victory over so proud & insulting an enimie.[8]

Recurrent warfare along the borders plus a spirited ferocity imprinted on each successive generation of colonists a need to legitimize their wars more and more. In the process, they developed a society that equated military exploits with heroism and strove to teach its young martial virtues. Indeed, a violent culture developed in all the colonies, but it was a paradoxical one. Ferocious brutality mingled with an enlightened rationality to limit war, but only against a worthy enemy.[9]

In addition to Amerindians, English provincials had encounters with their French and Spanish counterparts during the colonial wars. These proved to be just as bloody and brutal as their dealings with the Native Americans, but lacked some of the barbarity normally reserved for a non-Christian enemy. King William's War (1689-1697), Queen Anne's War (1701-1713), the War of Jenkins' Ear (1739-1742), King George's War (1744-1748), and the French and Indian War (1754-1763), witnessed the participation of both provincial and English forces.[10] The colonists saw the regulars at their worst, such as at Cartagena in 1740-1741. They also saw the redcoats at their best, as on the Plains of Abraham in 1759.[11] Overall, these wars were mutual learning experiences. The provincial Americans taught the regulars a lesson or two about light warfare, which emphasized stealth, mobility and flexibility. Meanwhile, the English regulars instructed the colonials in discipline.[12]

In the course of these wars, the provincial troops also grew accustomed to the aristocratic disdain of their English comrades-in-arms. British commanders like James Wolfe and Edward Braddock thought colonial soldiers to be inferior and worthless. They treated them with a certain amount of ill-disguised contempt. As a result, the colonials had to contend with an inferiority complex and felt that they had something to prove to their condescending English brothers.[13]

Before leaving the topic of the colonial wars, it must be remembered that they were not conflicts in the European sense. During this time, European war on a grand scale had not yet reached the American shore. In the colonies, the armies were much smaller as were the battlefields. Much of the fighting occurred along the frontiers. The small population of 1.6 million (1760) was spread out, and with an estimated 25% of each colony's population residing along the frontiers, very few people experienced war firsthand. Although limited war was in vogue during this Age of Reason in Europe, it could still be devastating to the landscape and civilian population. Armies demanded quarters and a plentiful food supply, imposed curfews, pressed men into service, and confiscated property. Provincial Americans had practically no experience with the bad facets of large armies, whether friendly or not.[14]

All this would change with the upcoming Revolutionary War. Much of the fighting occurred in heavily populated regions, not on the frontiers. Boston, Newport, New York, Philadelphia, Savannah, and Charles Town all experienced occupation by large royal armies. More of the colonial population than ever before faced war directly and witnessed all the accompanying discomforts and horrors. They realized that European warfare was not so limited at times after all. Moreover, they learned that some of the cruelty they inflicted upon the Amerindians was now being used upon them, and by fellow Britons to boot. The cruel war normally reserved for inferiors came back to haunt them.[15]

What the revolutionaries attempted in 1775 was indeed unprecedented. They had much to prove to the outside world, especially the mother country. Although eager for victory, they had to stay patient and conduct a defensive war. As a virtuous people, they needed to prove the legitimacy, honor, and respectability of their cause in order to avoid the stigma of being simple rebels. They had to maintain the ethos of the good, Christian soldier and follow through with virtue in word and deed. They needed to be self-restrained and to avoid any type of brutality and wanton revenge. Keeping the appearance of "injured innocence" and moral superiority through discipline was paramount to George Washington and the other revolutionary leaders. By conducting a just war, the enemy could be made to appear evil.[16]

An example of this process at work concerns the fate of an American deserter. On the night of July 8-9, 1779, a patrol under Captain Philip Reed of Lee's Legion captured three deserters near Stony Point, New York. The next morning, Washington approved the summary execution of one of the men, but Lieutenant Colonel Henry "Light-Horse Harry" Lee had the sentence already carried out. Lee had the deserter shot, and then ordered that his head be cut off and placed on top of the gallows at Smith's Cove. When Washington received Lee's full report on July 10, he instructed the lieutenant colonel to bury the body at once. He had two reasons for doing so. The American commander-in-chief believed that the decapitation would make the Continental Army appear as a tyrannical instrument of Congress. Furthermore, he wished to keep the headless corpse out of British hands, as the propaganda value of it would have been immense.[17]

The ministerial forces that came to America in 1775 brought their own violent heritage with them and had special experience in suppressing rebellions. The royal response to the uprisings in Ireland in the sixteenth and seventeenth centuries was extremely harsh. At the time of Lexington and Concord, the latest experience with rebellion to rock England was the famous Jacobite revolt of 1745. The "Forty-Five" was also met with much brutality and left an indelible mark upon the minds of the royal officials and troops involved. They undoubtedly came out of that experience with a view that "rebels" were not a normal enemy, that they were ungrateful subjects basking in their perfidy and who had to be dealt with in a harsh manner.[18]

The American rebellion which commenced in 1775 also dictated a swift imperial response. Although not as contemptible as "barbarian" Scottish Highlanders or "wild" Catholic Irishmen, rebellious Americans did arouse a strong antipathy among Englishmen. Yet, unlike European wars fought earlier in the century, this conflict mandated that royal strategists pay close attention to popular sentiment. The provincials had been long accustomed to direct participation in their respective governments.

Their democratic practices would ensure that this war would be less a contest over territory than a struggle for the political allegiance of the people. Sir William Howe and Sir Henry Clinton, the two British commanders-in-chief during much of the war, became keenly aware of this, with the latter writing that it was necessary "to gain the hearts and subdue the minds of America."[19]

The top echelon of royal officials might have realized this, but what is more important for our considerations are the military officers who actually took the field and faced the rebellion on a daily basis. Between 3,500 and four thousand British officers served in America. Two schools of thought concerning the rebellion developed among them. The conciliatory group adhered to a policy based upon moral reasons, an older sense of chivalry, and practical considerations. They asserted that mild treatment of the colonials would yield immense political dividends. Furthermore, many of these officers believed that the majority of the provincials were actually loyal at heart. In order to halt the revolutionary movement, the British only needed to win over the "deluded" Americans. The "hard-line" group was the exact opposite, demanding a tough approach in order to crush the rebellion. These "fire and sword" men saw destruction and devastation as an effective means of solving the problem.[20]

All British officers, like their American counterparts, had a sense of virtue. However, their type of virtue represented a different brand of public good, i.e. King and Country. The hard-liners took it to extremes and employed a more brutal version of it. After all, these colonials were rebels! Three officers who advocated "brutal virtue" are worthy of mention. Patrick Ferguson, Francis Rawdon, and Banastre Tarleton were all regular British officers who led Loyalists troops and exemplified brutal virtue at work. They had daily contact with their men in the field and evidently began to empathize with them enough to identify with their anger and desire for revenge.[21]

Banastre Tarleton in particular was a total affront to the American sense of virtue. Although both sides felt the nobility of their cause, Tarleton was more willing from the start to employ harsher methods to win. By his own admission, he was the total opposite of American virtue. He believed that "Coolness Apathy & Civil Law will never supply Hussars with Horses."[22] Rebel activity dictated the need to "discriminate with severity," although this could prove to be a "disagreeable exertion of authority."[23] For Tarleton, the need to uphold King and Country sanctioned brutal measures in the best European tradition. As a result, Tarleton and his Legion gave the rebellious colonials a type of warfare that they thought the latter deserved. The vainglorious Englishman clearly felt that his opponents brought upon themselves European war will all its accompanying horrors.[24]

What is more significant, though, is what this brutal virtue employed by Tarleton meant for the revolutionary movement. After 1779, Banastre Tarleton was the one of the most visible threats to the American moral cause. The British Legion commandant was enterprising, active, unrelenting, and usually victorious. His achievements at Monck's Corner, Lenud's Ferry, the Waxhaws, and Fishing Creek had profound implications. By defeating the Rebels in battle, he called into question their virtue, the absolute basis of their cause. By its very nature, virtue implies that something is good and righteous. However, American defeats at the hands of the British Legion inferred that the revolutionaries were doing something wrong and that their moral superiority was flawed.[25]

Furthermore, revenge is always a big temptation and Tarleton represented a serious threat to American efforts to restrain themselves. Unfortunately for the revolutionaries, they failed the test. The American goal from the start was to limit their violent impulses in order to appear as a civilized and virtuous people. However, Tarleton's Legion only incited the Rebels to respond with brutality.[26]

Tarleton was a real threat, physically, psychologically, and politically to the American cause. A French officer who observed the surrender ceremonies at York Town stated that civilians came from miles to see the British prisoners, particularly "le colonel Talton." Someone like Banastre Tarleton was a prime candidate for notoriety, especially because he led Loyalist troops. However, something else about the man is significant.[27]

During the Revolutionary War, each side saw the other as totally inferior in regards to honor, human worth, and virtue. A graphic example of this hatred at work concerns the ill-fated Major Patrick Ferguson. As he marched through the Carolina backcountry in the fall of 1780, he released a prisoner with a verbal message. He threatened to lay "waste with fire and sword" the settlements along the Watauga, Nolachucky, and Holston rivers. As is commonly known, the over-the-mountain men in these areas did not wait to let him fulfill his promise. After defeating Ferguson at King's Mountain, they reportedly gathered around his corpse and "in the most complete gesture of triumph, of revenge, of contempt," urinated upon it.[28] The survivors of his command fared little better and suffered innumerable abuses on their way to prison camps at Hillsboro, North Carolina.[29]

Simon Girty, Walter Butler, David Fanning, William Cuningham, and Benedict Arnold all betrayed some higher ideal of virtue in American eyes.[30] Such Loyalists provided a useful anti-image to Patriot virtue, but no matter how depraved they appeared, their actions could never justify independence. What the revolutionaries needed was a real *English* devil. Banastre Tarleton filled the bill admirably. One witness to the violence in South Carolina assuredly had Tarleton in mind when he wrote that "such scenes have been perpetrated by Officers whom I could Name, & whose families are amongst the first in Great Britain."[31]

For Americans, why Banastre Tarleton was so evil was not really that important. Most of them looked upon the Englishman as a base, incorrigible fellow. Tarleton's violence revealed not native courage but innate depravity. By condemning him, John Laurens extolled a more honorable code of conduct and in the process downplayed American involvement in a civil war.[32]

When the revolutionaries won the war, their cause instantly became justified and true. In the American psyche, the myth of injured innocence was maintained and affirmed. Furthermore, in a decidedly typical victor's mindset, it normally followed that their enemy had really been wrong and evil. The British had tried to oppress popular sovereignty and lost. Banastre Tarleton was definitely included in this equation. In the popular mind, he became an ogre, although there is no real quantitative or qualitative evidence that suggests his men committed more depradations than anyone else in the Revolutionary War.[33]

This is the main myth which surrounds Banastre Tarleton and the British Legion. It became part of the historiographical legacy of the Revolution. The roster of misdeeds assigned to Tarleton and the British Legion grew after the war, adding to their reputation and making them appear more and more sinister. They evolved into the perfect abstraction of imperfect virtue. Oral tradition has turned the young officer and his Legionnaires into "cruel myrmidons" who acted out the twisted mandates of a repressive king.[34]

We are left with the legacy of "Bloody Tarleton" because of this demonic myth. We cannot escape him. Although there is no direct evidence that contemporaries referred to him as "Bloody Tarleton," modern historians call him by that nickname.[35] Some scholars purposely distort his physical characteristics in an attempt to make him appear more monstrous. Two historians assert that his countenance ran "a little to grossness about the eyes and mouth," although all eighteenth century accounts make especial mention of its handsome qualities. In another history Tarleton appears as "the huge, dashing cavalryman," but again this is an exaggeration because all who actually met the man agree that he was small of stature.[36] Tarleton is accused of exhuming a corpse in order to "look upon the face of such a brave man" and of allowing his men to murder and mutilate a pregnant woman, but once more, there is no direct eyewitness evidence to sustain these accusations.[37]

Countless other stories abound. George Washington Parke Custis, in addition to the tale related at the opening of this chapter, recounts another dubious story concerning the Englishman. He maintains that at a house in Halifax, North Carolina, Mrs. Willie Jones made Tarleton's mangled hand the point of a severe joke. When the Briton called William Washington "an illiterate fellow," the noble American lady responded: "Ah, colonel, you ought to know better, for you bear on your person proof that he knows very well *how to make his mark!*"[38]

Mrs. Jones' was making reference to the Cowpens, where it was believed that Lt. Col. Washington wounded Tarleton in the hand. However, this is simply not true for Tarleton himself states that he was never wounded until the Battle of Guilford Courthouse, two months after Cowpens. After the later battle, he wrote: "I am hit *at last* in the right Hand and Arm."[39]

It appears that this story was intended as some type of metaphor. By distorting the facts behind Tarleton's mangled hand, the American cause could be made to appear more noble. Someone with obvious superior virtue (Washington) inflicted upon a "cruel and resentful" individual (Tarleton) a mark of retribution (the disfigured hand). In other words, American virtue wins over British tyranny.[40]

Another metaphor is available with the fanciful encounter between Tarleton and Mrs. Slocomb, the wife of an American officer. As the British Legion set up camp at the Slocomb plantation in North Carolina, the dragoon and the lady engaged in a lively but polite argument over the merits of her husband. When Tarleton called him a rebel, the lady replied: "No, sir, he is in the army of his country, and fighting against our invaders, therefore not a rebel." The Legion commander responded: "I fear we differ in opinion, madam. A friend to his country will be the friend of the king, our master." "Slaves only acknowledge a master in this country," rejoined Mrs. Slocomb.[41]

The argument continued along the same lines. Each time Tarleton made some type of derogatory comment, Mrs. Slocomb answered with a pithy comment, in effect destroying the validity of his assertions. The metaphor here is that American virtue can never be defeated.[42]

In and of themselves, these may seem like relatively minor points, but taken together they contribute to the myth surrounding the man and his regiment. Furthermore, something even more important occurs in the historiography of the Revolutionary War. It appears that over the years, "Bloody Tarleton" has become our defining perception of the man. Eighteenth-century Americans clearly loathed this English officer; but it has taken their descendants to put into words what they actually felt. Modern Americans have taken it upon themselves to continue and nurture the myth of injured innocence. An oral tradition has formed around Tarleton and the Legion. In the process, Americans have divorced themselves from the reality, which is that Banastre Tarleton is no more guilty or innocent of wanton devastation than anyone else who participated in that struggle. An illustration of this legacy at work and the contention between American and British notions of virtue can be easily found.[43]

Tarleton's participation in the battle at the Waxhaws, South Carolina, on May 29, 1780 is well known. Without going into too much detail, as this engagement will be discussed in much greater length in Chapter VII, let it be remembered that the British Legion made a rapid pursuit of an American force under Colonel Abraham Buford. When he arrived at the North Carolina – South Carolina border, Tarleton sent forth a flag of truce, offering Buford terms similar to those accepted by Major General Benjamin Lincoln at Charles Town earlier that month. He wrote that "if you are rash enough to reject them, the blood be upon your head."[44] This statement was hardly surprising, given eighteenth-century military etiquette and the character of the man who wrote it.[45] Nevertheless, the American colonel rejected the offer and in the ensuing mêlée, Tarleton's horse went down at the same time a white flag appeared in the American ranks. This event stimulated his Legionnaires "to a vindictive asperity not easily restrained,"[46] and they began to shoot and bayonet their opponents regardless of any attempts at surrender. The proud Legion officer wrote the Earl Cornwallis immediately after the battle, calling it a "complete success." His disdain for the Rebels was clearly apparent when he wrote "I have Cut 170 Off'rs and Men to pieces."[47] The earl had nothing but praise for this loyal soldier of the Crown.[48]

A similar incident involved Henry Lee. On February 25, 1781 along the Haw River in North Carolina, Lieutenant Colonel Henry Lee with his Legionnaires tricked Colonel John Pyle's Loyalists into believing that they were Tarleton's Legion. The two legions had nearly identical green coats and dragoon helmets. After some eager Rebel militiamen compromised the facade, Lee's Legion fell upon the Loyalists with all their fury. In the words of Lee:

> The conflict was quickly decided, and bloody on one side only...During this sudden recounter, in some parts of the line the cry of mercy was heard, coupled with assurance of being our best friends; but no expostulation could be admitted in a conjuncture so critical. Humanity even forbade it, as its first injunction is to take care of your own safety, and our safety was not compatible with that of the supplicants, until disabled to offend.[49]

In the two encounters, enemy losses greatly outnumbered those suffered by friendly forces. Each commander, employing his respective ideal of virtue, felt comfortable with his explanation of the events. Yet, the Waxhaws became known as a massacre, perpetrated by a bloodthirsty fiend. Meanwhile, Lee's actions along the Haw River became viewed as tragic but necessary. Although Lee and his Legion had given a poor showing of themselves and their cause by stooping to the level of their enemy, Lee's explanation was sufficient to allow the aura of superior virtue to shine through. In fact, his ideal of conspicuous virtue grew after the war to the extent that he became one of the real heroes of popular American culture.[50]

Lee's argument is readily accepted by many while Tarleton's explanation is quickly dismissed and discredited. It is generally believed that Banastre Tarleton purposely set out to massacre defenseless men and only needed an excuse to do so. Although Lee's argument technically could be used to back Tarleton's actions, the Waxhaws has never been explained in that manner. Popular culture and the myth of injured innocence simply cannot allow it.[51]

Banastre Tarleton in many respects was what the revolutionaries were searching for in an enemy. He not only strengthened their resolve, but he justified their cause in the long run. He and the British Legion fit the American search for an evil foe by adhering to a more brutal form of virtue. Over the years they have become a conduit for the American ideal of virtue to stay and grow in the collective consciousness of the nation.

The myth and reality of our subject can be clarified even more. The next two chapters will substantiate the above thesis by analyzing the areas where Tarleton has received the most condemnation: poor discipline amongst his troops and the implementation of a terror policy to subdue the South.

---

[1] *Recollections and Private Memoirs of Washington, by his adopted son, George Washington Parke Custis, with a memoir of the author, by his daughter; and illustrative and explanatory notes. by Benson J. Lossing.* (New York: Derby & Jackson, 1860), 251-252. This work also has other more fanciful stories about Tarleton; Robert D. Bass in *The Green Dragoon: The Lives of Banastre Tarleton and Mary Robinson* (New York: Henry Holt, 1957), 5, takes this story as if it was gospel truth. He repeats it nearly verbatim and without any critical approach.

[2] Custis, *Recollections and Private Memoirs of Washington,* 251-252. The author has searched high and low for any indication that the meeting actually took place. The memoirs of Tarleton, Laurens, Lafayette, and others reveal nothing on the subject. Gregory D. Massey, "A Hero's Life: John Laurens and the American Revolution" (Ph.D. diss., University of South Carolina, 1992), 467-474; Lafayette remembered that every sort of politeness was shown, "especially towards Lord

Cornwallis, one of the men of the highest character in England, who was considered to be their foremost general." Charlemagne Tower, Jr., *The Marquis De La Fayette in the American Revolution. With Some Account of the Attitude of France Toward the War of Independence*, 2 vols. (Philadelphia: J.B. Lippincott Company, 1895), 2:457; for values and manners among officers, see Christopher Duffy, *The Military Experience in the Age of Reason* (New York: Atheneum, 1988), 74-88; also see John E. Ferling, *A Wilderness of Miseries: War and Warriors in Early America* (Westport, Connecticut: Greenwood Press, 1980), 112; Robert Middlekauff, "Why Men Fought in the American Revolution," *Huntington Library Quarterly* 43 (Spring 1980): 145; French officers were more willing to overlook the dragoon's past behavior and invited him to dine with them. Bass, *The Green Dragoon*, 5.

[3] Protocol dictated that Lafayette refer Tarleton to Laurens. As Washington's aide-de-camp, John Laurens helped to negotiate the British capitulation at York Town. Once the surrender document had been signed on October 20, he had the responsibility of making sure that both sides adhered to its terms. Therefore, all English, German, and Loyalist prisoners fell under his jurisdiction. John Laurens, n.d. [1781-1782], "Surrender of Lord Cornwallis," William Jackson Papers, Sterling Memorial Library, Yale University, New Haven, Connecticut; following the encounter, Tarleton stalked away to his quarters, which he seldom left until his departure from Virginia. He was evidently well aware of how much the common American soldier hated him and asked for special protection from his captors. Custis, *Recollections and Private Memoirs of Washington*, 251-253; according to *London Ruddiman's Weekly Mercury* of January 30, 1782, the British cavalry officer returned to his quarters one day and discovered that his bed had been stabbed in several places. Whether or not this actually occurred is debatable.

[4] Charles Royster, *A Revolutionary People at War: The Continental Army and American Character, 1775-1783* (New York: WW Norton and Company, 1981), 22-23, 67; Richard A. Gabriel, *To Serve With Honor: A Treatise on Military Ethics and the Way of the Soldier* (Westport, Connecticut: Greenwood Press, 1982), 150, 154-173; the Renaissance meaning of virtue grew out of the old Roman concept of manly prowess. A virtuous man had "intellectual and moral audacity," feeling equally at home with women in the palace and soldiers in camp. Will Durant, *The Renaissance: A History of Civilization in Italy from 1304 - 1576 AD*, The Story of Civilization V (New York: Simon and Schuster,

1953), 580-581; Lester H. Cohen, *The Revolutionary Histories: Contemporary Narratives of the American Revolution* (Ithaca: Cornell University Press, 1980), 192, 195.

[5] John Morgan Dederer, *War in America to 1775 Before Yankee Doodle* (New York: New York University Press, 1990), 6, 80, 89, 103, 126-127; Ferling, *A Wilderness of Miseries*, 155-156, 159; for the Thirty Years' War, see Geoffrey Parker et al, *The Thirty Years' War*, rev. ed. (London: Routledge & Kegan Paul Ltd., 1987); in this violent age, death and dismemberment were regular features of life. See Michel Foucault, *Discipline and Punish: The Birth of the Prison*, trans. Alan Sheridan (Editions Gallimard, 1975; repr., New York: Vintage Books, 1979); for limited war, see Richard A. Preston et al, *Men in Arms: A History of Warfare and Its Interrelationships With Western Society*, 5th ed. (Fort Worth, Texas: Holt, Rinehart & Winston, 1991), 116-132; Russell F. Weigley, *The Age of Battles: The Quest for Decisive Warfare from Breitenfeld to Waterloo* (Bloomington: Indiana University Press, 1991); Duffy, *Military Experience in the Age of Reason*; Ira D. Gruber, "British Strategy: The Theory and Practice of Eighteenth-Century Warfare," in *Reconsiderations on the Revolutionary War; Selected Essays*, ed. Don Higginbotham (Westport, Connecticut: Greenwood Press, 1978), 14-31; Maarten Ultee, "Adapting to Conditions," in *Adapting to Conditions: War and Society in the Eighteenth Century*, ed. Maarten Ultee (The University of Alabama Press, 1986), 1-15.

[6] Dederer, *War in America to 1775*, 7; Ferling, *A Wilderness of Miseries*, 197-200; for warfare with the Amerindian, see Ian K. Steele, *Warpaths: Invasions of North America* (New York and Oxford: Oxford University Press, 1994); Patrick M. Malone, *The Skulking Way of War: Technology and Tactics Among the New England Indians* (Lanham, Maryland: Madison Books, 1991; repr., Baltimore and London: Johns Hopkins University Press, 1993); also consult Francis Jennings, "Savage War," in *The Invasion of America: Indians, Colonialism, and the Cant of Conquest* (Chapel Hill: University of North Carolina Press, 1975), 146-170.

[7] Dederer, *War in America to 1775*, 20-21, 127-129, 137-138, 175-176, 180. Durant, *The Renaissance*, 580-581.

[8] *Bradford's History "Of Plimoth Plantation." From the Original Manuscript. With a Report of the Proceedings Incident to the Return of the*

Manuscript to Massachusetts (Boston: Wright & Potter Printing Company, 1898), 425-426.

[9] Ferling, *A Wilderness of Miseries*, 197, 200; Dederer, *War in America to 1775*, 137-138, 143; Richard Maxwell Brown, "Violence and the American Revolution," in *Essays on the American Revolution*, eds. Stephen G. Kurtz and James H. Hutson (Chapel Hill: University of North Carolina Press, 1973), 81-120; Ofer Zur, "The Psychohistory of Warfare: The Co-Evolution of Culture, Psyche and Enemy," *Journal of Peace Research* 24 (1987): 129-132.

[10] These wars had their equivalents in Europe: War of the League of Augsburg (1688-1697), War of Spanish Succession (1702-1713), War of Austrian Succession (1744-1748), and the Seven Years' War (1756-1763). The War of Jenkins' Ear received its name from English sea captain Robert Jenkins, who claimed that Spanish officials cut off his ear in a naval skirmish. See Howard H. Peckham, *The Colonial Wars: 1689-1762* (Chicago: University of Chicago Press, 1964); Maurice Matloff, ed., *American Military History*, Army Historical Series (Washington, DC: Center of Military History, 1973), 18-40; Reed Browning, *The War of the Austrian Succession* (New York: St. Martin's Press, 1993); Francis Jennings, *Empire of Fortune: Crowns, Colonies & Tribes in the Seven Years War in America* (New York and London: WW Norton and Company, 1990).

[11] For Cartagena, see Richard Harding, *Amphibious Warfare in the Eighteenth Century: The British Expedition to the West Indies 1740-1742* (Woodbridge, Suffolk: The Boydell Press, 1991). The expeditionary army to this Colombian port city lost 7,195 men to sickness; British general James Wolfe captured Quebec on September 13, 1759. For the battle on the Plains of Abraham, see C.P. Stacey, *Quebec, 1759: The Siege and the Battle* (Toronto: Macmillan Company, 1959); the colonials also witnessed Braddock's defeat, one of the worst British military disasters ever to occur in North America. On July 9, 1755 near modern Pittsburgh, Pennsylvania, a French and Indian force ambushed General Edward Braddock and his army of 1,300 men. In the ensuing battle, the English suffered over nine hundred casualties. Consult Paul E. Kopperman, *Braddock at the Monongahela* (University of Pittsburgh Press, 1977).

[12] Dederer, *War in America to 1775*, 89-95, 136-140; for light warfare, consult *Journals of Major Robert Rogers* (London, 1765; repr., New York: Corinth Books, 1961); Eric Robson, "British Light Infantry in the Mid-Eighteenth Century: The Effect of American Conditions," *The Army Quarterly* 63 (1952): 209-222; J.F.C. Fuller, *British Light Infantry in the Eighteenth Century* (London, 1925); from the pre-1775 experience it is very possible that a need for legionary units became apparent to many officers. Duffy, *Military Experience in the Age of Reason*, 268-269, 280-288; discipline is covered in the excellent J.A. Houlding, *Fit for Service: The Training of the British Army, 1715-1795* (Oxford: Clarendon Press, 1981).

[13] Francis Jennings, *Empire of Fortune*, 220-221; Lee McCardell, *Ill-Starred General: Braddock of the Coldstream Guards* (Pittsburgh: University of Pittsburgh Press, 1958), 212; Captain John Knox, *An Historical Journal of the Campaigns in North-America, for the Years 1757, 1758, 1759, and 1760*, 3 vols. (London: W. Johnston and J. Dodsley, 1769), 1:145; Dederer, *War in America to 1775*, 139-140; the colonials also had some feelings of self-worth, especially since they captured Louisbourg in 1745 with minimal British aid. However, in 1748 this post on Cape Breton Island was returned to French control, causing dismay and anger among many New Englanders. John Adams wrote that British treatment of provincial officers and troops "made my blood boil in my veins." Ferling, *A Wilderness of Miseries*, 168, 172; John Shy, "American Society and Its War for Independence," in *Reconsiderations on the Revolutionary War*, ed. Higginbotham, 77-78.

[14] Dederer, *War in America to 1775*, 108, 143. European armies and battles in this era in no way compared to those of the Napoleonic era; Robert K. Wright, Jr., *The Continental Army*, Army Lineage Series (Washington, DC: Center of Military History, 1989), 3-8; Ferling, *A Wilderness of Miseries*, 56, 198-199. Ferling maintains the exact opposite, that because of the colonial wars, the American civilians had more experience than Europeans with the discomforts and horrors of military conflict. Given the intensity and duration of the numerous wars on the Continent in the eighteenth century, this does not seem likely; see Claude C. Sturgill, "The French Army in Roussillon, 1716-1720," in *Adapting to Conditions*, ed. Ultee, 16-25; Lee Kennett, *The French Armies in the Seven Years' War: A Study in Military Organization and Administration* (Duke University Press, 1967), 84; Frederick II

quipped: "We somewhat forget what brotherly love is whenever we make war." Four times more civilians than soldiers died in the War of Austrian Succession. Consult Browning, *War of Austrian Succession*, 8, 136, 289, 291-292, 319-320, 375-377. Duffy, *Military Experience in the Age of Reason*, 151-188, 268-288; Weigley, *The Age of Battles*, 195; Peter Paret, "The Relationship Between the Revolutionary War and European Military Thought and Practice in the Second Half of the Eighteenth Century," in *Reconsiderations on the Revolutionary War*, ed. Higginbotham, 153-155.

[15] The psychological implications of this are interesting. In being brutalized, one is also degraded and insulted, something that was always anathema to colonials. Ferling, *A Wilderness of Miseries*, 166, 169.

[16] William Fitzpatrick to Dr. Franklin, undated (October 1780?), in B.F. Stevens, comp., *Facsimiles of Manuscripts in European Archives Relating to America 1773-1783*, 25 vols. (Wilmington, DE: Mellifont Press, 1970), 10:954; Royster, *A Revolutionary People at War*, 17-18, 22-23, 67, 188; Royster, *Light-Horse Harry Lee and the Legacy of the American Revolution* (New York: Alfred A. Knopf, 1981), 29, 38, 45-46; Dederer, *War in America to 1775*, 119, 180, 203, 213; Ferling, *A Wilderness of Miseries*, 166, 168, 194-196, 199; Samuel Adams reflected: "Put your enemy in the wrong, and keep him so, is a wise maxim in politics, as well as in war." For this statement in addition to "injured innocence," see David Hackett Fischer, *Paul Revere's Ride* (New York: Oxford University Press, 1994), 42, 78-79, 327-329. Fischer makes an interesting observation concerning Paul Revere's account of events on the night of April 18-19, 1775. The Massachusetts Historical Society *Proceedings* (1798) published his narrative, but left out Revere's statement that he attempted to attack the British patrol when he first sighted it outside of Lexington. Fischer maintains that this was an aggressive impulse not consistent with the myth of American innocence; Middlekauff, "Why Men Fought in the American Revolution," 137; John Shy, "American Society and Its War for Independence," 78 and Higginbotham, "The American Militia: A Traditional Institution with Revolutionary Responsibilities," 83-103, both in *Reconsiderations on the Revolutionary War*, ed. Higginbotham; Shy, *A People Numerous and Armed: Reflections on The Military Struggle for American Independence* (Oxford University Press, 1976), 193-224; "The Military Institutions of Colonial America: The Rhetoric and the

Reality," in Don Higginbotham, *War and Society in Revolutionary America: The Wilder Dimensions of Conflict* (Columbia: University of South Carolina Press, 1988), 19-41; Royster, "Founding a Nation in Blood: Military Conflict and American Nationality," in *Arms and Independence: The Military Character of the American Revolution*, eds. Ronald Hoffman and Peter J. Albert (Charlottesville: University Press of Virginia, 1984), 25-49; Royster, "A Society and Its War," in *Adapting to Conditions*, ed. Ultee, 174-187.

[17] Royster, *A Revolutionary People at War*, 80-82.

[18] The traditional notion held that "rebellion was a sin against the ordained dispensation, a belief founded in classical antiquity and Christian scripture." Stephen Conway, "To Subdue America: British Army Officers and the Conduct of the Revolutionary War," *William and Mary Quarterly* 43 (1986): 396 (hereafter cited as *WMQ*); Dederer, *War in America to 1775*, 129, 132-133; rebels were "animals" and "vermin." Jennings, *Empire of Fortune*, 3-7; William A. Speck, *The Butcher: The Duke of Cumberland and the Suppression of the 45* (Oxford: Basil Blackwell, 1981), 148-162. The aftermath of the battle at Culloden Moor was bloody, with the fleeing Highlanders receiving no quarter. Nevertheless, Cumberland was successful and *that* is what mattered to the King. For the battle, see John Prebble, *Culloden* (New York: Atheneum, 1962); in 1746 nine Scottish rebels were hanged on Kennington Common. After five minutes had elapsed, the executioner cut them down and disemboweled each man. McCardell, *Ill-Starred General*, 99; some believed that "Rebellion according to Scripture is, as the Sin of witchcraft." Royster, *A Revolutionary People at War*, 13.

[19] Memo. of conversation, Feb. 7, 1776, Clinton Papers, William L. Clements Library, Ann Arbor, Michigan; Jeremy Black, *War for America: The Fight For Independence 1775-1783* (New York: St. Martin's Press, 1991), 13, 18-19; Stephen Conway, "To Subdue America," *WMQ* 43 (1986): 381-382; Conway, "British Army Officers and the American War for Independence," *WMQ* 41 (1984) : 265-276. Also see Conway's *The War of American Independence 1775-1783* (New York: St. Martin's Press, 1995), 117, 247; Armstrong Starkey, "Paoli to Stony Point: Military Ethics and Weaponry During the American Revolution," *Journal of Military History* 58 (January 1994) : 11; Higginbotham, "Military Leadership in the American Revolution," in *War and Society*,

84-105; Piers Mackesy, "What the British Army Learned," in *Arms and Independence*, eds. Hoffman and Albert, 191-215.

[20] Conway, "To Subdue America," *WMQ* 43 (1986): 382-395; John Shy, *A People Numerous and Armed*, 175-184.

[21] *Ibid.*, 383, 395-401; Patrick Ferguson is an unique case, as he became more conciliatory as time went along. See Howard H. Peckham, ed., *Sources of American Independence: Selected Manuscripts from the Collections of the William L. Clements Library*, 2 vols. (Chicago and London: University of Chicago Press, 1978), 2: 293-294, 307-310, 336-342. The Scotsman maintained that "America has never yet felt us in Earnest," but endeavored to keep his troops' marauding to a bare minimum; Starkey, "Paoli to Stony Point," *Journal of Military History* 58 (January 1994): 18-20; Higginbotham, "Reflections on the War of Independence, Modern Guerrilla Warfare, and the War in Vietnam," in *Arms and Independence*, eds. Hoffman and Albert, 20; Shy, "American Society and Its War for Independence," in *Reconsiderations on the Revolutionary War*, ed. Higginbotham, 80-81; Bernard Berelson and Gary A. Steiner, *Human Behavior: An Inventory of Scientific Findings* (New York: Harcourt, Brace & World, 1964), 241-286, 374-380.

[22] Tarleton to Captain John André, February 19, 1779, Clinton Papers.

[23] Tarleton to Lord Cornwallis, August 5, 1780, Lenau's Ferry, Cornwallis Papers, Public Record Office, Kew, 30/11/63, ff. 19-21 (hereafter cited as PRO); Lt. Col. Banastre Tarleton, *A History of the Campaigns of 1780 and 1781, in the Southern Provinces of North America* (London: T. Cadell, 1787), 100.

[24] Conway, "To Subdue America," *WMQ* 43 (1986): 395-407.

[25] For Tarleton's military successes, see his *History of the Campaigns;* Royster, *A Revolutionary People at War*, 11, 15, 115-116, 188.

[26] For American reactions to the "massacre" at the Waxhaws, see David Ramsay, *The History of the Revolution of South-Carolina, From a British Province to an Independent State*, 2 vols (Trenton: Isaac Collins, 1785), 2:109-110; also consult William Dobein James, *A Sketch of the Life of Brig. Gen. Francis Marion and a History of His Brigade From Its Rise in*

June 1780 until Disbanded in December, 1782 With Descriptions of Characters and Scenes Not Heretofore Published (Charleston, 1821), 38-41, Appendix 1-7; incidents of revenge can be found in John C. Dann, ed., *The Revolution Remembered: Eyewitness Accounts of the War for Independence* (Chicago: University of Chicago Press, 1980), 187-189, 201-203; *The Revolutionary War Sketches of William R. Davie*, ed. Blackwell P. Robinson (Raleigh: North Carolina Department of Cultural Resources, Division of Archives and History, 1976), 23; Higginbotham, "Reflections on the War of Independence, Modern Guerrilla Warfare, and the War in Vietnam," in *Arms and Independence*, eds. Hoffman and Albert, 1-24.

[27] Royster, "Founding a Nation in Blood: Military Conflict and American Nationality," in *Arms and Independence*, eds. Hoffman and Albert, 47-48; Ferling, *A Wilderness of Miseries*, 166; Cohen, *The Revolutionary Histories*, 185, 212, 214-219; Joachim du Perron, comte de Revel, *Journal particulieur d'une campagne aux Indes Occidentales (1781-1782)* (Paris: H. Charles-Lavauzelle, 1898?), 169.

[28] See M. M. Gilchrist, *Patrick Ferguson: "A Strange Adventurer, Tho' A Man of Some Genius,"* Scots' Lives Series (Edinburgh: National Museums of Scotland Publications, 2002), passim. They also stripped Ferguson's body of its clothing, evidently in quest for souvenirs. Lyman C. Draper, *King's Mountain and Its Heroes: History of the Battle of King's Mountain, October 7th, 1780, and the Events Which Led To It* (Cincinnati: Peter G. Thomson, 1881); Hank Messick, *King's Mountain: The Epic of the Blue Ridge "Mountain Men" in the American Revolution* (Boston: Little, Brown and Company, 1976), 152-153; "the mountaineers used every insult and indignity...towards the dead body of Major Ferguson." Tarleton, *History of the Campaigns,* 165; the released prisoner was named Samuel Phillips. See Peckham, ed., *Sources of American Independence*, 293-294. For the civil war in the South, see John S. Pancake, *This Destructive War: The British Campaign in the Carolinas, 1780-1782* (Tuscaloosa and London: University of Alabama Press, 1985). Also Robert M. Weir, "Rebelliousness: Personality Development and the American Revolution in the Southern Colonies," in *The Southern Experience in the American Revolution*, eds. Jeffrey J. Crow and Larry E. Tise (Chapel Hill: University of North Carolina Press, 1978), 25-54.

[29] Tarleton, *History of the Campaigns*, 165; *Diary of Lieut. Anthony Allaire, of Ferguson's Corps* (New York: New York Times, 1968); Christopher Ward, *The War of the Revolution*, 2 vols. (New York: Macmillan Company, 1952), 2:744-745; Ferling, *A Wilderness of Miseries*, 190.

[30] Simon Girty (1741-1818) led Indian raids in the Old Northwest. Thomas Boyd, *Simon Girty: The White Savage* (New York: Minton, Balch & Company, 1928); Walter Butler (1752?-1781) was a captain in Butler's Rangers, which operated in the upstate New York region. Howard Swiggett, *War Out of Niagara*, Empire State Historical Publication 20 (Port Washington, New York: Ira J. Friedman, 1963); David Fanning (1755-1825) and William Cuningham (d. 1787) commanded Loyalist partisan bands in the South. See *The Narrative of Colonel David Fanning*, ed. Lindley S. Butler (Charleston: Tradd Street Press, 1981) and J.B.O. Landrum, *Colonial and Revolutionary History of Upper South Carolina, Embracing for the Most Part the Primitive and Colonial History of the Territory Comprising the Original County of Spartanburg with a General Review of the Entire Military Operations in the Upper Portion of South Carolina and Portions of North Carolina* (Greenville, SC: Shannon and Company, 1897), 341-359; the treason of Major General Benedict Arnold (1741-1801) is well known. Willard Sterne Randall, *Benedict Arnold: Patriot and Traitor* (New York: William Morrow, 1990); Charles Royster, "'The Nature of Treason': Revolutionary Virtue and American Reactions to Benedict Arnold," *WMQ* 36 (1979): 163-193; Norman Gelb, *Less than Glory*, (New York: GP Putnam's Sons, 1984), 163; Conway, "To Subdue America," *WMQ* 43 (1986): 407.

[31] British bumbling also could not justify independence. Robert M. Weir, "'The Violent Spirit,' the Reestablishment of Order, and the Continuity of Leadership in Post-Revolutionary South Carolina," in *An Uncivil War: The Southern Backcountry during the American Revolution*, eds. Ronald Hoffman, Thad W. Tate, and Peter J. Albert (Charlottesville: University Press of Virginia, 1985), 78.

[32] Royster, "'The Nature of Treason,'" *WMQ* 36 (1979): 189; Morgan reflected upon his victory over the Legion commander at the Cowpens as follows: "Had not Britons during this Contest received so many Lessons of Humanity, I should flatter myself that this might teach them a little, but I fear they are incorrigible." Gen. Daniel Morgan to

General Nathanael Greene, Camp near Cane Creek, SC, Jan. 19, 1781, *The Papers of General Nathanael Greene*, ed. Richard K. Showman, 7 vols. to date (Chapel Hill: University of North Carolina Press, 1976-), 7:152-155; Custis, *Recollections and Private Memoirs of Washington*, 251-252; Arthur N. Gilbert, "Law and Honour Among Eighteenth-Century British Army Officers," *The Historical Journal* 19 (1976): 75-87; Higginbotham, "Military Leadership in the American Revolution," in *War and Society*, 88-89. Weir, "Rebelliousness," *The Southern Experience*, eds. Crow and Tise, 35, 37, 40-45.

[33] "It was generally observed of Tarleton and his corps, that they not only exercised more acts of cruelty than any one in the British army, but also carried further the spirit of depredation." James, *A Sketch of the Life of Brig. Gen. Francis Marion*, 64; "The terrible Tarleton...was one of the real villains of the Revolution." Elswyth Thane, *The Family Quarrel: A Journey Through the Years of the Revolution* (New York: Duell, Sloan and Pearce, 1959), 25, 100; Royster, *A Revolutionary People at War*, 115-116, 331-368; Royster, *Light-Horse Harry Lee*, 46; Royster, "'The Nature of Treason,'" *WMQ* 36 (1979): 190, 192-193; Charles Thomson, the first secretary of the American Congress, declined to write a history of the Revolution. Although a dedicated revolutionary, he did not feel comfortable with the complete truth of the era. "I could not tell the truth, without giving great offense. Let the world admire our patriots and heroes. Their supposed talents and virtues..., by commanding imitation, will serve the cause of patriotism and our country." Gelb, *Less than Glory*, 17; for the propaganda aspects of the Revolution, see Carl Berger, *Broadsides and Bayonets: The Propaganda War of the American Revolution* (1961; repr., San Rafael, CA: Presidio Press, 1976); Philip Davidson, *Propaganda and the American Revolution 1763-1783* (University of North Carolina Press, 1941); Wesley Frank Craven, *The Legend of the Founding Fathers* (New York: New York University Press, 1956); two examples of Revolutionary propaganda include Thomas Paine, *Common Sense and The Crisis* (Philadelphia: W. & T. Bradford, 1776; Albany: Charles R. & George Webster, 1792; repr., Garden City, New York: Anchor Books, 1973) and Mason Locke Weems, *The Life of George Washington; With Curious Anecdotes, Equally Honourable to Himself and Exemplary to His Young Countrymen*, 9th ed. (Philadelphia: Mathew Carey, 1809).

[34] "The stigma remains on *Tarleton's Legion alone*, that as often as they gained an advantage, and triumphed in success, the virtue of humanity was lost." Alexander Garden, *Anecdotes of the Revolutionary War in America, with Sketches of Character of Persons the Most Distinguished, in the Southern States, for Civil and Military Services* (Charleston: A.E. Miller, 1822), 259; James, *A Sketch of the Life of Brig. Gen. Francis Marion*, Appendix 3-4 ; Conway, "To Subdue America," *WMQ* 43 (1986): 407; John Adams wrote Benjamin Rush that "both tradition and history are already corrupted in America." Adams wrote this in 1811, less than one generation after the war. Two hundred years later, the warped perceptions of the American Revolution are still with us. See Michael Kammen, *Mystic Chords of Memory: The Transformation of Tradition in American Culture* (New York: Alfred A. Knopf, 1991), 13, 40; Syndney George Fisher, *The True Benjamin Franklin* (Philadelphia, 1899), 6; Philip Davidson, *Propaganda and the American Revolution*, 139-152, 365, 410; a "rational actor" model is employed by American propagandists and historians when writing about Banastre Tarleton. This theory "treats the actions of governments and large organizations as the acts of individuals. Further, it assumes that the individual actor...behaves rationally, in that he or she uses the most efficient means to pursue ends that are in his or her self-interest." For more on this interesting theory, consult James West Davidson and Mark Hamilton Lytle, *After the Fact: The Art of Historical Detection,* 3rd ed. (New York: McGraw-Hill, Inc., 1992), 279; Ferling, *A Wilderness of Miseries*, 190; Higginbotham, "Military Leadership in the American Revolution," "American Historians and the Military History of the American Revolution," and "The Early American Way of War: Reconnaissance and Appraisal," in *War and Society*, 88-89, 241-312.

[35] Bass, *The Green Dragoon*, 72, 83; Pancake, *This Destructive War*, 71; Hugh F. Rankin, "Cowpens: Prelude to Yorktown," *North Carolina Historical Review* 31 (July 1954): 346; Mark Mayo Boatner III, *Encyclopedia of the American Revolution* (New York, David McKay Company, 1966; repr., Mechanicsburg, PA: Stackpole Books), 1994, 82, 485, 1087; James L. Stokesbury, *A Short History of the American Revolution* (New York: William Morrow, 1991), 231-232, 233, 237.

[36] George F. Scheer and Hugh F. Rankin, *Rebels and Redcoats* (Cleveland and New York: World Publishing Company, 1957), 457; Willard M. Wallace, *Appeal to Arms: A Military History of the American*

Revolution (New York: Harper and Brothers, 1951), 209. For a contemporary account of Tarleton's physical appearance, see James Parton, *Life of Andrew Jackson*, 3 vols. (Boston and New York: Houghton, Mifflin and Company, 1859-1860), 1:83-84.

[37] Both of these stories will undergo further analysis in later chapters. For the disinterred body, see Joseph Johnson, *Traditions and Reminiscences Chiefly of the American Revolution in the South: Including Biographical Sketches, Incidents and Anecdotes, Few of Which Have Been Published, Particularly of Residents in the Upper Country* (Charleston: Walker and James, 1851), 162; also repeated in Bass, *The Green Dragoon*, 111; the tale of the butchered woman is in Jean-Baptiste-Antoine de Verger, "Journal of the Most Important Events that occurred to the French Troops under the command of M. le Comte de Rochambeau," in *The American Campaigns of Rochambeau's Army 1780, 1781, 1782, 1783*, trans. and eds. Howard C. Rice, Jr. and Anne S.K. Brown, 2 vols. (Princeton University Press, 1972), 1:137.

[38] Original emphasis. Custis, *Recollections and Private Memoirs of Washington*, 252n.

[39] Emphasis added. Tarleton to Dr. Collyer, N. Carolina April 10th [1781], in "New War Letters of Banastre Tarleton," ed. Richard M. Ketchum, *New York Historical Society Quarterly* 51 (January 1967): 81; the injury was caused by either a musket or rifle ball. As a result of this wound, part of Tarleton's right hand was later amputated. Bass, *The Green Dragoon*, 169-170.

[40] According to Custis, Tarleton spoke sarcastically of William Washington again, but this time in the presence of Mrs. Ashe, the sister of Mrs. Jones. With a sneer, the Legion officer said: "I would be happy to see Col. Washington." Mrs. Ashe instantly retorted: "If you had looked behind you, Colonel Tarleton, at the battle of the Cowpens, you would have enjoyed that pleasure." This rebuke caused the Englishman much anger, and when he placed his hand upon his sword, General Alexander Leslie intervened: "Say what you please, Mrs. Ashe, Colonel Tarleton knows better than to insult a lady in my presence." (The implication here is that Tarleton could be cruel enough to strike a lady.) Custis, *Recollections and Private Memoirs of Washington*, 252n; this story first appeared as "Anecdote of Colonel

Tarleton," *Philadelphia American Museum or Universal Magazine* 4 (1788): 94.

[41] This account is found in Johnson, *Traditions and Reminiscences*, 557-569. It first appeared in the *Charleston Courier*, September 3, 1842. The whole story, which takes place in 1781, is of doubtful veracity, especially since it claims that Patrick Ferguson was present. This is simply not possible because Ferguson had died the previous October.

[42] Johnson, *Traditions and Reminiscences*, 560-566. Mrs. Slocomb also makes Tarleton's hand the point of her wit. "Your old friend, Colonel Washington, who, although a perfect gentleman, it is said shook your hand very rudely, when last you met."

Banastre Tarleton also insulted Mercy Otis Warren. She revealed that he had "the effrontery afterwards in England, to boast in the presence of a lady of respectability, that he had killed more men, and ravished more women, than any man in America." Mercy Otis Warren, *History of the Rise, Progress and Termination of the American Revolution. Interspersed with Biographical, Political and Moral Observations*, 3 vols. (Boston: Manning and Loring, 1805), 2:197; after British forces occupied Charles Town in 1780, a woman found her home commandeered by the young cavalryman. Her request for the use of one or two of the rooms received this concise reply: "Madam, after mature deliberation, my eyes are so opened, and senses convinced, that the enemies of my country should not enjoy every convenience, that I hold it an act of propriety to retain the house in Broad-street, given me by the Commander in Chief for my sole accommodation. B. Tarleton." Alexander Garden, *Anecdotes of the Revolutionary War*, 269.

[43] Cohen, *The Revolutionary Histories*, 15, 18, 21, 219-229; in many wars it is common to see prominent individuals identified by nicknames. If they are friends, it makes them become more endearing, such as "Light-Horse Harry" Lee and "Mad Anthony" Wayne. If they are foes, it makes them seem more sinister, like "Bloody Bill" Cuningham and "No-Flint" Grey. Lt. Col. Henry Lee (1756-1818) commanded a legion in the American army. Royster, *Light-Horse Harry Lee*. Brig. Gen. Anthony Wayne (1745-1796) actually gained his nickname after the Battle of Fallen Timbers (1794). At this engagement, he routed a force of Native Americans and opened the Ohio Territory to white settlement. See Paul David Nelson, *Anthony Wayne: Soldier of the Early Republic* (Bloomington: Indiana University Press, 1985); Wright, *The*

Continental Army, 79; for William Cuningham, see footnote 30. Maj. Gen. Charles Grey (1729-1807) conducted a surprise bayonet assault on American troops at Paoli, Pennsylvania in 1777. He had some of his soldiers remove the flints from their firelocks; hence, his name. Ward, *War of the Revolution*, 1:358-359; one observer referred to all Americans during this era as "monsters left to the wild impulses of the wildest nature." J. Hector St. John Crevecoeur, *Sketches of 18th Century America*, eds. H.L. Bourdin et al. (New York, 1925), 183, 185-187.

[44] Tarleton, *History of the Campaigns*, 28-31, 77-78, 83.

[45] According to eighteenth century military custom, an enemy force summoned to surrender and which refuses to do so technically forfeits its right to quarter. Greg Novak, *A Guide to the American War of Independence in the North*, Campaign Book # 7A (Champaign, Illinois: Ulster Imports, 1990), 116-117.

[46] Tarleton, *History of the Campaigns*, 30-31.

[47] *Ibid.*, 83-84; one of his officers stated that "in three minutes after the attack was begun, there was not a rebel on the field that was not levelled with the ground." See "Account of Lieutenant Colonel Tarleton," *Gentleman's Magazine* (London), March 1781.

[48] Tarleton, *History of the Campaigns*, 80, 82; "Col. Tarleton knew, that having taken a command of the King's troops, the duty he owed to his country directed him to fight and conquer." *London Chronicle*, July 18, 1780.

[49] Henry Lee, *Memoirs of the War in the Southern Department of the United States*, 2 vols. (Philadelphia and New York: Bradford and Inskeep, 1812), 1:311-312.

[50] The apparent basis of the "massacre" story at the Waxhaws is a letter by Dr. Robert Brownfield to William D. James (n.d.) in the latter's *A Sketch of the Life of Brig. Gen. Francis Marion*, Appendix 1-7; Royster, *Light-Horse Harry Lee*, xi, 33, 45-46, 57; Lee claims to have killed only ninety of the enemy and hotly refutes any accusation of a "foul massacre." He states that "had the officer or the corps been capable of massacre, it was only necessary to have ordered pursuit, and

not a man of the enemy would have escaped." Lee, *Memoirs of the War*, 1:313; Starkey, "Paoli to Stony Point," 7-27.

[51] Joel W. Huffstetler, "Henry Lee and Banastre Tarleton: How Historians Use Their Memoirs," *The Southern Historian* 6 (Spring 1985): 12-19.

CHAPTER VII

Discipline

In the early spring of 1781, the English army under Lord Cornwallis began its advance into Virginia. As usual, the vanguard consisted of the British Legion. The line of march brought it through Halifax, North Carolina, where some of the royal troops engaged in the looting and plundering of homes. The next day, four miles north of the Roanoke River, Lieutenant Colonel Banastre Tarleton received an unexpected visit from Earl Cornwallis himself. Accompanied by six dragoons of his guard, his lordship rode up to the column and halted its march. Upon the arrival of some local inhabitants, the earl directed Lieutenant Colonel Tarleton to dismount his dragoons and line them up along the side of the road. Slowly, the general and the civilians walked down the line, carefully looking at each legionnaire. When they came to one particular sergeant and private, the civilians and the general held a hurried conversation in low tones. The two dragoons began to perspire and became nervous when the earl's guard detail seized them. Conducted back to Halifax, the two Legion soldiers stood before an impromptu general court martial. They were quickly found guilty of rape and robbery and then summarily executed.[1]

Poor discipline among the ranks of the British Legion is one area where the myths surrounding Tarleton and his men really manifest themselves. This story above can be read in two ways: namely that Banastre Tarleton allowed his men to wantonly plunder neighboring homes and to ravish local women, or, alternatively, that senior British commanders severely punished such behavior. Americans have generally opted for the first interpretation, but such an assessment is not altogether fair, let alone true. As the historian of another controversial figure in American history stated: "With the advantage of hindsight it is easy to abstract events from their context and to misconstrue their meaning."[2] This chapter will address the frequently asserted claim that the British Legion lacked discipline by attempting to restore the appropriate context. In the process, the author shall demonstrate that excesses of royal troops were indicative of larger problems and by no means limited to Tarleton's regiment.

The term "discipline" needs to be clarified. It refers to military training, and troops had discipline if they could properly stand at attention, march in column, load and fire their muskets, etc. Disciplined soldiers conducted themselves in a proper manner on and off the battlefield; above all else, they followed orders.

By today's standards, the military system which regulated discipline in the eighteenth-century British Army appears harsh. The earliest extant set of rules of war dates to 1642. These "articles of war" defined the rules and laws of war, such as the conduct of soldiers while on campaign, the policy on dividing plunder, exchanging prisoners, etc. They also established special courts to try cases.[3]

The General Courts Martial (GCM) rendered judgment upon major offenses, i.e. those that could result in execution or lashings of great magnitude. Murder, rape, robbery as well as mutiny and desertion represented the top five major crimes. As might be expected, many more petty transgressions occurred in the army. The Regimental Courts Martial (RCM) heard cases that dealt with gambling, drunkenness, absenteeism, straggling, personal appearance, and individual misbehavior.[4]

Two factors made this lower court unique. First, no transcripts or documentation of any kind were required for cases brought before this tribunal. Second, such informality allowed the officers of the regiment (usually five as opposed to thirteen for the GCM) to punish soldiers without regard for equity or law. For instance, given the choice between charging a soldier with desertion or neglect of duty, the regimental officers usually decreed the latter indictment and avoided the bureaucratic red tape of a GCM with all its accompanying transcripts, lawyers, royal review, and possible pardon. The speed of a RCM could be invaluable in the course of a campaign when a myriad of other concerns faced a regiment's officers. In 1718, military authorities attempted to codify RCM procedures. However, they placed no limit on the maximum sentences these courts could inflict upon convicted soldiers. Overall, the RCM became a device by which regiments punished men without the prying eyes of outsiders.[5]

The punishments administered by these courts, whether general or regimental, reflected the brutality of the age and the mindset of the criminal justice system. "Running the gauntlet" meant that a convicted soldier had to slowly walk down a line of two parallel rows of his comrades. As he passed, they would whip him with switches or the flats of their swords. In order to make him feel the full effect of the punishment, a noncommissioned officer with a musket and bayonet would walk slowly backwards in front of the condemned.[6]

To "piquet" a soldier entailed suspending him from a tree limb. As he dangled by his hands, a sharp pointed stake or piquet was placed at his feet. Of course, this occasionally resulted in permanent lameness. The wooden horse could also be physically impairing. This device resembled a carpenter's saw horse, but with the crossbar shaved to a sharp edge. A convicted soldier had to sit astride the horse for a certain period, often with weights tied to his legs to increase the pain.[7]

By 1750, these punishments fell out of vogue in the British Army and became increasingly replaced by the lash. The infamous "cat-o'-nine tails" was a whip with nine knotted cords which cut deep stripes on a prisoner's back. The practice of whipping someone with this ghastly instrument was described as giving a certain number of "stripes" or "lashes." British military code permitted up to one thousand lashes, and in rare cases even more.[8]

Starting in 1740, some restraints appeared during floggings. Soldiers lived through large numbers of lashes, say one thousand for desertion, because they were administered at intervals over several weeks and supervised by a surgeon. Furthermore, drummers now carried out the punishment. The rationale for all this is simple. Aside from being more humane, it saved a valuable if momentarily wayward soldier for future service. In addition, a drummer boy of thirteen or fourteen years of age did not have the upper body strength of an adult corporal or sergeant. The youth could not last long at full tilt when whipping his comrade. Of course, a drummer boy could also be more easily coerced into going easy on the condemned by the latter's friends. For example, American private Abram Meers of the Delaware Regiment once struck a drummer and accused him of whipping a convicted soldier in too severe a manner.[9]

Aside from these corporal punishments, other options included confinement or dismissal from service, but these occurred infrequently. Capital convictions usually happened more often and conveyed a stronger message, as in the case of Samuel Webb, a matross in the Royal Artillery. In March 1778 at Redoubt Number Eight outside New York City, he engaged in mutinous behavior by striking one Captain Campbell of the Thirty-Fifth Regiment. A GCM promptly passed a guilty verdict and sentenced Webb to death.[10]

Maintaining discipline and correcting offenses are necessities in any military organization. Regimental field officers, or the colonels, lieutenant colonels and majors, preferred to administer justice themselves with their own courts. On one level, a regiment represented a miniature society for officers and men alike. In this society, deference and loyalty flourished, friendships developed, and bravery and honor became basic character traits. *Esprit de corps* simply dictated that field officers take care of "their own" and rectify any problems.

On another level, the members of a regiment symbolized the family that many of the rank and file never had or would have. They, more than anyone else, realized that army life could be brutal, and they could sympathize with someone who "strayed." When enlisted personnel exhibited less than proper behavior, the company-grade officers, or the captains, captain-lieutenants, lieutenants, ensigns and cornets, usually became the first to know. However, whereas a field officer would probably call a Regimental Court Martial, a company-grade officer would be more inclined to let the matter pass with a warning or with assigning extra duty. What was apparently occurring here is that the company-grade officer had more direct contact with the rank and file and empathized with their plight. He realized that by reporting crimes or digressions of duty, he would place a soldier in a position to suffer a penalty which undoubtedly would be severe. Moreover, it must be remembered that a soldier represented valuable property to a regiment. It took anywhere from two to three years to train and season a soldier completely. Replacing him would be not only expensive but difficult, especially in wartime.[11]

Revolutionary War documents and correspondence make frequent note of a recurring problem: plundering. The term "plundering" as used in the eighteenth century was synonymous with marauding and pillaging. It signified the taking of valuables by forceful means, many times without the permission of one's commander. Plundering can be said to have come in three forms. Official plunder occurred when troops had written instructions to systematically seize grain and livestock. Officers supervised the confiscation and presented the civilian owners with promissory notes. Casual plunder was more subtle, and entailed such things as stealing fence rails for fires and letting horses graze in a farmer's pasture. Private plunder was simple robbery in which civilians were many times physically abused.[12]

Plunder differed from "booty," which meant collective spoils distributed to military or naval forces after an engagement. For instance, the cargo of a captured vessel would be distributed proportionally to the officers and crew of the capturing ship. During a siege, the land forces involved expected to share in the booty of confiscated property once the town fell.

A decidedly fine line existed between plunder and booty. All officers officially frowned upon the former, but allowed some of it from time to time. Meanwhile, the taking of booty or spoils became a time-honored tradition in eighteenth-century warfare. Many viewed it as the right and privilege of a conquering force.[13]

A good view of all this at work concerns the siege of Louisbourg in 1745. Before New England troops descended upon Cape Breton Island, their commanders had promised them all the booty once the garrison surrendered. When they reached the island, they quickly lost discipline in their zeal to procure plunder. Commodore Peter Warren of the Royal Navy urged Lieutenant General William Pepperrell to give "directions against plundering, *till leave given*, upon pain of death."[14] Once the French fortress fell, the colonial officers became worried because there grew "a great Noys and hubbub a mungst the Solders about the Plonder." The New Englanders nearly mutinied when it was learned that the second clause of the surrender terms prohibited the molestation of the population and that guards would be stationed at each civilian's home.[15]

Nevertheless, company-grade officers frequently turned a blind eye to what the French called *la maraude*, especially when it dealt with fresh food. "Supplementary field rations," as they were known, had to be taken by sheer necessity. Keeping an army supplied with food in the eighteenth century was a staggering task and shortages had to be countered by living off the land. All armies engaged in such behavior. To men consistently eating salted meat, rancid butter, and moldy bread, fresh produce and meat seemed like manna, and their desire for it was natural and justifiable. An American private named Algernon Roberts echoed such "wartime morality." He deemed plundering "a natural consequence attending camps." No one should be "so credulous as to believe the contrary."[16] Brigadier General James Murray, governor-general of Quebec at the close of the French and Indian War, had a more simplistic view: "Necessity has no law."[17]

Nonetheless, the fine line between plunder and booty must be remembered. Wanton pillaging was always just one step away and a soldier engaged in the removal of foodstuffs from a civilian's house might be tempted to liberate the owner of his silverware or to sexually assault his wife or daughter. If caught, he received punishment dependant upon who found him and the severity of his crime. If discovered by a junior officer, he could face light punishment. The field officer would probably insist upon a RCM while the provost marshal or army commander would be most unforgiving.[18]

Regimental commanders did attempt to redress the evil of plundering. A careful examination of the orderly book for Oliver De Lancey's Loyalist brigade from 1776 to 1778 reveals that practically every general and battalion order makes some reference to the plundering and marauding of the troops. The February 8, 1777 battalion orders state that officers and soldiers alike would be punished for dismantling fences for their cooking fires. On April 1, battalion orders announced that horses could not be pressed into service without the knowledge and approbation of the commanding officer. Nearly three months later on June 28, a decree proclaimed that the rank and file could not take fruit and other belongings of the populace without specific permission. Later in the summer of 1777, the complaints of the inhabitants became so great that Brigadier General De Lancey advised his officers to pay proper attention to the behavior of their men.[19]

Still, the "irregularities" continued and the orders were repeated. The frustration of the higher command is evident when one year later in the summer of 1778, De Lancey discovered that some of his soldiers had been clandestinely milking cows belonging to local farmers. The general ordered a GCM for such "infamous robberies" and promised no mercy for those involved. He also instructed his battalion commanders to furnish patrols around neighboring enclosures and pastures.[20]

The recurrence of these irregularities indicates a lack of supervision. Since the company or troop represented the basic unit of any British regiment, junior officers and noncommissioned officers (NCO's) had the responsibility of enforcing discipline. A captain and his two subaltern officers had only sixty-four men under their direct command, and many times less than that because of combat, disease, and desertion. Although it was impossible to supervise all the rank and file at all times, the company officers and NCO's still must take a large part of the blame for the poor behavior of their men.[21]

Other officers besides De Lancey had the same problem. Major General Alexander Leslie issued these general orders off Hampton Roads, Virginia in October 1780:

> As the Success of every Military operation principaly depends on ye. regularity of ye. troops employed, and as Plundering of any kind Strikes immediately at ye. Root of good discipline, Majr. G'. Leslie hopes that every [officer] he has the honor to Command will use his utmost exertion to prevent that unsoldier like vice.[22]

He went on and assured his men that all measures would be taken to procure fresh provisions and to distribute them in an equitable manner. Nevertheless, "the most exemplary Punishment" awaited any man found marauding or "breaking the rules of good order and discipline."[23]

Once the landings on the Virginia coast occurred, Leslie found that the troops "by no means answered his expectation with regard to regularity, & sobriety." He then re-issued the above general orders. Later, when his command linked up with Lord Cornwallis's troops in South Carolina, Leslie assured the troops that the earl was "most anxiously attentive" to obtain for them "every comfort that the nature of the service will admit of." On February 6, 1781, he decreed:

> Any officer who looks on with Indifference & does not do his Utmost to prevent the Shamefull Marauding Which has of late prevailed in the Army Will be Considered in a more Criminal light than the persons who Commit those Scandalous Crimes, which must bring disgrace & Ruin on his Majesty's Arms.[24]

Evidently, this warning had no effect because the depredations continued.[25]

Major Patrick Ferguson's "Proposed Plan for bringing the Army under strict discipline with regard to marauding" represents one of the more explicit British attempts to rectify this problem. Ferguson did feel that it was "necessary for the comfort, refreshment, & encouragement of the Troops in the field, that they be allowed to help themselves in some degree." While he saw nothing wrong with the confiscation of poultry, pigs, fruits and vegetables, he viewed the plundering of houses and the destruction of property as excessive. The Scottish officer suggested that any soldier or camp follower who entered a house without an officer should be arrested. Those who abused women or children would be executed, while persons who killed or removed livestock without orders would receive milder punishments. He also recommended that special detachments guard each dwelling along the army's line of march until it had passed. These detachments would collect delinquents and stragglers, receiving one dollar per prisoner. At the end of each day's march, immediate courts martial would convene, rendering on-the-spot punishments for those found guilty.[26]

By adhering to this plan, Ferguson maintained that the number of deserters and stragglers would decrease, the character and discipline of the army would be assured, and local farmers would lose a minimal amount of property without being abused or irritated. Ferguson also recommended that handbills be distributed to the populace, alerting them on what to expect.[27]

Aside from plundering, another major problem for eighteenth-century armies was desertion. During the Revolutionary War, it became particularly rampant. Major General Nathanael Greene lamented: "At the close of the war, we fought the enemy with British soldiers, and they fought us with those of America."[28] Numerous reasons lay behind why individuals left their units in the dark of the night or during the monotony of a march. The better food and pay of civilian life or another army always topped the list. An overly stern officer or the bullying of a fellow soldier represented another possibility. Of course, capture by enemy forces also tempted many. Prison conditions during this period, were, in a word, horrible. The dank and filthy conditions of a prison, with its accompanying meager rations and fatal diseases, did not appeal to many captured troops. The choice of enlisting in the opposing army became too much of a temptation for some. For example, many of the one thousand Rebel prisoners taken at Camden, South Carolina in August 1780 "volunteered" for service in Cornwallis's army.[29]

A deserter, if recaptured, would usually face a summary execution. In 1746, a British man-of-war captured two French transports off the coast of Scotland. English authorities found onboard a complete French regiment, with twenty-nine deserters from the British army in Flanders. A General Court Martial hastily convened at Whitehall. All twenty-nine received the death sentence, but only five were ordered to be shot. The twenty-nine threw dice on a drumhead, and the five who lost met their fate in Hyde Park on Wednesday morning, April 23, 1746.[30]

During the Revolutionary War, one out of four deserters from the British Army received the death sentence. The typical punishment for the others was one thousand lashes. Field officers and higher ranking officers such as brigadiers and division commanders would be more likely to make examples of deserters.

Company-grade officers would be less likely to inflict severe punishment. As stated earlier, it all depended upon who caught the wayward soldier. A good example of this occurred at Bunker Hill on June 17, 1775. Before the battle commenced, five redcoats bolted from the ranks of Lieutenant Colonel Robert Pigot's command and ran toward the American lines. They were quickly caught and brought before General William Howe. Mindful of maintaining discipline yet reluctant to lose five prime soldiers, Howe selected two at random and had them immediately hanged from a nearby tree.[31]

Despite such punishments, the fact remains that plundering and desertion were rampant in the British Army. By keeping this in mind, we can now turn to Banastre Tarleton and the British Legion.

First, there is simply no way that Banastre Tarleton could have known what each and every soldier in his Legion was doing all the time. The fact that he was constantly in the field with his men did not make him omnipresent or omniscient as some historians would have one believe.[32] Of course, as the commander of the British Legion he held ultimate responsibility for his men's actions. However, a good defense can be made for his limited knowledge of their activities.

As it advanced, the British Legion was akin to a beehive, swarming with green-coated members, coming and going—videttes, forage parties, messengers, patrols. Tarleton had no way of knowing what his men had perpetrated upon the local populace unless he actually witnessed the act(s) or the offended party came into his camp to complain. The latter possibility was a more than unlikely occurrence, especially since the British Legion moved fast and did not stay in one area for too long. The simple fear of the inhabitants also played a role.[33]

Tarleton probably learned of his soldiers' actions from rumors circulating around the neighboring communities or from other British officers. What he did with such information is uncertain. As mentioned earlier, regimental courts martial were impromptu and written records did not have to be kept. Furthermore, there is no letter book or order book for the British Legion in existence.[34] As an English officer and gentleman, it is likely that Tarleton punished his men for their more serious depredations. However, he made no attempts to conceal his hatred for the Rebel cause and he may have been more likely to overlook something that another officer would frown upon.[35]

Moreover, something else is at play with this one particular officer and his command. It may be surmised that Banastre Tarleton's diligent attendance with his legionnaires influenced him greatly. Like other leaders of Loyalist troops, he began to identify with the troops, which in turn helped to foster a strong corporate sense. Furthermore, close contact with his men undoubtedly intensified this young man's feelings of paternalism. As an officer coming from a wealthy family, he would have exhibited the prevailing aristocratic ethos. This sense of noblesse oblige could have occasionally lessened his desire to punish infractions. Meanwhile, the legionnaires became aware of this paternalistic concern for their welfare and reciprocated by viewing Banastre Tarleton as their champion. Their behavior outside Gloucester, Virginia on October 3, 1781 indicates this mindset. When the lieutenant colonel fell from his horse, the Legion dragoons broke formation and raced to his rescue.[36]

One area where poor discipline was rife with the British Legion had to do with foraging parties. As might be expected, this partially mounted unit always had a need for forage. During the southern campaigns, Lord Cornwallis repeatedly told the Legion commander to keep his dragoons at a distance from the main army, "as they would consume our whole substance in half an hour." In November 1780, parties in search of forage near Camden, South Carolina had to travel seventeen miles in order to find hay and oats. One month later, Tarleton stated: "We forage at a very great distance," for "not above six loads of forage" could be procured for seven miles around the Legion's encampment.[37]

In light of this situation, it is not too difficult to surmise what some foraging parties did once beyond the realm of direct supervision. Many plundered at will. Lieutenant Colonel John Simcoe of the Queen's Rangers noted: "It is impossible to protect any country from the depredations of foraging parties."[38] As the commander of a partially mounted corps, he too had ample opportunity to discover this for himself.

Just as Banastre Tarleton was ignorant about certain depredations, so was Lieutenant General Cornwallis himself. Since the British Legion usually formed the vanguard of his march, Lord Cornwallis had no direct control over this far-reaching, mobile corps. He would come upon the regions it traveled through only after it was gone. In fact, he probably saw the aftermath of Legion marauding long before Tarleton ever heard of it. However, as overall British commander, he too must take part of the blame, especially since he once told Tarleton, that as for provisions and forage, "you must live as well as you can."[39]

In his book, *A History of the Campaigns of 1780 and 1781, in the Southern Provinces of North America*, Banastre Tarleton never refutes any allegations about the "irregularities" or "excesses" of his men. In fact, he is quite open about them, as illustrated with the story related at the opening of this chapter. That is what makes this account all the more remarkable. In addition, Tarleton includes in his work the following admonishment from Cornwallis: "I must recommend it to you in the strongest manner to use your utmost endeavours to prevent the troops under your command from committing irregularities."[40]

What this rape-robbery story and Cornwallis's reproach indicate is that Banastre Tarleton was not exactly aware of all the Legion doings. His last comment about the execution of the two dragoons caught by Cornwallis reads as follows: "The immediate infliction of the sentence exhibited to the army and manifested to the country the discipline and justice of the British general." This is hardly the view of a man who disagrees with his superior's decision.[41]

A problem that plagued most regimental commanders, i.e. a lack of cooperation on the part of company-grade officers to punish enlisted personnel, also afflicted Tarleton. Such factors as a lack of replacements, distance from the main army and the provost marshal, and a desire to permit some plundering all played a role. On December 26, 1780, the Legion lieutenant colonel wrote a very revealing letter to his superior officer, which read in part: "I am sorry your Lordship has cause to complain of the plundering of the Legion. *The officers have kept me in ignorance or steps should have been taken immediately to suppress it.*"[42] These do not seem like the words of an officer trying to hide something.

There are numerous other stories concerning Legion depredations that, if taken with this information in mind, help refute the commonly held notion that Banastre Tarleton simply let his men run wild. After the Battle of Monck's Corner on April 14, 1780, three Legion dragoons entered a plantation house owned by a distinguished Loyalist and attempted to rape several women taking refuge there. The women fortunately escaped but not before one was slashed several times with a saber. They sought the protection of Lieutenant Colonel James Webster, who had the assailants immediately arrested and court-martialed. The three men then received severe floggings, although Major Ferguson thought instant death a more appropriate punishment.[43]

There is no way of being certain that Tarleton knew of this event at the plantation. The attack on Monck's Corner occurred at 3 a.m. and in the early morning darkness and confusion, much had to be done—collecting prisoners and badly needed horses, tending to the wounded, writing dispatches. It does not seem likely that Banastre Tarleton, a well-known dandy with the ladies, would condone such behavior from three missing dragoons. In this case, Tarleton was not the monster that popular history makes him out to be. The crime was committed by individuals acting on their own accord, without the presence of their leader.[44]

An explanation is available for another "infamous" incident. This time, in November 1780, the British Legion rode to the Pee Dee River area of South Carolina in order to suppress the activities of Francis Marion. The Legion commander selected the plantation of recently deceased Whig General Richard Richardson as the site for an ambush. However, the general's widow, as staunch a rebel as her beloved husband, sent her son to warn the approaching Marion, who then beat a hasty retreat through neighboring swamps. Tarleton discovered this before daylight and then chased the elusive partisan "for seven hours through swamps and defiles." After a pursuit of nearly thirty miles in which a glimpse of the quarry never materialized, the exasperated Tarleton and his exhausted legionnaires returned to Richardson's. There, he had the house looted and the livestock driven into the barns which were then consumed "in one general blaze."[45]

Undoubtedly, Banastre Tarleton was enraged that his plan had been betrayed. He possibly could have been feeling especially vengeful over the recent execution by the Rebels in New York of Colonel John André, a friend from earlier days in Philadelphia.[46] In any event, the lieutenant colonel wanted to make a point about rebels and how their perfidy would not be tolerated. He felt totally justified in his reaction, no matter how excessive it might seem. As he stated in a letter to a fellow English officer about the same time: "Nothing will serve these people but fire & sword."[47]

This argument is meant in no way to deny that the British Legion acted excessively at times or that it did not have a fair share of disreputable individuals. One legionnaire noted that "I never before had kept such bad company." After the war, Tarleton himself commented that "bad materials" comprised part of the rank and file. Although Loyalist soldiers were very capable of pillaging and marauding, part of the problem may have been deserters. Like most English regiments at the time, the Legion had a number of American deserters in its ranks, although the exact percentage is unknown. However, we do know of one specific case, that of Michael Docherty, which was indicative of the times. Docherty was the American soldier captured twice by the British and who volunteered each time for service in the royal army, once in the Seventeenth Regiment and once in Tarleton's Legion.[48]

Such an individual story illustrates the desperation of captured personnel to escape the horrible conditions of prison camps. Like

Docherty, most deserters had nothing to lose. Some in fact might have become so desperate as to jettison morals and engage in criminal behavior. As "criminals" and wanted men, they could easily justify exceeding the bounds of civilized warfare. By doing so, they could satiate all their desires, whether they be food, clothing, shelter, money, or sexual gratification.

Aside from plundering and desertion, the British Legion's frequent excessive use of force and occasional lackluster performance in combat are two other areas identified by historians as indicative of poor discipline. By looking at various well-known incidents, we can see how the troops fared and what occurred.

In the early morning bayonet assault on MacPherson's Plantation, South Carolina in March 1780, eager Legion infantrymen inadvertently attacked another Loyalist regiment. Ferguson's American Volunteers had arrived earlier the preceding night, found no enemy, and set up an encampment. Ferguson quickly managed to halt the fighting, but not before receiving a severe bayonet wound in his left arm.[49]

At Wahab's Plantation, North Carolina on September 21, 1780, eighty Rebel cavalrymen led by William Davie surprised the Legion cavalry. Caught in the process of saddling their mounts, the British panicked and fled. At Charlotte five days later, the Legion dragoons twice charged a stone wall held by the enemy. When ordered to do it a third time, they refused until Cornwallis himself pleaded with them.[50]

These two occurrences do not necessarily mean that the Legion lacked discipline; rather they illustrate two important points. First, by September of 1780 the British Legion had been in the field for the better part of nine months. The strain of near constant service must have been great. Second, Tarleton did not command at either of these engagements. At this time, he had malaria and his second-in-command, Major George Hanger, led the regiment in the field. "Lacking the inspiration of their proper leader," they performed poorly—an interesting observation as it indicates the charisma of Tarleton and the sway he held over his men. Lord

Cornwallis observed: "Indeed the whole of them are very different when Tarleton is present or absent."[51]

The Battle of Cowpens has already been discussed in a previous chapter. As may be remembered, when Tarleton ordered his dragoons to charge the oncoming horde of Americans, they twice failed to comply and then fled the field. Exhaustion from a harrowing two-week chase of Morgan's army may have played a role. Also, simple panic may have set in among the dragoons. Panic was and still is very contagious on the battlefield. Even the most experienced units could panic very easily, especially when as fatigued and hungry as the British were that cold morning in January 1781.[52] Critics of Tarleton frequently fail to acknowledge this possibility.

In addition, American deserters among the dragoons may have contributed to the hasty retreat. These "hired sabers of dubious worth," as one modern historian calls them, were "capable but not entirely reliable." Seeing a line of Americans charging downhill and sensing defeat in the air, they may have decided to embrace their first loyalty, i.e. their own lives. They knew all too well what would probably occur to them if captured. Once one deserter fled, another assuredly followed suit, and before long the true Loyalists among the Legion cavalry left too.[53]

What occurred at Tarrant's Tavern, North Carolina was partially caused by confusion. The Legion dragoons, fresh from their defeat along the Broad River and chided by their commander to "*remember the Cowpens*," charged down the lane near the tavern on February 1, 1781. The scene at the tavern was already chaotic before they arrived. Civilians and soldiers alike crowded the tavern and the road outside. Wagons loaded with personal possessions congested the road and made it nearly impassable. When the call went up "Tarleton is coming!," soldiers and civilians alike panicked and were caught out in the open. The Legionnaires, suddenly finding themselves in a crowd of people, probably could not prevent their saber blows from landing on several unfortunate civilians.[54]

The death of American Colonel Alexander Scammell outside York Town, Virginia in early October 1781 denotes "guilt by association." The morning after the British abandoned three outer redoubts, Lieutenant Allan Cameron and a small party of Legion cavalry surprised a reconnoitering force commanded by Scammell. Cameron instantly charged the enemy and "brought off Colonel Scammell, who was wounded in attempting to retreat." The Americans claimed that Scammell, who later died, was shot in the back for no good reason. However, Cameron and his troopers had express orders to take prisoners. The determination and excitement associated with capturing an enemy field officer could have contributed to Scammell's wound.[55]

Thomas Jefferson's house would have certainly fared a lot worse had the British Legion been totally bereft of discipline. The Legion lieutenant commanding the detachment sent to capture the Virginia governor in July 1781 ordered his men not to plunder Monticello in any way. Indeed, Jefferson himself noted that they stayed for eighteen hours and "preserved everything with sacred care."[56]

Yet, man's blatant and unwarranted inhumanity to man cannot be discounted in some of these above-mentioned incidents, especially since armies will always have their share of innately depraved individuals. The reader is reminded of the story of Moses Hall's grisly discovery as related in the first chapter of this work. Given that Hall's account is the only one available of the event, and that he appears to have been objective and honest, especially with his description of the six murdered Loyalists, one must take it at face value. Assuredly, it was extreme to bayonet a sixteen-year-old boy, as he could have been simply taken along on the march and let go at a later time.[57]

Another example of poor discipline involved the fate of one James Gillies, a fourteen-year-old bugler in Lee's Legion. On the morning of February 13, 1781, Gillies and his comrades encountered some British Legion dragoons five miles north of Guilford Courthouse, North Carolina. In the ensuing skirmish, the

Discipline

British horsemen easily chased down the bugler's jaded horse and sabered Gillies to death. Later, Lee's men discovered that the British troopers involved in this event were intoxicated.[58]

Next to the Cowpens, the Battle of the Waxhaws is what Banastre Tarleton and the British Legion are most well known for in the annals of Revolutionary War history. Much has been written about this engagement and many historians view it as a massacre. What happened on May 29, 1780 along the South Carolina -North Carolina border demands careful investigation.[59]

After Charles Town fell on May 12, 1780, Cornwallis ordered Lieutenant Colonel Tarleton to take his legion on a preliminary sweep through the South Carolina interior and to crush any lingering opposition. At the same time, a contingent of approximately four hundred Virginia Continentals and cavalry under Colonel Abraham Buford had been marching south toward Charles Town. These troops included both veterans and raw recruits.[60] When he learned of the capitulation, Buford quickly began to retreat out of South Carolina. Tarleton and 270 legionnaires made a 105-mile ride in fifty-four hours and caught Buford just south of the border with North Carolina in an area known as the Waxhaws.[61]

The confident Tarleton sent forward a flag of truce which exaggerated his force as seven hundred strong and which demanded that Buford surrender immediately. He offered the Rebel colonel terms similar to those accepted by American Major General Benjamin Lincoln at Charles Town. He concluded his summons as follows: "If you are rash enough to reject them, the blood be upon your head."[62]

Under the rules of eighteenth-century warfare, an enemy force called upon to surrender which fails to do so forfeits its right to quarter in any upcoming combat. When the American rejection of terms is combined with Tarleton's hard-line stance on the rebellion, it can be seen how the situation automatically became very foreboding for Buford and his men.[63]

Slaughter of Col. Buford's Regiment at Charleston, Waxhaws, May 29, 1780; line engraving, circa 1860-1870 (Anne S. K. Brown Military Collection, Brown University Library, Providence, R.I.)

After the passage of the truce flag, both sides began to deploy for battle. Buford sent his wagons and five artillery pieces, under the guard of a small contingent of troops, ahead on the road to Salisbury. His remaining soldiers took positions astride the road. Unfortunately, the terrain was an open wood and favored a cavalry assault. The British commander deployed his forces for a classic cavalry charge to be followed by a swift bayonet attack. Tarleton interspersed cavalry and dismounted infantry throughout his line, with instructions for the flanking units to envelope the American line.[64]

The kind of attack Tarleton intended and ultimately conducted was a truly bloody affair. A typical cavalry charge was based upon shock and occurred with the greatest possible velocity. For that reason, an encounter between cavalry and infantry was often one-sided. The cavalryman had a sevenfold advantage over the foot soldier in strength and weight.[65] Instant destruction usually announced itself with the pounding of those hooves. A military theorist of the time wrote of this moment: "Where do we find the kind of men who will stay calm at the terrible moment when they face the charge of a force of cavalry which happens to be well led?"[66]

The crucial zone for the foot soldiers occurred when the horsemen approached a distance of fifty to thirty paces from the infantry lines. At this distance, the most effective musket fire could be delivered before panic likely swept through the ranks.[67] The new recruits among the Virginia Continentals must have been nervous, more so than their veteran comrades.[68]

As the Legion advanced, American officers ordered the rank and file to hold their fire until Tarleton's horsemen were within ten yards. This was a fatal mistake on the part of Buford and his officers, for horsemen at full gallop could cover that distance in a second. The volley did not stay the momentum of the charge and the British crashed into the thin Rebel line. The Americans, unable to reload quickly enough, soon had the added problem of charging Legion infantry. The assault reduced the Continentals to what in another context has been described as "a purposeless crowd in a few instants."[69]

Both sides agreed that during the mêlée, Tarleton's horse was shot from under him at the same time the Americans hoisted a surrender flag. However, what occurred next has been debated for years by historians. British supporters assert that Tarleton's fall spurred the Legionnaires to exact revenge and kill all the Americans for their apparent treachery. American accounts dismiss the incident as a poor attempt on the part of Tarleton and his men to justify their inherent bloodthirstiness and depravity.[70]

One description of the battle sheds light upon this subject, but surprisingly it has never really been used before by historians. This eyewitness account not only backs up Tarleton's claim about the horse, but it is written by none other than Buford's adjutant, Colonel H. Boyer. What is even more remarkable is that this narrative first appeared in Alexander Garden's *Anecdotes of the American Revolution, Illustrative of the Talents and Virtues of the Heroes and Patriots, Who Acted the Most Conspicuous Parts Therein* (2nd series; Charleston: A.E. Miller, 1828), pages 135-138. Garden was not only a former member of Lee's Legion but a zealous patriot to boot.[71]

According to this narrative, after fifteen minutes of fighting Colonel Buford ordered Boyer to ride forward with a flag of truce. Boyer did so, but reluctantly since the shooting had not ceased. What happened next is best described in the adjutant's own words: "When close to the British commander, he delivered Beaufort's [Buford's] message, but a ball at the moment, striking the forehead of Tarlton's horse, he plunged, and both fell to the ground, the horse being uppermost."[72] The young British dragoon leader, enraged by what he perceived as Rebel treachery, ordered his men to kill Boyer. The Legionnaires then attempted to saber Boyer, but he escaped unhurt. Nearby American officers Captain John Stokes and Lieutenant Willison saw what had happened and then ordered their platoons to recommence firing. "The rage of the British soldiers, excited by the continued fire of the Americans, while a negotiation was offered by flag, impelled them to acts of vengeance that knew no limits."[73]

Tarleton reflected:

> The loss of officers and men was great on the part of the Americans, owing to the dragoons so effectually breaking the infantry, and to a report amongst the cavalry, that they had lost their commanding officer, which stimulated the soldiers to a vindicative asperity not easily restrained.[74]

Given the small number of troops involved on either side and the level expanse of the field, it is possible that a number of Legionnaires saw Tarleton's horse go down. As word spread of his "death," so did their rage.

The nakedly face-to-face quality of combat with bayonet and saber is difficult to convey to the modern reader. There is nothing pretty or ethical about it.[75] The psychological dimensions found on the field that spring day near Waxhaws, South Carolina are not overly complex. A Legion soldier, tired from a long chase yet animated by the charge, coming upon a Continental, demoralized by his ranks being broken, spelled disaster. The Legionnaire would not be receptive to enemy pleas for quarter after he witnessed or heard about his leader's apparent demise. The Continental, meanwhile, would be confused by the sight of some of his comrades surrendering while others still resisted. As a result, tragic misunderstanding and anger permitted a frenzy of bloodletting to feed upon itself.[76]

The British Legionnaires undeniably exhibited fierce loyalty to their leader on May 29, 1780. Their fury produced a high casualty ratio for such a small, short battle. British losses amounted to five killed and fourteen wounded. The American figures equaled 113 killed and 203 prisoners, 150 of whom were wounded. Tarleton always maintained that the slaughter commenced before he could remount another horse. Although probably dazed by his fall, he could have tried to take charge before the situation devolved into complete mayhem. He evidently let his anger get the best of him, at least for a while. Tarleton had little sympathy for Rebels; and, furthermore, these particular people had rejected his demand for surrender, a fact which technically absolved him of all guilt concerning their fate.[77]

The charge of "massacre" has been leveled by many, and how one views this engagement depends upon which side of the political fence one is sitting. Indeed, the Legionnaires acted excessively. The British commander's seeming lack of compassion in leaving the 150 wounded Americans on the field was actually a humane act. Banastre Tarleton and his men were many miles from the main army. (Cornwallis was still south of Camden, around forty miles north of Nelson's Ferry.) Camden, the nearest town of substantial size, was about forty miles away. His horses were jaded and his troops equally exhausted. He had only one surgeon with limited medical supplies and most of the wounded were unable to travel. The young Legion leader had no other choice but to parole the wounded Americans and to let the local populace succor them.[78]

The Rebels made much of the number of dead and wounded, while ignoring the flag incident. They also failed to admit that close combat with edged weapons was always bloody. Multiple wounds consistently appeared in such encounters.[79] Both Sir Henry Clinton and Earl Cornwallis praised the young man for his victory. However, at least one British official, Charles Stedman, while complimentary of the British Legion for its "activity and ardour," wrote that "the virtue of humanity was totally forgot."[80]

What partially influences the American conception of the "Waxhaws Massacre" is again a sense of injured innocence, notions of moral superiority, and simple propaganda. Banastre Tarleton became a villain and his legionnaires labeled "cruel myrmidons" for their deeds that day. Meanwhile, "Tarleton's Quarter!" became a catchword for no mercy. Further discussion of the effect of this battle upon the American cause is best reserved for the next chapter. What should be addressed now is another factor influencing American perceptions of this engagement.[81]

It is evident in the American view of the Waxhaws that some type of unresolved anxiety existed over the use of the bayonet. As a weapon, the bayonet was unfamiliar to provincial military culture. English regulars, meanwhile, developed a deadly proficiency in its use. By keeping this in mind, it is easy to see why the Revolutionary War produced more than just one "massacre."

On the night of September 20-21, 1777, Major General Charles Grey and six English regiments fell upon Anthony Wayne's division of 1,500 men bivouacked near Paoli Tavern, Pennsylvania. Grey ordered his men to march with unloaded muskets, and those who could not draw their rounds had to remove their flints. His men rushed into the encampment and killed or wounded approximately 150 Americans and took seventy to eighty prisoners. British losses numbered three killed and five wounded.[82]

This is the celebrated "Paoli Massacre," commonly described as the butchery of defenseless men, stabbed to death in their sleep. Like the Waxhaws, American claims of foul play obscured the brilliance of the attack and the regrettable consequences of close combat with sword and bayonet. This bayonet assault of September 1777 was the first of its kind during the war, and became the basis for exaggerated stories of massacres of helpless Americans. Other engagements such as Old Tappan (September 28-29, 1778) and Little Egg Harbor (October 14-15, 1778) received similar appellations.[83]

For most of the war, Americans had little proficiency in the use of the bayonet and viewed it with a certain amount of dread and horror. It became a brutal weapon, something which is also seen with the European's objection to the Native American tomahawk and British anger over the deliberate aim of American riflemen at their officers. Popular culture does not acknowledge the fact that the tomahawk and the rifle were no more barbarous than the sword and bayonet or vice versa.[84]

All regiments in the British Army, as well as in the American Army, had their moments of less than exemplary behavior. Why the British Legion's transgressions received such attention had to do with reasons already discussed. As a highly visible element of the British Army in dress, membership, and activity, it became noticeable to friend and foe alike. In addition, it had a young, ambitious leader who loathed all rebels and cared little for the niceties of war. The next chapter analyzes how Legion discipline affected the course of the war in the South.

---

[1] Lieutenant Colonel Banastre Tarleton, *A History of the Campaigns of 1780 and 1781, in the Southern Provinces of North America* (London: T. Cadell, 1787), 290. The names of the two dragoons are unknown.

[2] John Sugden, *Tecumseh's Last Stand* (University of Oklahoma Press, 1985), 120.

[3] Sylvia R. Frey, "Courts and Cats: British Military Justice in the Eighteenth Century," *Military Affairs* 43 (1979): 5-7; Arthur N. Gilbert, "The Regimental Courts Martial in the Eighteenth Century British Army," *Albion* 8 (1976): 50; Andrew Eliot, a Boston clergyman, noticed in early 1769 that for regular troops "discipline is so shockingly severe…" John Shy, *Toward Lexington: The Role of the British Army in the Coming of the American Revolution* (Princeton University Press, 1965), 279, 288-289, 413. An excellent recent study analyzing military discipline and corporate identity is Stephen Brumwell's *Redcoats: The British Soldier and War in the Americas, 1755-1763* (Cambridge: Cambridge University Press, 2002). See specifically pages 100-112, 119-127, and 179-190.

[4] Gilbert, "Regimental Courts Martial," 50-53; the American military justice system and Articles of War relied heavily upon English precedent. See James C. Neagles, *Summer Soldiers: A Survey and Index of Revolutionary War Courts-Martial* (Salt Lake City, Utah: Ancestry Inc., 1986), 1, 5, 7-9. This volume of American court martial cases has 3,315 entries. Nearly one out of six (593) pertained to officers.

[5] The 1735 Articles of War allowed a RCM to have only three commissioned officers when five could not be gathered. Gilbert, "Regimental Courts Martial," 50-53; also see Arthur N. Gilbert, "British Military Justice During the American Revolution," *The*

Eighteenth Century: Theory and Interpretation 20 (1979): 24-38; Shy, *Toward Lexington*, 344-345; Frey, "Courts and Cats," 9.

[6] For the brutality of the age, consult Michel Foucault, *Discipline and Punish: The Birth of the Prison*, trans. Alan Sheridan (New York: Vintage Books, 1979); the sentence of some condemned soldiers required them to make multiple trips down the gauntlet, while others had to carry fifteen or eighteen pound weights. Frey, "Courts and Cats," 8; Neagles, *Summer Soldiers*, 36-37; running the gauntlet was an ancient Roman tradition revived by Gustavus of Sweden. Punishment of soldiers by soldiers was a part of martial bonding. See John Morgan Dederer, *War in America to 1775 Before Yankee Doodle* (New York: New York University Press, 1990), 92.

[7] Different armies had their own variation of each punishment. Gilbert, "Regimental Courts Martial," 54n16; the piquet or "spicket" was occasionally used to derive information from captured enemy personnel. John C. Dann, ed., *The Revolution Remembered: Eyewitness Accounts of the War for Independence* (Chicago: University of Chicago Press, 1980), 188-189; John E. Ferling, *A Wilderness of Miseries: War and Warriors in Early America* (Westport, Connecticut: Greenwood Press, 1980), 117; "shaming" was another popular punishment. In December 1757, a court martial held in Nova Scotia found a British grenadier guilty of cowardice. The condemned had to sit on a wooden horse for a half hour each day for six days. He wore a petticoat and held a broom in his hand. A note pinned to his back read: "Such is the reward of my merit." The grenadier later became "a remarkable gallant soldier." Captain John Knox, *An Historical Journal of the Campaigns in North-America, for the Years 1757, 1758, 1759, and 1760*, 3 vols. (London: W. Johnston and J. Dodsley, 1769), 1:128-129.

[8] Flogging became appropriately also known as "putting on a new shirt." Until 1832, British courts had no real limitation on the number of lashes that they could impose. Frey, "Courts and Cats," 8; Gilbert, "Regimental Courts Martial," 61n32; during the American Revolution, 56.6% of the British GCM lash convictions resulted in one thousand stripes or more. The average number of lashes a soldier actually received was 791. Gilbert, "British Military Justice," 25. Also see Arthur N. Gilbert, "The Changing Face of British Military Justice, 1757-1783," *Military Affairs* 49 (1985): 80-84; after the flogging or gauntlet, some units would pass the regimental flag over the convicted

soldier in order to "purify" him. Lee Kennett, *The French Armies in the Seven Years' War: A Study in Military Organization and Administration* (Duke University Press, 1967), 84n66; the American Army initially employed the old Mosaic law of thirty-nine lashes. However, Washington realized that this did not represent enough of a deterrent. In 1776, he had the Articles of War changed to provide a higher maximum of one hundred lashes. Neagles, *Summer Soldiers*, 35-36; Charles Royster, *A Revolutionary People at War: The Continental Army and American Character, 1775-1783* (New York: WW Norton, 1981), 77-78; for high numbers of lashes, see the cases of William Short, Thomas Stanley, Ebenezer Holmes, John Connor, John Case and others in William Kelby, comp., *Orderly Book of the Three Battalions of Loyalists Commanded by Brigadier-General Oliver De Lancey 1776-1778* (Baltimore: Genealogical Publishing, 1972), 37, 52, 59, 61, 66-67. Lt. Gen. Henry Clinton's approval of the Short flogging read in part: "Put [it] in execution at such times and in such proportion as the officer commanding the regiment shall direct." Ferling, *A Wilderness of Miseries*, 115-116.

[9] Frey, "Courts and Cats," 8; see the eyewitness account of a flogging in Judge Advocate General Hughes to Secretary at War, March 3, 1723, War Office Records, Public Record Office, Kew, 71/15 (hereafter cited as PRO); in March 1755 at Hampton, Virginia, a deserter from the Royal Navy received 240 lashes on a Monday. The officer supervising the flogging ordered that the remaining 110 would be given the following Friday "or when he [the prisoner] shall be in condition to receive them." Lee McCardell, *Ill-Starred General: Braddock of the Coldstream Guards* (University of Pittsburgh Press, 1958), 151; Shy, *Toward Lexington*, 308-309n132; death did occur during many floggings. See the incidents in the *Quebec Gazette*, August 18, 1766 and the *Williamsburg Virginia Gazette*, September 8, 1766; a drummer in the Twentieth Regiment reportedly received thirty thousand lashes during his fourteen years at Gibraltar, four thousand of which he received in one year alone! He was reported as "hearty and well" in 1728. For this incredible story, consult T.H. McGuffie, *The Siege of Gibraltar 1779-1783* (London: B.T. Batsford, 1965), 82; as punishment for striking the drummer, Meers had to ask for his pardon in the presence of their commanding officer. Neagles, *Summer Soldiers*, 36, 201.

[10] A matross was an artillery soldier. The commander-in-chief approved Webb's sentence. Kelby, *Orderly Book of De Lancey's Three*

Battalions, 59-60. Gilbert, "Changing Face of Military Justice," 80-84. A soldier condemned to die usually received a volley from a firing squad which consisted of members from his own unit.

[11] For the distinction between field and company-grade officers, see Robert K. Wright, Jr., *The Continental Army* (Washington, DC: Center of Military History, 1989), 436, 437, 439; Sylvia R. Frey, *The British Soldier in America: A Social History of Military Life in the Revolutionary Period* (Austin: University of Texas Press, 1981), 132; Kennett, *The French Armies*, 28; Stephen Conway, "'The great mischief Complain'd of': Reflections on the Misconduct of British Soldiers in the Revolutionary War," *William and Mary Quarterly* 47 (1990): 387-390; during the 1700's, French inns proscribed "dogs, lackeys, prostitutes or soldiers." Dederer, *War in America*, 92-93; Shy, *Toward Lexington*, 344, 349n83; Frey, "Courts and Cats," 8-9; Gilbert, "Regimental Courts Martial," 57, 66; Christopher Duffy, *The Military Experience in the Age of Reason* (New York: Atheneum, 1988), 95; officers were governed by a different set of codes and rules. See Arthur N. Gilbert, "Law and Honour Among Eighteenth-Century British Army Officers," *The Historical Journal* 19 (1976): 75-87; Bernard Berelson and Gary A. Steiner, *Human Behavior: An Inventory of Scientific Findings* (New York: Harcourt, Brace & World, 1964), 241-286, 365-380, 443-449; Martin van Creveld, *Command in War* (Cambridge: Harvard University Press, 1985), 1-11.

[12] Bernhard A. Uhlendorf, trans., *Revolution in America: Confidential Letters and Journals 1776-1784 of Adjutant General Major Baurmeister of the Hessian Forces* (Rutgers University Press, 1957), 21-22, 65, 95, 99-100, 124-125, 185, 284, 338-339, 363, 442; Royster, *A Revolutionary People*, 73; *The American Journal of Ambrose Serle, Secretary to Lord Howe 1776-1778*, ed. Edward H. Tatum, Jr. (San Marino, California: Huntington Library, 1940), 72, 74, 77, 86-87, 175, 198, 245-246; Frey, "Courts and Cats," 8-9.

[13] Uhlendorf, *Revolution in America*, 21-22; *Journal of Serle*, 176. Marauding and the quest for spoils could alienate the population. For a discussion of the ramifications of these activities, see the next chapter.

Contrary to popular belief, criminals and other "scum of the earth" did *not* make up the majority of the rank and file in the British Army. For that reason, one just cannot simply dismiss plundering as the activities of such disreputable individuals. See Frey, *The British Soldier in America*, 6-7, 13, 16, 72-74, 111; also consult Stephen R. Conway,

"The Recruitment of Criminals into the British Army, 1775-81," *Bulletin of the Institute of Historical Research* 58 (May 1985): 46-58.

[14] Emphasis added. George A. Rawlyk, *Yankees at Louisbourg* (Orono: University of Maine Press, 1967), 39, 142.

[15] Ibid., 150, 155-156; for another example of problems arising over plunder, see Sir Henry Clinton, *Memorandums, etc. etc., Respecting The Unprecedented Treatment Which the Army Have Met With Respecting Plunder Taken After A Siege, And of Which Plunder The Navy Serving With The Army Divided Their More Than Ample Share, Now Fourteen Years Since* (London, 1794). The bone of contention seems to have been Rebel ships and merchandise surrendered at Charles Town in May 1780.

[16] Royster, *A Revolutionary People*, 74; in late 1757, French troops called the commander of the Army of the Lower Rhine *Pere la maraude*. Kennett, *French Armies*, 44-45, 83-84; Claude C. Sturgill, "The French Army in Rousillon, 1716-1720" and Lawrence E. Babits, "Greene's Strategy in the Southern Campaign, 1780-1781," both in Maarten Uhltee, ed., *Adapting to Conditions: War and Society in the Eighteenth Century* (The University of Alabama Press, 1986), 16-25, 135-149; Reed Browning, *The War of the Austrian Succession* (New York: St. Martin's Press, 1993), 8, 136, 189, 289, 291-292, 319-320, 376; Peter Paret, "The Relationship Between the Revolutionary War and European Military Thought and Practice in the Second Half of the Eighteenth Century," in Don Higginbotham, ed., *Reconsiderations on the Revolutionary War: Selected Essays* (Westport, Connecticut: Greenwood Press, 1978), 144-157; Frey, "Courts and Cats," 9; for British supply problems during the war, see R. Arthur Bowler's excellent *Logistics and the Failure of the British Army in America, 1775-1783* (Princeton University Press, 1975).

[17] Knox, *An Historical Journal*, 2:246nl; Dederer, *War in America*, 100. *A Letter from Lieut. Gen. Sir Henry Clinton, K.B. To the Commissioners of Public Accounts, Relative to Some Observations in their Seventh Report, Which may be judged to imply Censure on the late Commanders in Chief of His Majesty's Army in North America* (London: J. Debrett, 1784), 18-19.

[18] In August 1777 near Elk River, Maryland, General Howe himself found some troops pillaging local homes. A few he had hanged on the spot while the others were flogged "within an inch of their lives." Uhlendorf, *Revolution in America*, 95, 99-100.

[19] It is interesting to note that most of the cases in this orderly book dealing with marauding were heard before a GCM. De Lancey's Brigade was stationed on Long Island, New York during this period. Kelby, *Orderly Book of De Lancey's Three Battalions*, 5, 9, 21, 28.

[20] *Ibid.*, 34-35, 39, 50, 85, 89, 94, 99, 110-111.

[21] A subaltern was a company-grade officer below the rank of captain, such as a lieutenant, ensign, or cornet. A typical English company during wartime had one captain, one lieutenant, one ensign or cornet, three sergeants, three corporals, two musicians, and fifty-six privates. Three of the last were actually "contingent men," fictitious names carried on the rolls. Their pay was used to care for the regiment's orphans and widows. Wright, *The Continental Army*, 48-49, 439.

[22] A. R. Newsome, "A British Orderly Book, 1780-1781," *North Carolina Historical Review* 9 (1932): 60, 164.

[23] *Ibid.*

[24] *Ibid.*, 165, 289-290, 296-297.

[25] The troops should not bear the sole blame. As in all armies of the time, camp followers—bat men or servants, sutlers, soldiers's wives and companions, plus occasional prostitutes—committed a large share of the depredations. *Ibid.*, 366, 368-369, 370, 377-379, 381.

[26] Ferguson's detailed plan is found in Howard H. Peckham, ed., *Sources of American Independence: Selected Manuscripts from the Collections of the William L. Clements Library*, 2 vols. (Chicago and London: University of Chicago Press, 1978), 2:336-342.

[27] Ferguson claimed that "the necessity of our wants would reconcile them to as unavoidable." *Ibid.*, 2:339-342; other royal officers had similar plans to stem pillaging. See Uhlendorf, *Revolution in America*, 102; Newsome, "A British Orderly Book," 297, 366, 377-379; the Rebel armies had their own problem with marauders. See the individual cases of James Carey, David Hall, Jonathan Young and others in Neagles, *Summer Soldiers*, 98, 151, 280.

[28] For the quote, see John S. Pancake, *This Destructive War: The British Campaign in the Carolinas, 1780-1782* (Tuscaloosa: University of Alabama Press, 1985), 217; two out of every ten American soldiers deserted from Washington's army. Ferling, *A Wilderness of Miseries*, 109; Neagles, *Summer Soldiers*, 69, 99, 150, 200, 249, 280; Lord Rawdon, commander of the Volunteers of Ireland, became so exasperated with desertion that he issued a harsh manifesto to halt it. He ordered that any civilian found aiding a deserter would be flogged and deported to the West Indies. He also placed a bounty on each runaway—ten guineas for his head, but only five if the culprit was brought in alive. Rawdon's superiors did not find this decree too appealing and had him rescind it. See Rawdon to Major Rugeley, Camden, July 1, 1780, and Rawdon to Cornwalllis, December 5, 1780, both in Colonial Office Records, PRO, 5/101, 283-284, 413. The Volunteers of Ireland reportedly consisted of deserters from the American army. William B. Willcox, ed., *The American Rebellion: Sir Henry Clinton's Narrative of His Campaigns, 1775-1782, With an Appendix of Original Documents* (New Haven: Yale University Press, 1954), 110-111. Pulaski's Legion contained many German prisoners of war taken at Saratoga, New York in 1777. Leszek Szymanski, *Casimir Pulaski: A Hero of the American Revolution* (1979; repr., New York: Hippocrene Books, 1994), 188-189.

[29] For POWs, see Betsey Knight, "Prisoner Exchange and Parole in the American Revolution," *William and Mary Quarterly* 48 (1991): 201-222, and Catherine Prelinger, "Benjamin Franklin and American Prisoners of War in England during the American Revolution," *William and Mary Quarterly* 32 (1975): 261-294; Pancake, *This Destructive War*, 107; see the case of American deserter Michael Docherty in Alexander Garden, *Anecdotes of the Revolutionary War in America, With Sketches of Character of Persons the Most Distinguished, in the Southern States, For Civil and Military Services* (Charleston: A.E. Miller, 1822), 396-398; the British many times sent deserters to garrison remote, disease-ridden posts such as Gibraltar and those in the West Indies. See Uhlendorf, *Revolution in America*, 77; Frey, *The British Soldier in America*, 72-73, 185n105; McGuffie, *Siege of Gibraltar*, 82; the depredations of the notorious Chasseurs Britanniques, a regiment formed from French deserters during the Napoleonic wars, are well recounted in the *Washington National Intelligencer*, July 5, 1813; also consult Jac Weller, *Wellington in the Peninsula 1808-1814* (Nicholas Vane, 1962). This British regiment participated in the June 1813 raid on Hampton, Virginia during the War of 1812.

30 The possible fate awaiting deserters if caught may very well have contributed to the stubborn nature of the fighting in the southern campaigns. Pancake, *This Destructive War*, 217; the execution of the five unfortunates is found in McCardell, *Ill-Starred General*, 98; a similar situation is found in Kennett, *French Armies*, 83.

31 Gilbert, "The Changing Face of British Military Justice," 83; Gilbert, "British Military Justice," 31-32; Thomas J. Fleming, *Now We Are Enemies: The Story of Bunker Hill* (New York: St. Martin's Press, 1960), 200-201; in October 1768, Maj. Gen. Thomas Gage had a deserter named Ames shot on Boston Commons. He then ordered all the regiments in the garrison to file past the corpse, just in case anyone missed the point. Shy, *Toward Lexington*, 153, 164, 307-308, 362-363, 413.

32 Stephen Conway, "To Subdue America: British Army Officers and the Conduct of the Revolutionary War," *William and Mary Quarterly* 43 (1986): 395. For the traditional interpretation, see Walter B. Edgar, *Partisans and Redcoats: The Southern Conflict That Turned the Tide of the American Revolution* (New York: William Morrow, 2001) and John Buchanan, *The Road to Guilford Courthouse: The American Revolution in the Carolinas* (New York: Wiley, 1997). Edgar and Buchanan also repeat the usual unsubstantiated stories about Tarleton and the Legion.

33 A vidette was a mounted sentry. Anthony J. Scotti, Jr., "'This Disagreeable Exertion of Authority': Banastre Tarleton and the British Legion in the Southern Campaigns, 1780-1781" (MA thesis, Wake Forest University, 1991), 58-59.

34 *Ibid.*; the *Orderly Book of Captain [Thomas] Scott's Company of the British Legion* is in the Andre de Coppet Collection at Princeton University Library. However, this volume only covers the early years of the company, before Captain Scott resigned his commission and the regiment went South. A Captain John B. Scott is listed in Murtie June Clark, *Loyalists in the American Southern Campaign of the Revolutionary War*, 3 vols. (Baltimore: Genealogical Publishing Company, 1981), 3:379.

35 Gilbert, "Law and Honour," 75-87; Tarleton to Cornwallis, August 5, 1780, Leneu's Ferry, Cornwallis Papers, PRO, 30/11/63, ff. 19-21;

Tarleton, *History of the Campaigns*, 100. Major James Craig, the commanding officer on John's Island, SC, had a sergeant of the British Legion executed for plundering. He made an example of the Legionnaire in order to "check so violent a breach of good order and discipline." Major General Alexander Leslie to Sir Henry Clinton, camp near Charles Town, January 29, 1782, Carleton Papers, the Royal Institution of Great Britain, vol. 23, No. 52, 6pp. (microfilm) (hereafter cited as Carleton Papers); Berelson and Steiner, *Human Behavior*, 374-380; Van Creveld, *Command in War*, 5-9, 16, 274-275; John Keegan, *The Mask of Command* (New York: Viking, 1987), 1-11.

[36] Conway, "'The great mischief Complain'd of,'" 388-390; Frey, *The British Soldier in America*, 111, 132; Berelson and Steiner, *Human Behavior*, 241-286, 374-380, 442-449; Keegan, *The Mask of Command*, 10-11; "I should wish to have as many of the Militia as possible sent to Colonel Tarleton. If anybody can put spirit into them he will." Lord Cornwallis to Colonel John Harris Cruger, November 25, 1780, Wynnesborough, in Robert D. Bass, *The Green Dragoon: The Lives of Banastre Tarleton and Mary Robinson* (New York: Henry Holt, 1957) 123; at Gloucester Point, the uhlans or lancers of Lauzun's Legion almost killed the young Englishman before his men arrived. Tarleton's Legion also exhibited a profound sense of loyalty at the Waxhaws in May 1780. Tarleton, *History of the Campaigns*, 30-31, 377. Also see *Memoirs of the Duc de Lauzun*, trans. C. K. Scott Moncrieff (London: George Routledge and Sons, 1928), 207-208.

[37] Cornwallis to Tarleton, Winnsboro, November 13, 1780, 30/11/82, ff. 37-38; Lt. Col. George Turnbull to Cornwallis, Camden, November 12, 1780, 30/11/4, ff. 102-103; Tarleton to Cornwallis, Daniels Plantation, December 26, 1780, 30/11/4, ff. 404-405; Tarleton to Cornwallis, Woodwards, December 14, 1780, 30/11/4, ff. 325-326, all in the Cornwallis Papers, PRO.

[38] Lieut. Col. J. G. Simcoe, *A History of the Operations of a Partisan Corps Called the Queen's Rangers* (New York, 1844; repr., New York: New York Times and Arno Press, 1968), 37-38; Uhlendorf, *Revolution in America*, 139.

[39] Cornwallis to Tarleton, Winnsboro, November 8, 1780, Cornwallis Papers, Pro, 30/11/82, ff. 10-11.

[40] Tarleton, *History of the Campaigns*, 38.

[41] *Ibid.*, 290.

[42] Emphasis added. Tarleton to Cornwallis, Daniels Plantation, December 26, 1780, Cornwallis Papers, PRO, 30/11/4, ff. 404-405.

[43] *Diary of Lieut. Anthony Allaire, of Ferguson's Corps* in Lyman C. Draper, *King's Mountain and Its Heroes: History of the Battle of King's Mountain, October 7th, 1780, and the Events Which Led To It* (Cincinnati: Peter G. Thomson, 1881), 491. James Ferguson, *Two Scottish Soldiers, a Soldier of 1688 and Blenheim, a Soldier of the American Revolution and a Jacobite Laird and His Forbears* (Aberdeen: D. Wyllie and Son, 1888), 79. This story is repeated in Bass, *The Green Dragoon*, 74-75. The plantation in question was Fair Lawn and it belonged to Sir John Colleton.

[44] The amorous adventures of young Banastre Tarleton are well noted in Bass, *The Green Dragoon*, 37-41 and Sir George Otto Trevelyan, *The American Revolution*, 3 vols. (New York: Longmans, Green, and Company: 1898-1907), 3:281, 285; most officers felt very strongly about rape and would impose the harshest penalty upon the perpetrators. Few if any would ignore sexual assaults on local women as did Lord Francis Rawdon on Staten Island in September 1776. He dismissed the victims as "so little accustomed to these vigorous methods that they don't bear them with the proper resignation." However, out of all fairness to Rawdon, this may have been a poor attempt at a crude joke because he later enforced strict discipline among his troops in the South. Conway, "To Subdue America," 394-95; Kelby, *Orderly Book of De Lancey's Three Battalions*, 86; *Letters of Eliza Wilkinson*, ed. Caroline Gilman (New York, 1839; repr., New York: New York Times and Arno Press, 1969), 30; Richard A. Gabriel, *To Serve With Honor: A Treatise on Military Ethics and the Way of the Soldier* (Westport, Connecticut: Greenwood Press, 1982), 29, 150, 154-174, 227.

[45] Tarleton, *History of the Campaigns*, 172; Francis Marion to General Gates, Benbow's Ferry, November 26, 1780, in *The Papers of the Continental Congress: 1774-1789*, comp. John Butler (Washington, DC: US Government Printing Office, 1978) M247, reel 174, i154, vol. 2: 334 (microfilm) (hereafter cited as *PCC*); "Letters of John Rutledge," ed. Joseph Barnwell, *The South Carolina Historical and Genealogical Magazine*

18 (1917): 44; the Legion commandant did *not* exhume the corpse of General Richardson as Robert Bass and others claim. *The Green Dragoon*, 110-111.

[46] Bass made this very perceptive point. *The Green Dragoon*, 111; André's involvement in the Benedict Arnold conspiracy is well known. He met the fate of a spy on October 2, 1780. See Willcox, *The American Rebellion*, 457-466.

[47] Tarleton to Turnbull, near Singletons, November 5, 1780, Cornwallis Papers, PRO, 30/11/4. ff. 63-64.

[48] Tarleton to the Duke of York, Richmond, September 28, 1801, in Bass, *The Green Dragoon*, 407; Garden, *Anecdotes of the Revolutionary War in America*, 396-398, 409. In 1780-1781, a Legion court martial gave one thousand stripes to a deserter named Wade from Rocky Mount, NC. He died under the lash. Docherty never explained how he avoided being executed for desertion. One theory is that desertion had become so rampant that the junior officers simply ignored his transgression. They might have sympathized too with his plight and quietly re-admitted him into the ranks. The fact that recruits were getting scarce may have also played a role. It is interesting to note that Docherty was wounded each time he was taken prisoner. The dates of his enlistment in the British Legion (September 3, 1780) and his subsequent capture at the Cowpens (officially reported on February 23, 1781) are verified in Muster Rolls of Captain Donald McPherson's Company, British Legion, Infantry, from October 25, 1780 to December 24, 1780, and from October 25, 1781 to December 24, 1781. See PRO 30/55, Doc. 10253 and Loyalist Regiment Muster Rolls, 1777-1783, Public Archives of Canada, Ottawa, Ontario, RG8I "C" Series, Vol. 1884 (hereafter cited as PAC); for other Legion deserters, see Lewis Nicola to J. Jay, July 10, 1779, *PCC*, M247, reel 180, i163, p.72 (microfilm).

[49] Ferguson gave the man who wounded him some money as a reward for his sense of duty. Commending the man's spirit, he said: "We should have known our friends sooner from their mode of attack." Ferguson, *Two Scottish Soldiers*, 76-77. *Diary of Lieut. Anthony Allaire*, in Draper, *King's Mountain*, 485-486.

[50] Blackwell P. Robinson, ed., *The Revolutionary War Sketches of William R. Davie* (Raleigh: North Carolina Department of Cultural Resources, Division of Archives and History, 1976), 21-26; Major George Hanger, in command of the Legion at Charlotte, deemed it "a trifling insignificant skirmish," but admitted he should have sent the infantry in first to clear the town. Major George Hanger, *An Address to the Army; in Reply to Strictures, by Roderick M'Kenzie (Late Lieutenant in the 71st Regiment) on Tarleton's History of the Campaigns of 1780 and 1781* (London: James Ridgway, 1789), 55-58; Franklin and Mary Wickwire, *Cornwallis: The American Adventure* (Boston: Houghton Mifflin Company, 1970), 198-199.

[51] The "inspiration" quote is from M. F. Treacy, *Prelude to Yorktown: The Southern Campaign of Nathanael Greene, 1780-1781* (Chapel Hill: University of North Carolina Press, 1963), 45. The Cornwallis quote can be found in Bass, *The Green Dragoon*, 107; Tarleton, *History of the Campaigns*, 159; Hanger received a wound in the Charlotte affair. Hanger, *An Address to the Army*, 54.

[52] Tarleton, *History of the Campaigns*, 210-222; at the Battle of Hobkirk's Hill, South Carolina on April 25, 1781, the First Maryland, a crack Continental unit, broke and fled for no apparent reason. Christopher Ward, *The War of the Revolution*, 2 vols. (New York: Macmillan, 1952), 2:806; Richard A. Gabriel, *The Painful Field: The Psychiatric Dimension of Modern War* (Westport, Connecticut: Greenwood Press, 1988), 1-2, 7, 13-14, 21, 31-32, 63; a soldier's battle efficiency reaches a peak after three to five months of combat experience; it inevitably decreases thereafter. Berelson and Steiner, *Human Behavior*, 266-286, 446, 448-449.

[53] Treacy, *Prelude to Yorktown*, 98.

[54] Original emphasis. Tarleton, *History of the Campaigns*, 225-226; Burke Davis, *The Cowpens-Guilford Courthouse Campaign* (Philadelphia: J. B. Lippincott Company, 1962), 89-91.

[55] Tarleton, *History of the Campaigns*, 375; Scammell's close ties to Washington and former position as Adjutant General made his death all the more shocking. James Thacher, *Military Journal of the American Revolution, From the Commencement to the Disbanding of the American Army; Comprising a Detailed Account of the Principal Events and Battles of the*

Revolution, With Their Exact Dates, And a Biographical Sketch of the most Prominent Generals (Hartford, Connecticut, 1862; repr., New York: New York Times and Arno Press, 1969), 289-291.

[56] *The Writings of Thomas Jefferson: Being His Autobiography, Correspondence, Reports, Messages, Addresses, And Other Writings, Official and Private*, ed. H. A. Washington, 9 vols. (Washington, DC: Taylor and Maury, 1853-1854), 2:425-426. The Legion officer's name was McLeod. Jefferson managed to escape capture by fleeing his home just minutes before the Legion detachment arrived.

[57] Dann, *The Revolution Remembered*, 202.

[58] Henry Lee, *Memoirs of the War in the Southern Department of the United States*, 2 vols. (Philadelphia and New York: Bradford & Inskeep & Inskeep and Bradford, 1812), 1:283-284. The deaths of other "harmless youths" at the hands of British legionnaires have grown out of this incident. For the peaceful Quaker boy shot down in his own front yard, see George F. Scheer and Hugh F. Rankin, *Rebels and Redcoats* (Cleveland and New York: World Publishing Company, 1957), 402. The murder of pious William Strong as "he trudged along with his Bible under his arm" is attributed to a Legion detachment commanded by Captain Christian Huck. The story of this young man's death is found in Bass, *The Green Dragoon*, 88. Both stories are very suspect and probably the results of good old Yankee propaganda.

[59] The basis of the massacre story is a letter by Dr. Robert Brownfield to William Dobien James. It reads in part:

> The demand for quarters, seldom refused to a vanquished foe, was at once found to be in vain; —not a man was spared—and it was the concurrent testimony of all the survivors, that for fifteen minutes after every man was prostrate. They went over the ground plunging their bayonets into every one that exhibited any signs of life, and in some instances, where several had fallen one over the other, these monsters were seen to throw off on the point of the bayonet the uppermost, to come at those beneath...

The missive is located in William Dobein James, A.M., *A Sketch of the Life of Brig. Gen. Francis Marion and a History of His Brigade From Its*

Rise in June 1780 until Disbanded in December, 1782 With Descriptions of Characters and Scenes Not Heretofore Published (Charleston, 1821; repr., Marietta, Georgia: Continental Book Company, 1948), Appendix, pp.1-7.

The similarity of early Waxhaws accounts is quite remarkable and has helped to perpetuate the massacre myth. See for instance the following histories: David Ramsay, *The History of the Revolution of South-Carolina, From a British Province to an Independent State*, 2 vols. (Trenton: Isaac Collins, 1785), 2:109-110; William Gordon, *The History of the Rise, Progress, and Establishment, of the Independence of the United States of America: Including an Account of the Late War; and of the Thirteen Colonies, From Their Origin to that Period*, 4 vols. (London: Charles Dilly and James Buckland, 1788), 3:360-361; John Lendrum, *A Concise and Impartial History of the American Revolution. To Which is Prefixed, a General History of North and South America. Together with an Account of the Discovery and Settlement of North America, and a View of the Progress, Character, and Political State of the Colonies previous to the Revolution*, 2 vols. (Boston: I. Thomas and E.T. Andrews, 1795), 2:289-290; John Marshall, *The Life of George Washington, Commander in Chief of the American Forces, During the War Which Established the Independence of His Country, and First President of the United States*, 5 vols. (Philadelphia: C.P. Wayne, 1804-1807; repr., Fredericksburg, Virginia: Citizens' Guild of Washington's Boyhood Home, 1926), 3:179-181; Abiel Holmes, *The Annals of America, From the Discovery by Columbus in the Year 1492, to the Year 1826*, 2 vols. (Cambridge: Hilliard and Brown, 1829), 2:309.

[60] Tarleton, *History of the Campaigns*, 27; J. Tracy Power, "'The Virtue of Humanity Was Totally Forgot': Buford's Massacre, May 29, 1780," *South Carolina Historical Magazine*, 93 (January 1992): 5-7. Buford's troops included members of the First, Second, and Third Virginia Regiments and the First and Second Virginia Detachments. A unit of Lt. Col. William Washington's Third Continental Dragoons also accompanied Buford's command. For the Virginia units, see *The Orderly Book of Captain Benjamin Taliaferro 2d Virginia Detachment Charleston, South Carolina, 1780*, ed. Lee A. Wallace, Jr. (Richmond: Virginia State Library, 1980), 5-6, 8-9, 12, 16, 18, 24, 108-109, 155. In late April 1780, Buford was at Nelson's Ferry on the Santee River, about thirty miles from Orangeburg, South Carolina.

[61] The British troops included 130 cavalry and one hundred mounted infantry of Tarleton's Legion plus forty troopers from the Seventeenth

Light Dragoons. A three-pounder cannon also accompanied this detachment. Tarleton, *History of the Campaigns*, 25, 27-29, 83.

[62] *Ibid.*, 28-29, 77-78.

[63] No matter how absurd it may seem today, proper etiquette in warfare was very important to the eighteenth-century military. The ramifications of not accepting a surrender offer can be seen with the slaughter of the American garrison at Fort Griswold, New London, Connecticut, on September 6, 1781. Frances M. Caulkins, *History of New London, Connecticut: From the First Survey of the Coast in 1612, to 1852* (New London: Press of Case, Tiffany and Company, 1852), 545-570. The British took the fort on the third attempt and after suffering heavy casualties, including three officers killed and three wounded. They then burned New London as well as Groton. Browning, *The War of the Austrian Succession*, 319-320; Greg Novak, *A Guide to the American War of Independence in the North*, Campaign Book #7A (Champaign, Illinois: Ulster Imports, 1990), 116-117. The American garrison at Charles Town was refused the honors of war (leaving with flags flying, drums playing a proper march, etc.) because as rebels, the Americans were not true belligerents. Gregory D. Massey, "A Hero's Life: John Laurens and the American Revolution" (Ph.D. diss., University of South Carolina, 1992), 468-469. In July 1776, Washington refused to receive some dispatches from General Howe because they did not acknowledge his military rank. They were addressed to "George Washington, Esquire." Henry Steele Commager and Richard B. Morris, eds., *The Spirit of 'Seventy-Six: The Story of the American Revolution as told by Participants*, 2 vols. (Indianapolis and New York: Bobbs-Merrill Company, 1958), 1:426-428.

[64] Tarleton, *History of the Campaigns*, 29-30; Power, "'The Virtue of Humanity,'" 8.

[65] Duffy, *The Military Experience*, 215, 222-224, 228. The strength and weight of a horseman was counterbalanced by the infantryman being crammed into a given frontage. While cavalry ranks had at least three foot files (or spaces between men in line), infantry lines had only two foot files. In addition, a six-foot long musket with bayonet had a better reach than a three foot sword. Nevertheless, neither of these factors mattered at the Waxhaws because the American line was so thin and

the raw recruits among its ranks could not effectively halt the horsemen once they broke through.

⁶⁶ Duffy, *Military Experience*, 215; Gabriel, *The Painful Field*, 1-2, 31-32; Ofer Zur, "The Psychohistory of Warfare: The Co-Evolution of Culture, Psyche and Enemy," *Journal of Peace Research* 24 (1987): 125-134.

⁶⁷ Duffy, *Military Experience*, 215.

⁶⁸ Gabriel, *The Painful Field*, 1-2, 30.

⁶⁹ John Keegan, *The Face of Battle: A Study of Agincourt, Waterloo, and the Somme* (London: Penguin Books, 1978), 154; Tarleton, *History of the Campaigns*, 30-31, Power, "'The Virtue of Humanity,'" 8-10.

⁷⁰ Ramsay, *The History of the Revolution of South-Carolina*, 2:109-110; Brownfield letter in James, *A Sketch of the Life of Marion*, Appendix, 2-6.

⁷¹ Garden's *Anecdotes of the American Revolution, Illustrative of the Talents and Virtues of the Heroes and Patriots, Who Acted the Most Conspicuous Parts Therein* is not to be confused with his earlier work entitled *Anecdotes of the Revolutionary War in America, With Sketches of Character of Persons the Most Distinguished, in the Southern States, For Civil and Military Services* (Charleston: A.E. Miller, 1822). An adjutant was a staff officer who handled a regiment's daily paperwork and supervised guard and work details. Wright, *The Continental Army*, 435.

⁷² Garden, *Anecdotes of the American Revolution, Illustrative of the Talents...*, 138. This was a rather well-aimed stray shot. It is not beyond the realm of possiblity that one of Washington's dragoons did this out of revenge for Tarleton's earlier brutal attacks upon the Third Continentals at Monck's Corner and Lenud's Ferry. Ward, *War of the Revolution*, 2:701-703.

⁷³ Garden, *Anecdotes of the American Revolution, Illustrative of the Talents...*, 138.

⁷⁴ Tarleton, *History of the Campaigns*, 30-31. According to one expert, such behavior is indicative of "battle stress." Gabriel, *The Painful Field*, 13. For the "justice of the rank and file" during the raid on Lexington

and Concord, Massachusetts, see David Hackett Fischer, *Paul Revere's Ride*, (New York and Oxford: Oxford University Press, 1994), 258. British troops, enraged by American sniping, looted and burned homes along the line of retreat. Many civilians died in the rampage.

[75] The author has been to the Waxhaws battle site. Robert Middlekauff, "Why Men Fought in the American Revolution," *Huntington Library Quarterly* 43 (Spring 1980): 140-146; Armstrong Starkey appears to be influenced by American notions of virtue in his "Paoli to Stony Point: Military Ethics and Weaponry During the American Revolution," *Journal of Military History* 58 (January 1994): 7-27. His claims that the Americans exhibited higher moral standards in close combat are unconvincing. Whig involvement in the southern campaigns is proof enough to the contrary. Starkey's article on page 11 includes an excerpt from Mark Helprin's *A Soldier of the Great War* (1991), which given the discussion of the Waxhaws, is worth repeating:

> In bayonet training throughout the world, the soldier who wields the bayonet is ordered to scream as he drives the blade through. Civilians assume that the cry is meant to terrify the opponent, but it isn't. It's meant to bridge your natural reluctance to push a long blade into a living human being, and to cover the sound of steel cutting into flesh and bone. As dreadful as is the task, should your enemy be coming at you, you accomplish it so readily and remorselessly that, how can I describe it? It seems no more difficult or disturbing than say, lighting a match.

[76] Scotti, "'This Disagreeable Exertion of Authority,'" 64-65; Zur, "The Psychohistory of Warfare," 129-132; Starkey, "Paoli to Stony Point," 14-16. In a similar incident, the British soldiers at Fort Griswold claimed that they saw a white flag over the American ramparts long before the Rebels stopped firing. Caulkins, *History of New London, Connecticut*, 545-570.

Unlike in his MA thesis, the author here has decided not to explain this encounter between Legionnaire and Continental with a theory developed by the zoologist Heini Hediger. The author became interested with Hediger's theory of animal behavior after reading John Keegan's *The Face of Battle*. On pages 166-182, Keegan uses the hypothesis to justify some of the fighting at La Haye Sainte and

Hougoumont during the battle of Waterloo, June 18, 1815. According to Hediger, all animals are governed by the principle of *critical reaction*. If a threat of bodily harm is offered *beyond* a certain distance, the intended recipient will retire. If it is offered *within* a certain distance, the recipient will react violently. These distances are known as "flight distance" and "critical distance," respectively. After several inquiries, however, the author discovered that most zoologists disagree with the applicability of Hediger's theory to human beings. They assert that too many other variables are involved—number of enemy and friendly soldiers, morale, fatigue, ammunition supply, training, etc. Nevertheless, Keegan's use of Hediger's work is still very intriguing. Also see Keegan, *A History of Warfare* (New York: Alfred A. Knopf, 1993), 84.

The author is indebted to the staffs of Riverbanks Zoo and Garden, Columbia, South Carolina and the North Carolina Zoological Park at Asheboro, North Carolina for their comments on this subject. More on the critical reaction theory can be found in Heini Hediger, *The Psychology and Behavior of Animals in Zoos and Circuses*, trans. Geoffrey Sircom (New York: Dover Publications, 1968), and Heini Hediger, *Wild Animals in Captivity: An Outline of the Biology of Zoological Gardens*, trans. Geoffrey Sircom (New York: Dover Publications, 1964); Berelson and Steiner, *Human Behavior*, 663.

[77] Power, "'The Virtue of Humanity,'" 9-10; Tarleton, *History of the Campaigns*, 30; Keegan maintains that an "extra-specific" factor is at work in an encounter like this one. He suggests that men on horseback feel superior to and different from men on foot, and thus have less qualms about killing them out of hand. This superiority complex derives from the traditional and well known animosity between cavalrymen and infantrymen. In armies of the time, mounted troops frequently suppressed infantry mutinies. Keegan, *The Face of Battle*, 203. For the ethos of the man on horseback, see Winston Churchill to Lord Randolph Churchill, September 10 [1893], [53 Seymour Street], and Winston to Lady Randolph, May 1, [1894], Sandhurst, both in Randolph S. Churchill and Martin Gilbert, eds., *Winston S. Churchill*, 8 vols. (London: Heinemann, 1966-1988), 1:209-210, 226.

[78] What has contributed to the massacre story is that most of these wounded undoubtedly died. Until the twentieth century, the four big killers on any battlefield were shock and bleeding, tetanus, gas gangrene, and septicemia or blood poisoning. The last three would kill

80 to 100% of those infected within three to ten days. Given the primitive medical knowledge of the Revolutionary era, it does not seem likely that many of the American wounded from the Waxhaws survived a fortnight. See Richard Gabriel and Karen Metz, *From Sumer to Rome: The Military Capabilities of Ancient Armies* (New York: Greenwood Press, 1991), 97-99. Keegan, *A History of Warfare*, 361; Eric Carlton, *Massacres: An Historical Perspective* (Cambridge: Scolar Press, 1994), 4, 6, 177. Surgeons were sent for from Charlotte and Camden. Tarleton captured 2 wagons with ammunition and 26 others loaded with clothing, arms, cartridges, cartridge boxes, flints, and camp equipage. These were trophies to be brought back to Cornwallis, and carrying wounded Americans in the wagons would be a military mistake for several reasons: it would entail abandoning valuable materiel; it would take too much time; and it would have only called more attention to brutal British actions. See Tarleton, pp. 31-32, 84.

[79] Dr. Brownfield made special note of wounds received by Lieutenant Pearson, Ensign Cruit, and Captain John Stokes. James, *A Sketch of the Life of Marion*, Appendix, 3-6. American General Thomas Pinckney visited the Waxhaws wounded and asserted that they had on average sixteen wounds per man. Sgt. Mitchell carried the regimental colors at the battle and received mild treatment at the hands of Legion Captain David Kinloch. Garden, *Anecdotes of the American Revolution, Illustrative of the Talents...*, 139-140; Starkey, "Paoli to Stony Point," 15-16.

[80] "I have Cut Off'rs and Men to pieces." Tarleton, *History of the Campaigns*, 80-84; Stedman, a commissary in Cornwallis' army, had a personal vendetta against Tarleton. His comments about the younger man drip with sarcasm and are in response to Tarleton's postwar criticisms of the earl. Charles Stedman, *The History of the Origin, Progress, and Termination of the American War*, 2 vols. (London, 1794; repr., New York: New York Times and Arno Press, 1969), 2:193, 324-325.

[81] James, *A Sketch of the Life of Marion*, Appendix, 4; Ramsay, *The History of the Revolution of South-Carolina*, 2:110.

[82] Hence his nickname, "No-Flint" Grey. Ward, *War of the Revolution*, 1:358-359; Starkey, "Paoli to Stony Point," 7-9.

[83] At Old Tappan, New York, General Grey's force surprised some American dragoons under Lt. Col. George Baylor as they slept in three barns. The British bayoneted thirty-six and captured forty Rebels. Only thirty-seven managed to escape. Major Patrick Ferguson conducted the attack upon Little Egg Harbor, New Jersey. Like Paoli and Old Tappan, it was a night assault. Ferguson's men killed fifty of Pulaski's Legion and took five prisoners.

The fact that all three of the attacks occurred at night might have something to do with the high number of American casualties. Most night attacks during the Revolutionary War were exceptionally bloody. Ferguson observed of the Little Egg Harbor raid: "It being a night attack Little Quarter could be given." Ward, *War of the Revolution*, 2:616-618; Starkey, "Paoli to Stony Point," 7-8, 22, 26.

[84] Ward, *War of the Revolution*, 1:469n21; Starkey, "Paoli to Stony Point," 13-15.

CHAPTER VIII

Terror

Several stories concerning Lieutenant Colonel Banastre Tarleton are found in Alexander Garden's 1828 book on the American Revolution. One of them deals with the fate of a young boy at British headquarters in March 1781. Like the Laurens-Tarleton encounter described previously, this account is apocryphal, but interesting nonetheless.[1]

A few days before the Battle of Guilford Courthouse, British soldiers brought in a local youth for questioning. Asked about the location of the American army, he responded: "You will find it soon enough." The English officers assembled in the headquarters tent looked at each other, some of them amused at this display of youthful arrogance. However, Tarleton immediately became exasperated at the boy's impertinence and drawing his cavalry saber, cut off one of the lad's fingers. He then demanded: "Will you now tell me where is Greene?" The young American, "with [a] steady and undaunted countenance," replied: "You will know time enough." The British lieutenant colonel became even more angry and repeated his action, but with as little success. Three more times the question was posed, and three more fingers had to be removed by the lieutenant colonel of dragoons, "considered the pride of the army—its greatest ornament."[2]

This story is more than likely American propaganda. There is simply no way that any British officer could have perpetrated such a deed in front of his peers, especially Charles, Earl Cornwallis. Furthermore, there is no corroborative evidence to sustain Garden's claim. Like the stories of Mrs. Slocomb and others, it is a metaphor for the victory of American noble virtue over British brutal virtue. Nonetheless, no matter how fanciful the account may be, it is a good example of the use of terror to achieve some desired goal, in this case information.[3]

The fact that participants of the Revolutionary War in the South employed terror is well noted. Both Whig and Tory contributed to the violence, and it is not important who did what first.[4] However, the consistency of British terror and the extent of it are debatable. Moreover, Banastre Tarleton's role in the implementation of such a policy of terror needs clarification in order to dispel any myths.

A state of intense fear, or what can be called terror, undoubtedly existed in the Southern colonies prior to the royal invasion of 1780. Once the British Army appeared, the civil war between Tory and Whig escalated. Unfortunately, the British commander on the scene, Lieutenant General Charles Cornwallis, did not possess the necessary resources to deal with the situation.[5]

Lord Cornwallis (1738-1805) is one of the more interesting figures to come out the Revolutionary War. Sir George Otto Trevelyan described him as "an English aristocrat of the finest type...enlightened, tolerant and humane."[6] A courageous and magnanimous leader, he was a gentleman in the truest sense. He is best remembered for his defeat at York Town in 1781 and his later achievements as governor-general of India.[7]

However, Earl Cornwallis, simply by virtue of who he was, had no place in a civil war. One must empathize with the man, for he had a truly frustrating assignment. His natural inclination for compassion frequently conflicted with his appointed task of maintaining control and quelling the rebellion. His lordship discovered that to punish the disloyal and reward the faithful was not as simple as it seemed, especially in a civil war where loyalties were not easily discernible.[8]

Sir Henry Clinton wrote of the need "to gain the hearts & subdue the minds of America."[9] Unlike European wars fought earlier in the eighteenth century, the Revolutionary War demanded that military strategists pay close attention to popular sentiment. The democratic practices of the colonial governments allowed common Americans to have a say in most matters affecting their lives. A long-established militia organization even enhanced their ability for direct involvement. "These distinctive features of American life ensured that the war was less a struggle for territory on the European model than a contest for the political allegiance of the people."[10]

Unfortunately for the British, their cause had lost the battle over popular sentiment by 1780.[11] Furthermore, Lord Cornwallis had only a vague notion on how to suppress the revolutionaries. He realized that something had to be done to punish the Rebels. On September 24, 1780, he wrote to a subordinate:

> I am clearly of opinion, that in a civil war there is no admitting of neutral characters, & that those who are not clearly with us, must be so far considered against us, as to be disarmed, and every measure taken to prevent their being able to do mischief.[12]

Yet, the earl's humane nature made him inconsistent in this regard, and he would many times not follow through with his threats. As a result, he sent an ambiguous message to friend and foe alike.[13]

The British campaign to subdue the southern colonies has been compared by one historian to William T. Sherman's march through the same area eighty-four years later. Although not as systematic as that of the Union commander, the march of Cornwallis was nonetheless devastating. The earl certainly saw nothing wrong with the destruction of plantations found to have caches of arms and ammunition. Nevertheless, he did not tolerate looting.[14]

Part of the earl's problem had to do with plundering. As discussed in the previous chapter, some plundering was considered justifiable. Nevertheless, the civilian population did not always understand. As early as January 1777, a British official noted that Whig newspapers had turned the poor conduct of royal troops to their own benefit.[15] Another contemporary asserted that plundering did "infinitely more to maintain the rebellion than to smother it."[16]

Patrick Ferguson realized that wanton plundering could have a detrimental effect. It not only hurt the discipline of the army, but terrorized the loyal members of the population and alienated them. Nevertheless, he asserted that the homes of all rebel civil magistrates and soldiers should be plundered in an orderly manner. "By this means the soldier would at times be gratified by a just booty without hurting discipline." As a result, two goals would be achieved—the halt of indiscriminate plunder and the punishment of active and virulent Rebels.[17]

Like all army commanders, Earl Cornwallis knew that his men plundered local areas for foodstuffs. The sad but unavoidable acts of war he could tolerate somewhat. The senseless pillaging of homes, however, disturbed him greatly because such activity added to the sense of terror in the region and was politically counterproductive. In July 1780, he wrote a letter Lieutenant Colonel Thomas Brown, warning him to keep a better eye on his soldiers. Near the end of the letter, he appealed to the man's sense of honor: "I never entertained a doubt of your performing with the utmost zeal, your duty to your king and country."[18]

Justifiable plundering was in essence a form of limited terror. It acted as a warning, giving the disloyal faction of the population a taste of things to come. Cornwallis felt that it was beneficial overall, just as he regarded out-and-out punishment of rebellious activity. A month after the above correspondence, following a small uprising near Camden, South Carolina, Cornwallis had his aide-de-camp pen this letter to two field commanders. Lieutenant Haldane wrote:

> His Lordship desires that you will most rigidty (*sic*) put in execution his orders relative to the treatment of the persons concerned in this last general revolt, but if these should be many of the description ordered to be hanged, you will be pleased to execute several of the ringleaders and detain the others in prison until Lord Cornwallis's pleasure is known.[19]

Even then, his lordship had an inconsistent approach to limited terror. His compassion frequently tempered his stern side. For instance, as he led the Thirty-Third Foot through the small town of Darby, Pennsylvania on November 18, 1777, Rebel snipers fired out of a house and killed his sergeant major. The troops then entered the dwelling and bayoneted everyone inside.[20] However, several years later in South Carolina, English troops under Cornwallis captured three rebel militiamen who had previously taken the oath of allegiance to the crown. Sentenced to death, they received a last-minute pardon from Cornwallis. Given such inconsistent behavior, it is not difficult to see why a Loyalist would become disgusted with the British, while a Rebel would mock royal authority and become less intimidated.[21]

More of this ambivalence became apparent during the Virginia operations. In June 1781, the British Army under Cornwallis encamped for ten days at Thomas Jefferson's residence at Elk Hill. The troops consumed all the livestock and confiscated thirty slaves. Upon leaving, the earl had not only the house burnt, but also the fences and all the unharvested crops. Furthermore, the soldiers "carried off all the horses capable of service; of those too young for service [they] cut the throats." The plantation was rendered "an absolute waste." As the house commanded a view of the entire area, the British general "must have seen every fire." Moreover, Jefferson asserted that Cornwallis treated the rest of the neighborhood in a similar manner, "but not with that spirit of total extermination with which he seemed to rage over my possessions." Undoubtedly, Thomas Jefferson fell into Major Ferguson's classification of an "active and virulent" Rebel.[22]

The revolutionaries pounced upon anything which undermined the British position in this civil war. They would eagerly transmit not only reports of battles, but also rumors of marauding and tales of murder. Exaggerations and outright lies became commonplace.[23] The Americans also made the most of Cornwallis's ambivalent stance on the use of terror. In the summer of 1780, they intercepted a British dispatch courier and published two letters which had a profound effect upon British efforts in the South.

One missive pertained to the treatment of deserters. On July 1, 1780, the commanding officer at Camden wrote Henry Rugeley, a colonel of Loyalist militia. In this letter, Lord Francis Rawdon promised to whip, imprison, or deport anyone found aiding and abetting deserters. Also, he placed a ten guinea bounty on the head of any deserter from his own regiment, the Volunteers of Ireland. Five guineas would be given for a live deserter.[24]

Rawdon had his orders read to all the militia companies under his command. Along with some other officers, he made up this manifesto in order to "act upon the fears and prejudices of the vulgar." He intended his bluff to frighten the populace and would-be deserters, but he had no real intention of ever carrying it out. Lord Rawdon knew he had no authority to deport civilians to the West Indies. Moreover, he certainly could not encourage them to stalk and kill royal soldiers. Cornwallis quickly had the younger officer repeal his orders, but the damage had already been done. In the long run, this letter as well as the second one had a damaging effect.[25]

Unlike Rawdon's decree, Cornwallis's August 18, 1780 letter to Lieutenant Colonel John Harris Cruger was not meant for public consumption. In the course of the letter, his lordship stated that it was necessary to punish with the "greatest rigour" those who broke their oath of allegiance to the crown. They would be imprisoned while their property was destroyed or given to plundered Loyalists. Furthermore, any militiaman who served with the British Army and then defected to the enemy would be hanged.[26]

While Cornwallis's orders were harsh but not entirely unjust, the Rebels used them to their advantage. There is substantial evidence which suggests that they altered this document until it "breathed wanton oppression." First, they changed the recipient's name to Lieutenant Colonel Nisbet Balfour, a regular British officer. Cruger was a Loyalist who commanded a battalion in De Lancey's Brigade. This letter would be more effective if a regular officer could be made to appear brutal. Second, the forgers took the harshest sounding parts out of context and thereby changed an almost casual letter into an official and methodical statement of British policy.[27]

George Washington himself received the two letters and made a direct complaint to Sir Henry Clinton in New York. Nathanael Greene also voiced his outrage to Lord Cornwallis. Overall, the whole business damaged the British cause in the South. By trying to scare the Rebels with words, Rawdon and Cornwallis gained local and undeserved reputations for cruelty. Many Rebels became more adamant in their stance while some neutrals finally decided to back the revolution. Consequently, pacification became difficult to maintain.[28]

It can be argued that terror is most effective when it is inconsistently employed. By not always following the same course of action and punishing your enemies, you confuse them and undermine their resolve. The Mongols exhibited this during their invasion of Europe in the thirteenth century. However, beyond a certain point terror is not required to maintain domination. The "trick," as it may be termed, is to know when terror becomes excessive and is no longer necessary.[29]

During the British campaigns in the South, there was no discernible moment because the violence continually fed upon itself. It was not an easy situation to confront, just as Union General Ulysses S. Grant discovered during his operations in western Tennessee in the summer of 1862. In his attempt to suppress secessionist activity, Grant employed the traditional yet unwritten rules of war. They stipulated that armies of occupation must respect the persons and property of civilians. In turn, all communities were responsible for the actions of their members, and the occupying army could inflict punishment on any community which did not demonstrate respect. "Armies which did not make war on civilians must not themselves be warred on by civilians."[30]

Part of this equation is, of course, the common soldier. Many times during the Revolutionary War he acted on his own initiative. Ingrained habits of obedience and discipline in the ranks did not necessarily compel all enlisted personnel to respect the property of their enemies. Poorly disciplined individuals represented a problem in all armies. Another factor in this situation is the sense of "otherness," especially in a civil war where Whig and Tory saw each other as less than human. The populace as well as the physical environment often appeared to British soldiers not only hostile but deserving of rough treatment. Hard war was not necessarily inevitable, but as the fighting progressed many commanders naturally became more numb to the violence and more ruthless in outlook. Enlisted men, sensing this directly from their company-grade officers, oftentimes implemented their own retaliatory policy.[31]

In 1780-1781, the gentleman's war was over in America. By that time, the conciliatory group among British officers had lost its voice. The achievements of this group were only ephemeral. In the civil war raging in the South, the "fire and sword" element among royal officers held sway. A low regard for colonists, deep aversion to rebellion, frustration over guerrilla warfare and the conflict's duration, desire for vengeance, plus simple anger all played a role in increasing the number of hard-liners. Granted, there existed no concerted policy of destruction like Sherman's march through Georgia during the Civil War or the ravaging of the Palatinate in the Thirty Years' War. Yet, if one looks carefully at how the war was actually fought on the local level, one can see how hard-line behavior influenced the course of events.[32]

There were never enough supporters of restraint in the British Army, especially in the lower echelons of the army's hierarchy. Officers with a hard-line attitude often exercised a significant influence at the local level. By burning homes and laying waste farms, they left a more enduring impression than all the restraint shown by their conciliatory comrades. In the process, not only did the American population become more terrorized but the patriot press had much to write about.[33]

Considering these developments, it is possible to get a clearer picture of Cornwallis vis-à-vis his subordinates. It is a matter of no great importance but of some interest to note that three of the earl's chief subordinates—Ferguson, Rawdon, and Tarleton—fell into the hard-line category. Given his personality and his ambiguous stance on terror, someone like Cornwallis inadvertently gave such individuals much leeway in the manner in which they conducted operations against the enemy.[34]

Banastre Tarleton is a prime case in point. A young, energetic, and ambitious officer, he commanded Cornwallis's sole cavalry regiment. Being detached from the main army and the winner of impressive victories, Tarleton could engage in more questionable activities than other field commanders. His attitude toward the rebellion plus the tactics of the very mobile British Legion contributed to the terror. He espoused the traditional imperial response to rebellion, and unlike Patrick Ferguson, for instance, he would follow through with his rhetoric of punishing the disloyal.[35]

Tarleton's Legionnaires undoubtedly sensed their leader's attitude. After all, he promised them "the plunder of the leaders of the faction."[36] Lord Cornwallis knew all too well what the British Legion, this "necessary evil," could do in the hands of young Tarleton. What he could not bring himself to do, he allowed his favorite subordinate to accomplish. His lordship clearly saw the Legion as contributing to the terror. He revealed his sentiments in a letter to his aide-de-camp, dated November 13, 1780: "I find the terror as great as possible. Tarleton alone can settle matters."[37]

At another time, Cornwallis wrote Lord Rawdon at Camden: "Cavalry acts chiefly upon the nerves & if once it losses its terror, it loses its' greatest force."[38] Nevertheless, the earl could not tolerate excessive behavior and would occasionally warn his dragoon leader to keep a better eye on his men. Tarleton, meanwhile, would apologize when even he felt his men were totally out of line.[39]

The American response to British terror is not difficult to gauge. Granted, it worked for a while and the militia was intimidated, but not for long since it continued to come out.[40] In fact, there are several good examples of how the terror employed by Tarleton backfired on him.[41]

Thomas Sumter had resigned his commission as lieutenant colonel of the Second South Carolina Regiment in 1778. He then returned home to live the life of a simple country gentleman. A British Legion detachment changed all that for him on May 28, 1780 when it burned his house in the High Hills of the Santee. Sumter quickly rejoined his former comrades and began forming militia companies west of the Catawba River.[42]

The "justice of the rank and file" exhibited at the Waxhaws the very next day "gave a more sanguinary turn to the war." "Tarleton's Quarter" became a catchword for "no mercy" and it gave subsequent battles a more vicious tinge. Indeed, American commanders at King's Mountain in October had a difficult time in restraining their men from implementing it.[43]

The operations of Captain Christian Huck also exasperated the situation. Many historians portray him as a "miniature Tarleton." Lorenzo Sabine calls him the "Swearing Captain," because he supposedly once declared that "God Almighty was turned Rebel; but if there were twenty Gods on their side, they should all be conquered."[44] Whether or not he actually said this is debatable, although his pillaging of homes is not. Unfortunately for the captain, his actions stirred up much resentment. In July 1780, he led a detachment of Legion dragoons, New York Volunteers, and

Loyalist militia on a raid through the upper Broad River area. At Williamson's Plantation, South Carolina, on July 11, a force of Rebel militia surrounded his encampment during the night. Attacking at dawn the next day, they killed Huck and thirty or forty of his men, wounded a similar number, and dispersed the rest.[45]

No better example of the failure of terror to achieve its goal can be seen than with the fate of John Postell. A member of the Charles Town garrison, he was paroled at its surrender and went home. Two weeks after his return, two dragoons of the British Legion came to his door and demanded his "full blooded stone horse [stallion]." Postell produced his copy of the parole and refused to give up the animal, but the two dragoons took it anyway. Several months later in mid-October 1780, three more dragoons appeared at his home, but this time he was not there. They seized:

> The only gelding I had left fit to ride, three negroe boys, plundered my house, abused my wife, told her they were going in search of me, and if they found me they would take my life, invited all my negroes to go to Camden to them promising them rewards if they would, and that I should never get them again...[46]

Upon his return home, Postell found his distraught wife and saw all the damage. At that very moment he decided to "seek refuge" with Francis Marion's partisans. As he later described it: "If the treatment above mentioned did not discharge me of a parole given as mine was, It was my misfortune to mistake the matter, however be it as it will, what I have done could not be avoided by me...."[47]

Banastre Tarleton and his green-coated regiment undoubtedly contributed to the level of terror in the South, and in the process gained undying infamy. Henry Lee maintains that Tarleton had become such a hated figure at the end of the war, that he had to request special protection from his former enemies. In his *Memoirs*, Lee gleefully relates how the Englishman approached a French officer and requested that American militia not participate in the surrender ceremonies at Gloucester Point.[48]

The extent to which Banastre Tarleton employed terror is not as excessive as it has been portrayed. American popular culture has seen fit to exaggerate the extent of several Legion depredations to make the perpetrators appear truly barbaric and evil. Two of the better known stories concerning Tarleton and his men are the apparent result of verbal rumor and American propaganda. Neither one has any corroborative evidence.

The first such story pertains to the Richardson plantation. Tarleton and some dragoons visited the site in early November 1780. According to an 1845 account which is repeated by at least three historians, the Legion commander committed a most ghoulish deed upon the Richardson family. He reportedly had the body of the recently deceased General Richard Richardson removed from its grave. His pretext for doing such a ghastly thing was so "that he might examine the features of a man of his decided character," although Joseph Johnson maintains that Tarleton was actually looking for the family silverware.[49]

This story is suspect for many reasons. The person who first related it was the Honorable John Peter Richardson II (1801-1864), grandson of General Richardson and governor of South Carolina from 1840 to 1842. He obviously could not have been a witness because he was born twenty-one years after the fact. He evidently heard about Tarleton's visit to his grandfather's home from his father, James Burchill Richardson (1770-1836), also a governor of South Carolina (1802-1804). James Burchill was present when the Legionnaires looted the home. In fact, when an officer tried to remove the deceased general's saddle, ten-year-old James Burchill jumped upon it. The British became "amused at what they called the impudence of the little rebel" and let him keep it. Nevertheless, James Burchill Richardson never left any written account of what actually happened at his father's plantation.[50]

In fact, there does not exist a direct eyewitness to the event. Major Richard Richardson, Francis Marion, and William Dobein

James all visited the house right after Tarleton and his men departed. None of these individuals ever mentioned that the British officer disinterred the six-week-old corpse.[51]

Why Banastre Tarleton would take the time and effort to do such a thing seems uncertain. As an English officer and gentleman, he would have shown more respect for the dead and the family's feelings than the 1845 account suggests, regardless of how angry he was with the widow Richardson. He already made his point to the family by looting and then burning their home along with all the other structures on the plantation. To assign two or three dragoons to dig up a corpse would be time consuming. This detachment was in an area infested with Rebel partisans and many miles from Cornwallis's main army. The argument that he was looking for the family silverware does not seem feasible. Assuredly, the Richardsons could have found a better hiding place than the grave of a loved one.[52]

John P. Richardson II might have gotten this story from his father. The image is not too hard to conjure up: A father and his small son sitting in front of a fireplace on a cold wintry night as the former relates the evil doings of a certain Lieutenant Colonel Tarleton. It is possible that both father and son got the idea for the ghoulish deed from a statement made by Governor John Rutledge right after Tarleton's raid. Rutledge asserted that the young Briton "exceeded his usual Barbarity, ... & this because he pretended to believe, that the poor old Genl. was with the Rebel-Army, *tho', had he open'd his grave, before the Door, he might have seen the Contrary.*"[53]

Another source which may have influenced Richardson's tale is a newspaper report. The Patriot press at the time simply abounded with such stories, many of them untrue. For example, one newspaper in February 1777 reported that British troops liked to open family vaults and scatter the bones of the deceased. Jonathan W. Austin repeated the same assertion in his *Oration, Delivered at Boston, March 5, 1778*: "They have ransacked the silent repositories, and the remains of one that was once amiable and captivating, flung about as food for the birds of the air."[54]

Much of what we know of the Revolution is derived from propaganda. The people who wrote such information gave expression to ideas and fears that had been germinating for years. Furthermore, "the most important motive in war psychosis is not reason or justice, or even self-interest, but hate."[55]

Simple hatred of the enemy is apparent in the second example. This account matches Richardson's tale in sheer barbarity and cruelty. However, it too is suspect because it only circulated among four French officers and is not corroborated by any American accounts.

All four authors agree that as the French army debarked in Virginia in early September 1781, it came upon a countryside devastated by the British. At one particular estate, somewhere between Jamestown and Hampton, a pregnant woman was found murdered. Which French troops actually first came upon the grisly sight is uncertain. Jean-Baptiste-Antoine de Verger, a sous-lieutenant in the Royal Deux-Ponts Régiment, recalled:

> I was nearly an eyewitness to the atrocities committed by the English. Some of Tarleton's dragoons, after pillaging a house, violated a young woman who was pregnant. After fastening her to a door, one of them split open her belly with a sabre, killing the infant, then wrote over the door the following inscription, which I saw:
> *You dam rebel's Whore,*
> *you shall never bear enny more.*[56]

Verger also mentions that the wells in the area had been poisoned by the English, who had thrown corpses into them.[57]

Of the four accounts, Verger's is the only one which blames Tarleton's Legionnaires directly. However, he never claims to have actually seen the body and the written warning. Karl Gustaf Tornquist, a Swede serving in the French navy, relates essentially the same story: "A pregnant woman was found murdered in her bed through several bayonet stabs; the barbarians had opened both her breasts and written above the bed canopy: 'Thou shalt never give birth to a rebel.' In another room was just as horrible a sight, five cut-off heads, arranged on a cupboard...."[58]

A sous-lieutenant in the Régiment d'Infanterie de Monsieur, Joachim du Perron, Comte de Revel, added his own twist to the atrocity. He not only remembered the murdered woman, but desecrated graves as well. "Les tombeaux étaient ouverts, les ossements en avaient été retirés et jetés çà et là." (The tombs were opened and the bones thrown here and there).[59]

The fourth version is the work of an anonymous author and appeared in Amsterdam in 1782. It defends François Joseph Paul, Comte de Grasse, the French admiral who conducted operations in the Chesapeake, and may very well be attributed to his pen. The author asserts that Lord Cornwallis commanded "an army which had committed atrocities to the point even of killing a woman, opening her, taking out the child she bore in her womb, and hanging it to a tree, with this inscription: *Thou shalt not breed traitors.*"[60]

There are several reasons why this gruesome story is suspicious. If soldiers of the infamous "Colonel Talton" actually committed this despicable act, then why does only one author state so? Is it that Verger was picking the most convenient scapegoat? Also, too many discrepancies are present, especially with the location and date of the crime. Verger claims that it occurred sometime on or after September 18, 1781 near Jamestown, while Tornquist maintains that it happened around September 2 "on a beautiful estate 2 miles from Hampton." Jamestown and Hampton are approximately thirty miles apart.[61]

The location of the woman, her baby, and the inscription also differ with each account. In fact, the exact wording of the sign varies. Moreover, each author attempts to outrage his readers with lurid ancillary details: corpses dumped in drinking wells (Verger), five severed heads on a cupboard (Tornquist), plundered graves and scattered bones (Du Perron), and a fetus hanging from a tree (anonymous).[62]

It is interesting to note that these French officers demonstrated a profound admiration for America and its people. This may have influenced them to write about the "godless behaviour" of the enemy. In addition, it is noteworthy that Tornquist, Du Perron and the anonymous author were naval officers and they may have been repeating a story which circulated among their kind. They may have also read Verger's journal before they penned their own accounts. No Americans make mention of this horrible crime, and this is the most damning evidence against the Frenchmen's claim. Patriot newspapers would have certainly repeated the details of the discovery while American officers and soldiers would have recorded it in their correspondence and journals. However, outside this group of four Frenchmen, everyone else is silent on the matter.[63]

The propaganda value of such a tale is immense. Like the disinterring of corpses, reports concerning the abuse of women received much attention in the press, and French officers may have read about them prior to the Chesapeake operations. One account in particular circulated throughout the states. British soldiers reportedly attacked women at Maidenhead, Hopewell, and Woodbridge during the occupation of New Jersey in 1776-1777. No female was safe, including a seventy-year old, a young girl, and a pregnant woman.[64]

Lieutenant Colonel Banastre Tarleton acted out the role of a loyal subject to his King. He rode through the southern campaigns a proud figure, chastising all those who would not submit to Crown law. He had an appointed task to do, and if his actions seemed brutal and left rebellious colonists without food or shelter, then so be it. He assuredly helped to increase the level of terror in the South, but he was not the sole instigator. Tarleton was but one actor in a play with many members in the cast. Why American popular culture has chosen him as the star of this play entitled "Terror" is because of who he was — a young, arrogant, ambitious favorite of a British general.[65]

Be that as it may, one can assert that terror never worked in suppressing disloyal activity in the southern colonies. That fact became all too apparent to the British army at York Town, Virginia on October 19, 1781. Banastre Tarleton assuredly felt the sting of the American victory over British terror when he was humbled in the streets of the town four days later. As the Legion commandant and the Baron de Vioménil rode down the main street of York Town on their way to dinner, a steward of a local planter stepped in front of them. Recognizing the Englishman's horse as belonging to his master, the steward demanded that Tarleton dismount. The embarrassed Englishman tried to plead with the American, but the latter was adamant. As the steward led the animal away, nearby American civilians began to smirk and laugh. A French officer then had his orderly dismount and give his steed to the red-faced Tarleton.[66]

---

[1] Alexander Garden, *Anecdotes of the American Revolution, Illustrative of the Talents and Virtues of the Heroes and Patriots, Who Acted the Most Conspicuous Parts Therein*, 2nd Series (Charleston: A.E. Miller, 1828), 129-130, 135-139; also see Garden's earlier *Anecdotes of the Revolutionary War In America, With Sketches of Character of Persons the Most Distinguished, in the Southern States, for Civil and Military Services* (Charleston: A.E. Miller, 1822), 259, 267, 269, 284-288, 397-398, 409.

[2] Garden, *Anecdotes of the American Revolution, Illustrative of the Talents,...* (1828), 129-130.

[3] Garden attributes the story to an unnamed lieutenant of the Seventy-First Highlanders. *Ibid.*; for the fanciful encounter between Tarleton and the noble Mrs. Slocomb, see Joseph Johnson, *Traditions and Reminiscences Chiefly of the American Revolution in the South: Including Biographical Sketches, Incidents and Anecdotes, Few of Which Have Been Published, Particularly of Residents in the Upper Country* (Charleston: Walker and James, 1851), 557-569; for the snide remarks of Mrs. Willie Jones and Mrs. Ashe, consult *Recollections and Private Memoirs of Washington, by his adopted son, George Washington Parke Custis, with a memoir of the author, by his daughter; and illustrative and explanatory notes. by Benson J. Lossing* (New York: Derby and Jackson, 1860), 252. Discussions of all three accounts are found in Chapter VI.

[4] For the civil war and how it terrorized the South, see John S. Pancake, *This Destructive War: The British Campaign in the Carolinas, 1780-1782* (Tuscaloosa: University of Alabama Press, 1985); Henry Lumpkin, *From Savannah to Yorktown: The American Revolution in the South* (Columbia: University of South Carolina Press, 1981); John Richard Alden, *The South in the Revolution: 1763-1789*, History of the South Series 3 (Louisiana State University Press, 1957); Don Higginbotham, *The War of American Independence: Military Attitudes, Policies, and Practice, 1763-1789* (New York: Macmillan Company, 1971); Dan L. Morrill, *Southern Campaigns of the American Revolution* (Baltimore: The Nautical and Aviation Publishing Company, 1993); Norman Gelb, *Less than Glory* (New York: GP Putnam's Sons, 1984), 172; John Shy, "American Society and Its War for Independence" and Don Higginbotham, "The American Militia: A Traditional Institution with Revolutionary Responsibilities," both in Don Higginbotham, ed., *Reconsiderations on the Revolutionary War: Selected Essays* (Westport, Connecticut: Greenwood Press, 1978), 72-103; "Daniel Morgan: Guerrilla Fighter" and "Reflections on the War of Independence, Modern Guerrilla Warfare, and the War in Vietnam," both in Don Higginbotham, *War and Society in Revolutionary America: The Wider Dimensions of Conflict* (Columbia: University of South Carolina Press, 1988), 132-173; Richard Maxwell Brown, "Violence and the American Revolution" and John Shy, "The American Revolution: The Military Conflict Considered as a Revolutionary War," in Stephen G. Kurtz and James H. Hutson, eds., *Essays on the American Revolution* (Chapel Hill: University of North Carolina Press, 1973), 81-156; Charles Royster, "A Society and Its War," Maarten Ultee, ed., *Adapting to Conditions: War and Society in the Eighteenth Century* (University of Alabama Press, 1986), 174-187; Ira D. Gruber, "Britain's Southern Policy" and Clyde R. Ferguson, "Functions of the Partisan-Militia in the South During the American Revolution: An Interpretation," in Robert W. Higgins, ed., *The Revolutionary War in the South: Power, Conflict, and Leadership. Essays in Honor of John Richard Alden* (Duke University Press, 1979), 205-258; Lieutenant Colonel Louis D.F. Frasché, "Problems of Command: Cornwallis, Partisans and Militia, 1780," *Military Review* 57 (April 1977): 60-74; Robert M. Weir, "'The Violent Spirit,' the Reestablishment of Order, and the Continuity of Leadership in Post-Revolutionary South Carolina," in Ronald Hoffman, Thad W. Tate, and Peter J. Albert, eds., *An Uncivil War: The Southern Backcountry during the American Revolution* (Charlottesville: University Press of Virginia, 1985), 70-98; also consult

Jeffrey J. Crow and Larry E. Tise, eds., *The Southern Experience in the American Revolution* (Chapel Hill: University of North Carolina Press, 1978).

[5] David Ramsay, *The History of the Revolution of South-Carolina, From a British Province to an Independent State*, 2 vols. (Trenton, New Jersey: Isaac Collins, 1785); Mercy Otis Warren, *History of the Rise, Progress and Termination of the American Revolution. Interspersed with Biographical, Political and Moral Observations*, 3 vols. (Boston: Manning and Loring, 1805); *Letters of Eliza Wilkinson*, ed. Caroline Gilman (New York, 1839; repr., New York: New York Times and Arno Press, 1969), 28-31, 39-43, 88-89; Hannah Arendt, *On Violence* (New York: Harcourt, Brace & World, 1969, 1970), 4, 51, 54-55. Also consult Chapter IV of this book.

[6] Quoted in Christopher Ward, *The War of the Revolution*, 2 vols. (New York: Macmillan, 1852), 1:282-283.

[7] For an excellent view of this intriguing man, see Franklin and Mary Wickwire, *Cornwallis: The American Adventure* (Boston: Houghton Mifflin Company, 1970).

[8] *Ibid.*, 173-175. For wavering loyalties of the militia, see "Colonel Robert Gray's Observations on the War in Carolina," *The South Carolina Historical and Genealogical Magazine* 11 (July 1910): 139-159.

[9] Memo. of conversation, February 7, 1776, Clinton Papers, William L. Clements Library, University of Michigan, Ann Arbor, Michigan; Ira D. Gruber, "British Strategy: The Theory and Practice of Eighteenth-Century Warfare," in Higginbotham, ed., *Reconsiderations on the Revolutionary War*, 22-30; "Military Leadership in the American Revolution," in Higginbotham, *War and Society*, 84-89.

[10] Stephen Conway, "To Subdue America: British Army Officers and the Conduct of the Revolutionary War," *William and Mary Quarterly* 43 (1986): 381 (hereafter cited as *WMQ*); also see Conway's "British Army Officers and the American War for Independence," *WMQ* 41 (1984): 265-276, and *The War of American Independence 1775-1783* (New York: St. Martin's Press, 1995), 117, 247. "Revolutionary violence is less an instrument of physical destruction than one kind of persuasion." John Shy, "The American Revolution: The Military Conflict Considered as a Revolutionary War," in

Kurtz and Hutson, eds., *Essays on the American Revolution*, 126; American Major General Charles Lee emphasized the need to maintain morale and to create the proper attitude among the civilian population. John Shy, "Charles Lee: The Soldier as Radical," in *George Washington's Generals*, ed. George Athan Billias (New York: William Morrow, 1964), 34; Maarten Ultee, Adapting to Conditions," in Ultee, ed., *Adapting to Conditions*, 2; Peter Paret, "The Relationship Between the Revolutionary War and European Military Thought and Practice in the Second Half of the Eighteenth Century," in Higginbotham, ed., *Reconsiderations on the Revolutionary War*, 153-155; Jeremy Black, *War for America: The Fight For Independence 1775-1783* (New York: St. Martin's Press, 1991), 18-19, 65-66, 195, 249.

[11] Shy, "American Society and Its War for Independence," in Higginbotham, ed., *Reconsiderations on the Revolutionary War*, 79-81; Conway, "To Subdue America," 401-407; Paul H. Smith, *Loyalists and Redcoats: A Study in British Revolutionary Policy* (Chapel Hill: University of North Carolina Press, 1964), 169, 173-174; Robert McCluer Calhoon, *The Loyalists in Revolutionary America: 1760-1781* (New York: Harcourt Brace Jovanovich, 1965), 493-494, 499; Piers Mackesy, *The War for America 1775-1783* (Cambridge: Harvard University Press, 1964), 343.

[12] Cornwallis to Lieutenant Colonel John Harris Cruger, September 24, 1780, Cornwallis Papers, Public Record Office, Kew, 30/11/80, ff. 5-6 (hereafter cited as PRO).

[13] Wickwire, *Cornwallis*, 173-174; "In an auction of terror the rebels could always outbid him." Mackesy, *War for America*, 343-344.

[14] For the march of Sherman during the Civil War, consult Clement Dowd, *Life of Zebulon B. Vance* (Charlotte: North Carolina: Observer Printing and Publishing House, 1897), 469-472, among other sources.

[15] *The American Journal of Ambrose Serle, Secretary to Lord Howe 1776-1778*, ed. Edward H. Tatum, Jr. (San Marino, California: Huntington Library, 1940), 176, 245-246. After two men were hanged and five others severely flogged in August 1777 for marauding, Serle noted that "if this had been done a year ago, we should have found its advantages."

[16] Bernhard A. Uhlendorf, trans, *Revolution in America: Confidential Letters and Journals 1776-1784 of Adjutant General Major Baurmeister of the Hessian Forces* (Rutgers University Press, 1957), 22.

[17] Howard H. Peckham, ed., *Sources of American Independence: Selected Manuscripts from the Collections of the William L. Clements Library*, 2 vols. (Chicago and London: University of Chicago Press, 1978), 2:341-342.

[18] Cornwallis to Brown, Charleston, July 21, 1780, Cornwallis Papers, PRO, 30/11/78, ff. 38-39. General Orders dated at Smith's Plantation, North Carolina, March 4, 1781, reminded all His Majesty's troops to treat Loyalists with kindness and respect. A. R. Newsome, "A British Orderly Book, 1780-1781," *North Carolina Historical Review* 9 (1932): 183, 277, 280, 289-290, 293, 296-297, 366, 368-370, 377-379, 381; Lieutenant Colonel Banastre Tarleton, *A History of the Campaigns of 1780 and 1781, in the Southern Provinces of North America* (London: T. Cadell, 1787), 290.

[19] Lieutenant Haldane to Lieutenant Colonel George Turnbull or Major Patrick Ferguson, Camden, August 20, 1780, Cornwallis Papers, PRO, 30/11/79, ff. 25-26.

[20] Armstrong Starkey, "Paoli to Stony Point: Military Ethics and Weaponry During the American Revolution," *Journal of Military History* 58 (January 1994): 18.

[21] Roger Lamb, *Memoir of His Own Life* (Dublin: J. Jones, 1811), 261. The *Memoir* of the ubiquitous Sergeant Lamb is an insightful look into the life of a common British soldier. A member of the Twenty-Third or Royal Welch Fusiliers, he participated in Burgoyne's expedition and the southern campaigns. He managed to avoid imprisonment by twice escaping to New York City; "Colonel Robert Gray's Observations," 144-145; Lawrence E. Babits, "Greene's Strategy in the Southern Campaign, 1780-1781," in Ultee, ed., *Adapting to Conditions*, 138; Charles Stedman, *The History of the Origin, Progress, and Termination of the American War*, 2 vols. (London, 1794; New York: New York Times and Arno Press, 1969), 2:198-199.

[22] By contrast, the Legionnaires who visited Monticello at roughly the same time disturbed nothing at all. *The Writings of Thomas Jefferson:*

Being His Autobiography, Correspondence, Reports, Messages, Addresses, And Other Writings, Official And Private, ed. H.A. Washington, 9 vols. (Washington, DC: Taylor & Maury, 1853-1854), 2:425-427; Tarleton, *History of the Campaigns*, 295-298.

[23] Royster, "A Society and Its War," in Ultee, ed., *Adapting to Conditions*, 178. Also see Philip Davidson, *Propaganda and the American Revolution 1763-1783* (University of North Carolina Press, 1941), 139, 143-144, 356, 365-366; Carl Berger, *Broadsides and Bayonets: The Propaganda War of the American Revolution* (1961; repr., San Rafael, California: Presidio Press, 1976), 147-150; Gelb, *Less than Glory*, 14.

[24] Rawdon to Rugeley, July 1, 1780, Cornwallis Papers, PRO, 30/11/95, f. 9.

[25] Wickwire, *Cornwallis*, 178-179.

[26] The letter, in its original form, appears in Charles Ross, ed., *Correspondence of Charles, First Marquis Cornwallis*, 3 vols., 2nd ed. (London: John Murray, 1859), 1:56-57.

[27] The altered missive is found in the Cornwallis Papers, PRO, 30/11/95, f. 10; Wickwire, *Cornwallis*, 179-180.

[28] Greene to Lord Cornwallis, Charlotte, North Carolina, December 17, 1780, in *The Papers of General Nathanael Greene*, Richard K. Showman, ed., 7 vols. to date (Chapel Hill: University of North Carolina Press, 1976-), 6:591-593; Wickwire, *Cornwallis*, 179-181.

[29] For the Mongols, see James Chambers, *The Devil's Horsemen: The Mongol Invasion of Europe* (New York: Atheneum, 1985); Arendt, *On Violence*, 55-56.

[30] For Grant, see Bruce Catton, *Grant Moves South* (Boston: Little, Brown, and Company, 1960), 291-294. Bernard Berelson and Gary A. Steiner, *Human Behavior: An Inventory of Scientific Findings* (New York: Harcourt, Brace & World, 1964), 241-286.

[31] See Catton, *Grant Moves South*, 291-294. The foreign nature of the American should not be overemphasized, although his provincialism

seemed peculiar to many Englishmen. John Morgan Dederer, *War in America to 1775 Before Yankee Doodle* (New York: New York University Press, 1990), 137-140; John Shy, *Toward Lexington: The Role of the British Army in the Coming of the American Revolution* (Princeton University Press, 1965); Berelson and Steiner, *Human Behavior*, 363-380, 443-449, 659-667; David Hackett Fischer, *Paul Revere's Ride* (New York and Oxford: Oxford University Press, 1994), 258.

[32] Conway, "To Subdue America," 395-405.

[33] *Ibid.*, 403-407; Stephen Conway, "'The great mischief Complain'd of': Reflections on the Misconduct of British Soldiers in the Revolutionary War," *WMQ* 47 (1990): 376-377, 387-390. Black, *War for America: The Fight for Independence*, 18, 189, 249.

[34] Another officer who could be placed in this group is Major James Wemyss of the Sixty-Third Foot. One historian asserts that he was second only to Tarleton as the "most hated man in the British army." In early September 1780, he reportedly burned a path seventy miles long and fifteen miles wide between Kingstree and Cheraw, South Carolina. He met defeat at the hands of Thomas Sumter on November 9, 1780 at Fishdam Ford, South Carolina. Badly wounded in the fight, Wemyss returned home to England where he disappeared totally from the *Army Lists* in 1789. Robert Bass, *The Green Dragoon: The Lives of Banastre Tarleton and Mary Robinson* (New York: Henry Holt, 1957), 105, 116 popularizes Wemyss's notoriety. Also see Paul David Nelson, *General James Grant: Scottish Soldier and Royal Governor of East Florida* (Gainesville: University of Florida Press, 1993), 3, 76, 81-82, 85, 98, 115, 119.

[35] Ferguson on many occasions vacillated between the conciliatory and hard-line schools of thought. In August 1778, he wanted to lay waste large tracts of Connecticut, exempting only "the houses (but not the Crop or moveables) of known Loyalists." After his raid upon the New Jersey coast two months later, he explained to Clinton that "no manner of Insult or Injury has been offered to the peaceable Inhabitants." At another time he stated: "America has never yet felt us in Earnest." Later in the southern campaigns, he promised to lay waste the settlements along the Watauga, Nolachucky, and Holston rivers. If not for Kings Mountain, he might well have made good on his threats.

Peckham, ed., *Sources of American Independence,* 2:293-294, 308, 310; Ferguson to Clinton, October 10, 15, 1778, Colonial Office Records, PRO, 5/96, 177, 179; Conway, "To Subdue America," 383; Major General Alexander Leslie to Lt. Col. Nisbet Balfour, Charlestown, January 25, 1781, Alexander Leslie Letterbook, 1781-1782, Nisbet Balfour Letters, January-December 1781, South Carolina Department of Archives and History, Columbia, South Carolina (microfilm); nine Culloden rebels in 1746 endured the traditional response to insurrection. After being hanged on Kennington Common, each was cut down before he died. They were then disemboweled and beheaded. Lee McCardell, *Ill-Starred General: Braddock of the Coldstream Guards* (Pittsburgh: University of Pittsburgh Press, 1958), 99; Conway, "British Army Officers," 276; Martin van Creveld, *Command in War* (Cambridge: Harvard University Press, 1985), 5-16, 274-275.

[36] Tarleton to Cornwallis, August 5, 1780, Leneau's Ferry, Cornwallis Papers, PRO, 30/11/63, ff. 19-21; Tarleton, *History of the Campaigns,* 100-101; Berelson and Steiner, *Human Behavior,* 370, 372, 374, 443-449; John Keegan, *The Mask of Command* (New York: Viking, 1987), 1-11.

[37] Cornwallis to Lieutenant John Money, November 13, 1780, Winnsborough, Cornwallis Papers, PRO, 30/11/4, ff. 112-113.

[38] Cornwallis to Rawdon, July 15, 1780, Charleston, Cornwallis Papers, PRO, 30/11/78, ff. 18-19.

[39] Tarleton, *History of the Campaigns,* 38, 290; Tarleton to Cornwallis, December 26, 1780, Daniels Plantation, Cornwallis Papers, PRO, 30/11/4, ff. 404-405; Major General Alexander Leslie to Sir Henry Clinton, January 29, 1782, camp near Charles Town, Carleton Papers, in the Royal Institution of Great Britain, vol. 23, No. 52, 6pp. (microfilm) (hereafter cited as Carleton Papers).

[40] Instances of Tarleton's Legion intimidating the militia can be located in Francis Marion to Gen. Horatio Gates, November 26, 1780, Benbow's Ferry, *The Papers of the Continental Congress: 1774-1789,* comp. John Butler (Washington, DC: US Government Printing Office, 1978), 1p., Copy, M247, reel 174, i154, vol. 2, p. 334 (microfilm) (hereafter cited as *PCC*); Henry Lee, *Memoirs of the War in the Southern Department*

of the United States, 2 vols. (Philadelphia and New York: Bradford & Inskeep & Inskeep & Bradford, 1812), 1:315; Major Ichabod Burnet to Colonel Henry Lee, Jr., February 2, 1781 Camp at Mask's Ferry, NC (On Pee Dee), *The Papers of General Nathanael Greene*, 7:234-235; John C. Dann, ed., *The Revolution Remembered: Eyewitness Accounts of the War for Independence* (Chicago: The University of Chicago Press, 1980), 201-203.

[41] Robert Middlekauff, "Why Men Fought in the American Revolution," *Huntington Library Quarterly* 43 (Spring 1980): 143-144, 147-148; Starkey, "Paoli to Stony Point," 20-27; Blackwell P. Robinson, ed., *The Revolutionary War Sketches of William R. Davie* (Raleigh: North Carolina Department of Cultural Resources, Division of Archives and History, 1976), 23; for Rebel reaction to earlier Legion activity, see Robert Kyff, "Tarleton's Raid on Bedford and Poundridge," *The Westchester Historian* 44 (Summer 1968), 56-58.

[42] This occurred when Tarleton and the Legion passed through the area on their way to find Buford. Nisbet Balfour reported that he had received "many and wonderful complaints of men cloathed in green plundering singly every house they come across or can get at..." Pancake, *This Destructive War*, 81-82; Bass, *The Green Dragoon*, 88.

[43] Ramsay, *The History of the Revolution of South-Carolina*, 2:110; Fischer, *Paul Revere's Ride*, 258; the American riflemen at Kings Mountain yelled "Give them Buford's play!" Lyman C. Draper, *King's Mountain and Its Heroes: History of the Battle of King's Mountain, October 7th, 1780, and the Events Which Led To It* (Cincinnati: Peter G. Thomson, 1881), 282; Dann, ed., *The Revolution Remembered*, 201-203; for a similar example of the justice of the rank and file, consult Reed Browning, *The War of the Austrian Succession* (New York: St. Martin's Press, 1993), 319-320. On September 16, 1747, the French stormed the Dutch city of Bergen-op-Zoom and went on a rampage through the streets; Pancake, *This Destructive War*, 120.

[44] Lorenzo Sabine, *Biographical Sketches of Loyalists of the American Revolution, With an Historical Essay*, 2 vols. (Boston: Little, Brown and Company, 1864), 1:552-553; Bass, *The Green Dragoon*, 88-89.

45 It is said that the Rebel militia pursued the fleeing Loyalists for fifteen miles. Huck or Houk had orders to "push the rebels as far as he deemed convenient." Two houses he looted near Williamson's belonged to Colonel William Bratton and Captain John McClure. These officers formed the militia force which surrounded the Loyalist's command. Ward, *The War of the Revolution*, 2:708-709; Pancake, *This Destructive War*, 83-84; for Tarleton's reaction to Huck's fate, see Tarleton, *History of the Campaigns*, 92-93, 101.

46 John Postell. Charleston Jail. Statement re his actions while a prisoner. June 24, 1781, *PCC*, 4p., Copy, M247, reel 175, i155, vol. 2, pp. 294-295.

47 *Ibid.*, 295-296.

48 Lee, *Memoirs*, 2:362; it is well known that George Washington allowed Cornwallis to send the sloop *Bonetta* to New York after the surrender had occurred. The English earl insisted upon and received the following stipulations: that it be permitted to sail without examination and that it carry "such soldiers as I may think proper to send as passengers in her." It would not be surprising if members of the British Legion comprised part of her 250 passengers. See Henry Steele Commager and Richard B. Morris, eds., *The Spirit of 'Seventy-Six: The Story of the American Revolution as told by Participants*, 2 vols. (Indianapolis and New York: The Bobbs-Merrill Company, 1958), 2:1241; Lieut. Col. J.G. Simcoe, *A History of the Operations of a Partisan Corps Called the Queen's Rangers* (New York, 1844; New York: New York Times and Arno Press, 1968), 254; a Hessian officer reported that on December 8, 1781, a cartel ship from York Town arrived in New York and carried 111 Anspach, Hessian, and English officers. Fifty more persons, wishing to escape "the inevitable revenge of the rebels," had secreted themselves in the hold. Uhlendorf, trans., *Revolution in America*, 479-480; "Lt. Col. Tarleton: His Character," *The Cambridge (Massachusetts) General Repository and Review* 3 (January 1813), 106; American cavalry leader William Washington called his personal red banner "Tarleton's Terror." Lumpkin, *From Savannah to Yorktown*, 218-219; John Shy, *A People Numerous and Armed: Reflections on the Military Struggle for American Independence* (Oxford University Press, 1976), 1-19, 225-254.

[49] Letter of the Honorable John P. Richardson, Clarendon, September 29, 1845, in Joseph Johnson, *Traditions and Reminiscences*, 161-162; the story is repeated in Edward McCrady, *The History of South Carolina in the Revolution 1775-1783*, 2 vols. (New York and London: The Macmillan Company, 1901-1902), 1:816-819; Robert Bass is another historian who does not question the veracity of this tale. *The Green Dragoon*, 110-111.

[50] John P. Richardson II is not to be confused with his son John Peter Richardson III (1831-1899), also a South Carolina governor (1886-1890). *Governors of South Carolina: 1776-present* (Greenville: Greenville News-Piedmont Company, 1988), 6, 15, 27; Johnson, *Traditions and Reminiscences*, 162.

[51] General Richard Richardson had three sons: Richard, James Burchill, and John. Richard was the eldest. Johnson, *Traditions and Reminiscences*, 162-163, 165; Francis Marion to Gen. Horatio Gates, Benbow's Ferry, November 26, 1780, PCC, 1p., Copy, M247, reel 174, i154, vol. 2, p.334; William Dobein James, A.M., *A Sketch of the Life of Brig. Gen. Francis Marion and a History of His Brigade From Its Rise in June 1780 until Disbanded in December, 1782 With Descriptions of Characters and Scenes Not Heretofore Published* (Charleston, 1821; Marietta, Georgia: Continental Book Company, 1948), 61-64. James was a member of Marion's command.

[52] Arthur N. Gilbert, "Law and Honour Among Eighteenth-Century British Army Officers," *The Historical Journal* 19 (1976): 75-87; Richard A. Gabriel, *To Serve With Honor: A Treatise on Military Ethics and the Way of the Soldier* (Westport, Connecticut: Greenwood Press, 1982), 29, 150, 157, 227. If they did place the silverware in the grave, who then would be the more barbaric and ghoulish—the family for hiding it there or Tarleton for looking? The Whig argument about the silverware refutes the myth of injured innocence. Fischer, *Paul Revere's Ride*, 327-344; Gelb, *Less than Glory*, 11-12, 17; Charles Royster, "Founding a Nation in Blood: Military Conflict and American Nationality," in Ronald Hoffman and Peter J. Albert, eds., *Arms and Independence: The Military Character of the American Revolution* (Charlottesville: University Press of Virginia, 1984), 47-48; Charles Royster, *A Revolutionary People at War: The Continental Army and American Character, 1775-1783* (New York: WW Norton and Company, 1981), 188.

[53] Emphasis added. "Letters of John Rutledge," ed. Joseph Barnwell, *The South Carolina Historical and Genealogical Magazine* 18 (1917): 44. The exhumation of bodies was not unknown in the colonial era. William Byrd II of Virginia, looking for guidance during a time of deep personal turmoil, opened his father's grave in 1710. Kenneth A. Lockridge, *The Diary, and Life, of William Byrd II of Virginia, 1674-1744* (Chapel Hill and London: University of North Carolina Press, 1987), 43-44; in September 1775, American officers in search of talismans opened the coffin of Reverend George Whitefield, a renowned figure of the Great Awakening. They then removed his collar and wristbands. Charles Royster, "'The Nature of Treason': Revolutionary Virtue and American Reactions to Benedict Arnold," *WMQ* 36, (1979): 163.

[54] The newspaper was the *Freeman's Journal* and it reported that this very event occurred at least twice. In Davidson, *Propaganda and the American Revolution*, 366-367, 410; Wesley Frank Craven, *The Legend of the Founding Fathers* (New York: New York University Press, 1956), 60; Berger, *Broadsides and Bayonets*, 147.

[55] Davidson, *Propaganda and the American Revolution*, 139, 142-145, 365-366, 410; "American Historians and the Military History of the American Revolution" and "The Early American Way of War: Reconnaissance and Appraisal," both in Higginbotham, *War and Society*, 242-246, 264-265.

[56] A sous-lieutenant or sublieutenant was equivalent to an ensign in an English regiment. Verger's "Journal of the Most Important Events that occurred to the French Troops under the Command of M. le Comte de Rochambeau" is found in *The American Campaigns of Rochambeau's Army 1780, 1781, 1782, 1783*, trans. and eds. Howard C. Rice, Jr. and Anne S.K. Brown, 2 vols. (Princeton University Press, 1972), 1:137. In his manuscript (MS, p. 95) Verger gives the inscription in English, followed by his French translation of it.

[57] *Ibid.*

[58] Karl Gustaf Tornquist, *The Naval Campaigns of Count De Grasse During the American Revolution 1781-1783*, trans. Amandus Johnson

(Philadelphia: Swedish Colonial Society, 1942), 57. Tornquist's journal was first published in 1787 by the Swedish Naval Society. He apparently participated in the landings along the James River, which began on September 2; Barbara W. Tuchman cites Tornquist in *The First Salute* (New York: Alfred A. Knopf, 1988), 266-267; the Swede is also cited in Christopher Hibbert, *Redcoats and Rebels: The American Revolution Through British Eyes* (New York: Avon Books, 1991), 273.

[59] Joachim du Perron, Comte de Revel, *Journal particulier d'une campagne aux Indes Occidentales (1781-1782)* (Paris: H. Charles-Lavauzelle, ca. 1898), 124-125. The journal has entries from May 1780 to August 1782. The inscription read: "Tu n'enfanteras plus de rebelles." Du Perron was assigned to a marine detachment on the *Languedoc*, a ship in the French fleet. During the siege of York Town, he served on the Gloucester side of the York River.

[60] *Operations of The French Fleet under the Count De Grasse in 1781-2 As Described In Two Contemporaneous Journals* (New York, 1864), 78. This volume actually contains three journals. The first manuscript is hostile to de Grasse and is attributed to the Chevalier de Goussencourt, an apparent pseudonym. The second account relates the tale of the murdered woman while the third one pertains to the naval battle with British Vice Admiral George Brydges Rodney in the Saintes Passage, April 9-12, 1782. Like the second journal, the third account is also anonymous; Tuchman, *The First Salute*, 266.

[61] Verger, "Journal," in *American Campaigns of Rochambeau's Army*, 1:137; Tornquist, *Naval Campaigns of De Grasse*, 56-57; Du Perron asserts that it occurred on September 2 at Jamestown. *Journal particulier d'une campagne...*, 124-125.

[62] Verger, "Journal," in *American Campaigns of Rochambeau's Army*, 1:137; Tornquist, *Naval Campaigns of De Grasse*, 56-57; Du Perron, *Journal particulier d'une campagne...*, 124-125; *Operations of The French Fleet*, 78.

[63] "The inhabitants are in general a fine people, capable of sacrificing everything to satisfy an idea once adopted." Tornquist, *Naval Campaigns of De Grasse*, 14-15, 58, 76; America had no unfaithful women, according to the author of *Operations of the French Fleet*, 87-88.

[64] Davidson, *Propaganda and the American Revolution*, 368-369.

[65] James, *A Sketch of the Life of Francis Marion*, 64; "the Butcher Tarleton" can be seen in Don Cambou, *The American Revolution: The Birth of the Republic*, Part III, hosted by Bill Kurtis, Arts and Entertainment (North Hollywood, CA: Greystone Communications, Inc., 1994), documentary.

[66] The steward was a Mr. Day and the owner Sir Peyton Skipwith. Tarleton had injured his leg in a cavalry skirmish earlier in the month and pleaded "the extent of his injuries." Bass, *The Green Dragoon*, 5; James Thacher, *Military Journal of the American Revolution, From the Commencement to the Disbanding of the American Army; Comprising a Detailed Account of the Principal Events and Battles of the Revolution, With Their Exact Dates, And a Biographical Sketch of the most Prominent Generals* (Hartford, Connecticut: Hurlbut, Williams and Company, 1862; repr., New York: New York Times and Arno Press, 1969), 292. A surgeon in the Continental Army, Thacher witnessed the siege of York Town; Royster, *A Revolutionary People*, 115-116.

CHAPTER IX

Epilogue and Conclusions

The career of the British Legion did not abruptly end at York Town. It followed a more gradual course. After the surrender, the remnants of the unit went into cantonments on Long Island, New York. There, the populace soon complained about the depredations of certain green-coated soldiers. Lieutenant Colonel John Simcoe vehemently denied that his Queen's Rangers had participated in any wrongful acts, and he in turn accused the British Legion. The evidence suggests that the latter did indeed engage in plundering. On August 7, 1782, Jacobus Cropsey made a written complaint to the new British commander-in-chief, Sir Guy Carleton. He requested the removal of Legion soldiers from his house and barn. They had not only pulled up his corn and stolen his poultry, but they had killed some of his horses and used the flesh to feed their hounds.[1]

After the articles of peace had been signed on November 30, 1782, the British Legion, like all other provincial regiments, became earmarked for disbandment. On September 15, 1783, 208 officers and men of the unit embarked for Nova Scotia and one final muster. Most of these men received small plots of land as compensation for their service.[2]

As for Banastre Tarleton, he did not accompany his men to the site of their final muster. By that time, he had already returned home on parole. On January 18, 1782 he rode into London as a minor celebrity, and his postwar career proved to be equally active if not glorious.[3]

Ten days after his return, young Tarleton sat for the well-known Reynolds portrait. He then embarked upon a carefree social life. He had met young William Henry, Duke of Clarence, in New York before his departure. Now, back in England, Tarleton quickly became the boon companion of the duke and his brother George, the Prince of Wales. He drank and gambled heavily until monetary woes led to a few months of voluntary debtor's exile in France.[4]

It was during this time that the young and dashing Tarleton began a relationship with Mary Robinson, the famous actress and poetess. Known by her stage name, "Perdita," she was also the former companion of the Prince of Wales and the Duc de Lauzun. The young beauty of the stage found him simply enchanting and for fifteen years the couple were lovers. His marriage to Susan Priscilla Bertie on December 17, 1798 left Mary absolutely devastated.[5]

In 1787, Tarleton, with the aid of Mary's gifted pen, wrote *A History of the Campaigns of 1780 and 1781, in the Southern Provinces of North America*. An excellent and thoroughly insightful history, it is marred by the author's vanity and politics. In several passages he portrays his former superior in an unfavorable light. Earl Cornwallis deeply felt these aspersions on his character and wrote to his brother: "Tarleton's is a most malicious and false attack; he knew and approved the reasons for several of the measures which he now blames...I know it is very foolish to be vexed about these things, but yet it touches me in a tender point."[6]

The publication produced much rancor. An officer taken prisoner at the Cowpens, Lieutenant Roderick MacKenzie, published his own work within the same year entitled, *Strictures on Lt. Col. Tarleton's History of the Campaigns....* George Hanger, in turn, came to the defense of his good friend Tarleton with *An*

Address to the Army; in Reply to Strictures, by Roderick M'Kenzie.... The instigator of all this, meanwhile, remained undaunted. When Brooks's Club blackballed Tarleton for his criticism of Lord Cornwallis, the Prince of Wales formed his own club in opposition.[7]

The former commandant of the British Legion continued his military career but never saw combat again. He gradually rose through the ranks with the aid of his political connections. On November 18, 1790, he became a "colonel in the Army,"[8] and four years later on October 3, major general. His rank of lieutenant general was dated January 1, 1801 while that of general was January 21, 1812.[9] He also served as commandant of the Cork Military District in southern Ireland (1801-1803) and Severn Military District in western England (1803-1809). On February 23, 1808, he became governor of Berwick and Holy Island.[10]

Banastre Tarleton also dabbled in politics, although he made for a mediocre politician. He sat for seven sessions in Parliament for his home city of Liverpool, even defeating his brother John in 1796. Occasionally, he would wear his Legion uniform to the Commons. A staunch Whig until 1805, he is best remembered for his defense of the slave trade and his criticism of Sir Arthur Wellesley.[11]

In later life, Tarleton made several attempts to gain special recognition from the king. In January of 1815, the Order of the Bath was enlarged to include those officers who had distinguished themselves after 1803. Tarleton viewed this as a great injustice, and wrote to Earl Bathurst, Secretary for War. In his detailed letter, the aging general recounted his numerous activities during the American rebellion.[12] As a measure to soothe Tarleton's wounded pride, the Prince Regent created him a baronet on January 23, 1816.[13] At the coronation of King George IV on May 20, 1820, Tarleton became a Knight Grand Cross of the Order of the Bath.[14]

Sir Banastre Tarleton spent his remaining years at his estate in Leintwardine, Shropshire, wracked by gout and rheumatism. When the weather permitted, he would fish in the Teme River.

He died peacefully on January 16, 1833, at the age of seventy-nine.[15]

It is truly ironic that Banastre Tarleton, such a notorious figure in the American psyche, should die of old age. The image of an old man quietly fishing from a row boat does not equate with the American idea of a bloody fiend riding through the Carolina countryside. In the past two hundred years, historians have reconciled this dichotomy by making Tarleton into a conduit for a larger issue: the justice of the American cause and its virtue.

His personality helped. Young, ambitious, and arrogant, this Englishman had a no-nonsense approach to his appointed task. He employed a more brutal sense of virtue than his American counterparts, echoing the old imperial response to rebellion. In addition, he led a Loyalist regiment which saw much service. For a long time, the Green Horse was the only mounted British regiment in the South. The British Legion was a new kind of military organization, not seen in America prior to this time. Its mobility and distinctive dress also added to its mystique.[16]

Banastre Tarleton clearly inspired his men. In November 1780, Cornwallis wrote to Lieutenant Colonel John Harris Cruger: "I should wish to have as many of the Militia as possible sent to Colonel Tarleton. If anybody can put spirit into them he will."[17] Tarleton supplied the charisma while his soldiers reciprocated with a profound sense of loyalty. Overall, the British Legion served its master well and became one of the better Loyalist battalions raised by royal officials. Yet the war decimated its ranks, and in the end a Native American adage rings true for the Legion as well as other Loyalist regiments: "If they are to be killed, they are too many; if they are to fight, they are too few."[18]

To heap the most heinous acts upon the British Legion and its commandant is not realistic. There is simply no way of proving that Tarleton and his Legionnaires committed the most and the worst depredations of the war. As has been observed of the War of Austrian Succession: "It would be misleading to suggest that brutal behavior by soldiers was either typical or widely condoned. But it was not infrequent...and if it was rarely authorized, it was even more rarely punished."[19]

As a field commander, Tarleton was no more guilty or innocent of his men's actions than any other British or American officer. He had no regard for civil opinion when it conflicted with his duty. From his perspective, terror produced immediate results. For instance, during the raids on Poundridge and Bedford, New York in July 1779, he warned enemy militiamen that if they persisted in their sniping, he would burn neighboring houses. When he made good on his threat, the sniping stopped. Cornwallis observed that partisan activity in the low country of South Carolina ceased for nearly a month after Tarleton rode through the area in November 1780. Nevertheless, the effects of terror were only transitory. Once the Whigs had time to ruminate on the actions of Tarleton's Legion, they responded with equal if not more fury, as Moses Hall, Anthony Allaire, and others affirmed.[20]

The Legion commander subscribed to the view that the British Army in North America "behaved with a moderation which may have been to its detriment."[21] The terror was never sufficient for his purposes. The Americans, meanwhile, found it excessive. The Laurens-Tarleton encounter at York Town, although fictitious, expresses their stance. In the American view, no military or civil office could possess qualities of its own. Rather, the right kind of man gave dignity to the office, or in other words, "the character of the office-holder defined the office."[22] Tarleton gave the impression of being the cruel messenger of a repressive king, capable of the most reprehensible acts, including the defiling of graves and the murder of pregnant women.[23]

Professor Alan Taylor in his review of John Demos' *The Unredeemed Captive* makes an analogy between the book's protagonists (the Indians) and a black hole. He states: "We know their presence, just as we do a black hole's, primarily by their effects on nearby objects, in this case documents colonists made."[24] The same analogy can be made for our subject.

Tarleton has been vilified in American historiography. He gained notoriety during the war and since that time he has become the perfect model of the devil incarnate. Where this all originated is with an attempt by the revolutionaries to personify the "evil" confronting America. Thomas Paine did this in *Common Sense* when he called King George III "the Royal Brute of Britain." By the same token, the colonials were presented as having the virtue which made America great, as demonstrated by Mason Locke Weems in *Life and Memorable Actions of George Washington* (1800).[25]

For that reason, Tarleton has been grouped with the likes of Walter Butler, William Cuningham, David Fanning, Simon Girty, and Benedict Arnold. However, he differed from these individuals in a significant way. The perception of Tarleton as an ogre is more than a mere progression in the historiography of the Revolution. Tarleton the fiend is a political and psychological manifestation of Whig fears. Loyalists, although deluded in their beliefs, did not represent enough of a threat, politically, militarily, or psychologically. Revolutionaries needed a real "English devil" to justify their actions to the world and themselves. Tarleton filled the bill admirably.

The interception and alteration of Lord Cornwallis's August 18, 1780 letter to Lieutenant Colonel John Harris Cruger revealed the Whig philosophy. This missive contained instructions for suppressing the rebellion. Whig forgers not only altered its contents but replaced Cruger's name with that of Lieutenant Colonel Nisbet Balfour. They had good reason for doing so. As a regular British officer, Balfour symbolized the tyrannical threat to America, more so than the Tory Cruger.[26]

Banastre Tarleton was and still is a convenient scapegoat, and by focusing on him, Americans have obscured their own participation in a cruel war.[27] One contemporary, the London publisher Charles Dilly, viewed him in a criminal light. In 1785, Dilly hesitated to sell David Ramsay's nationalistic *History of the Revolution of South-Carolina*.... He feared angry British mobs as well as possible lawsuits. Said Dilly: "The war being over, the hazard of publication might enable the criminals instead of receiving punishment (I mean Tarleton and others of his sanguinary cast) to call it down on the publisher."[28]

Nevertheless, the term "Bloody Tarleton" did not originate until long after the war. In 1957, Robert Duncan Bass coined the phrase in his eloquent biography of Tarleton. This professor of English literature relied heavily upon previous historians who refined colonial perceptions of the dragoon leader and made him appear more brutish.[29] With the publication of *The Green Dragoon: The Lives of Banastre Tarleton and Mary Robinson*, "Bloody Tarleton" became a part of American heritage and the national psyche. There is now no way of escaping him. A recent documentary on the American Revolution even refers to him as "the Butcher Tarleton."[30]

We are left with the legacy of "Bloody Tarleton," created through propaganda, national chauvinism, oral history, and occasionally complete fabrication.[31] The historiography of the American Revolution has created this image, based upon the Whig abstraction of brutal or imperfect virtue. "Bloody Tarleton" is both myth *and* reality. American popular culture assures the man's infamy. Not surprising, he remains a relatively obscure figure in Great Britain.[32]

This book began with the story of a septuagenarian named Moses Hall. He submitted his application for a pension two years after another septuagenarian peacefully died in Leintwardine, Shropshire, England. In the twilight of their years, Moses Hall and Banastre Tarleton undoubtedly had the same basic memories of the Revolutionary War: the sound of musketry, the smell of Carolina pine, the taste of salt pork, the feel of a warm camp fire on a cold winter's night. As for their more philosophical reminiscences, we have seen fit to remember for them.

---

[1] The Legion returned to New York aboard the sloop *Bonetta* and other cartel ships. Some members had to wait until after the preliminary peace agreement had been signed in order to be

exchanged. Lieut. Col. J. G. Simcoe, *A History of the Operations of a Partisan Corps Called the Queen's Rangers* (New York, 1844; repr., New York: Arno Press, 1968), 254, 257-258; Bernhard A. Uhlendorf, trans., *Revolution in America: Confidential Letters and Journals 1776-1784 of Adjutant General Major Baurmeister of the Hessian Forces* (Rutgers University Press, 1957), 479-480, 487, 530; Jacobus Cropsey to Gen. Sir Guy Carleton, Narrows, August 7, 1782, Carleton Papers, the Royal Institution of Great Britain, vol. 25, No. 1, 1p. (microfilm) (hereafter cited as Carleton Papers). Before the receipt of Cropsey's letter, orders had been issued for the British Legion to set up bivouac at Jamaica, New York. G. G. Ludlow to Major Frederick MacKenzie, Denyses, August 10, 1782, Carleton Papers, vol. 25, No. 2, 1p. After York Town, some elements of the British Legion were incorporated into the King's American Dragoons under Lt. Col. Benjamin Thompson. Col. Benjamin Thompson to Lt. Gen. Alexander Leslie, Duxcents Plantation (SC), February 25, 1782, Carleton Papers, vol. 53, No. 128, 4pp. Philip Katcher and Michael Youens, *The American Provincial Corps 1775-1784*, Men-at-Arms Series (Reading, England: Osprey, 1973), 39-40.

[2] This figure includes 169 cavalry and thirty-nine infantry. Embarkation return, September 15, 1783, Colonial Office Records, Public Record Office, Kew, 5/111, f. 149 (hereafter cited as PRO). Esther Clark Wright, "The Evacuation of the Loyalists from New York in 1783," *The Nova Scotia Historical Review* 4 (1984): 24-25; George Hanger, *The Life, Adventures, and Opinions of Col. George Hanger*, 2 vols. (London: J. Debrett, 1801), 2:437; Carleton to Brigadier General H.E. Fox, New York, September 12, 1783, vol. 49, No. 141, 4p., Carleton to Lieutenant Colonel Glasier, 4th Battalion, 60th Regiment of Foot, New York, September 12, 1783, Vol. 49, No. 146, 1p., Governor John Parr to Carleton, Halifax, September 20, 1783, vol. 49, No. 204, 4pp, all in the Carleton Papers. Some Legionnaires had problems with back pay while others had their property confiscated by the American government. See the memorial of Sergeant Nathaniel Underhill to Lt. Gen. James Robertson, New York, July 19, 1782, vol. 25, No. 120, 2p., memorandum for making out a warrant to Captain Charles Handfield for payment to NCOs and privates of the British Legion, discharged and going to England (267 pounds, 4 shillings, 1.5 pence), in August 25 to October 24, 1783 British Legion pay abstracts, vol. 28, No. 110, 1p., Maurice Morgann to Lt. Col. Banastre Tarleton, July 9, 1783, vol. 47,

No. 192, 1p., Assistant Surgeon Joseph Skinner to Carleton, New York, October 21, 1783, vol. 52, No. 134, 1p., all in the Carleton Papers. Lorenzo Sabine, *Biographical Sketches of Loyalists of the American Revolution, With an Historical Essay*, 2 vols. (Boston: Little, Brown and Company, 1864), 1:546, 552-553, 569, 2:80, 387, 434, 489, 596.

[3] Major George Hanger supervised the disbandment of the regiment. Hanger, *The Life of Col. Hanger*, 2:437. On his way home, a French privateer captured the merchant ship carrying Tarleton. He and two other officers had to pay four hundred guineas as ransom. Robert D. Bass, *The Green Dragoon: The Lives of Banastre Tarleton and Mary Robinson* (New York: Henry Holt, 1957), 7. *London Ruddiman's Weekly Mercury* of January 2, 1782, reported: "It must give pleasure to every lover of this country, to be assured, that by a letter from the gallant Col. Tarleton to his brother, now in Ipswich, that distinguished character was in perfect health in the middle of last month, and is daily expected in England."

[4] It is interesting to note that the painting depicts Tarleton in a half-stooping position, hiding his right hand. J.R. Smith engraved the portrait in mezzotinto the same year. The Smith mezzotinto can be seen in Henry P. Johnston, *The Yorktown Campaign and the Surrender of Cornwallis, 1781* (New York, 1881), 226-227. William Henry was the third son of King George III. When the commander of the Green Horse met him, the duke was a sixteen-year-old midshipman aboard the *Prince George.* Tarleton also developed a friendship with Frederick, the Duke of York. Bass, *The Green Dragoon*, 6-9, 266. King George III did not like the Prince of Wales's wild behavior and frowned upon his friendship with Banastre Tarleton. The Prince was eight years younger and became awed by the dragoon's stories. Tarleton's later attacks upon Earl Cornwallis, a favorite at court, also did not endear him to His Royal Majesty. "Sir Banastre Tarleton," *Blackwoods Magazine* 116 (October 1874), 441; during this time the young colonel of dragoons made frequent pleas to his family to pay off his debts. See the Tarleton family correspondence in Bass, *The Green Dragoon*, 209-224, 450. For the family's business ventures after 1783, see the Tarleton Papers, Liverpool Record Office, 920 TAR 4/5, 4/10, 4/26, 4/41, 5/11, 5/12 (microfilm). The Napoleonic wars ruined Banastre's brothers. Both John and Thomas filed for bankruptcy before they died.

[5] Lady Jane Tarleton did not approve of Mary Robinson. Bass, *The Green Dragoon*, 9, 42, 128-138, 194-240, 312, 318-320, 328-333, 374, 387, 389, 392, 401. Mary Robinson died on December 26, 1800 after a prolonged illness. She was only forty-two years old. Her parting shot at the man who left her was a novel entitled *The False Friend*, published in February 1799. The main character had the name of "Treville." The Duc de Lauzun described her as "gay, lively, open, and a good creature." *Memoirs of the Duc de Lauzun*, trans. C.K. Scott Moncrieff (London: George Routledge and Sons, 1928), 211. Susan Priscilla was barely twenty when she wed the forty-four year old major general. A natural daughter of Robert Bertie, fourth Duke of Ancaster, she had a dowry reported at twenty thousand pounds sterling. The marriage produced no children.

[6] Lieutenant Colonel Banastre Tarleton, *A History of the Campaigns of 1780 and 1781, in the Southern Provinces of North America* (London: T. Cadell, 1787). In 1796, Tarleton had a second edition published. Contrary to Robert Bass's claim (*The Green Dragoon*, 367), the 1796 version does mention the Cowpens. An original copy of the second edition can be found in the Rare Books Room of the Alderman Library at the University of Virginia, Charlottesville. In the above quote, his lordship was making reference to Kings Mountain. "My not sending relief to Colonel Ferguson, although he was positively ordered to retire, was entirely owing to Tarleton himself; he pleaded weakness from the remains of a fever, and refused to make an attempt, although I used the most earnest intreaties." Earl Cornwallis to the Bishop of Lichfield and Coventry, Calcutta, Dec. 12, 1787, *Correspondence of Charles, First Marquis Cornwallis*, 13 vols., ed. Charles Ross, 2nd ed. (London: John Murray, 1859), 1: 315-316. During this time, Lord Cornwallis declined to ask Tarleton to join his staff in India because of the latter's political affiliations. Bass, *The Green Dragoon*, 248-252. Tarleton's *History* added to the controversy over who actually lost the war in America. For the pamphlet war between Sir Henry Clinton and Earl Cornwallis, see Benjamin Franklin Stevens, comp. and ed., *The Campaign in Virginia 1781. An exact Reprint of Six rare Pamphlets on the Clinton-Cornwallis Controversy with very numerous important Unpublished Manuscript Notes By Sir Henry Clinton K.B. and the Omitted and hitherto Unpublished portions of the Letters in their Appendixes added from the*

Original Manuscripts, 2 vols. (London: 4 Trafalgar Square, Charing Cross, 1888).

[7] MacKenzie makes especial note of the Cowpens and the "five errors" committed by the British commander. Roderick MacKenzie, *Strictures on Lt. Col. Tarleton's History of the Campaigns of 1780 and 1781, in the Southern Provinces of North America; Wherein Characters and Corps are Vindicated from Injurious Aspersions, and Several Important Transactions Placed in Their Proper Point of View* (London: R. Faulder, 1787); Major George Hanger, *An Address to the Army; in Reply to Strictures, by Roderick M'Kenzie (Late Lieutenant in the 71st Regiment) on Tarleton's History of the Campaigns of 1780 and 1781* (London: James Ridgway, 1789); the Prince's club was called Dover House. General Grant to Earl Cornwallis, April 6, 1788, *Correspondence of Cornwallis*, ed. Ross, 1:372-378.

[8] Unlike a regular colonelcy, this commission did not entitle the owner to the command of a specific regiment. W. Y. Carman, "Banastre Tarleton and the British Legion," *Journal of the Society for Army Historical Research* 62 (1984): 128; previously on December 25, 1782, Tarleton received the permanent rank of lieutenant colonel of "Light Dragoons, America." This culminated an effort to gain recognition for the British Legion and to procure half-pay for its officers. Murtie June Clark, ed., *Loyalists in the American Southern Campaign of the Revolutionary War*, 3 vols. (Baltimore: Genealogical Publishing Company, 1981), 3:343; Order for forming a Corps of Cavalry, under the Command of Lieut. Colonel Commandant Tarleton, December 25, 1782, War Office Records, PRO, 26/31, f. 328; Commissions for the following Gentlemen to be Officers in a Regiment of Light Dragoons, Home Office Records, PRO, 51/146, f. 57. Twenty-four officers are listed in this document.

[9] In 1799, Major General Tarleton was sent to Portugal but quickly obtained his recall because of the lack of activity in the area. Robert H. Vetch, "Sir Banastre Tarleton, 1754-1833," *The Dictionary of National Biography*, 22 vols., eds. Sir Leslie Stephen and Sir Sidney Lee (London: Oxford University Press, 1921-1922), 19:368; Captain Walter Harold Wilkin, *Some British Soldiers in America* (London: Hugh Rees, LTD., 1914), 149; the *London Gazette* of December 31, 1811 announced his rank of general by brevet; Benson J. Lossing, *The Pictorial Field-*

Book of the Revolution, 2 vols. (New York, 1855), 2:401 erroneously gives the date for the major general commission as 1817.

[10] Vetch, "Sir Banastre Tarleton," *Dictionary of National Biography*, 19:368; Wilkin, *Some British Soldiers*, 149; Bass, *The Green Dragoon*, 404-405, 408, 411; Tarleton also held colonelcies in the following regiments: Durham Fencible Cavalry (commission date: May 11, 1799), Twenty-Second Light Dragoons (January 8, 1801), Twenty-First Light Dragoons (April 29, 1802), and the Eighth or Royal Irish Hussars (January 15, 1818).

[11] Except for a brief respite in 1806-1807, he sat in Parliament continuously from 1790 to 1812. Reportedly, the former Legion officer would raise his mangled hand in the streets of Liverpool during election time in order to remind his constituents of what he had sacrificed for King and Country. James B. Atlay, "Tarleton of the Legion," *Cornhill Magazine* (August 1905), 246-247; "Sir Banastre Tarleton," *Blackwoods Magazine*, 449; by this time, Tarleton's gambling and political activities had finally alienated his family. Bass, *The Green Dragoon*, 364, 429; some give Tarleton the credit for calling Wellesley the "Sepoy General." Wellesley, the later Duke of Wellington, coolly handled Tarleton's criticism of his operations in Portugal. He replied that "he would much rather follow his example in the field than his advice in the senate." For Tarleton's parliamentary career, see *The Annual Register, or a View of the History, Politics, and Literature, For the Year, 1792; 1795; 1796; 1797; 1798; 1803; 1804; 1806; 1808; 1809; 1810; 1812* (London, 1799-1813). His argument that the slave trade was profitable for Liverpool is in volume xxxiv (1792), pp. 149, 152-153. The verbal sparring with Wellesley is in volume li (1809), p. 60.

[12] Vetch, "Sir Banastre Tarleton," *Dictionary of National Biography*, 19:368; in his letter to Bathurst, the aging Tarleton related how the British Legion marched over 1200 miles during the entire southern campaigns. Tarleton to the Earl Bathurst, Secretary for War, Leintwardine, Ludlow, January 27, 1815, in Bass, *The Green Dragoon*, 443-446.

[13] This was during the time of George III's mental illness. The Prince of Wales (the future George IV) held the throne as regent. Carman, "Banastre Tarleton and the British Legion," 128; the award of the

baronetcy was announced on November 6, 1815, but it was not actually bestowed until January 23, 1816. Wilkin, *Some British Soldiers*, 149; because Tarleton had no children, he proposed collateral descent for the baronetcy. He wished for his favorite nephew, "Thomas Tarleton, Esquire, of Bolesworth Castle, in the county of Cheshire, and heirs male of his body lawfully begotten." The Herald's College denied the request. Bass, *The Green Dragoon*, 447-448; John Burke and John Bernard Burke, *A Genealogical and Heraldic History of the Extinct and Dormant Baronetcies of England, Ireland, and Scotland*, 2nd ed. (London: John Russell Smith, 1844), 518-519. This source erroneously gives the date as November 6, 1818. Because Sir Banastre died without issue, his baronetcy expired in January 1833.

[14] Carman, "Banastre Tarleton and the British Legion," 128; Vetch, "Sir Banastre Tarleton," *Dictionary of National Biography*, 19:368; Bass, *The Green Dragoon*, 451. Neither of these two royal honors admitted Tarleton to the peerage or nobility. A baronetcy was merely a hereditary knighthood. Valentine Heywood, *British Titles: The Use and Misuse of the Titles of Peers and Commoners, with Some Historical Notes*, 2nd ed. (London: Adam and Charles Black, 1953), 119-125, 134, 137.

[15] A relative of the family remembered "a fine, but rather stern and rugged looking old man,...confined by gout to his chair and his crippled hands further deformed by the loss of a thumb and forefinger of one of them in the American war." Bass, *The Green Dragoon*, 442, 452. Vetch, "Sir Banastre Tarleton," *Dictionary of National Biography*, 19:368 and Wilkin, *Some British Soldiers*, 148, give his death date as January 25. This is actually the date of his burial.

[16] Stephen Conway, "British Army Officers and the American War for Independence," *William and Mary Quarterly* 41 (1984): 265-276; Lawrence Linfield Stirling, "Banastre Tarleton: A Reevaluation of His Career in the American Revolution" (MA thesis, Louisiana State University and Agricultural and Mechanical College, August 1964), 74. Stirling makes a good attempt at diminishing the image of "Bloody Tarleton" in American history; Anthony J. Scotti, Jr., "'This Disagreeable Exertion of Authority:' Banastre Tarleton and the British Legion in the Southern Campaigns, 1780-1781" (MA thesis, Wake Forest University, May 1991), 82-83; the British Legion represented "precisely the kind of force Britain was always lacking in sufficient

numbers throughout the war, especially useful in the Southern terrain." Don Higginbotham, *The War of American Independence: Military Attitudes, Policies, and Practice, 1763-1789* (New York: The Macmillan Company, 1971), 367.

[17] Cornwallis to Cruger, November 25, 1780, Wynnesborough, in Bass, *The Green Dragoon*, 107, 123. Sir Henry Clinton to Lord George Germain, May 15, 1780, Charleston, *Documents of the American Revolution: 1770-1783*, ed. K. G. Davies, 21 vols., Colonial Office Series (Dublin: Irish University Press, 1972-1981), 18:91.

[18] Mohawk chief Theyanoguin or Hendrick made this observation of colonial troops before they marched into a French ambush along the shores of Lake George, New York in 1755. Francis Parkman, *The Conspiracy of Pontiac and the Indian War after the Conquest of Canada*, 2 vols: The Library of America (Boston: Little, Brown and Company, 1851; repr., New York: Viking Press, 1991), 1:437. Bernard Berelson and Gary A. Steiner, *Human Behavior: An Inventory of Scientific Findings* (New York: Harcourt, Brace & World, 1964), 370, 372, 374-379, 662-666; John Keegan, *The Mask of Command* (New York: Viking Press, 1987), 10-11; Martin van Creveld, *Command in War* (Cambridge: Harvard University Press, 1985), 5-6, 8-9, 16, 274-275. Anthony J. Scotti, Jr., "British Victory" and "Loyalists," in *History in Dispute: The American Revolution, 1763-1789*, edited by Keith Krawczynski (Columbia, S.C.: Manly/Farmington Hills, Michigan: St. James, 2002).

[19] Reed Browning, *The War of the Austrian Succession* (New York: St. Martin's Press, 1993), 376; William Dobein James, *A Sketch of the Life of Brig. Gen. Francis Marion and a History of His Brigade From Its Rise in June 1780 until Disbanded in December, 1782 With Descriptions of Characters and Scenes Not Heretofore Published* (Charleston, 1821; Marietta, Georgia: Continental Book Company, 1948), 64; Berelson and Steiner, *Human Behavior*, 367.

[20] Robert Kyff, "Tarleton's Raid on Bedford and Poundridge," *The Westchester Historian* 44 (Summer 1968): 53; Cornwallis to Clinton, Wynnesborough, December 3, 1780, in *Lieutenant-General Sir Henry Clinton, K.B., Observations on Some Parts of the Answer of Earl Cornwallis to Sir Henry Clintons Narrative* (London: J. Debrett, 1783), 47; John C. Dann, ed., *The Revolution Remembered: Eyewitness Accounts of the War for*

Independence (Chicago and London: University of Chicago Press, 1980), 201-203; *Diary of Lieut. Anthony Allaire, of Ferguson's Corps*, in Lyman C. Draper, *King's Mountain and Its Heroes: History of the Battle of King's Mountain, October 7th, 1780, and the Events Which Led To It* (Cincinnati: Peter G. Thomson, 1881), 484-515; Jeremy Black, *War for America: The Fight For Independence 1775-1783* (New York: St. Martin's Press, 1991), 18-19; Stephen Conway, *The War of American Independence 1775-1783* (New York: St. Martin's Press, 1995), 247. During the War of 1812, the British again discovered that the tactics of retaliation only strengthened American resolve. Walter Lord, *The Dawn's Early Light* (Baltimore and London: Johns Hopkins University Press, 1972), 315.

[21] John E. Ferling, *A Wilderness of Miseries: War and Warriors in Early America* (Westport, Connecticut: Greenwood Press, 1980), 192.

[22] "Military Leadership in the American Revolution," in Don Higginbotham, *War and Society in Revolutionary America: The Wider Dimensions of Conflict* (Columbia: University of South Carolina Press, 1988), 88-89; Maarten Ultee, "Adapting to Conditions," in Maarten Ultee, ed., *Adapting to Conditions: War and Society in the Eighteenth Century* (The University of Alabama Press, 1986), 5-6; a description of the Laurens-Tarleton encounter is in Chapter VI.

[23] Tarleton to Captain John André, February 19, 1779, Sir Henry Clinton Papers, William L. Clements Library, University of Michigan, Ann Arbor, Michigan; Tarleton to Cornwallis, August 5, 1780, Leneau's Ferry, in Cornwallis Papers, Public Record Office, Kew, 30/11/63, ff. 19-21 (hereafter cited as PRO); Joseph Johnson, *Traditions and Reminiscences Chiefly of the American Revolution in the South: Including Biographical Sketches, Incidents and Anecdotes, Few of Which Have Been Published, Particularly of Residents in the Upper Country* (Charleston: Walker and James, 1851), 162; Jean-Baptiste-Antoine de Verger, "Journal of the Most Important Events that occurred to the French Troops under the Command of M. le Comte de Rochambeau," in *The American Campaigns of Rochambeau's Army 1780, 1781, 1782, 1783*, trans. and eds. Howard C. Rice, Jr. and Anne S. K. Brown, 2 vols. (Princeton University Press, 1972), 1:137.

[24] Alan Taylor, "A Review of *The Unredeemed Captive: A Family Story From Early America*. By John Demos. (New York: Alfred A. Knopf, 1994)," in *William and Mary Quarterly* 52 (July 1995): 518.

[25] Howard Swiggett, *War Out of Niagara*, Empire State Historical Publication 20 (Port Washington, New York: Ira J. Friedman, 1963), vii-viii, xx; Thomas Paine, *Common Sense and The Crisis* (Philadelphia: W. & T. Bradford, 1776; Albany: Charles R. & George Webster, 1792; repr., Garden City, New York: Anchor Books, 1973), 41; by 1850, fifty-nine editions of Weems's "biography" had been printed. *The Life of George Washington; With Curious Anecdotes, Equally Honourable to Himself and Exemplary to His Young Countrymen*, 9th ed. (Philadelphia: Mathew Carey, 1809); John Morgan Dederer, *War in America to 1775 Before Yankee Doodle* (New York: New York University Press, 1990), 23; "The American Revolution Today," in John Shy, *A People Numerous and Armed: Reflections on The Military Struggle for American Independence* (Oxford University Press, 1976), 8-9.

[26] Cornwallis to Cruger, August 18, 1780, in *Correspondence of Cornwallis*, ed. Ross, 1:56-57; Cornwallis to Balfour, August 18, 1780, in Cornwallis Papers, PRO, 30/11/95, f. 10; Robert M. Weir, "'The Violent Spirit,' the Reestablishment of Order, and the Continuity of Leadership in Post-Revolutionary South Carolina," in Ronald Hoffman, Thad W. Tate, and Peter J. Albert, eds., *An Uncivil War: The Southern Backcountry during the American Revolution* (Charlottesville: University Press of Virginia, 1985), 78; L. Edward Purchell, *Who was Who in the American Revolution* (New York: Facts On File, 1993), 74-75, 121, 157-158, 189; Charles Royster, "'The Nature of Treason': Revolutionary Virtue and American Reactions to Benedict Arnold," *William and Mary Quarterly* 36 (1979):163-193; Arnold is in essence an embarrassment. He was truly a remarkable soldier, "but it goes against the grain to think so highly of turncoats." Norman Gelb, *Less than Glory* (New York: GP Putnam's Sons, 1984), 163.

[27] *The South Carolina Royal Gazette* (Charleston), February 9, 16, and April 17, 24, 1782, reported the execution of thirteen Loyalist prisoners in Orangeburgh. After killing one of them, a Rebel guard said that he had never seen "a son of a bitch bleed so much in his life." Ferling, *A Wilderness of Miseries*, 105-108, 154-169, 189-190, 196; attempts at justifying American actions can be found in Henry Lee, *Memoirs of the*

War in the Southern Department of the United States, 2 vols. (Philadelphia and New York: Bradford & Inskeep & Inskeep & Bradford, 1812); Hank Messick, *King's Mountain: The Epic of the Blue Ridge "Mountain Men" in the American Revolution* (Boston: Little, Brown and Company, 1976), 152-153; also see Joel W. Huffstetler, "Henry Lee and Banastre Tarleton: How Historians Use Their Memoirs," *The Southern Historian* 6 (1985): 12-19.

[28] Arthur H. Shaffer, *To Be An American: David Ramsay and the Making of the American Consciousness* (Columbia: University of South Carolina Press, 1991), 102; Weir, "'The Violent Spirit,'" in Hoffman et al, eds. *An Uncivil War*, 78.

[29] "Tarleton's Quarter!" originated during the war. See David Ramsay, *The History of the Revolution of South-Carolina, From a British Province to an Independent State*, 2 vols. (Trenton: Isaac Collins, 1785), 2:110; "Anecdote of Colonel Tarleton," *Philadelphia American Museum or Universal Magazine* 4 (1788): 94; "Lt. Col. Tarleton: His Character," *Cambridge (Massachusetts) General Repository and Review* 3 (January 1813): 106; Alexander Garden, *Anecdotes of the Revolutionary War in America, with Sketches of Character of Persons the Most Distinguished, in the Southern States, for Civil and Military Services* (Charleston: A.E. Miller, 1822), 259; George Washington Parke Custis, *Recollections and Private Memoirs of Washington, by his adopted son, George Washington Parke Custis, with a memoir of the author, by his daughter; and illustrative and explanatory notes. by Benson J. Lossing* (New York: Derby and Jackson, 1860), 251-253; Willard M. Wallace, *Appeal to Arms: A Military History of the American Revolution* (New York: Harper and Brothers, 1951), 209; Christopher Ward, *The War of the Revolution*, 2 vols. (New York: Macmillan, 1952), 2:701; Hugh F. Rankin, "Cowpens: Prelude to Yorktown," *North Carolina Historical Review* 31 (July 1954): 346; George F. Scheer and Hugh F. Rankin, *Rebels and Redcoats* (Cleveland: World Publishing Company, 1957), 457.

[30] Robert D. Bass, *The Green Dragoon: The Lives of Banastre Tarleton and Mary Robinson* (New York: Henry Holt, 1957); "Bloody Tarleton" can be viewed in Don Cambou, *The American Revolution: The Birth of the Republic*, Part III, hosted by Bill Kurtis, Arts and Entertainment (North Hollywood, CA: Greystone Communications, Inc., 1994), documentary; Elswyth Thane, *The Family Quarrel: A Journey Through the Years of the*

Revolution (New York: Duell, Sloan and Pearce, 1959), 25, 100; Bart McDowell, *The Revolutionary War* (Washington, DC, National Geographic Society, 1967), 165; Higginbotham, *The War of American Independence*, 361; "Bloody Ban" can be found in John S. Pancake, *This Destructive War: The British Campaign in the Carolinas, 1780-1782* (Tuscaloosa and London: University of Alabama Press, 1985), 71 and Craig L. Symonds, *A Battlefield Atlas of the American Revolution* (Baltimore: Nautical and Aviation Publishing, 1986), 80; James L. Stokesbury, *A Short History of the American Revolution* (New York: William Morrow, 1991), 231-232; "the Butcher Tarleton" is also in Christopher Hibbert, *Redcoats and Rebels: The American Revolution Through British Eyes* (New York: Avon Books, 1991), 263-264, 266; J. Tracy Power, "'The Virtue of Humanity was Totally Forgot': Buford's Massacre, May 29, 2780," *South Carolina Historical Magazine* 93 (January 1992), 5; a comical rendition of the Englishman is done in Alan Alda, *Sweet Liberty*, starring Alan Alda, Michael Caine, Bob Hoskins, and Michelle Pfeiffer, 107 min., Color, Rated PG (Los Angeles, CA: MCA/Universal Home Video, Inc., 1986), movie; the novelist Dewey Lambdin also refers to Tarleton's reputation in *The French Admiral* (New York: Pinnacle Books, 1990), 27, 30-31. Another recent documentary is a bit more objective. See Carol L. Fleisher, director, *The Revolutionary War,* narrated by Charles Kuralt, The Learning Channel (Bethesda, Md.: Discovery Communications, 1995).

[31] Philip Davidson, *Propaganda and the American Revolution 1763-1783* (Chapel Hill: University of North Carolina Press, 1941), 366; Wesley Frank Craven, *The Legend of the Founding Fathers* (New York: New York University Press, 1956), 2, 60, 166; Gelb, *Less than Glory*, 11-12, 14, 17, 172; Lester H. Cohen, *The Revolutionary Histories: Contemporary Narratives of the American Revolution* (Ithaca: Cornell University Press, 1980), 15, 185, 192, 195, 197, 219-229; Michael Kammen, *Mystic Chords of Memory: The Transformation of Tradition in American Culture* (New York: Alfred A. Knopf, 1991), 3, 13, 17, 25, 38-39. Also see Kammen's *A Season of Youth: The American Revolution and the Historical Imagination* (New York: Alfred A. Knopf, 1978), 186-222.

[32] "What people believe to be true about their past is usually more important in determining their behavior and responses than truth itself." Kammen, *Mystic Chords*, 38-39; William Seymour, *The Price of*

Folly: British Blunders in the War of American Independence (London: Brassey's 1995), passim.

BIBLIOGRAPHY

Primary Sources

Unpublished Manuscripts

Colonial Williamsburg, Inc., Williamsburg, Virginia
    British Headquarters Papers

Library of Congress, Manuscripts Division, Washington, DC
    Nathanael Greene Papers
    George Washington Papers

Liverpool Record Office, Liverpool, England
    Tarleton Papers (microfilm)

National Archives, Washington, DC
    Papers of the Continental Congress (microfilm)

New-York Historical Society, New York, New York
    M.S. Almanack for the year 1783, compiled by Bernhard de Wiederhold

Princeton University Library, Manuscript Division, Department of Rare Books and Special Collections, Princeton, New Jersey
    Orderly Book of Captain Scott's Company of the British Legion, Andre de Coppet Collection

Public Archives of Canada, Ottawa, Ontario
    Loyalist Regiment Muster Rolls, 1777-1783

Public Record Office, Kew, Richmond, Surrey, England
    Colonial Office Records
    Cornwallis Papers (microfilm)
    Home Office Records
    War Office Records

South Carolina Department of Archives and History, Columbia, South Carolina
    Sir Guy Carleton Papers (microfilm)
    Alexander Leslie Letterbook, 1781-1782, Nisbet Balfour, Letters (microfilm)

South Caroliniana Library, University of South Carolina, Columbia, South Carolina
    Charleston, Revolutionary War Collection
    Sir Henry Clinton Manuscripts
    Ninety-Six District Papers

Sterling Memorial Library, Yale University, New Haven, Connecticut
    William Jackson Papers

William L. Clements Library, University of Michigan, Ann Arbor, Michigan
    Sir Henry Clinton Papers

Newspapers and Periodicals

The Annual Register, or a View of the History, Politics, and Literature, For the Year 1780, 1781, 1791, 1792, 1795, 1796, 1797, 1798, 1803, 1804, 1806, 1808, 1809, 1810, 1812 (London).

Army List, 1780

Army List, 1781

Boston New England or Independent Chronicle, August 10 and September 7, 1780.

Cambridge Chronicle and Journal (England), January 2, 1779.

Cambridge (Massachusetts) General Repository and Review, 3 (January 1813).

Charleston Courier, September 3, 1842.

Charleston South Carolina Royal Gazette, February 9, 16, April 17, 24, 1782.

Gentleman's Magazine (London), March 1781.

Ipswich (Connecticut) Journal, October 21, 1780.

London Chronicle, July 18, October 14, 1780; March 29, 1781.

London Gazette Extraordinary, July 5, October 9, 1780; December 31, 1811.

New York Packet, November 22, 1781.

New York Royal Gazette, June 3, July 8 and 11, 1778; June 16, July 7, 1779; December 26, 1781; June 29, July 20, 1782; April 12, 1783.

Petersburg Intelligencer

Philadelphia American Museum or Universal Magazine, 4 (1788).

Philadelphia Pennsylvania Packet, February 17, 1781.

Quebec Gazette, August 18, 1766.

Ruddiman's Weekly Mercury (London), January 2 and 30, 1782.

Washington National Intelligencer, July 5, 1813.

Williamsburg Virginia Gazette, September 8, 1766.

Collected Documents

American Material from the Tarleton Papers in the Liverpool Record Office. Intro. P.D. Richardson. British Records Relating to America in Microform. Ed. W.E. Minchinton. University of Hull, 1974.

Atkinson, C.T. "British Forces in North America, 1774- 1781: Their Distribution and Strength." *Journal of the Society for Army Historical Research* 16 (1937): 3-23; 19 (1940): 163-166; 20 (1941): 190-192.

Butler, John, comp. *The Papers of the Continental Congress: 1774-1789*. Washington, DC: US Government Printing Office, 1978.

Chesnutt, David R. and C. James Taylor, eds. *The Papers of Henry Laurens*. 14 vols. to date. Columbia: University of South Carolina Press, 1968- .

Clark, Murtie June, ed. *Loyalists in the American Southern Campaign of the Revolutionary War*. 3 vols. Baltimore: Genealogical Publishing Company, 1981.

Clark, Walter, ed. *The State Records of North Carolina*. 26 vols. Goldsboro, NC: Nash Brothers, 1886-1907.

Correspondance du Lord G. Germain, Avec Les Généraux Clinton, Cornwallis et les Amiraux dans la station de l'Amérique, avec plusieurs lettres interceptées du Général Washington, du Marquis de la Fayette et de M. de Barras, chef d'Escadre. Berne: Chez la Nouvelle Société Typographique, 1782.

Cumberland, Duke of. "Standing orders for the dragoons, circa 1755." *Journal of the Society for Army Historical Research* 23 (1945): 98-106.

Davies, K.G., ed. *Documents of the American Revolution: 1770-1783*. Colonial Office Series. 21 vols. Dublin: Irish University Press, 1972-1981.

Fitzpatrick, John, ed. *The Writings of George Washington: 1745-1799*. 39 vols. Washington, DC: US Government Printing Office, 1931-1944.

Godfrey, Carlos E. "Muster Rolls of Three Troops of Loyalist Light Dragoons." *The Pennsylvania Magazine of History and Biography* 34 (1910): 1-8.

Historical Manuscripts Commission Great Britain. *Report on American Manuscripts in the Royal Institution of Great Britain*. Intro. George A. Billias. 4 vols. Boston: Gregg Press, 1972.

Idzerda, Stanley J., ed. *Lafayette in the Age of the American Revolution: Selected Letters and Papers, 1776-1790*. 5 vols. to date. Ithaca: Cornell University Press, 1977- .

Journals of the House of Commons, 1547-1803. 57 vols. London, 1803.

Kelby, William, comp. *Orderly Book of the Three Battalions of Loyalists Commanded by Brigadier-General Oliver De Lancey 1776-1778*. New York: New-York Historical Society, 1917; repr., Baltimore: Genealogical Publishing, 1972.

Ketchum, Richard M., ed. "New War Letters of Banastre Tarleton." *New-York Historical Society Quarterly* 51 (January 1967): 61-81.

Murdoch, David H., ed. *Rebellion in America: A Contemporary British Viewpoint, 1765-1783*. Santa Barbara, California and Oxford, England: Clio Books, 1979.

Myers, Theodorus Bailey. *Cowpens Papers, Being Correspondence of General Morgan and the Prominent Actors*. Charleston, 1881.

Neagles, James C. Summer Soldiers: *A Survey and Index of Revolutionary War Courts-Martial*. Salt Lake City, Utah: Ancestry, Inc., 1986.

Newsome, A.R. "A British Orderly Book, 1780-1781." *North Carolina Historical Review* 9 (1932): 57-78, 163-186, 273-298, 366-392.

Peckham, Howard H., ed. *Sources of American Independence: Selected Manuscripts from the Collections of the William L. Clements Library*. 2 vols. Chicago and London: University of Chicago Press, 1978.

Showman, Richard K., ed. *The Papers of General Nathanael Greene*. 7 vols. to date. Chapel Hill: University of North Carolina Press, 1976- .

Stevens, B.F., comp. *B.F. Stevens's Facsimiles of Manuscripts in European Archives Relating to America 1773-1783*. London, 1889-1895. Wilmington, Delaware: Mellifont Press, 1970.

Wallace, Lee A. Jr., ed. *The Orderly Book of Captain Benjamin Taliaferro 2d Virginia Detachment Charleston, South Carolina, 1780*. Richmond: Virginia State Library, 1980.

Memoirs, Narratives, and Similar Materials

The American Campaigns of Rochambeau's Army 1780, 1781, 1782, 1783. Trans. and eds. Howard C. Rice, Jr. and Anne S.K. Brown. 2 vols. Princeton University Press, 1972.

The American Journal of Ambrose Serle, Secretary to Lord Howe 1776-1778. Ed. Edward H. Tatum, Jr. San Marino, California: Huntington Library, 1940.

Archibald Robertson, Lieutenant-General Royal Engineers: His Diaries and Sketches in America 1762-1780. Ed. Harry Miller Lydenberg. New York: New York Public Library, 1930.

Barnwell, Joseph W., ed. "Letters of John Rutledge." *The South Carolina Historical and Genealogical Magazine* 18 (1917): 42-49.

Churchill, Randolph S. and Martin Gilbert, eds. *Winston S. Churchill*. 8 vols. London: Heinemann, 1966-1988.

Clinton, Sir Henry. *The American Rebellion: Sir Henry Clinton's Narrative of His Campaigns, 1775-1782, with an Appendix of Original Documents*. Ed. William B. Willcox. New Haven: Yale University Press, 1951.

———. *A Letter from Lieut. Gen. Sir Henry Clinton, K.B. To the Commissioners of Public Accounts, Relative to Some Observations in their Seventh Report, Which may be judged to imply Censure on the late Commanders in Chief of His Majesty's Army in North America*. London: J. Debrett, 1784.

———. *Memorandums, etc. etc., Respecting The Unprecedented Treatment Which the Army Have Met With Respecting Plunder Taken After A Siege, And of Which Plunder The Navy Serving With The Army Divided Their More Than Ample Share, Now Fourteen Years Since*. London, 1794.

———. *Narrative of the Campaign in 1781 in North America*. London, 1783. Philadelphia: John Campbell, 1865.

———. *Observations on Mr. Stedman's History of the American War*. London: J. Debrett, 1794.

———. *Observations on Some Parts of the Answer of Earl Cornwallis to Sir Henry Clinton's Narrative*. London: J. Debrett, 1783.

"Colonel Robert Gray's Observations on the War in Carolina." *The South Carolina Historical and Genealogical Magazine* 11 (July 1910): 139-159.

Commager, Henry Steele and Richard B. Morris, eds. *The Spirit of 'Seventy-Six: The Story of the American Revolution as Told by Participants*. Indianapolis and New York: Bobbs-Merrill Company, 1958.

Comte de Revel, Joachim du Perron. *Journal particulieur d'une campagne aux Indes Occidentales (1781-1782)*. Paris: H. Charles-Lavauzelle, 1898 (?).

Cornwallis, Earl. *An Answer to That Part of the Narrative of Lieutenant-General Sir Henry Clinton, K.B. Which Relates to the Conduct of Lieutenant-General Earl Cornwallis, During the Campaign in North-America, in the Year 1781*. London, 1783. Philadelphia: John Campbell, 1865.

Custis, George Washington Parke. *Recollections and Private Memoirs of Washington, by his adopted son, George Washington Parke Custis, with a memoir of the author, by his daughter; and illustrative and explanatory notes. by Benson J. Lossing*. New York: Derby and Jackson, 1860.

Dann, John, ed. *The Revolution Remembered: Eyewitness Accounts of the War for Independence*. Chicago: University of Chicago Press, 1980.

Davie, William Richardson. *Instructions to be Observed for the Formations and Movements of the Cavalry*. Halifax, North Carolina: Abraham Hodge, 1799.

_____. *The Revolutionary War Sketches of William R. Davie*. Ed. Blackwell P. Robinson. Raleigh: North Carolina Department of Cultural Resources, Division of Archives and History, 1976.

"Demonstration Against Charleston, South Carolina, in 1779. Journal of Brigade Major F. Skelly." *Magazine of American History* (August 1891): 152-154; (November 1891): 392-393.

The Diary, and Life, of William Byrd II of Virginia, 1674-1744. Ed. Kenneth A. Lockridge. Chapel Hill and London: University of North Carolina Press, 1987.

Diary of Lieut. Anthony Allaire, of Ferguson's Corps. New York: New York Times, 1968.

"Extracts from the Journal of Lieutenant John Bell Tilden, Second Pennsylvania Line, 1781-1782." Ed. John Bell Tilden Phelps. *Pennsylvania Magazine of History and Biography* 19 (1895): 51-63, 208-233.

Garden, Alexander. *Anecdotes of the American Revolution, Illustrative of the Talents and Virtues of the Heroes and Patriots, Who Acted the Most Conspicuous Parts Therein.* 2nd Series. Charleston: A.E. Miller, 1828.

_____. *Anecdotes of the Revolutionary War in America, with Sketches of Character of Persons the Most Distinguished, in the Southern States, for Civil and Military Services.* Charleston: A.E. Miller, 1822.

Hanger, Major George. *An Address to the Army; in Reply to Strictures, by Roderick M'Kenzie (Late Lieutenant in the 71st Regiment) on Tarleton's History of the Campaigns of 1780 and 1781.* London: James Ridgway, 1789.

_____. *The Life, Adventures, and Opinions of Col. George Hanger.* 2 vols. London: J. Debrett, 1801.

Heitman, Francis B. *Historical Register of Officers of the Continental Army During the War of the Revolution.* Washington, DC, 1914. Baltimore: Genealogical Publishing Company, 1982.

James, William Dobein, A.M. *A Sketch of the Life of Brig. Gen. Francis Marion and a History of His Brigade From Its Rise in June 1780 until Disbanded in December, 1782 With Descriptions of Characters and Scenes Not Heretofore Published.* Charleston, 1821. Marietta, Georgia: Continental Book Company, 1948.

Johnson, Joseph. *Traditions and Reminiscences Chiefly of the American Revolution in the South: Including Biographical Sketches, Incidents and Anecdotes, Few of Which Have Been Published, Particularly of Residents in the Upper Country.* Charleston: Walker and James, 1851.

Johnson, William. *Sketches of the Life and Correspondence of Nathanael Greene.* 2 vols. Charleston, South Carolina, 1822.

The Journal and Order Book of Captain Robert Kirkwood of the Delaware Regiment of the Continental Line. Ed. Rev. Joseph Brown Turner. Wilmington: The Historical Society of Delaware, 1910.

Journals of Major Robert Rogers. London, 1765. New York: Corinth Books, 1961.

Knox, Captain John. *An Historical Journal of the Campaigns in North-America, for the Years 1757, 1758, 1759, and 1760.* 3 vols. London: W. Johnston and J. Dodsley, 1769.

Lamb, Roger. *Memoir of his own Life.* Dublin: J. Jones, 1811.

Lee, Henry. *Memoirs of the War in the Southern Department of the United States.* 2 vols. Philadelphia and New York: Bradford & Inskeep & Inskeep & Bradford, 1812.

Letters of Eliza Wilkinson. Ed. Caroline Gilman. New York, 1839. New York: New York Times and Arno Press, 1969.

Luvaas, Jay ed., and trans. *Frederick the Great on the Art of War.* New York: The Free Press, 1966.

MacKenzie, Roderick. *Strictures on Lt. Col. Tarleton's History of the Campaigns of 1780 and 1781, in the Southern Provinces of North America; Wherein Characters and Corps are Vindicated from Injurious Aspersions, and Several Important Transactions Placed in Their Proper Point of View.* London: R. Faulder, 1787.

Memoirs of the Duc de Lauzun. Trans. C.K. Scott Moncrieff. London: George Routledge and Sons, 1928.

Memoirs of the Marshall Count De Rochambeau. Paris, 1838. New York: New York Times and Arno Press, 1971.

Moultrie, William. *Memoirs of the American Revolution, So Far As It Related to the States of North and South-Carolina, and Georgia.* 2 vols. New York: David Longworth, 1802.

The Narrative of Colonel David Fanning. Ed. Lindley S. Butler. Charleston: Tradd Street Press, 1981.

"New Documentary Light on Tarleton's Raid: Letters of Newman Brockenbrough and Peter Lyons." Ed. John Cook Wyllie. *The Virginia Magazine of History and Biography* 74 (1966): 452-461.

Operations of The French Fleet under the Count De Grasse in 1781-2 As Described In Two Contemporaneous Journals. New York, 1864.

Paine, Thomas. *Common Sense and The Crisis.* Philadelphia: W. & T. Bradford, 1776; Albany: Charles R. & George Webster, 1792; repr., Garden City, New York: Anchor Books, 1973.

Pembroke, Henry Earl of. *Military Equitation: Or, a Method of Breaking Horses, and Teaching Soldiers to Ride.* 3rd ed. London: E. Easton, 1778.

Ramsay, David. *The History of the Revolution of South-Carolina, From a British Province to an Independent State.* 2 vols. Trenton, New Jersey: Isaac Collins, 1785.

Ross, Charles, ed. *Correspondence of Charles, First Marquis Cornwallis.* 3 vols. 2nd ed. London: John Murray, 1859.

St. John de Crevecoeur, J. Hector. *Sketches of Eighteenth Century America.* Eds. H.L. Bourdin et al. New York, 1925.

Secretary of the Commonwealth. *Bradford's History "Of Plimoth Plantation." From the Original Manuscript. With a Report of the Proceedings Incident to the Return of the Manuscript to Massachusetts.* Boston: Wright and Potter Printing Company, 1898.

Seymour, William. "A Journal of the Southern Expedition, 1780-1783." *Pennsylvania Magazine of History and Biography* 7 (1883): 286-298.

Simcoe, Lieut. Col. J.G. *A History of the Operations of a Partisan Corps Called the Queen's Rangers.* New York, 1844. New York: New York Times and Arno Press, 1968.

Stedman, Charles. *The History of the Origin, Progress, and Termination of the American War.* 2 vols. London, 1794. New York: New York Times and Arno Press, 1969.

Stevens, Benjamin Franklin, comp. and ed. *The Campaign in Virginia 1781. An exact Reprint of Six rare Pamphlets on the Clinton-Cornwallis Controversy with very numerous important Unpublished Manuscript Notes By Sir Henry Clinton K.B. And the Omitted and hitherto Unpublished portions of the Letters in their Appendixes added from the Original Manuscripts.* 2 vols. London, 1888.

Tarleton, Lieutenant Colonel Banastre. *A History of the Campaigns of 1780 and 1781, in the Southern Provinces of North America.* London: T. Cadell, 1787.

———. *A History of the Campaigns of 1780 and 1781, in the Southern Provinces of North America.* 2nd ed. London: T. Cadell, 1796.

Thacher, James. *Military Journal of the American Revolution, From the Commencement to the Disbanding of the American Army; Comprising a Detailed Account of the Principal Events and Battles of the Revolution, With Their Exact Dates, And a Biographical Sketch of the most Prominent Generals.* Hartford, Connecticut, 1862. New York Times and Arno Press, 1969.

Tornquist, Karl Gustaf. *The Naval Campaigns of Count De Grasse During the American Revolution 1781-1783.* Trans. Amandus Johnson. Philadelphia: Swedish Colonial Society, 1942.

Uhlendorf, Bernhard A., trans. and ed. *Revolution in America: Confidential Letters and Journals 1776-1784 of Adjutant General Major Baurmeister of the Hessian Forces.* Rutgers University Press, 1957.

———. *The Siege of Charleston, With an Account of the Province of South Carolina: Diaries and Letters of Hessian Officers From the von Jungkenn Papers in the William L. Clements Library.* University of Michigan Publications, History and Political Science 12. Ann Arbor: University of Michigan Press, 1938.

Warren, Mercy Otis. *History of the Rise, Progress, and Termination of the American Revolution. Interspersed with Biographical, Political and Moral Observations.* 3 vols. Boston: Manning and Loring, 1805.

Weems, Mason Locke. *The Life of George Washington; With Curious Anecdotes, Equally Honourable to Himself and Exemplary to His Young Countrymen.* 9th ed. Philadelphia: Mathew Carey, 1809.

Wheeler, Richard, comp. *Voices of 1776.* New York: Thomas Y. Crowell, 1972.

The Writings of Thomas Jefferson: Being His Autobiography, Correspondence, Reports, Messages, Addresses, And Other Writings, Official and Private. Ed. H.A. Washington. 9 vols. Washington, DC: Taylor and Maury, 1853-1854.

"The Yorktown Campaign. Journal of Captain John Davis, of the Pennsylvania Line." *Pennsylvania Magazine of History and Biography* 5 (1881): 290-311.

Secondary Sources

Books

Alden, John Richard. *The South in the Revolution: 1763- 1789.* A History of the South Series 3. Louisiana State University Press, 1957.

Arendt, Hannah. *On Revolution.* New York: Viking Press, 1963.

──────. *On Violence.* New York: Harcourt, Brace and World, Inc., 1969, 1970.

Babits, Lawrence E. *A Devil of a Whipping: The Battle of Cowpens* (Chapel Hill: University of North Carolina Press, 1998).

Bancroft, George. *History of the United States, From the Discovery of the American Continent.* 10 vols. 1834-1874. Boston: Little, Brown and Company, 1861-1875.

Barzun, Jacques and Henry F. Graff. *The Modern Researcher*. 4th ed. San Diego: Harcourt Brace Jovanovich, 1985.

Bass, Robert D. *Gamecock: The Life and Campaigns of General Thomas Sumter*. New York: Henry Holt, 1961.

_____. *The Green Dragoon: The Lives of Banastre Tarleton and Mary Robinson*. New York: Henry Holt, 1957.

_____. *Ninety-Six: The Struggle for the South Carolina Back Country*. Lexington, South Carolina: Sandlapper Store, 1978.

_____. *Swamp Fox: The Life and Campaigns of General Francis Marion*. New York: Henry Holt, 1959.

Berelson, Bernard and Gary A. Steiner. *Human Behavior: An Inventory of Scientific Findings*. New York: Harcourt, Brace & World, 1964.

Berger, Carl. *Broadsides and Bayonets: The Propaganda War of the American Revolution*. 1961. San Rafael, California: Presidio Press, 1976.

Billias, George Athan, ed. *George Washington's Generals*. New York: William Morrow and Company, 1964.

Black, Jeremy. *War for America: The Fight For Independence 1775-1783*. New York: St. Martin's Press, 1991.

Boatner, Mark Mayo III. *Encyclopedia of the American Revolution*. New York: David McKay Company, 1966; repr., Mechanicsburg, Pennsylvania: Stackpole Books, 1994.

Bowler, R. Arthur. *Logistics and the Failure of the British Army in America, 1775-1783*. Princeton: Princeton University Press, 1975.

Boyd, Thomas. *Simon Girty: The White Savage*. New York: Minton, Balch and Company, 1928.

Browning, Reed. *The War of the Austrian Succession*. New York: St. Martin's Press, 1993.

Brumwell, Stephen, *Redcoats: The British Soldier and War in the Americas, 1755-1763* (Cambridge: Cambridge University Press, 2002).

Buchanan, John, *The Road to Guilford Courthouse: The American Revolution in the Carolinas* (New York: Wiley, 1997).

Burke, John and John Bernard Burke. *A Genealogical and Heraldic History of the Extinct and Dormant Baronetcies of England, Ireland, and Scotland*. 2nd ed. London: John Russell Smith, 1844.

Calhoon, Robert M. *The Loyalists in Revolutionary America: 1760-1781*. New York: Harcourt Brace Jovanovich, 1965.

Carlton, Eric. *Massacres: An Historical Perspective*. Cambridge: Scolar Press, 1994.

Catton, Bruce. *Grant Moves South*. Boston: Little, Brown and Company, 1960.

Caulkins, Frances M. *History of New London, Connecticut: From the First Survey of the Coast in 1612, to 1852*. New London: Press of Case, Tiffany and Company, 1852.

Chambers, James. *The Devil's Horsemen: The Mongol Invasion of Europe*. New York: Atheneum, 1985.

Cohen, Lester H. *The Revolutionary Histories: Contemporary Narratives of the American Revolution*. Ithaca: Cornell University Press, 1980.

Conway, Stephen. *The War of American Independence 1775-1783*. New York: St. Martin's Press, 1995.

Craven, Wesley Frank. *The Legend of the Founding Fathers*. New York: New York University Press, 1956.

Crow, Jeffrey J. and Larry E. Tise, eds. *The Southern Experience in the American Revolution*. Chapel Hill: University of North Carolina Press, 1978.

Curtis, Edward E. *Organization of the British Army in the American Revolution*. New Haven, Connecticut, 1926.

Darling, Anthony D. *Red Coat and Brown Bess*. Historical Arms Series 12. Bloomfield, Ontario: Museum Restoration Service, 1970.

Davidson, James West and Mark Hamilton Lytle. *After the Fact: The Art of Historical Detection*. 3rd ed. New York: McGraw-Hill, Inc., 1992.

Davidson, Philip. *Propaganda and the American Revolution 1763-1783*. University of North Carolina Press, 1941.

Davis, Burke. *The Cowpens-Guilford Courthouse Campaign*. Philadelphia: J.B. Lippincott Company, 1962.

Dederer, John Morgan. *War in America to 1775 Before Yankee Doodle*. New York: New York University Press, 1990.

Dowd, Clement. *Life of Zebulon B. Vance*. Charlotte, North Carolina: Observer Printing and Publishing House, 1897.

Draper, Lyman C. *King's Mountain and Its Heroes: History of the Battle of King's Mountain, October 7th, 1780, and the Events Which Led To It*. Cincinnati: Peter G. Thomson, 1881.

Duffy, Christopher. *The Military Experience in the Age of Reason*. New York: Atheneum, 1988.

Dupuy, Trevor N., Curt Johnson, and David L. Bongard. *The Harper Encyclopedia of Military Biography*. New York: HarperCollins, 1992.

Durant, Will. *The Renaissance: A History of Civilization in Italy from 1304-1576 AD*. The Story of Civilization V. New York: Simon and Schuster, 1953.

Edgar, Walter B., *Partisans and Redcoats: The Southern Conflict That Turned the Tide of the American Revolution* (New York: William Morrow, 2001).

Ferguson, James. *Two Scottish Soldiers, a Soldier of 1688 and Blenheim, a Soldier of the American Revolution and a Jacobite Laird and His Forbears*. Aberdeen: D. Wyllie and Son, 1888.

Ferling, John E. *A Wilderness of Miseries: War and Warriors in Early America*. Westport, Connecticut: Greenwood Press, 1980.

Fischer, David Hackett. *Paul Revere's Ride*. New York: Oxford University Press, 1994.

Fisher, Syndney George. *The True Benjamin Franklin*. Philadelphia, 1899.

Fiske, John. *The American Revolution*. 2 vols. Boston: Houghton, Mifflin and Company, 1891.

Fleming, Thomas J. *"Downright Fighting": The Story of Cowpens*. Official National Park Handbook 135. Washington, DC: US Department of the Interior, 1988.

_____. *Now We Are Enemies: The Story of Bunker Hill*. New York: St. Martin's Press, 1960.

Fortescue, Sir John. *A History of the British Army*. 13 vols. London: 1899-1930. New York: AMS Press, 1976.

Foucault, Michel. *Discipline and Punish: The Birth of the Prison*. Trans. Alan Sheridan. New York: Vintage Books, 1979.

Frey, Sylvia R. *The British Soldier in America: A Social History of Military Life in the Revolutionary Period*. Austin: University of Texas Press, 1981.

_____. *Water from the Rock: Black Resistance in a Revolutionary Age*. Princeton: Princeton University Press, 1991.

Fuller, J.F.C. *British Light Infantry in the Eighteenth Century*. London, 1925.

Gabriel, Richard A. *The Painful Field: The Psychiatric Dimension of Modern War*. Westport, Connecticut: Greenwood Press, 1988.

_____. *To Serve With Honor: A Treatise on Military Ethics and the Way of the Soldier*. Westport, Connecticut: Greenwood Press, 1982.

Gabriel, Richard and Karen Metz. *From Sumer to Rome: The Military Capabilities of Ancient Armies*. New York: Greenwood Press, 1991.

Gelb, Norman. *Less than Glory*. New York: GP Putnam's Sons, 1984.

Gipson, Lawrence Henry. *The Triumphant Empire: Britain Sails Into the Storm, 1770-1776*. The British Empire Before the American Revolution 12. New York: Alfred A. Knopf, 1965.

Gilchrist, M. M., *Patrick Ferguson: "A Strange Adventurer, Tho' A Man of Some Genius,"* Scots' Lives Series (Edinburgh: National Museums of Scotland Publications, 2002).

Gordon, William. *The History of the Rise, Progress, and Establishment, of the Independence of the United States of America: Including an Account of the Late War; and of the Thirteen Colonies, From Their Origin to that Period*. 4 vols. London: Charles Dilly and James Buckland, 1788.

Governors of South Carolina: 1776-present. Greenville: Greenville News-Piedmont Company, 1988.

Grotius, Hugo. *The Rights of War and Peace*. Trans. A.C. Campbell. New York: M. Walter Dunne, 1901.

Harding, Richard. *Amphibious Warfare in the Eighteenth Century: The British Expedition to the West Indies 1740-1742*. Woodbridge, Suffolk: The Boydell Press, 1991.

Hediger, Heini. *The Psychology and Behavior of Animals in Zoos and Circuses*. Trans. Geoffrey Sircom. New York: Dover Publications, 1968.

_____. *Wild Animals in Captivity: An Outline of the Biology of Zoological Gardens*. Trans. Geoffrey Sircom. New York: Dover Publications, 1964.

Heywood, Valentine. *British Titles: The Use and Misuse of the Titles of Peers and Commoners, with Some Historical Notes*. 2nd ed. London: Adam and Charles Black, 1953.

Hibbert, Christopher. *Redcoats and Rebels: The American Revolution Through British Eyes*. New York: Avon Books, 1991.

Higginbotham, Don. *Daniel Morgan: Revolutionary Rifleman*. Chapel Hill: University of North Carolina Press, 1961.

_____, ed. *Reconsiderations on the Revolutionary War: Selected Essays*. Westport, Connecticut: Greenwood Press, 1978.

_____. *The War of American Independence: Military Attitudes, Policies, and Practice, 1763-1789*. New York: Macmillan Company, 1971.

_____. *War and Society in Revolutionary America: The Wider Dimensions of Conflict*. Columbia: University of South Carolina Press, 1988.

Higgins, W. Robert, ed. *The Revolutionary War in the South: Power, Conflict, and Leadership. Essays in Honor of John Richard Alden*. Duke University Press, 1979.

Hildreth, Richard. *The History of the United States of America*. 6 vols. 1849-1852. New York: Harper and Brothers, 1877-1880.

Hoffman, Ronald and Peter J. Albert, eds. *Arms and Independence: The Military Character of the American Revolution*. Charlottesville: University Press of Virginia, 1984.

Hoffman, Ronald, Thad W. Tate and Peter J. Albert, eds. *An Uncivil War: The Southern Backcountry during the American Revolution*. Charlottesville: University Press of Virginia, 1985.

Holmes, Abiel. *The Annals of America, From the Discovery by Columbus in the Year 1492, to the Year 1826*. 2 vols. Cambridge: Hilliard and Brown, 1829.

Houlding, J. A. *Fit for Service: The Training of the British Army, 1715-1795*. Oxford: Clarendon Press, 1981.

Jennings, Francis. *Empire of Fortune: Crowns, Colonies and Tribes in the Seven Years War in America*. 1988. New York: WW Norton, 1990.

———. *The Invasion of America: Indians, Colonialism, and the Cant of Conquest*. Chapel Hill: University of North Carolina Press, 1975.

Johnston, Henry P. *The Yorktown Campaign and the Surrender of Cornwallis, 1781*. New York, 1881.

Kammen, Michael. *Mystic Chords of Memory: The Transformation of Tradition in American Culture*. New York: Alfred A. Knopf, 1991.

———. A Season of Youth: *The American Revolution and the Historical Imagination*. New York: Alfred A. Knopf, 1978.

Katcher, Philip R. N. *Encyclopedia of British, Provincial, and German Army Units: 1775-1783*. Harrisburg, Pennsylvania: Stackpole Books, 1973.

Katcher, Philip and Michael Youens. *The American Provincial Corps 1775-1784*. Men-at-Arms Series. Reading, England: Osprey, 1973.

Keegan, John. *The Face of Battle: A Study of Agincourt, Waterloo and the Somme*. London: Penguin Books, 1978.

———. *A History of Warfare*. New York: Alfred A. Knopf, 1993.

———. *The Mask of Command*. New York: Viking Press, 1987.

Kennett, Lee. *The French Armies in the Seven Years' War: A Study in Military Organization and Administration*. Duke University Press, 1967.

Kirkland, Thomas J. and Robert M. Kennedy, *Historic Camden*, 2 volumes (Columbia, S.C.: State Company, 1905 and 1926).

Kopperman, Paul E. *Braddock at the Monongahela*. University of Pittsburgh Press, 1977.

Kurtz, Stephen G. and James H. Hutson, eds. *Essays on the American Revolution*. Chapel Hill: University of North Carolina Press, 1973.

Lambdin, Dewey. *The French Admiral*. New York: Pinnacle Books, 1990.

Lambert, Robert Stansbury. *South Carolina Loyalists in the American Revolution*. Columbia: University of South Carolina Press, 1987.

Landrum, J. B. O. *Colonial and Revolutionary History of Upper South Carolina, Embracing for the Most Part the Primitive and Colonial History of the Territory Comprising the Original County of Spartanburg with a General Review of the Entire Military Operations in the Upper Portion of South Carolina and Portions of North Carolina*. Greenville, SC: Shannon and Company, 1897.

Langguth, A.J. *Patriots: The Men Who Started the American Revolution*. New York: Simon and Schuster, 1988.

Lee, Henry Jr. *The Campaign of 1781 in the Carolinas*. Philadelphia, 1824.

Lefferts, Lieutenant Charles M. *Uniforms of the American, British, French, and German Armies in the War of the American Revolution, 1775-1783*. New York, 1926. Old Greenwich, Connecticut: WE Inc., 1971.

Lendrum, John. *A Concise and Impartial History of the American Revolution. To Which is Prefixed, a General History of North and South America. Together with an Account of the Discovery and Settlement of North America, and a View of the Progress, Character, and Political State of the Colonies previous to the Revolution*. 2 vols. Boston: I. Thomas and E.T. Andrews, 1795.

Lord, Walter. *The Dawn's Early Light*. Baltimore and London: Johns Hopkins University Press, 1972.

Lossing, Benson J. *The Pictorial Field-Book of the Revolution*. 2 vols. New York, 1855.

Lumpkin, Henry. *From Savannah to Yorktown: The American Revolution in the South*. Columbia: University of South Carolina Press, 1981.

Mackesy, Piers. *The War for America 1775-1783*. Cambridge: Harvard University Press, 1964.

Malone, Patrick M. *The Skulking Way of War: Technology and Tactics Among the New England Indians*. Plimoth Plantation, 1991.

Marshall, John. *The Life of George Washington, Commander in Chief of the American Forces, During the War Which Established the Independence of His Country, and First President of the United States*. 5 vols. Philadelphia, 1804-1807. Fredericksburg, Virginia: Citizens' Guild of Washington's Boyhood Home, 1926.

Matloff, Maurice, ed. *American Military History*. Army Historical Series. 1973. Washington, DC: US Government Printing, 1985.

May, Robin and G.A. Embleton. *The British Army in North America 1775-1783*. Men-at-Arms 39. London: Osprey, 1974.

McCardell, Lee. *Ill-Starred General: Braddock of the Coldstream Guards*. University of Pittsburgh Press, 1958.

McCrady, Edward. *The History of South Carolina in the Revolution, 1775-1783*. 2 vols. New York: Macmillan Company, 1901-1902.

McDowell, Bart. *The Revolutionary War*. Washington, DC: National Geographic Society, 1967.

McGuffie, T. H. *The Siege of Gibraltar 1779-1783*. London: B. T. Batsford, 1965.

McNeill, William H. *The Pursuit of Power: Technology, Armed Force, and Society since A.D. 1000*. Chicago: University of Chicago Press, 1982.

Messick, Hank. *King's Mountain: The Epic of the Blue Ridge "Mountain Men" in the American Revolution*. Boston: Little, Brown and Company, 1976.

Millis, Walter. *Arms and Men: A Study in American Military History*. New York: GP Putnam's Sons, 1956.

Mollo, John. *Uniforms of The American Revolution in Color.* Blandford Press, 1975. New York: Sterling Publishing Company, 1991.

Morrill, Dan L. *Southern Campaigns of the American Revolution.* Baltimore: The Nautical and Aviation Publishing Company, 1993.

Morse, Jedidiah. *Annals of the American Revolution; Or a Record of the Causes and Events Which Produced, and Terminated in the Establishment and Independence of the American Republic. Interspersed with Numerous Appropriate Documents and Anecdotes.* Hartford, 1824.

Nelson, Paul David. *Anthony Wayne: Soldier of the Early Republic.* Bloomington: Indiana University Press, 1985.

_____. *General James Grant: Scottish Soldier and Royal Governor of East Florida.* Gainesville: University Press of Florida, 1993.

Newlin, Algie I. *The Battle of New Garden.* Greensboro, North Carolina: The North Carolina Friends Historical Society and the North Carolina Yearly Meeting of Friends, 1977.

Novak, Greg. *A Guide to the American War of Independence in the North.* Campaign Book #7A. Champaign, Illinois: Ulster Imports, 1990.

The Oxford English Dictionary. Prepared by J.A. Simpson and E.S.C. Weiner. 20 vols. 2nd ed. Oxford: Clarendon Press, 1989.

Pancake, John S. *This Destructive War: The British Campaign in the Carolinas, 1780-1782.* Tuscaloosa: The University of Alabama Press, 1985.

Parker, Geoffrey et al. *The Thirty Years' War.* Rev. ed. London: Routledge and Kegan Paul Ltd., 1987.

Parkman, Francis. *The Conspiracy of Pontiac and the Indian War after the Conquest of Canada.* 2 vols. The Library of America. Boston: Little, Brown and Company, 1851; repr., New York: Viking Press, 1991.

Parton, James. *Life of Andrew Jackson*. 3 vols. Boston and New York: Houghton, Mifflin and Company, 1859-1860.

Peckham, Howard H. *The Colonial Wars: 1689-1762*. Chicago: University of Chicago Press, 1964.

Pitkin, Timothy. *A Political and Civil History of the United States of America, From the Year 1763 to the Close of the Administration of President Washington, in March, 1797: Including A Summary View of the Political and Civil State of the North American Colonies, Prior to that Period*. 2 vols. 1828. New Haven: Hezekiah Howe and Durrie and Peck, 1831.

Prebble, John. *Culloden*. New York: Atheneum, 1962.

Preston, Richard A., Alex Roland, and Sydney F. Wise, eds. *Men in Arms: A History of Warfare and Its Interrelationships with Western Society*. 5th ed. Forth Worth, Texas: Holt, Rinehart and Winston, Inc., 1991.

Quarles, Benjamin. *The Negro in the American Revolution*. Chapel Hill: University of North Carolina Press, 1961.

Randall, Willard Sterne. *Benedict Arnold: Patriot and Traitor*. New York: William Morrow and Company, 1990.

Rawlyk, George A. *Yankees at Louisbourg*. Orono: University of Maine Press, 1967.

Robson, Eric. *The American Revolution in its Political and Military Aspects (1763-1783)*. New York: Oxford University Press, 1955.

Royster, Charles. *Light-Horse Harry Lee and the Legacy of the American Revolution*. New York: Alfred A. Knopf, 1981.

_____. *A Revolutionary People at War: The Continental Army and American Character, 1775-1783*. New York: WW Norton and Company, 1981.

Sabine, Lorenzo. *Biographical Sketches of Loyalists of the American Revolution, With an Historical Essay*. 2 vols. Boston: Little, Brown and Company, 1864.

Scheer, George F. and Hugh F. Rankin. *Rebels and Redcoats.* Cleveland: World Publishing Company, 1957.

Seymour, William. *The Price of Folly: British Blunders in the War of American Independence.* London: Brassey's, 1995.

Shaffer, Arthur H. *To Be An American: David Ramsay and the Making of the American Consciousness.* Columbia: University of South Carolina Press, 1991.

Shy, John. *A People Numerous and Armed: Reflections on The Military Struggle for American Independence.* Oxford University Press, 1976.

_____. *Toward Lexington: The Role of the British Army in the Coming of the American Revolution.* Princeton University Press, 1965.

Simms, William Gilmore. *The Partisan: A Romance of the Revolution.* Chicago: Belford, Clarke and Company, 1887.

_____. *The Revolutionary War in South Carolina: An Anthology.* Comp. Stephen Meats. Columbia: Southern Studies Program, University of South Carolina, 1975.

Smith, Paul H. *Loyalists and Redcoats: A Study in British Revolutionary Policy.* Chapel Hill: University of North Carolina Press, 1964.

Speck, W. A. *The Butcher: The Duke of Cumberland and the Suppression of the 45.* Oxford: Basil Blackwell, 1981.

Stacey, C. P. *Quebec, 1759: The Siege and the Battle.* Toronto: Macmillan Company, 1959.

Steele, Ian K. *Betrayals: Fort William Henry and the "Massacre."* New York and Oxford: Oxford University Press, 1990.

_____. *Warpaths: Invasions of North America.* New York and Oxford: Oxford University Press, 1994.

Stember, Sol. *The Bicentennial Guide to the American Revolution.* 3 vols. New York: Saturday Review Press, 1974.

Stephen, Sir Leslie and Sir Sidney Lee, eds. *The Dictionary of National Biography*. 22 vols. Oxford: Oxford University Press, 1921-1922.

Stokesbury, James L. *A Short History of the American Revolution*. New York: William Morrow, 1991.

Sugden, John. *Tecumseh's Last Stand*. University of Oklahoma Press, 1985.

Swiggett, Howard. *War Out of Niagara*. Empire State Historical Publication 20. Port Washington, New York: Ira J. Friedman, 1963.

Symonds, Craig L. *A Battlefield Atlas of the American Revolution*. Baltimore: The Nautical and Aviation Publishing Company, 1986.

Szymanski, Leszek. *Casimir Pulaski: A Hero of the American Revolution*. 1979. New York: Hippocrene Books, 1994.

Thane, Elswyth. *The Family Quarrel: A Journey Through the Years of the Revolution*. New York: Duell, Sloan and Pearce, 1959.

Tower, Charlemagne, Jr. *The Marquis De La Fayette in the American Revolution. With Some Account of the Attitude of France Toward the War of Independence*. 2 vols. Philadelphia: J.B. Lippincott, 1895.

Treacy, M.F. *Prelude to Yorktown: The Southern Campaign of Nathanael Greene, 1780-1781*. Chapel Hill: University of North Carolina Press, 1963.

Trevelyan, Sir George Otto. *The American Revolution*. 3 vols. New York: Longmans, Green, and Company: 1898- 1907.

Troiani, Don. *Military Buttons of the American Revolution*. Gettysburg, Penn.: Thomas Publications, 2001.

_____. *Soldiers In America 1754-1865*. Mechanicsburg, Penn.: Stackpole Books, 1998.

Troxler, Carole Watterson. *The Loyalist Experience in North Carolina*. Raleigh: North Carolina Department of Cultural Resources, Division of Archives and History, 1976.

Tucker, George. *The History of the United States, From Their Colonization to the End of the Twenty-Sixth Congress, In 1841*. 4 vols. Philadelphia: J.B. Lippincott and Company, 1856-1857.

Ultee, Maarten, ed. *Adapting to Conditions: War and Society in the Eighteenth Century*. Tuscaloosa: The University of Alabama Press, 1986.

Van Creveld, Martin. *Command in War*. Cambridge: Harvard University Press, 1985.

Wallace, Willard M. *Appeal to Arms: A Military History of the American Revolution*. New York: Harper and Brothers, 1951.

Ward, Christopher. *The War of the Revolution*. 2 vols. New York: Macmillan Company, 1952.

Weigley, Russell F. *The Age of Battles: The Quest for Decisive Warfare from Breitenfeld to Waterloo*. Bloomington: Indiana University Press, 1991.

Weir, Robert M. *Colonial South Carolina: A History* (New York: KTO Press, 1983).

Weller, Jac. *Wellington in the Peninsula 1808-1814*. Nicholas Vane, 1962.

Wickwire, Franklin and Mary. *Cornwallis: The American Adventure*. Boston: Houghton Mifflin Company, 1970.

Wilkin, Captain Walter Harold. *Some British Soldiers in America*. London: Hugh Rees, LTD., 1914.

Willcox, William B. and Walter L. Arnstein. *The Age of Aristocracy: 1688 to 1830*. 4th ed. A History of England. Toronto: D.C. Heath and Company, 1983.

Windrow, Martin and Gerry Embleton. *Military Dress of the Peninsular War (1808-1814)*. London: Ian Allan, 1974.

Wood, W. J. *Battles of the Revolutionary War 1775-1781*. Chapel Hill: Algonquin Books, 1990.

Wright, Robert K. Jr. *The Continental Army. Army Lineage Series*. Washington, DC: Center of Military History, 1989.

Wrong, George M. *Washington and His Comrades in Arms: A Chronicle of the War of Independence*. New Haven: Yale University Press, 1921.

Dissertations, Theses, and Scholarly Papers

Babits, Lawrence E. "Continentals in the British Legion, August 1780-October 1781," paper presented at Guilford Courthouse National Military Park, Greensboro, N.C., March 16, 2001.

Daso, Major Dik A. "Chariots, Chivalry, and Cockpits: Evolution of the Fighter Pilot, 500 BC - AD 1918, 1993" [photocopy]. Author, Columbia, South Carolina.

Massey, Gregory D. "A Hero's Life: John Laurens and the American Revolution." Ph.D. diss., University of South Carolina, 1992.

Scotti, Anthony J. Jr. "'This Disagreeable Exertion of Authority': Banastre Tarleton and the British Legion in the Southern Campaigns, 1780-1781." MA thesis, Wake Forest University, 1991.

———. "The Myths of Bloody Tarleton," paper presented at the Banastre Tarleton Symposium, Kershaw County Historical Society and Historic Camden Revolutionary War Site, Camden, S.C., April 26, 2002.

Stirling, Lawrence Linfield. "Banastre Tarleton: A Reevaluation of His Career in the American Revolution." MA thesis, Louisiana State University and Agricultural and Mechanical College, 1964.

Articles

Atlay, James B. "Tarleton of the Legion." *Cornhill Magazine* (August 1905): 229-248.

Bauer, Frederic G. "Notes on the Use of Cavalry in the American Revolution." *US Cavalry Association Journal* 47 (1938): 136-143.

Carman, W.Y. "Banastre Tarleton and the British Legion." *Journal of the Society for Army Historical Research* 62 (1984): 127-131.

Carter, William H. "A British Dragoon in the American Revolution." *The Cavalry Journal* 32 (October 1923): 400-411.

Chamberlain, Mellon. "Memorial of Captain Charles Cochrane, A British Officer in the Revolutionary War," *Proceedings of the Massachusetts Historical Society*, May 1891.

Conway, Stephen R. "British Army Officers and the American War for Independence." *William and Mary Quarterly* 41 (1984): 265-276.

_____. "'The great mischief Complain'd of': Reflections on the Misconduct of British Soldiers in the Revolutionary War." *William and Mary Quarterly* 47 (1990): 370-390.

_____. "The Recruitment of Criminals into the British Army, 1775-81." *Bulletin of the Institute of Historical Research* 58 (May 1985): 46-58.

_____. "To Subdue America: British Army Officers and the Conduct of the Revolutionary War." *William and Mary Quarterly* 43 (1986): 381-407.

Farley, M. Foster. "The 'Old Wagoner' and the 'Green Dragoon.'" *History Today* 25 (1975): 190-195.

Frasché, Lieutenant Colonel Louis D.F. "Problems of Command: Cornwallis, Partisans and Militia, 1780." *Military Review* 57 (April 1977): 60-74.

Frey, Sylvia R. "Courts and Cats: British Military Justice In The Eighteenth Century." *Military Affairs* 43 (1979): 5-11.

Gilbert, Arthur N. "British Military Justice During the American Revolution." *The Eighteenth Century: Theory and Interpretation* 20 (1979): 24-38.

_____. "The Changing Face of British Military Justice, 1757-1783." *Military Affairs* 49 (1985): 80-84.

_____. "Law and Honour Among Eighteenth-Century British Army Officers." *The Historical Journal* 19 (1976): 75- 87.

_____. "The Regimental Courts Martial in the Eighteenth Century British Army." *Albion* 8 (1976): 50-66.

Haarmann, Albert W. "Some Notes on American Provincial Uniforms, 1776-1783." *The Loyalist Gazette* 29 (Spring 1991): 21-27.

Hayes, John T. "The Connecticut Light Horse, 1776-1783." *Military Collector and Historian* (Winter 1970): 109-112.

Huffstetler, Joel W. "Henry Lee and Banastre Tarleton: How Historians Use Their Memoirs." *The Southern Historian* 6 (1985): 12-19.

Knight, Betsey. "Prisoner Exchange and Parole in the American Revolution." *William and Mary Quarterly* 48 (April 1991): 201-222.

Kyff, Robert. "Tarleton's Raid on Bedford and Poundridge." *The Westchester Historian* 44 (Summer 1968): 49-58.

Middlekauff, Robert. "Why Men Fought in the American Revolution." *Huntington Library Quarterly* 43 (Spring 1980): 135-148.

Power, J. Tracy. "'The Virtue of Humanity Was Totally Forgot': Buford's Massacre, May 29, 1780." *South Carolina Historical Magazine* 93 (January 1992): 5-14.

Prelinger, Catherine. "Benjamin Franklin and American Prisoners of War in England during the American Revolution." *William and Mary Quarterly* 32 (1975): 261-294.

Rankin, Hugh F. "Cowpens, Prelude to Yorktown." *North Carolina Historical Review* 31 (1954): 336-369.

Robson, Eric. "British Light Infantry in the Mid-Eighteenth Century: The Effect of American Conditions." *The Army Quarterly* 63 (1952): 200-222.

Royster, Charles. "'The Nature of Treason': Revolutionary Virtue and American Reactions to Benedict Arnold." *William and Mary Quarterly* 36 (1979): 163-193.

Scotti, Anthony J. Jr. "British Victory," in *History in Dispute: The American Revolution, 1763-1789*, edited by Keith Krawczynski (Columbia, S.C.: Manly/Farmington Hills, Michigan: St. James, 2002).

_____. "'The Lost Sons': British Legion Light Infantry in the Revolutionary War." *The Loyalist Gazette* 33 (Spring 1995): 24-26.

_____. "Loyalists," in *History in Dispute: The American Revolution, 1763-1789*, edited by Keith Krawczynski (Columbia, S.C.: Manly/Farmington Hills, Michigan: St. James, 2002).

Simpson, Alan. "The Legends of Carter's Grove—Fact or Fiction?" *Colonial Williamsburg* 11 (1989): 32-38.

"Sir Banastre Tarleton." *Blackwoods Magazine* 116 (October 1874): 432-449.

Smith, Paul H. "David Ramsay and the Causes of the American Revolution." *William and Mary Quarterly* 17 (1960): 51-77.

_____. "The American Loyalists: Notes on Their Organization and Numerical Strength." *William and Mary Quarterly* 25 (1968): 259-277.

Smy, William A. "Standards, Guidons and Colours of the British Army and Provincial Corps During the American Revolution." *The Loyalist Gazette* 31 (Spring 1993): 16-25.

Starkey, Armstrong. "Paoli to Stony Point: Military Ethics and Weaponry During the American Revolution." *Journal of Military History* 58 (January 1994): 7-27.

Taylor, Alan. "A Review of The Unredeemed Captive: A Family Story From Early America. By John Demos. (New York: Alfred A. Knopf, 1994)," *William and Mary Quarterly* 52 (July 1995): 517-519.

Tiedemann, Joseph S. "Patriots by Default: Queens County, New York, and the British Army, 1776-1783." *William and Mary Quarterly* 43 (January 1986): 35-63.

Weir, Robert M. "North Carolina's Reaction to the Currency Act of 1764." *North Carolina Historical Review* 40 (April 1963): 183-199.

Wright, Esther Clark. "The Evacuation of the Loyalists from New York in 1783." *The Nova Scotia Historical Review* 4 (1984): 5-25.

Zur, Ofer. "The Psychohistory of Warfare: The Co-Evolution of Culture, Psyche and Enemy." *Journal of Peace Research* 24 (1987): 125-134.

Documentaries and Movies

Alda, Alan. *Sweet Liberty*. Starring Alan Alda, Michael Caine, Bob Hoskins, and Michelle Pfeiffer. 107 min. Color. Rated PG. Los Angeles, CA: MCA/Universal Home Video, Inc., 1986. Videocassette.

Cambou, Don. *The American Revolution: The Birth of the Republic*. Part III. Hosted by Bill Kurtis. Arts and Entertainment. North Hollywood, CA: Greystone Communications, Inc., 1994. Documentary.

Emmerich, Roland, director. *The Patriot*. Starring Mel Gibson, Heath Ledger, and Jason Isaacs. 165 min. Color. Rated R. Culver City, CA: Sony Pictures Entertainment, 2000. Videocassette.

Fleischer, Carol L., director. *The Revolutionary War*. Narrated by Chareles Kuralt. The Learning Channel. Bethesda, Md.: Discovery Communications, 1995. Documentary.

INDEX

Index entries found in footnotes are designated by *n#* and are immediately followed by the page number on which that footnote can be found.

ACCOUTREMENTS, The Best Were Acquired For The Legion 99
ADAMS, John, Quoted About History 3
ADJUTANT, Defined *n71* 195
ADJUTANT GENERAL, Responsibilities *n41* 64
ALLAIRE, Anthony 235
AMERICAN LEGION, Formed By Benedict Arnold 36 Numerical Strength *n14* 54
AMERICAN REGIMENTS, Numerical Order *n41* 64
AMERICAN VOLUNTEERS OR RANGERS, *n18* 28 74 170
AMHERST, Lord Jeffrey (Baron) 19-20 Denied Tarleton's Promotion 19-21
ANDRÉ, Col John 21 And Benedict Arnold *n46* 190 Clinton's Adj Gen *n18* 28 Friend Of Tarleton's, Executed 169
ARMIES, Large Demands On Landscape And Civilians 130
ARNOLD, Brig Gen Benedict 236 A Remarkable Soldier *n26* 246 And American Legion 36 *n14* 54 In Virginia *n14* 107 Opposite Of Patriot Virtue 134 Treason Vs Virtue *n30* 148
ASHE, Mrs *n40* 151
BABY, Dropped In Woods 102
BACKHOUSE, Daniel Partnership With The Tarletons *n5* 24 Liverpool Mercantile Family *n5* 24

BALFOUR, Lt Col Nisbet, 207 236 Comment On Plundering *n41* 225
BANCROFT, George, Historian 103
BASKING RIDGE, Tarleton's Capture Of Lee 16 20
BASS, Robert D, Biographer Of Tarleton 4 103 Originated The Term "Bloody Tarleton" 103-104 237 Poetic License *n72* 122-123 Romanticized Biographies *n5* 10
BATH, Order Of The 232
BATHURST, Earl, Sec'y For War 232
BATTLE EFFICIENCY, Peaks After Three To Five Months Of Combat Experience *n52* 191
"BATTLE STRESS," *n74* 195-196
BAURMEISTER, Carl Leopold 102-103
BAYLOR, Lt Col George, Surprised By Bayonet Attack *n83* 199
BAYONET, Considered The Key To Victory 47 Legion And Ranger Training 35 Training And Military Ethics *n75* 196 Use, Unfamiliar To American Provincials 179
BAYONET ATTACK, In Darby Pennsylvania 205
BAYONET INCIDENT, 2 79 *n25* 90
BEAUFORT, Local Horses Used 98
BELFIELD ESTATE, In Dominica Owned By Tarleton *n2* 23
BERGER, Jean-Baptiste-Antoine De, Pregnant Woman Murder Story 214
BERTIE, Robert, Fourth Duke Of Ancaster (Father of Susan Priscilla) *n5* 240
BERTIE, Susan Priscilla, Married Tarleton 232 Large Dowry *n5* 240

BERWICK AND HOLY ISLAND, Tarleton Governor Of 232
BIGGIN'S BRIDGE, *n33* 111
BLACK DRAGOONS, Independent Troop Of *n15* 55
BLACK PIONEERS, 38 *n22* 58
BLACK RIVER, 91
BLACKSTOCKS HILL, 44 Killed And Wounded *n16* 86 Number Of Horses Lost 98 Tarleton Outnumbered 77 *n15* 85
"BLOODY," Usage And Meaning *n59* 117-118
"BLOODY BAN," *n73* 123
"BLOODY TARLETON," 135 137 *n72* 123 Origin Of The Term 102-103 237
BONETTA, (Sloop), Legion Returned To New York *n1* 237
"BOOTY," And Plunder 160-161
BOYER, Col H, Buford's Adjutant 176 Escaped Injury At Waxhaws 176
BRADDOCK, Maj Gen Edward *n11* 142 Remarks About Colonials 46
BRADDOCK'S DEFEAT, *n11* 142
BRADFORD, William, Justified War 128
BRADLEY, James, Guided Tarleton To River Fords *n24* 89
BRANDYWINE CREEK, Docherty Captured 38
BRATTON, Col William, And Pursuit Of Huck *n45* 226
BREVET STATUS, *n13* 27
BRITISH ARMY, Chronically Undermanned *n26* 59 Number Of Horse Regiments *n9* 52 Problems And Dispersal 73 Unprepared For Mobile Warfare 73
BRITISH BUMBLING, *n31* 148

BRITISH FIRST REGIMENT OF FOOT GUARDS, 21
BRITISH LEGION, 1 22 *n15* 55 *n41* 64 Activities In The South 19 92 After Cowpens 41 American Attitude Toward 95 And Lee's, Similar Appearance 34 *n24* 89 And Tarleton's "Hard-line" Attitude Contributed To The Terror 209 At Waxhaws *n1* 7 Attrition Rate 39 Battles And Skirmishes Listed 72 Brief Career In The South 72 Cavalry Troops 40 Coats Described *n10* 53 Commanded By Cathcart *n18* 28 Composition Of 36-37 Creation Of 40 Decline In Numbers By 1783 42 Depredations 168 Depredations Exaggerated 212 Disbandment In 1783 231 Disease, Desertion, Etc 42 Distribution In The South *n4* 81 Early Operations In The North 47-48 Evil Characterization 2 4 139 209 Exaggerations Of Strength *n26* 59 Excessive Force At Waxhaws 178 Excessive Use Of Force 170 Fatigued By Constant Duties *n12* 85 Fear Of 95 Four Companies Survived War *n31* 61 French Experience With 96 Full Potential Yet To Be Reached 49 Green Uniforms 34 Headgear Described *n11* 53 High Mobility In The South 92 Highly Visible 75 Impressive Forced Marches 78 In Charles Town Expedition 72 In New York 47 Inadvertent Bayonet Attack On Ferguson's Regiment 170 Intimidation, Agility, And Mobility 34-35 Intoxicated Troopers Sabered Young Bugler 173 Known As "Green Horse" 34 Lacked Tarleton's Leadership While He Was Ill 170 Leadership And Reliability 44 Little Known Of Officers And Men 37 Long Distances Covered *n4* 105 Marched Over 1200 Miles During Southern Campaigns *n12* 242

INDEX

BRITISH LEGION, (cont.)
  Members And Others Wished To Escape Rebel Revenge *n48* 226 Mystique 234 Myth And Reality 6 Newly Formed Loyalist Corps 19 Numbers After Cowpens & Yorktown 62-63 Numbers After Cowpens *n9* 106 Numerical Strength 36 39-42 Occasional Lackluster Performance 170 Officers 38 Organization Of 35-36 Origins 32-34 Outnumbered At Various Battles *n15* 85 Placed Upon Regular Establishment 43 Plundering On Long Island After York Town 231 Poor Discipline In Regard To Foraging Parties 165 Quartered At Setalket NY 48 Quick Stunning Victories 94 Raid On Poundridge And Bedford NY 48 Reputation For Wanton Killing 31 Sense Of Being An Elite Unit 47 Sent To Southern Provinces 19 Standard Works On *n2* 8 Strain Of Constant Duty 78 170 Tarleton's 74 Training And Discipline 46 Two Dragoons Executed For Rape And Robbery 155 Wartime Establishment 39
BROOKS'S CLUB, Blackballed Tarleton For Criticism Of Cornwallis 232
BROWN, Lt Col Thomas, Warned By Cornwallis 204
BROWNE, Ens George (Regular) 37
BROWNFIELD, Dr Robert *n59* 192
BRUCCOLI, Matthew J *viii*
BRUNSWICK DRAGOON REGIMENT PRINZ LUDWIG ERNST, *n9* 53
BRUTAL VIRTUE, 132
BRUTALITY, Of The Age *n6* 181
BUCKS COUNTY LIGHT DRAGOONS, Or Volunteers 40
BUFORD, Col Abraham *n1* 7 97 At Waxhaws 79 Caught By Tarleton During Retreat From SC 173 At Waxhaws 175 Horses Died In Pursuit 99 Massacre *n60* 193 Ordered Boyer With Flag Of Truce At Waxhaws 176 Refused To Surrender 173 See also, "REMEMBER BUFORD"
BUFORD'S PLAY, Slogan, "Give Them Buford's Play" *n43* 225
BULLOCK, Isaac 38
BURGOYNE, Maj Gen John, Surrender At Saratoga *n2* 49
BURNET, Maj Ichabod, Comments About Legion 95 Overestimated Legion Strength 21 108
BURWELL, Carter *n1* 80
BUTLER, Walter 236 Compared To Tarleton *n2* 7 Opposite Of Patriot Virtue 134
BYRD, William II, Exhumed Father's Body *n53* 228
CALEDONIAN VOLUNTEERS, 40-41 Recruiting *n32* 61
CAMDEN, 92 94 Americans Chased After Battle 79 Docherty Captured 38 Report In English Newspapers *n34* 112
CAMERON, Lt Allan, Charged Scammell's Americans 172
CAMPBELL, Capt, Struck By Samuel Webb 158
CAPE BRETON ISLAND, *n13* 143
CAREY, James *n27* 185
CARLETON, Sir Guy 231
CARLSON, R 13 Roxanne *viii*
CARTAGENA, *n11* 142
CARTER'S GROVE, Archaeological Evidence *n1* 80 Mansion Near Williamsburg *n1* 80 Possibly Occupied By Tarleton *n1* 80
CAT-O'-NINE-TAILS, 158

CATHCART, Lord William Schaw, Adj Gen *n18* 21 28 33 39 41 43 *n5* 51 *n19* 56 Creation Of British Legion 40 Maj Invalided *n41* 64 Returned To Thirty-Eighth Reg After Illness 43 Temporary Quartermaster General 43
CATHCART'S LEGION, 43 59
CAVALRY, Advantage Over Infantry *n65* 194 American, Grievous Losses 94 And Terror 210 Lack Of, Due To Low Provincial Turnout *n5* 82 Necessity Of *n5* 81 Superiority Complex *n77* 197 Three Types *n6* 51 Time Needed For Training *n5* 82 Use In American Revolution *n4* 81
CAVALRYMEN And Infantrymen, Animosity Between *n77* 197
CHAPMAN, Abraham 38 Amos 38 Samuel *n22* 58
CHARLOTTE, Davie At 94 Dragoons Under Davie Refused To Charge The Enemy 170
CHARLOTTESVILLE, Tarleton's Raid On 97
CHASSEUR, (Light Infantry) *n15* 55
CHASSEURS, Emmerick's 36
CHASSEURS À CHEVAL, *n6* 51
CHASSEURS BRITANNIQUES, Depredations *n29* 186
CHEVAUX LÉGERS, *n6* 51
"CHIVALRIC ENCOUNTERS," 47
CHOISY, Brig Gen Claude Gabriel De 96
"CHRISTIAN SPARTA," 3 *n3* 8
CHRISTIANITY, And Colonial Wars 128-129
CHURCH-BURNING, No Documentation *n9* 11 Scene In "The Patriot" Movie 5

CLARENCE, William Henry, Duke Of, Friend Of Tarleton 232
CLAYTON, Trading Ship Owned By John Tarleton *n3* 24
CLINTON, Sir Henry 20-22 33 41 43 72 *n4* 81 206 And Loss At Cowpens 100 And "Pamphlet War" With Cornwallis *n47* 115 *n6* 240 And Short Flogging 182 Awareness Of Political Struggle 132 Issues Decrees 74 One Of Tarleton's Benefactors 19 Praise For Tarleton And Simcoe 44 Praised Tarleton After Waxhaws 178 Realized Need To Win Popular Sentiment 203 Tarleton A Favorite Of 97
COFFIN, Elijah, Quaker Boy *n46* 65
COLLETON, Sir John *n43* 189
COLONIAL SOLDIERS, Disdained By English Aristocrats 129 Inferiority Complex 129
COLONIAL WARS, Different From European Conflicts 129 Involved Few Of Population 130
COMMISSARY, Definition *n45* 115
COMMISSIONS, Dating Of, In Order To Grant Seniority 21 Multiple *n12* 27 Regular And Provincial Or Local 18-20
COMMON SOLDIER, Obedience And Discipline 208
CONGAREE RIVER, *n10* 84 Horses To Be Bought 99
CONNELLY, Owen *vii*
"CONTINGENT MEN," *n16* 56
COOK, Zoe R *viii*
CORK MILITARY DISTRICT, Tarleton Commandant Of 232
CORNWALLIS, Charles, Earl, Lord, Lt Gen 20 15 45 47 91-92 138 *n7* 206 219 Allowed Legion To Choose Best Horses 99 Ambiguity 203-205 Ambiguous But Had "Hard-line" Subordinates 209 And Loss At Cowpens 100 And "Pamphlet War" With Clinton *n47* 115 *n6* 240

CORNWALLIS (cont.)
  Angered By Tarleton's Comments *n12* 85 Campaign In South Compared To Sherman's March 203 Comments About Kings Mountain *n6* 240 Comments On Legion Prisoners 93 Comments On Tarleton's Leadership 171 Comments On Tarleton *n37* 112 Comments To Tarleton After Cowpens 100-101 Confidence In Tarleton 234 Could Lose Patience With Tarleton 100 Did Not Tolerate Looting 204 Forced To Order Dragoon Charge At Charlotte 170 Has Two Dragoons Arrested 155 Hurt By Tarleton's Criticisms 232 Letter To Cruger Re Punishment For Deserters 206-207 Ignorant Of Certain Depredations 167 Pardoned Traitors 205 Praise For Tarleton 19-20 Praised Tarleton After Waxhaws 178 Protective Of British Legion 99 Relied Heavily On Tarleton 75 *n38* 112 Tarleton A Favorite Of 97-98 Tarleton Had A Close Relationship 97 Would Not Tolerate Excessive Force 210
CORNWALLIS LETTERS, Intercepted And Published 206 236 Altered For Propaganda Purposes *n26* 222
COUGHRAN, (Cochrane) Capt Charles, Career Of *n28* 110 Maj 96
"COWBOYS" (LOYALISTS), *n57* 68
COWPENS, 2-3 97 173 American Bravery *n17* 86 American Deserters Among Dragoons Fled 171

COWPENS (cont.)
  American Perspective *n17* 87 Comments *n37* 112 Defense Of Tarleton *n17* 87 Docherty Captured 38 Effect On British Legion Numbers 41 Exhaustion And Panic Played A Part 171 Failure *n47* 115 *n17* 78 86 Infantry Files *n17* 87 Infantry Lack Of Cohesion *n17* 86 Legion Infantry Not All Lost *n37* 62 Low Point In Tarleton's Career 100 MacKenzie Notes Five Errors Of Tarleton *n7* 241 News Of Defeat In Charles Town 101 Not In Second Edition Of Tarleton's *History Of The Campaigns n6* 240 Ramsay's Commentary *n56* 117 Stigma On Tarleton's Reputation 100 *n46* 115 Tarleton Not Wounded 136 Tarleton's Concern For Wounded 45 Tarleton's Impetuosity 77 Vilification Of Tarleton *n17* 87
CRAIG, Maj James, Had Plunderer Executed *n35* 187 Joanna *vii*
CRIMINALS, Not The Majority Of The British Army *n13* 183-184
"CRITICAL DISTANCE," *n76* 197
CROPSEY, Jacobus, Complained About Legion Soldiers 231
CRUGER, Lt Col John Harris 234 236 Letter From Cornwallis Re Deserters 206-207
CRUIT, Ens, Wounds Received At Waxhaws *n79* 198
CUIRASSIER (HEAVY) CAVALRY, *n6* 51
CULLODEN, Rebels Hanged And Disemboweled *n35* 224 Rebels Received No Quarter *n18* 145
CUNINGHAM, William "Bloody Bill" *n72* 123 *n43* 152 236 *n30* 148 Opposite Of Patriot Virtue 134
CUSTIS, George Washington Parke, Historian 103 Dubious Story About Tarleton 136 *n40* 151
DARK, Thomas, Compared To Tarleton *n5* 105

DAVID FANNING'S LOYALIST MILITIA, *n5* 105
DAVIE, Col William Richardson *n8* 83 Surprise Attack On Legion At Wahab's Plantation 78 170 Comments On British Legion 94 Ruthlessness *n15* 107
DAVIS, John 102
DAY, Mr, Steward Who Demanded Tarleton Give Back Horse *n66* 230
DE GRASSE, *n60* 229 Pregnant Woman Murder Story 215
DEFECTORS, Punishment 207
DELANCEY, Brig Gen Oliver 21 *n18* 28 Frustrated With Plundering 161-162
DELANCEY'S BRIGADE, Numerical Strength 39
DENOVAN, Lt Jeremiah (Regular) 37
DEPREDATIONS, Also Committed By Camp Followers, Bat Men, Servants, Wives, Prostitutes *n25* 185
DESECRATION OF GRAVES, Reported By Du Perron 215 Reported In Patriot Press 213
DESERTER, Execution And Decapitation By Lee, Propaganda Value 131 Execution Approved By Washington 131 Flogged To Death *n48* 190 Ordered Shot By Gage *n31* 187
DESERTERS, *n20* 57 *n28* 186 American In Legion Ranks 169 At Bunker Hill 165 Execution *n30* 187 Had Nothing To Lose By Joining Other Side 170 Might Have Become Criminals 170 Percentage Of Legion Not Known 37 Rawdon's Harsh Measures *n28* 186 Treatment In Rawdon Letter 206

DESERTION, A Major Problem 164 Punishments 164-165 Reasons 164
"DEVIL INCARNATE," 103 *n4* 24
DILLY, Charles, Viewed Tarleton In Criminal Light 236
DISCIPLINE, 155 From Company-grade Officers 159 Responsibility Of Field Officers 159 Responsibility Of NCO's 162
DISINTERRED BODY, *n37* 151 See also, EXHUMATION
DOCHERTY, Alternate Spellings *n24* 58 Michael, American Deserter *n63* 119 *n29* 186 Avoided Execution For Desertion *n48* 190 Enlisted In British Legion 38 Served On Both Sides 169-170
DRAFTED, Meaning Transfer Of Troops *n9* 52
DRAGOON (MEDIUM) CAVALRY, *n6* 51
DRAGOONS, Description 33 Naming Of *n5* 24-25
DU PERRON, 216 Joachim *n59* 229 Pregnant woman Murder Story 215
DUDLEY, Guilford 102
DUN, Pvt John 37
DUNLAP, Capt, Received Rejected Accoutrements *n43* 114
EDWARDS, Capt, James (Regular) 37 40
EIGHTY-SECOND REGIMENT, Mounted Infantry 84
ELIZABETH, Trading Ship Owned By John Tarleton *n3* 24
ELK HILL, (Jefferson's Home) Destroyed *n32* 111 Laid Waste By Cornwallis 205
EMMERICK, Lt Col Andreas, And Chasseurs 36 Recruiting Advertisement *n15* 55
ESPRIT DE CORPS, 159 In British Legion 46 49
ETIQUETTE, In 18th Century Warfare *n63* 194
EUROPEAN CAVALRY BATTLES, *n4* 81

INDEX

EXECUTION, Of Loyalist Prisoners *n27* 246 See also, DESERTER, DESERTERS, DESERTION

EXHUMATION, Of Bodies In Colonial Times *n53* 228 See also, DISINTERRED BODY

FAIR LAWN PLANTATION *n43* 189

FALLEN TIMBERS, Battle Of *n43* 152

FANNING, David 236 *n30* 148 Opposite Of Patriot Virtue 134

FANNY, Brigantine Owned By John Tarleton 14

FERGUSON, Maj Patrick 22 *n18* 28 46 *n53* 67 A "Hard-liner" 209 And Punishment 168 Advocate Of Brutal Virtue 132 Bayonet Attack At Little Egg Harbor *n83* Became More Conciliatory *n19* 146 Comment On Plundering 204 Dealing With Plundering 163-164 *n27* 185 Defeat And Contempt At Kings Mtn 134 Did Not Always Follow Through With Punishment 209 Killed At Kings Mtn 75 *n8* 83 *n28* 147 199 No Relief At Kings Mountain *n6* 240 Rewarded Man Who Wounded Him *n49* 190 Vacillated Between Conciliatory And "Hard-line" Schools Of Thought *n35* 223 Wounded By Bayonet 170

FERGUSON, James, Historian *n15* 86 102

FERGUSON'S AMERICAN VOLUNTEERS, Inadvertently Attacked By Legion 170

FIELD OFFICERS, And Company-grade *n11* 183

FIFTH AMERICAN REGIMENT, 43

FIFTY-FOURTH FOOT, *n18* 56

"FIGHTER PILOT MENTALITY," 47

FIRING SQUAD, *n10* 183

FIRST CONTINENTAL CAVALRY, (Bland's) *n10* 106

FIRST DRAGOON GUARDS, *n12* 27

FIRST MARYLAND, Broke And Ran *n52* 191

FISHING CREEK, Number Of Horses Lost 98 Report In English Newspapers *n34* 112 Surprise Attack 77 Tarleton Outnumbered *n15* 85

"FLIGHT DISTANCE," *n76* 197

FLOGGING, 168 And Death *n9* 182 As Punishment 158 *n8* 181 Carried Out By Drummers 158 Deserter *n9* 182 Maximum Lashes Raised By Washington 182

FORT GRANBY, Location *n10* 84

FORT GRISWOLD, British Attack And Slaughter *n63* 194

FORT MOTTE, Location *n10* 84

FORT WATSON, Location *n10* 84

"FORTY-FIVE," The, 131

FOURTH CONTINENTAL CAVALRY, (Moylan's) *n10* 106

FREDERICK THE GREAT, Quote *n4* 81 Use Of Light Infantrymen *n6* 52

FRENCH, Admiration For America And Its People 216 Military Assistance, *n24* 109 Views Of Tarleton 96

FRENCH AND INDIAN WAR, 129

GAGE, Maj Gen Thomas, Contempt For *n3* 8 Had A Deserter Shot *n31* 187

GARDEN, Alexander, Former Member Of Lee's Legion 176 Historian 103

GATES, Horatio 92

GENTLEMAN'S WAR, End Of 208

GEORGE III, King, Frowned Upon Prince Of Wales's Friendship With Tarleton *n4* 239 "Royal Brute Of Britain" 236 Time Of Mental Illness *n13* 242

GEORGE IV, King *n1* 49 232

GEORGIA LIGHT DRAGOONS (RANGERS), *n15* 55
GERMAIN, Lord George 19-20 Comments On Leadership 43
GERMAN AUXILIARIES, Percentage Of Legion Not Known 37
GILDART, Capt Francis (Cavalry) 40
GILLES' NORTH CAROLINA DRAGOONS, *n15* 55
GILLIES, James, Young Bugler Sabered To Death 172-173
GIRTY, Capt Simon (Butler's Rangers) *n30* 148 236 Opposite Of Patriot Virtue 134
GORDON, William, Historian 103
GRANT, Ulysses S *n30* 222 And Armies Vs Civilians 208
GRAVE ROBBING, 103
GRAY, Robert 103
GREEN, Pvt Isaac 38 *n23* 58
"GREEN HORSE," 49 British Legion Became Known As 34 See BRITISH LEGION
GREEN SPRING FARM, Lafayette's Camp *n24* 89
GREENE, Maj Gen Nathanael 206 Comments On Tarleton 92-93 Comment On Desertion 164
GRENADIERS, *n14* 54 *n6* 51-52
GREY, Maj Gen Charles "No-Flint" *n43* 152-153 33 179 *n82* 198
GUILFORD COURTHOUSE, 44 Bugler Sabered Near 172 Tarleton Wounded 136
HALDANE, Lt 205
HALL, David *n27* 185
HALL, Moses *n1* 7 71 79 *n25* 90 103 235 237 And Discovery Of Bayoneted Loyalists 172 Fear Of Tarleton's Legion 95 Finds Boy Bayoneted By Legionnaire 2 Recalls Prisoner Murders 1

HAMILTON'S NORTH CAROLINA VOLUNTEERS, Mounted *n10* 84
HANGER, Maj George 45 *n47* 66 71 Fourth Baron Coleraine *n1* 49 Anecdote 31 And Dragoons' Refusal To Charge 78 And Lauzun Became Friends After War *n1* 49 At Charlotte *n50* n51 191 Capt Tarleton Urged His Promotion 97 Defended Tarleton 232 Felt He Was Unjustly Treated 21 Poor Performance Of Legion At Charlotte *n18* 88 Rambunctious Lifestyle *n1* 49 Supervised Disbandment Of Legion *n3* 239 Tarleton's Second-in-command 170 Yellow Fever 44
HANGING ROCK, Battle Fought Between Americans *n19* 88 Legion Infantry Charge 78
HARCOURT, Lt Col William 15 16 18
"HARD-LINE" ATTITUDE, Reasons For 208-209
"HARD-LINE" OFFICERS, Left A More Enduring Impression Than Conciliatory Comrades 209
"HATMEN," *n6* 51
HAW RIVER, 79 *n24* 89
HIGHLANDERS, *n14* 54
HILDRETH, Richard, Historian 103
HILL, Janet E *viii*
HILLSBORO, North Carolina, Prisoners Abused 134
HISTORIOGRAPHY, 236 *n34* 150 And Brutal Virtue 237 Natural Progression 104
HISTORY, Americans' View Of Their Own 3 5 *n4* 9
HOBKIRK'S HILL, First Maryland Broke And Ran *n17* 87 *n52* 191
HOLMES, Abiel, Historian 103
HONORS OF WAR, *n63* 194
HORRY'S HORSE, *n10* 106
HORSE GRENADIER GUARDS, *n9* 52
HORSE GUARDS, *n9* 52
HORSES, A Precious Commodity 98-99 Captured At Monck's Corner 98 *n40* 113

INDEX

HORSES (cont.)
  Died In Pursuit Of Buford 99
  Exact Number In Legion Not Known *n45* 115 Killed By Hot Climate And Rapid Marches 99 Losses *n39* 113 Needed For Loyal Militia *n43* 114 Prohibited From Leaving Charles Town 98 Purchased From Civilians 99
HOVENDEN, Alternate Spellings *n29* 60 Capt Richard (Cavalry) 38 40
HOWE, Sir (Lord) William 21-22 33 Awareness Of Political Struggle 132 Did Not Acknowledge Washington's Military Rank *n63* 194 Flogged And Hanged Plunderers *n18* 184 Had Two Deserters Hanged At Bunker Hill 165
HUCK, Capt Christian (Dragoons), 38 A Miniature Tarleton 210 "The Swearing Captain" *n44* 114 210 Pursued By Militia For 15 Miles *n45* 226 Stirred Up Much Resentment 210
HUGER, Brig Gen Isaac *n10* 106
HUSSAR (LIGHT) CAVALRY, *n6* 51
HUSSARS, *n14* 54 *n15* 55
INFECTION, And Death Rate At Waxhaws *n78* 197
"INJURED INNOCENCE," 178 *n16* 144 *n52* 227 Concept Important To Washington 130-131 Myth Was Maintained And Affirmed 135 137
JACOBITE REVOLT, Of 1745, Affected British View Of Rebels 131
JAGERS (YAGERS), Light Infantry And Riflemen *n15* 55
JAMES, Capt Jacob (Cavalry) 38 40 *n22* 58 A Horse Thief *n39* 113

JAMES, William Dobein *n8* 106 *n59* 192 At Richardson Home 213
JEFFERSON, Thomas, An "Active And Virulent" Rebel 206 Elk Hill Home Destroyed *n32* 111 Legion Was Ordered Not To Plunder Monticello 172 Monticello Spared 97 *n32* 111 Terrified By Near Capture *n32* 111 *n56* 192
JENKINS, Robert *n10* 142
JOHNSON, Joseph, Historian 102-103 212
JONES, Mr *n40* 151 Mrs Willie 136
JORDAN, Ens William (Regular) 37
JOURNALS, Anonymous *n60* 229
KING'S AMERICAN DRAGOONS, 36 Recruiting *n15* 55 Some Elements Of British Legion Incorporated *n1* 238
KING'S AMERICAN RANGERS, Regular Establishment 43
KING'S AMERICAN REGIMENT, *n41* 64 Known Maximum Strength 39
KING'S DRAGOON GUARDS, (First) 15 *n55* 68
KING'S MEN, Many Joined Provincial Units 74
KING'S ROYAL REGIMENT OF NEW YORK, Numerical Strength 39
KING GEORGE'S WAR, 129
KING WILLIAM'S WAR, 129
KINGS MOUNTAIN, *n13* 85 *n60* 118 210
KINGSBRIDGE, Tarleton's Skirmish With Indians 18 20
KINLOCH, Capt David, Cared For Wounded Man *n79* 198
KINSTREE, Tarleton At 92
KOVACIK, Charles *vii*
LAFAYETTE, Marquis De 125 Spies Sent To His Camp By Tarleton *n24* 89 Urged Stroke Against Tarleton 94 Worried About Enemy Cavalry *n14* 107 Wrote Of Need For Dragoons 94

LAMB, Sgt Roger, Memoir *n21* 221
LAMM, Anderson *viii*
LANCERS, *n6* 51
LAND GRANT, In Lieu Of Levy Money *n3* 50
LAURENS, Henry 14
LAURENS, Lt Col John 125 134 Reportedly Admonished Tarleton *n4* 24 126 Aide-de-camp 14
LAUZUN, Armand-Louis De Gontaut-Biron, Duc De *n1* 31 49 232 Became Friends With Hanger and Tarleton After War *n1* 49 Died Under The Guillotine *n1* 49 Protests Another's Promotion 21 Relationship With Mary Robinson *n1* 49 Wished To Meet Legion Troops 95
LAUZUN'S LEGION, *n36* 187 Nearly Captured Tarleton *n16* 108
LAYMAN, Richard *viii*
LEE, Gen Charles, Captured At White's Tavern 16 Folly And Imprudence *n7* 25 Comments On American Cavalry *n40* 113
LEE, Lt Col Henry "Light Horse Harry" 95 *n43* 131 152 Comment On Tarleton 211 Tricked Pyle's Loyalists At Haw River 138
LEE'S LEGION, 33 Uniforms Similar To British Legion *n11* 53 *n24* 89
LEGION, Description 33 Fear Of 102 Frequent Need For New Kits *n43* 114 Kind Acts 96-97 Scattered Detachments *n12* 85 Strenuous Campaigns 79
LEGIONNAIRES, Back Pay And Property Confiscation Of *n2* 238 Extreme Loyalty 45 Occasionally Tried To Hide Identity 79 Psychological Tricks 79

"LEINTWARDINE," Tarleton's Estate In Shropshire 232
LENDRUM, John, Historian 103
LENUD'S FERRY, 94 Horses Captured 98 Surprise Attack 77 Tarleton Outnumbered *n15* 85
LESLIE, Maj Gen Alexander 151 Orders Against Plundering 162
"LETHAL DELUSION," 3 *n3* 8
LIGHT DRAGOONS, *n14* 54 *n6* 51
LIGHT INFANTRY, *n14* 54 *n6* 52 Description 33 The Elite Of Any Regiment *n6* 51
LIMITED TERROR, 204-205
"LIMITED WAR," 130 *n5* 141 Practiced In Europe 127
LINCOLN, Maj Gen Benjamin 137
LITTLE EGG HARBOR, Night Attack, 179 *n83* 199
LIVERPOOL BLUES, *n14* 27
LOCKWOOD, Maj Ebenezer 48
LONDON GAZETTE EXTRAORDINARY, Comments On Tarleton 97
LOUIS XVI, King Of France 21
LOUISBOURG, Capture In 1745 *n13* 143
LOYALIST FORCES, Greater Semblance To Regulars 33 Land Grants, Pay Bounties, Etc 32 Reforms Regarding Officers 32 Revamped Policy Toward 32 Troops, Great Need For 32 *n2* 50 Uniforms Changed From Green To Red 32-33
LOYALISTS, A Desperate Lot 45-46 British Policy Was Unrealistic *n3* 50-51 Confusion Over Definition *n18* 56 Contempt Of British Soldiers 46 Defined *n1* 7 Percent Of Population *n3* 50 73 Percentage Of Legion Not Known 37 Percentage Of Population In The South *n6* 82 Support Overestimated 73
MACKENZIE, Lt Roderick 232 Critic Of Tarleton 98 Criticized Tarleton After Cowpens 101 Infantry Comment 78

INDEX

MACKENZIE, Simon Paul *vii*
MACPHERSON'S PLANTATION, Ferguson Bayoneted *n15* 86 Night Attack 77
MANCHESTER REGIMENT, (72nd) *n12* 27
MANCHESTER VOLUNTEERS, *n12* 27
MANNERS, Peculiarity In Eighteenth-Century *n1* 49
MARION, Francis (Swamp Fox) 5 74 *n8* 83 92 168 At Richardson's Plantation 212 Biography By Bass 4 Comments About Tarleton 93 95 Joined By John Postell 211
MARSHALL, John, Historian 103
MARTIN, Gov Alexander (NC) *n5* 105
MATROSS, Definition *n10* 182
MAWHOOD, Col Charles *n12* 27
MCARTHUR, Maj Archibald, Criticized Tarleton 101
MCCLURE, Capt John, And Pursuit Of Huck *n45* 226
MCCRIMMIN, Lt Donald (Regular) 37
MCDONAL, Lt James 37
MCDONALD, Capt Charles (Infantry) 40 Sgt Peter 37 Lt Sorrel (Regular) 37
MCLEOD, Legion Officer Who Raided Monticello *n56* 192
MCPHERSON, Capt Donald (Regular) 37-38 40
METAPHOR, American Noble Virtue Over British Brutal Virtue 202
MILES, Francis, Trumpeter 37
MILITIA, Wavering Loyalties *n8* 219
MILLAR, Capt Thomas *n30* 111
MILLER, Capt 97 *n30* 111 John Ens (Regular) 37 *n30* 111 Thomas *n30* 111 Capt Thomas (Regular) 37 Infantry Capt 40

MISCHIANZA, (A Ball Given When Clinton Replaced Howe) 22*n18* 28
MITCHELL, Sgt, Carried Regimental Colors At Waxhaws *n79* 198
MONCK'S CORNER, 94 Horses Seized *n40* 113 Night Attack 77 Remnants *n10* 106
MONEY, Lt John, Wounded *n46* 65
MONGOLS, *n29* 222 Employed Inconsistent Terror Techniques 207
MONTICELLO, Jefferson's Home, Not Harmed 97 *n32* 111 172 *n22* 221
MORAL SUPERIORITY, 178
MORGAN, Brig Gen Daniel 3 45 Chased For Two Weeks By Legion 171 At Cowpens *n17* 87 94 Reflections On Victory At Cowpens *n32* 148 Resigned After Cowpens *n12* 107
MORSE, Jedidiah, Historian 103
MOULTRIE, William, Historian 103 *n55* 117
MOUNTED INFANTRY, Need For *n10* 84
MOUNTED TROOPS, Psychology Of *n55* 68 Superiority Complex 47
MURRAY, Brig Gen James 161
MYTH, Defined 4 *n6* 10
MYTH-MAKING PROCESS, 4-5 *n7* 10
MYTHS, Abandoned Baby 4 *n5* 9 Crazed Horse 4 *n5* 9-10 Quaker Boy 4 *n4* 9 Richardson Incident 4 *n5* 10 See also, DISINTERRED BODY and, PREGNANT WOMAN
NAPOLEONIC ERA, *n14* 143
NATIVE AMERICANS, And Colonial Wars 129 And Influence Of "Limited War" 127-128
NEUTRAL GROUND, Terrorized *n57* 68
NEW JERSEY VOLUNTEERS, Numerical Strength 39
NEW YORK VOLUNTEERS, *n41* 64 Known Maximum Strength 39 Regular Establishment 43 Turnbull's 74
NICKNAMES, *n43* 152-153

NIGHT ATTACKS, *n83* 199
NINETY-SIX DISTRICT, *n7* 82
  Widows And Orphans 74
NORTH CAROLINA
  PROVINCIALS, At Hanging
  Rock *n19* 88
"OFFICER CLASS," *n12* 27
OGILVY, Alternate Spellings *n29*
  60 Capt David (Cavalry) 40
OLD TAPPAN, 179 Bayonet
  Attack *n83* 199
"ON COMMAND," Meaning On
  Detached Duty *n36* 62
PAINE, Thomas 236
PANCAKE, John, Calls Tarleton
  "Bloody Ban" 104
PAOLI MASSACRE, Bayonet
  Attack *n8* 25 *n43* 153 179 *n83*
  199
PARKER, Marie *viii*
PAROLE, Definition *n9* 83 Often
  Broken *n1* 104
PARTISAN, Definition *n8* 83
PARTISAN BANDS, 74
PARTON, James, Calls Tarleton
  "Devil Incarnate" 103
PATERSON, Brig Gen James *n4*
  81
PATRIOT, Defined *n1* 7
PEARSON, Lt, Wounds Received
  At Waxhaws *n79* 198
PEPPERREL, Lt Gen William
  160
PHILADELPHIA (CHESTER
  COUNTY) LIGHT
  DRAGOONS, 40
PHILADELPHIA LIGHT
  DRAGOONS, First Troop 40
PHILIPS, Samuel, A Released
  Prisoner 147
PICKENS, Andrew 74 *n8* 83
PINCKNEY, Gen Thomas,
  Visited Wounded Men At
  Waxhaws *n79* 198
PIONEER TROOPS, *n22* 58
PIQUET, As Punishment 157 *n7*
  181 See also, SPICKET

PITKIN, Timothy, Historian 103
PLAINS OF ABRAHAM, Battle Of *n11*
  142
PLUNDERING, 159-163 165-166 *n15*
  184 Alienation Of Population *n13*
  183 And Food 160 At Louisbourg
  160 British Legion Sgt Executed
  n35 187 Detrimental Effect 204
  Hanging And Flogging *n15* 220
  Justifiable As A Form Of Limited
  Terror 204 Rebel Problems *n27* 185
  Three Forms 159-160
POPULATION, American, In
  Revolutionary Period *n6* 82
PORT ROYAL ISLAND, Legion
  Landing On 98
POSTELL, John 99 Fear Of Tarleton's
  Legion 95 Home Plundered By
  Dragoons 211 Statements As
  Prisoner *n23* 109 Mrs 95
POUNDRIDGE-BEDFORD RAID,
  n58 69 *n28* 110 Forced March 78
  Use Of Terror 235
PREGNANT WOMAN, Murder Of 96
  n27 109-110 *n37* 151 214 Story In
  Anonymous Journal *n60* 229
PREVOST, Maj Gen Augustine *n60* 69
PRINCE OF WALES LOYAL
  AMERICAN VOLUNTEERS, *n19*
  88
PRISON CAMPS, Desperately Avoided
  169-170
PRISONERS, Of Legion Cruelly
  Treated 93 Often Sent To Garrison
  Undesirable Posts *n29* 186
PROMOTIONS, *n15* n17 28 Analysis
  Of Quickness Of Tarleton's 20
PROPAGANDA, 202 212 214 237 *n33*
  149 *n34* 150 *n58* 192 Attacks At
  Maidenhead, Hopewell, And
  Woodbridge 216 Waxhaws 178
PROVINCIALISM, of Americans
  Seemed Peculiar To Many
  Englishmen *n31* 223
PROVINCIALS, Not "Associators" Or
  Militiamen *n3* 50

INDEX

PROVOST MARSHAL, Responsibilities *n55* 68
PSYCHOLOGY, Of Brutalization *n15* 144
PULASKI'S LEGION, 33 *n10* 106 Attacked By Ferguson *n83* 199
PUNISHMENT, And Purification *n8* 182 Capital 158 Company-grade Officers Reluctant To Inflict 167-168 Corporal 157-158 Part Of Martial Bonding *n6* 181
PYLE, Col John, Loyalist *n1* 7 *n24* 89 138
QUAKER BOY, Murder *n58* 192
QUARTERMASTER GENERAL, Responsibilities *n41* 64
QUEEN'S OWN LIGHT DRAGOONS, (Sixteenth) 15
QUEEN'S RANGERS, 21 34 40 167 *n15* 55 *n17* n18 28 *n4* 81 *n41* 64 Esprit De Corps *n50* 66 High Turnover *n20* 57 In Charles Town Expedition 72 In New York 47 Known Maximum Strength 39 Leadership And Reliability 43 44 Organized Like A Legion 36 Placed Upon Regular Establishment 43 Quartered At Oyster Bay NY 48 Simcoe's Recruited Prisoners 37 Sister Regiment To British Legion 35 Thorough Training 35 Uniforms Similar To Legion *n11* 53 Wartime Establishment 39
QUEEN ANNE'S WAR, 129
RAMSAY, David, Historian 103 *n56* 117 *n60* 118 236
RANGER INFANTRY, Organization *n14* 54
RANK AND FILE, Portion Of Regiment 36
RAPE, *n44* 189
RAWDON, Lord Francis *n18* 28 33 Lord Moira *n5* 51 A "Hard-liner" 209 Advocate Of Brutal Virtue 132 Cautioned About Legion 99 Deserter Punishment Letter 206 Harsh Measures For Deserters *n28* 186 Ignored Sexual Assaults On Women At Staten Island *n44* 189 Reproached By Cornwallis 100
REBELLION, As A Sin *n18* 145
REBELLIONS, Conciliatory Group 132 English Attitudes Towards 131-132 "Hard-line" Group 132 Two Schools Of Thought 132
REBELS, Had To Be Dealt With In A Harsh Manner 131
REDUCTION, Meaning Disbandment Of Regiment *n3* 50
REED, Capt Philip 131
REGIMENT, English Organization Of *n6* 51 Members As Family 159
REGIMENT D'INFANTERIE DE MONSIEUR, 96 215
REGIMENTAL COURT MARTIAL, Punishments 157-158 Uniqueness And Speed 157
REGULAR ESTABLISHMENT, Five Provincial Regiments 42
REGULARS, In The British Legion 37 Percentage Of Legion Not Known 37
"REMEMBER BUFORD," 1 *n1* 7
REVEL, Comte De 96
REVENGE, And Torture, *n8* 83 Incidents Of *n26* 147
REVERE, Paul *n16* 144
REVOLUTIONARY WAR, In Heavily Populated Areas 130 Involved Much Of Population 130
REYNOLDS, Sir Joshua, Portrait Of Tarleton 12-13 *n1* 22 232
RICHARDSON, Gen Richard 93 168 Body Or Silverware Exhumed 212-213 *n52* 227 Dug Up By Tarleton? 4 Corpse Not Exhumed *n45* 190 House Burned By Tarleton 169

RICHARDSON, James Burchill, Impudent Child 212
RICHARDSON, John Peter II 212-213
RICHARDSON, Mrs, Not Spared By Tarleton 93 Widow 97 Warned Marion 169
RIFLEMEN, $n14$ 54
ROBERTS, Algernon, Comment On Plundering 161
ROBERTSON, Archibald 103
ROBINS, Lt William 37
ROBINSON, Mary (Perdita), Love Interest Of Tarleton 4 $n1$ 49 232 Wrote Novel $n5$ 240
ROCHAMBEAU, Lt Gen Comte De, Comment On Tarleton 96 $n26$ 109 Visited Cornwallis 125
RODNEY, Vice Adm George Brydges $n60$ 229
ROUSSELET, Capt John (Infantry) 40
ROYAL DEUX-PONTS REGIMENT, 96
ROYAL GARRISON BATTALION, 37
ROYAL LIVERPOOL VOLUNTEERS, $n12$ 26
ROYAL REGIMENT OF HORSE GUARDS (BLUE), $n9$ 52
RUGELEY, Henry, And Deserter Punishment Letter 206
RUNNING THE GAUNTLET, As Punishment 157
RUTLEDGE, Gov John 102 213
SALEM, On The Black River, Tarleton At 92
SANDFORD, Alternate Spellings $n29$ 60 Capt Thomas (Cavalry) 40 96 $n29$ 110
SANFORD, Capt 96
SANTEE RIVER, 91-92 $n10$ 84
SCAMMELL, Col Alexander, Close Ties To Washington $n55$ Killed Outside York Town 172 191 Shot By Dragoons $n61$ 118

SCOTT, Capt John B $n34$ 187
SCOTTI, Anthony J Jr $viii$ 34 Laura $viii$
SECOND CONTINENTAL DRAGOONS, 48
SEVEN YEARS' WAR, $n10$ 142
SEVENTEENTH LIGHT DRAGOONS, 16 34 $n18$ 28 56 In Charles Town Expedition 72 Kept Red Uniform Coats 42 Trained Hussars $n39$ 63
SEVENTEENTH REGIMENT OF FOOT, 38
SEVENTH REGIMENT, 45 Michael Docherty In 169
SEVENTY-FIRST-HIGHLANDERS, Criticized Tarleton 101
SEVENTY-NINTH REGIMENT, 20
SEVENTY-SECOND REGIMENT, $n12$ 27
SEVENTY-SIXTH REGIMENT, Mounted Infantry $n10$ 84
SEVERN MILITARY DISTRICT, Tarleton Commandant Of 232
SEYMOUR, William 102
"SHAMING," As Punishment $n7$ 181
SHELDON, Col Elisha 48
SHERMAN'S MARCH, 208 $n13$ 220
SHOWALTER, Dennis vii
SIMCOE, Col John Graves 21 22 $n18$ 28 35 45-46 Accused British Legion Of Depredations 231 Comment On Plundering 167 Considered Bayonet The Key To Victory 47 His Equipment Went To Legion 100 Leadership And Charisma 44
SIMCOE'S QUEENS RANGERS, Equipment Appropriated 43 114 Green Uniforms 34
SIMMS, William Gilmore, Historian 103
SINGLETON'S MILLS, 92
SIXTEENTH LIGHT DRAGOONS, 34 $n18$ 56 Returned To England 73
SIXTY-THIRD REGIMENT, At Blackstocks Hill 77 Mounted Infantry 84
"SKINNERS" (REBELS), $n57$ 68

INDEX

SKIPWITH, Sir Peyton, Owner Of Horse Tarleton Was Riding *n66* 230
SLOCOMB, Mrs, Argument With Tarleton 136 *n42* 152 202
SLOPER, Lt Col Robert *n6* 25
SMITH, J R, Made Mezzotint Likeness Of Tarleton *n1* 22
SNOW ISLAND, Location *n7* 105
SOUS-LIEUTENANT, Definition *n27* 109 Equivalent To An Ensign *n56* 228
SOUTH, Politically Different From North 73
SOUTH CAROLINA, Invasion 73
SOUTH CAROLINA LOYALISTS, *n15* 55
SOUTH CAROLINA RANGERS, At Hanging Rock *n19* 88
SPEED AND MILEAGE, On Horse And Foot *n20* 88
SPICKET, SPICKETING, *n8* 83 As Punishment *n7* 181 see also PIQUET
SPIES, *n24* 89
STANLEY, Adj Thomas (Regular) 37
STEDMAN, Charles, Comment On Waxhaws 178 Criticized Tarleton 101 Despised Tarleton *n50* 116 Vendetta Against Tarleton *n80* 198
STEWART, Capt Charles *n60* 69 Company In Savannah 49
STEWART, Patrick Capt (Infantry) 37 40 *n60* 69
STEWART'S PROVINCIAL DRAGOONS, *n15* 55
STOKES, Capt John, At Waxhaws 176 Wounds Received At Waxhaws *n79* 198
STONY POINT, Docherty Captured 38
STRONG, William, Murder *n58* 192
SUBALTERN, Definition *n21* 185
SUBLIEUTENANT, Equivalent To An Ensign *n56* 228
SUGAR, Silver Age Of *n2* 23
SUMTER, Thomas (Carolina Gamecock) 74 *n8* 83 At Blackstocks Hill 77 At Fishing Creek *n15* 85 At Hanging Rock *n19* 88 Biography By Bass 4 Home Was Burned By British Legion 210
SUPPLY PROBLEMS, British *n16* 184
SUTHERLAND, Capt William 41
TACTICS, Analyzed By Simcoe 35
TARLETON, Lt Col Banastre 14 37 39 78-79 (Banestre) In King's Dragoon Guards 18 "The Butcher" *n73* 123 *n10* 84 A Convenient Scapegoat 236 A Cruel Villain *n33* 149 A Favorite Of His Superiors 17 20 22 97 99 A "Hard-liner" 209 A Real "English Devil" To Justify Revolution 134 139 236 A Triple Threat To American Cause 133 Ability To Inspire His Men 234 Advocated Brutal Virtue 132 Accusations Not Supported By Eyewitnesses 135 Active Social Live After The War 232 Activities In The South 92 American View Of 92-93 Amorous Adventures *n44* 189 And Exhumed Body Story 212-213 And Mrs Slocomb, Metaphor Of American Virtue 136-137 And Susan Had No Children *n5* 240 Appearance Described 13 *n1* 23 *n71* 122 *n36* 151 Argument With Mrs Ashe *n40* 151 Arrogance, Ability, And Skill 22 As A Field Commander 235 Asked Special Protection After York Town *n3* 140 At Brandywine And Germantown 17 At Forts Washington And Lee 16 At Lenud's Ferry 91 At Monmouth Courthouse 17 At Oxford 15 At Waxhaws *n1* 7 175 At White Plains 16 Attempts To Portray Him As A Monster *n71* 122 132

TARLETON (cont.)
  Attitude Toward Rebellion 91-92 Baronetcy Expired *n13* 243 Blames Cornwallis Re Ferguson *n12* 85 Boastfulness *n64* 120 British Views Of 97 Burns Richardson's House 169 Captain Of 79th Foot (Royal Live 18 Captures Lee At White's Tavern 16 Cast As Star Terrorist 216 Chases Marion 169 Comment On Waxhaws 177 Comments About Field Formation *n17* 86 Confronts Laurens 126 Considered A Cruel Individual 103 Considered Bayonet The Key To Victory 47 Cotibuted To Terror 211 Continued To Rise Through The Ranks After The War 232 Cornet 15-16 Cowpens Low Point In His Career 100 Criticized For Cowpens 101 Cut Off Boy's Fingers 201 Date Of Lt Col Commission *n15* 28 Dates Of Various Commissions 19 Death 233 *n14* 243 Defended Slave Trade 232 Demanded Impressment Of Equipment 100 Demonstrations Of Bravery 44 Described As Handsome In 18th Century Accounts 135 Devastation Caused By *n18* 108 Eager To Please His Superiors 20 Early Life 13-15 Early Military Service 15-16 Employed Brutal Virtue Echoing Old Imperial Response To Rebellion 234 Energy 47 Evil Characterization 1-5 Exploits In English Newspapers *n34* 112 Family Business Ventures *n4* 239 Fanciful Encounter With Mrs Slocomb, Mrs Jones, And Mrs Ashe *n3* 217

TARLETON (cont.)
  Fanciful Stories *n1* 139 Favoritism And Jealousy 100 Feared For His Safety After Yorktown 93 Feared Less By Continentals *n17* 108 French Views Of 96 Friends With Lauzun After The War *n1* 49 Friendship With Other Officers 22 Gained Rank By Merit 17 His Name Used To Frighten Children 102 His Place In American Psyche 237 *History Of The Campaigns* 232 *n6* 240 Horse On Staircase Story 71 Humiliated By Planter's Steward 217 *n66* 230 Ideal For Loyalist Regiment 20 Ignorant Of Certain Depredations 167 Ill During Battle Of Kings Mountain *n6* 240 Impersonated William Washington *n24* 89 In London After Surrender At York Town 232 In Old Age *n14* 243 In Painting *n4* 239 Insults To Women *n40* 151 Insults To Women *n42* 152 Interaction With Peers 20 Jealousy And Resentment Of 21 Leadership Of Legion 43-44 Loved The High Life *n9* 26 Motivated By Ambition 20 Myth And Reality 6 Near Princeton And Trenton 16 Pride In His Regiment 46 Quickly Rose Through The Ranks 17 Somewhat Reckless 18 Volunteers For North America 15-16 With Howe At Elk River 16 Knighted 232 *n14* 243 Labeled A Villain After Waxhaws 178 Leadership And Charisma 44 Made Lt Col Of British Legion 19 Malaria *n18* 88 Malaria Or Yellow Fever 44 *n47* 65-66 Mangled Hand *n11* 242 Mangled Hand Joke And Metaphor 136 Married To Susan Priscilla Bertie 232 Mezzontint *n1* 22 Military Successes *n25* 146 Mobility Of 79 Myth And Historiographical Legacy 135-137 Near Fatal Fever *n37* 112 Negative Comments *n50-54* 116

INDEX

TARLETON (cont.)
No Regard For Civil Opinion 235 Not Asked To Join Cornwallis' Staff In India n6 240 Not Invited To Visit Other Officers 125 Ordered Legionnaires To Kill Boyer 176 Outnumbered At Various Battles n15 85 Paroled Wounded Americans At Waxhaws 178 Perceptions Influenced By Operations 80 Perfect Model Of "The Devil Incarnate" 236 Pleas For Help With Debts n4 239 Praised By Clinton And Cornwallis After Waxhaws 178 Proclamation Of Pardon n3 104 Psychological Impact Of His Mobility 79 Ranks n8 n9 n10 241 Relied Upon Shock And Pursuit 77 Requested Court-martial n48 115 Rescued By His Legionnaires n48 66 Resentful Temper n70 121 Resentment And Jealousy Of 102 Responsibility For Discipline 165 Right Hand Amputated n39 151 Rumor Of Wounding n25 109 Sat For Reynolds Portrait 232 Sat For Seven Sessions In Parliament 232 Sat In Parliament n11 242 Satirized In "Sweet Liberty" n30 248 Secrecy Of Numbers 79 Seen By Americans As The Cruel Messenger Of A Repressive King 235 Sent To Portugal n9 241 Sent To Southern Provinces 19 Set Fire To Homes In New York 48 Ship Captured By French Privateer n3 239 Skirmish With Indian n12 27 Skirmish With Stockbridge Indians 18 Stamina 44 Standard Works On n2 8

TARLETON (cont.)
String Of Successes n38 112 Susan Priscilla 232 The Butcher 237 The Butcher n65 230 The Opposite Of American Sense Of Virtue 132-133 Thought Small Detachments Detrimental 99 Unaware Of Some Dragoon Depredations 168 Vilified In American Historiography 236 Worried About The Past n49 116 Wounded n46 65

TARLETON, Bridget, Sister Of Banastre n2 23

TARLETON, Clayton, Brother Of Banastre n2 23 n5 24

TARLETON, Jane, Sister Of Banastre n2 23

TARLETON, Jane, Lady, Mother Of Banastre 15 17 Did Not Approve Of Mary Robinson n5 240 Purchased Cornetcy n5 24

TARLETON, John Sr, Father Of Banastre 13 n2 23 Bankrupt After Napoleonic Wars n4 239 Mayor Of Liverpool 14 Prosperity 14 Ships Owned By n3 24 West Indies Merchant Trader 14

TARLETON, John Jr, Brother Of Banastre n2 23 Defeated By Brother Banastre In Parliament 232

TARLETON, Thomas, Brother Of Banastre 15 17 n2 23 n5 24 Bankrupt After Napoleonic Wars n4 239

TARLETON, Thomas, Nephew Of Banastre n13 243

TARLETON, William, Brother Of Banastre n2 23

"TARLETON'S GREEN HORSE," Actually Cathcart's Legion 43

TARLETON'S LEGION, Intimidating The Militia n40 224 Loyalty Demonstrated n36 187 Numerical Strength 41

"TARLETON'S QUARTER," 102 178 210 n29 246 Origins Of Expression n60 118

"TARLETON'S TERROR,"
William Washington's Banner
n48 226
TARRANT'S TAVERN,
Dragoons Were Fresh From
Defeat 171 People Panicked
95 Surprise Attack 77 Tarleton
Outnumbered *n15* 85
TARRENT'S TAVERN,
"Remember The Cowpens"
n19 108
TAVINGTON (TARLETON),
Col William 5
TAWES, Capt *n60* 69
TAYLOR, John 102
TEMPERATURE, Southern,
Well Suited For Cavalry 72
TERROR, 201 And The Patriot
Press 209 Created Equal If
Not More Furious Responses
235 Effects Only Transitory
235 Employed By Both Sides
During Revolutionary War 202
Failure Of 211 In The South
n4 218 Inconsistent 207
Knowing When To Employ
207 Produced Immediate
Results 235 Sometimes
Backfired On Tarleton 210
Tarleton's Role 202 209
TERROR POLICY, Of British
Legion 2
THACHER, James, Surgeon In
Continental Army 102 *n66* 230
THE ANNUAL REGISTER, *n33*
111 Comments On Tarleton
97 Report About Cowpens 100
THE GREEN DRAGOON,
Biography Of Tarleton 104
THE LONDON CHRONICLE,
Comments On Tarleton 97
THE PARTISAN, Novel 103
THE PATRIOT, Movie,
Inaccuracies Of 5
THIRD CONTINENTAL
CAVALRY, (Baylor's) *n10* 106
THIRTY YEARS' WAR, 208

THIRTY-SEVENTH FOOT, *n18* 56
THIRTY-THIRD FOOT, In Darby
Pennsylvania 205
THOMPSON, Lt Col Benjamin 36 *n1*
238
TILDEN, John Bell 102
TOPOGRAPHY, North American,
Brought Need For Legion 34
Unsuited To European War 33
Problems Presented 34 Southern,
Well Suited For Cavalry 72
TORNQUIST, Karl Gustaf 216
Comments About Americans *n63*
229 *n58* 229 Pregnant Woman
Murder Story 214
TORRENCE'S TAVERN, (Tarrant's
Tavern) *n19* 108
TORY, Defined *n1* 7
TROTTER, John, Cornetcy Purchased
From *n5* 24
TRUELOVE, John T 35 *viii*
TRUMBULL, Rebel Frigate 38
TUCKER, George, Historian 103
TWENTY-THIRD REGIMENT,
Mounted Infantry *n10* 84
"USABLE PAST, " 3 *n3* 8
VERGER, Jean-Baptiste-Antoine De 96
VERNON, Capt Nathaniel (Cavalry) 38
40*n22* 58
VIDETTE, Definition *n33* 187
VILLAINS, Shocking And Intriguing
To Americans *n3* 8
VIOLENCE, Growing Numbness
Toward, As War Progressed 208
VIOMÉNIL, Baron De 217
VIRTUE, American And British Styles
127 136-138 American, Called Into
Question After Defeats 133 Faltered
In Vengeance On Tarleton 133
American Ideal 139 American Sense
Of 132-133 And Courage 127 And
Cruelty In War 126 And
Development Of Violent Culture
129 And Perception Of "Bloody
Tarleton" 126 As Defined By
Tarleton Vs Laurens 126 Concepts
Of 134

INDEX

VIRTUE (cont.)
  Eighteenth-Century
  Definition 126-127 Important
  For Revolutionaries And Their
  Cause 130 Renaissance
  Meaning *n4* 140
VOLONTAIRES ETRANGERS
  DE LA MARINE, *n1* 49
VOLUNTEERS OF IRELAND,
  33 *n18* 28 *n20* 57 *n41* 64
  Deserters In 37 Known
  Maximum Strength 39
  Punishment For Deserters 206
  Regular Establishment 43
  Wartime Establishment 39
VOLUNTEERS OF NEW
  ENGLAND, *n15* 55
VON HINRICHS, Capt Johann
  59
VON STEUBEN, Maj Gen
  Frederick 94
WAHAB'S PLANTATION, 78
  n18 88 Davie At 94 Davie's
  Ruthlessness *n14* 107 Legion
  Cavalry Fled Attack 170
WALES, Prince Of, Formed His
  Own Club 232 Friend Of
  Tarleton 232 Future King
  George IV *n13* 242
WALLACE, Willard, Description
  Of Tarleton *n71* 122
WAR, Eighteenth-Century
  Custom Regarding Refusal To
  Surrender and Forfeit of
  Quarter *n45* 153 173 Etiquette
  And Conduct 125-126 *n2* 139-
  140 *n3* 140
WAR OF AUSTIRAN
  SUCCESSION, *n14* 144 234
WAR OF JENKINS' EAR, 129
  n10 142
WAR OF SPANISH
  SUCCESSION, *n10* 142
WAR OF THE LEAGUE OF
  AUGSBURG, *n10* 142
"WARRANT MEN," *n16* 56

WARREN, Mercy Otis, Historian 103
  Insulted By Tarleton *n42* 152
WARREN, Commodore Peter 160
WASHINGTON, Gen George, Allowed
  Cornwallis To Send Sloop To New
  York After Surrender *n48* 226
  Comments On Arnold *n14* 54
  Military Rank Not Acknowledged
  By Howe *n63* 194 Received
  Cornwallis' Intercepted Letters 207
  Visited Cornwallis 125
WASHINGTON, Lt Col William 94
  n10 106 136 *n48* 226 Escape At
  Lenud's Ferry *n15* 85 Some Of His
  Dragoons With Buford *n60* 193
  Tarleton Impersonated *n24* 89
  Tarleton Spoke Sarcastically *n40* 151
WATEREE RIVER, *n10* 84
WAXHAWS, 210 *n1* 7 *n34* 112 *n78* 198
  American Reactions To *n26* 146
  American View And Bayonet Use
  179 American Vs British Views 176
  Basis Of Massacre Story *n50* 153-154
  Bayonet And Saber Battle 177
  Bayonet Charge *n17* 108 Cavalry
  Charge *n65* 194-195 Forced March
  79 Losses 177 Loyalty Of
  Legionnaires 45 Massacre Story *n59*
  192-193 Number Of Horses Lost 98
  Ramsay's Commentary *n60* 118
  Psychological Dimensions 177
  Tarleton Outnumbered *n15* 85
  Tarleton's Horse Shot From Under
  Him 176-177 Tarleton's Pursuit And
  Defeat Of Buford 137-138 Viewed
  As A Massacre By Many 173 178
WAXHAWS VS HAW RIVER,
  Massacres Viewed Differently 138-139
WAYNE, Maj Gen "Mad" Anthony 94
  n43 152 179 And Paoli Massacre *n8*
  25 In Chesterfield Courthouse Area
  n12 107
WEBB, Matross Samuel, Executed For
  Mutinous Behavior 158
WEBSTER, Lt Col James, Punished
  Legionnaires 168

WEEMS, Mason Locke, *Life Of Washington* 236
WEIR, Robert *vii*
WELLESLEY, Sir Arthur 232
WELLINGTON, Wellesley, Duke Of, Comment On Tarleton *n11* 242
WEMYSS, Maj James 84 *n34* 223
WHIG, Defined *n1* 7
WHITEFIELD, Rev George, Exhumation Of *n53* 228
WILKINSON, Eliza 96 *n61* 119
WILLET, Walter 38 99
WILLIAMS, John, Judge *n5* 105 Opinion Of Tarleton 92

WILLIAMSON'S PLANTATION, Huck Killed *n44* 114 211
WILLISON, Lt, At Waxhaws 176
WILSON, Robert, Portrait Of Tarleton *n1* 23
WINNSBORO, 92
WOLFE, Maj Gen James *n11* 142 Commemorative Badge Of 17th *n39* 63 Remarks About Colonials 46
WOODEN HORSE, As Punishment 157
YORK, Frederick, Duke Of *n4* 239
YOUNG, Jonathan *n27* 185

About the Author

Anthony J. Scotti Jr. has History degrees from Greensboro College (BA, 1987), Wake Forest University (MA, 1991), and the University of South Carolina (Ph.D., 1995). His major field of study was colonial America, specifically the Revolutionary War. He is currently employed with the publishing firm Bruccoli Clark Layman/Manly, Inc. in Columbia, S.C., where he is the editor of the award winning *American Decades, American Eras, World Eras,* and *History in Dispute* series of books. The author is also an adjunct History instructor at Midlands Technical College and he has written several scholarly articles. In addition, he is the president, treasurer, and regimental historian of the British Legion, a reenactment unit based out of Raleigh, N.C. The author is married and resides in Irmo, S.C.

Other Revolutionary War Titles from Heritage Books

WILLIAM WASHINGTON, CAVALRYMAN OF THE REVOLUTION

Steven E. Haller

The story of the Revolutionary War in the Carolinas has been incomplete without a biography of Lt. Col. William Washington, cousin of George Washington. A frequent foe of Tarleton, here is the other side of the story! 2001, 239 pp., illus., maps, full name index, paper, $28.00, #H1803

REVOLUTIONARY RANGERS: DANIEL MORGAN'S RIFLEMEN AND THEIR ROLE ON THE NORTHERN FRONTIER, 1778-1783

Richard B. LaCrosse, J.r, with introduction by Harry Kels Swan

"Author-rifleman Richard LaCrosse, Jr. contributes in this essay a vital but forgotten chapter of our national Revolutionary War history. The significance of these farm-bred and trained soldiers, who employed American-made rifles in winning the war along this northern frontier, can now be assessed by students of our Revolution. In this splendid essay author LaCrosse has contributed a readable and accurate portrait of a little-known and less appreciated segment of the American Revolution." 2002, 221 pp., appends., illus., fullname index, paper $17.95, #L2052

A VINDICATION OF MY CONDUCT: THE COURT MARTIAL TRIAL OF LT. COL. GEORGE ETHERINGTON OF THE 60TH OR ROYAL AMERICAN REGIMENT HELD ON THE ISLAND OF ST. LUCIA IN THE WEST INDIES, OCTOBER 1781 AND THE EXTRAORDINARY STORY OF THE SURRENDER OF THE ISLAND OF ST. VINCENT'S IN THE BRITISH CARIBBEAN DURING THE AMERICAN REVOLUTION

Dr. Todd E. Harburn and Rodger Durham

2002, c235 pp., illus., fullname index, $16.95, H2092

FREE CATALOG!!
www.heritagebooks.com / 1-800-398-7709